15713

WITHDRAWN

The
Garland Library
of
War and Peace

The
Garland Library
of
War and Peace

Under the General Editorship of

Blanche Wiesen Cook, *John Jay College, C.U.N.Y.*

Sandi E. Cooper, *Richmond College, C.U.N.Y.*

Charles Chatfield, *Wittenberg University*

We Can Be Friends

by
Carl Marzani

Forward by
Dr. W. E. B. DuBois

Illustrated by
Fred Wright

with a new Introduction
for the Garland Edition by
Barton J. Bernstein

Garland Publishing, Inc., New York
1971

CALVIN T. RYAN LIBRARY
U. OF NEBRASKA AT KEARNEY

The new introduction for this
Garland Library Edition is Copyright © 1971, by
Garland Publishing Inc.
24 West 45 St., New York, N.Y. 10036

———————

All Rights Reserved

———————

International Standard Book No. 0-8240-0294-6

Library of Congress No. LC-78-147500

Printed in the United States of America

Introduction

−*a*

Had Carl Marzani not become a Communist and been persecuted for his political beliefs, he could have been an American success story. Born in Rome in 1912, he came to America at the age of twelve when his family fled Fascism. He grew up in a working class family in Scranton, Pennsylvania, excelled in high school and won a scholarship to Williams College, where he was elected to Phi Beta Kappa as a junior and served as an editor of the literary magazine. Granted a fellowship by Williams upon graduation, he studied at Oxford for two years, briefly fought against Franco in Spain, and then joined the British Communist Party.[1]

Returning to the United States, he joined the Communist Party in New York City at the time of the Nazi-Soviet Non-Aggression Pact in 1939. For the young Marzani, unlike so many who then left the party in bitterness and confusion, the Nazi-Soviet alliance made good sense. He agreed with Winston Churchill's analysis that it was practical international politics. Marzani had (as he later recalled) watched the "ruling groups appease Hitler in Spain, Austria,

---

[1]*Information on Marzani is drawn from his autobiography in progress, "The Education of a Reluctant Radical," ch. vi. (Hereafter cited as "Education.")*

INTRODUCTION

Czechoslovakia, gambling with their national interests to strengthen Hitler for his long-advertised showdown with Bolshevism. Their so-called appeasement was, in fact, complicity." When the West rebuffed Stalin's overtures for an anti-Nazi alliance, the Soviets, Marzani concluded, had little choice but to accept Hitler's offer and turn Germany's aggression toward the West. Unlike the Daily Worker *of that day, he could not agree that the pact was "a weapon for peace"; rather, it was a harbinger of war.*[2]

He joined the party, he writes, very much in the "frame of mind" that Claud Cockburn, the former British Communist, explains in his autobiography:

> *When I became a Communist, it never crossed my mind that Communism was going to solve all the problems of humanity. I did not think, even, that it would do more than a little good here and there. I did think that without it the crack-up of civilization everyone spoke of was going to occur sooner rather than later. I saw Communism . . . as essentially a conservative force – a means of conserving civilized human values. Nor do I regard that assumption, or gamble, as having been merely ludicrous. I still quite often meet people who tell me quite sincerely, that they 'simply cannot understand' why or how I should ever have become a Communist. Their incomprehension can suggest that perhaps they never looked closely at their political faces in the mirror of our times.*[3]

[2]*"Education," ch. vi, p. 8.*
[3]*Claud Cockburn,* View from the West *(New York, 1962), p. 137, quoted by Marzani, "Education," ch. vi, p. 9.*

6

INTRODUCTION

Living and organizing on New York's East Side, Marzani found the Communist Party an accepted and open part of the community. There was no espionage, conspiracy, or subversion. The party organized teenage clubs, ran dances and movies, held forums, and also tried to solve the local people's problems with welfare, employment, and housing. Communist leaders pleaded and petitioned for traffic lights, pressured landlords over faulty wiring and broken stairs, assisted applicants for relief and work projects, and protested against police brutality. In Marzani's section, the party, like its Democratic and Republican competitors, often served as an intermediary between the poor and the system.[4]

Most party members, he recalls, used their own names. In his own case, because he had a position teaching economics at New York University and feared having newspapers associate his name with the party, he used a pseudonym (Tony Wales) to safeguard his job. Many on the East Side, however, knew him by both names, and he even kept both on his mailbox.[5]

As a party member, he found intellectual excitement, felt relevant and useful, and enjoyed the sense of political power. Marzani served as a branch organizer, a section literature director, educational director, and even briefly as section organizer for the East Side. But slowly he became more critical of the

[4] *"Education," ch. vi, pp. 16-27.*
[5] *"Education," ch. vi, pp. 27-28.*

7

"establishment" within the party, resented the use of power for unworthy purposes, and objected to the intellectual rigidity. He never lost his conviction, however, that the rank and file were generally quite open-minded and thoughtful, and he still believes that the party contributed significantly to the education of its members, especially those with little formal education.[6]

His own departure was hastened when he was directed, and agreed, to frame and help expel as a Trotskyite a very independent-minded member who had been firing off critical memoranda to Earl Browder, then the party's General Secretary, who was angered by the criticism and gave orders to "dump him." Marzani's departure from the party came soon after the Nazi attack upon the Soviet Union in June 1941. As educational director of his section, he had promptly written and circulated a leaflet analyzing the event. To his distress, he was scolded by the party's New York leader who feared that this statement would be interpreted as party doctrine. In turn, Marzani was offended by the pettiness of the bureaucracy and by the ossification of its thought. Within a few months he left by mutual agreement when he helped establish a local community council to support England and France ("East Side Conference to Defend America — Crush Hitler"). Though he had embarked upon the project at the party's urging,

[6] *"Education," ch. vi, pp. 26-50.*

8

he resigned *"from the party since in my opinion, no one subject to party discipline could freely serve another semi-political grouping."* His stated reason, at first rejected by the party which threatened in retaliation to expel him, was ultimately, but uneasily, accepted.[7]

Independent of the party but still wedded to the anti-fascist cause, Marzani went to work for the Office of Strategic Services (OSS) three months after Pearl Harbor. He passed Intelligence screenings but ran into trouble later in 1942 when the FBI submitted a report on his earlier Communist activities and affiliations and he was questioned, under oath, about these matters by the FBI and the Civil Service Commission. Marzani denied all earlier connections with the party — allegedly on the advice of senior officials in OSS who feared fascism, not communism, and viewed the investigation as part of a bureaucratic struggle between the FBI and OSS for control of foreign intelligence. In 1946, the issue briefly arose once again after he had been transferred to the State Department. Marzani claims that he disposed of the matter in an informal meeting without actually denying his past, but the State Department official later claimed, under oath, that Marzani had explicitly denied his Communist past.[8]

---

[7] *"Education,"* ch. vi, pp. 51-57, and quotation at p. 56.
[8] *Marzani to Bernstein, May 13 and June 8, 1971. He actually joined the Office of Coordinator of Information, a predecessor of OSS.*

9

INTRODUCTION

Disillusioned with American foreign policy by 1946, Marzani prepared to leave the State Department and to make political films. In the summer, while on leave, he produced for the left-wing United Electrical Workers (UERMWA-CIO) "Deadline for Action," a bitter indictment of the electrical industry, big business in general, and postwar foreign policy. The film condemned General Electric and Westinghouse for their connections with Axis firms, charged big business with union-busting after the war, asserted that a few major economic groups (Morgan, Mellon, Rockefeller, etc.) controlled the economy, and warned that America's foreign policy was conceived so that "Big Business could dominate the world." As the cameras flashed to Congress and to Winston Churchill, who had recently given his "Iron Curtain" address at Fulton, Missouri, the narrator declared, "These are the men who are now conducting atomic diplomacy. The President himself shared a platform with Winston Churchill when he called for an Anglo-American alliance against Russia. Is this what millions died for?" Put simply, the message was incipient fascism at home and imperialism abroad. The film gained attention within the labor movement, reportedly upset some major businesses (especially General Electric), provoked some red-baiting, and led Marzani to conclude that he had a future in making political films.[9]

[9]*Marzani to Bernstein, May 13, 1971; "Education," ch. viii, pp. 64-71.*

10

INTRODUCTION

On November 15, Marzani resigned from State, but he was notified later that he had been discharged on December 20. In January 1947 he was indicted, and in May he was convicted, in federal court, under Section 80 of Title 18 of the Federal Code (called the "fraud" section) for having falsely denied (in 1942, 1943, and 1946) that, among other charges, he had been a member of the Communist Party in 1940 and 1941, that he had attended its meetings and participated in its activities, and that he had used the pseudonym of "Tony Whales." Presumably the government had not sought an indictment for perjury because (1) the statute of limitations, which barred prosecutions after three years, exempted the events of 1942-43; and (2) the alleged questioning of 1946 had been conducted without witnesses and without placing Marzani under oath, thereby failing to meet the conditions (sworn testimony before witnesses) for perjury. The fraud section did not require declarations under oath and had been extended by suspending the statute of limitations in order to allow prosecutions for acts (involving war contracts) committed in the early war years.[10]

In the trial, Marzani contended that he had not been asked (nor answered) questions in 1946 about earlier Communist Party connections and that he was innocent of all charges. "I never made any secret of

[10] 71 Fed. Supp. 615. The government erred in referring to Marzani's cover name as Whales, rather than Wales, which suggests that there were no documents on his activities of 1940-41.

11

INTRODUCTION

my beliefs — I was antifascist and pro-labor but no member of the Communist Party," he declared. This denial was obviously a lie. Years later he explained that he felt that his only effective legal defense was to lie. Had he only been indicted for the events of 1942-43, he would have pleaded not guilty and admitted his earlier Communist party membership and activities, for his attorneys were reasonably sure that the extension of the fraud statute (suspension of the statute of limitations) would not hold up in a higher court. But had he admitted that he had been a member of the party and that he lied under oath in 1942-43, he feared that the jury would have been more likely to believe (as the government charged) that he had been queried about these matters again in 1946 and that he had again lied. Why should a jury believe that a man who lied about one aspect of his past was not lying again? The largely black jury, as it turned out, did believe the government witnesses and convicted Marzani for "fraud" in 1942-43 and 1946.[11]

[11] *For Marzani's statement, New York Times, May 21, 1947. On the strategy, Marzani to Bernstein, May 13 and June 8, 1971. Nine members of the jury were black, and three witnesses testifying to Marzani's prewar Communist activities and membership were black. One of the witnesses, Marzani claims, was a police spy and agent provocateur who had organized a section of the National Negro Congress on the East Side and then turned in their names. The second, according to Marzani, was a former member of the Communist Party who had held a job in civil service and was subject to the same prosecution as Marzani. The third, again according to Marzani, was a former C.P. official, who falsely claimed to have been Marzani's superior. (Marzani to Bernstein, May 13, 1971) J. Anthony Panuch, Deputy Assistant Secretary of State for Administration, was the witness on the questioning in 1946.*

12

INTRODUCTION

The Court of Appeals reduced his conviction to two counts on the grounds that the statute of limitations was not suspended in this case and, therefore, the government could not prosecute him for the statements of 1942-43. The Supreme Court, considering his case twice, split each time on the two remaining counts, 4-4, thereby upholding the decision of the appeals court. Under the law, he could have been sentenced to twenty years and fined $20,000, but he was sentenced to one-to-three years, a sentence still considerably more harsh than those meted out for other "frauds" by federal employees convicted of lying about their age, education, or experience.[12]

Carl Marzani was an early casualty of the Cold War. True, he had lied to the FBI and the Civil Service Commission and maybe even to the State Department, but his prosecution certainly did not contribute directly to American security, for he was indicted after his resignation. The Marzani case, however, may have served other purposes. Perhaps the indictment and conviction were designed to serve as a warning to others in the government to answer

[12] *168* F2d *133, 83* U.S. App. D.C. 78; *335 U.S.* 895; *336 U.S.* 922. *In the Court of Appeals, the main brief was submitted by Allan R. Rosenberg, Warren Sharfman, and Charles E. Ford. The National Lawyers Guild and the Civil Rights Congress submitted separate briefs as* amici curiae *on behalf of Marzani. Osmond K. Kraenkel and Rosenberg submitted the main brief to the Supreme Court on each appeal. On the first appeal to the high court, the National Lawyers Guild again entered a brief as* amicus curiae. *Arthur Garfield Hays argued the appeal in the circuit court and Fraenkel argued the appeal in the Supreme Court.*

loyalty investigations truthfully. Probably the successful prosecution did help to establish the credibility of the administration's recently conceived loyalty-and-security program, and perhaps the "exposure" of Marzani was also designed to present to the American people evidence of the Truman administration's dedication to anti-Communism and of the falseness of GOP charges that the Fair Deal was "soft on Communism." Marzani, himself, believed that these were all substantial factors in his prosecution, but he also stressed that the FBI, which had been rebuffed earlier, and General Electric, a major target of his film, had also been out to get him.[13]

Some liberals were deeply troubled by the prosecution of Marzani. I. F. Stone, the crusading journalist, believed in Marzani's innocence, challenged the evidence (which included the use of paid government informers), criticized the judge for barring inquiries useful to Marzani's defense, and condemned the administration for launching a political "witch hunt." Undoubtedly, Stone would have reached the same final conclusion, and still viewed the prosecution as a repudiation of liberalism, even if he had known that Marzani had been a Communist. Eleanor Roosevelt, upon reading of the case, acknowledged that she could not judge Marzani's innocence but feared "that our civil liberties are being endangered. Through fear and undisciplined prejudice, we are becoming the

[13] *Marzani to Bernstein, May 13, 1971.*

14

very thing which we have condemned other people for being." Congressman Adolph J. Sabath, who also saw the beginning of a red scare and the abridgment of civil liberties, declared, "The latest sordid episode in the decline of human freedom in our beloved country is the conviction of Carl Marzani." "Under the present hysteria," announced Arthur Garfield Hays, the civil liberterian attorney who argued Marzani's appeal, "any liberal and progressive minded person is likely to be recklessly charged with being a Communist."[14]

Their protests may have alerted some to real dangers in American life, and cases like Marzani's convinced some Americans then, and some historians later, that the Truman administration was partly responsible for the postwar red scare and McCarthyism. But these protests did not aid Marzani, who served thirty-two months in federal penitentiaries. Customarily only twenty-seven months would have been served, but he lost five months of good behavior when he tried to smuggle a manuscript out of prison.[15]

[14] *Stone, "A New Weapon for Witch-Hunters," Nation (July 12, 1947), pp. 33-35; Eleanor Roosevelt, "My Day," quoted in Committee in Defense of Carl Marzani,* The Case of Carl Marzani *(1947), p. 11; Sabath in* Congressional Record, *80 Congress, 1 Session (July 26, 1947), p. A3992; Hays in* The Case of Carl Marzani, *p. 5. On the efforts of I.F. Stone and others to secure Marzani's release after he had served one year, see* National Guardian, *March 22, 1950.*

[15] *See, for example, Athan Theoharis,* Seeds of Repression: Harry S. Truman and the Origins of McCarthyism *(Chicago, 1971); Bernstein, "America in War and Peace: The Test of Liberalism," in Bernstein, ed.,* Towards A New Past: Dissenting Essays in American History *(New York, 1968), pp. 308-312.*

INTRODUCTION

After prison, he served on the staff of the United Electrical Workers until he was forced out in a purge of leftists in 1954, then became active in a publishing house which became Marzani and Munsell, and finally in 1968, turned to earning a living as a contractor and builder remodelling brownstones when a fire destroyed the small publishing firm. He now devotes most of his time to writing, and in the past fifteen years he has published a novel, The Survivor *(1958), on the postwar State Department and the red scare; a translation and commentary on the brilliant Italian Marxist, Antonio Gramsci,* The Open Marxism of Antonio Gramsci *(1957); pamphlets on the Bay of Pigs, on bomb shelters, and on Vietnam; a book (with Victor Perlo) arguing for disarmament,* Dollars and Sense of Disarmament *(1960); a volume on ecology,* To Heal the Wounded Earth *(1971); and is about halfway through a study of George Orwell.*[16]

We Can Be Friends, *mostly researched and written while in prison, is an eloquent statement for those who continued to believe that accommodation with the Soviet Union was possible. Based upon a close study of publicly available sources, it was the first*

[16]*Cameron Associates, predecessor of Marzani and Munsell, published the novel and the study of Gramsci. William R. Scott published the study of ecology. Marzani and Munsell published the volume on disarmament as well as* Cuba vs. the CIA *(1961), written with Robert Light;* Shelter Hoax *(1962); and* The Conscience of the Senate *(1965). Other recent pamphlets are:* The Unspeakable War *(Labor Committee for Peace in Vietnam, 1966);* Stop the War! *(Prometheus Paperbacks, 1968);* Withdraw *(American Documentary Films, 1970); and* The Threat of Neo-Fascism *(American Documentary Films, 1971).*

16

volume-length history from the left which sought to explain in some detail the origins of the Cold War and blamed it on America. Like I.F. Stone, whose bold volume on the Korean War almost went unpublished, Marzani had to scratch around for a publisher and finally, with the aid of the United Electrical Workers and some friends, established Topical Books to publish the volume. In order to reach a working class audience, Marzani recast the text into simple sentences, removed some of the qualifications, and tried (as he later explained) to walk the "slippery tightrope" of popularizing his thought without vulgarizing it.[17]

The book appeared with jacket copy by former congressman Vito Marcantonio, chairman of the American Labor Party, which was the New York wing of the Progressive Party, with a foreword by W.E.B.DuBois, former Progressive candidate for the Senate, and with "puffs" by Paul Sweezy, co-editor of the independent-Marxist Monthly Review, *which had published a chapter earlier in 1952, and by Richard Sasuly, author of* I.G. Farben. We Can Be Friends *was a selection of the Liberty Book Club, established by novelist Howard Fast with Communist Party support. The book was priced generally at $1 in paper and $3.50 in cloth, but generous discounts*

[17] *Marzani to Bernstein, May 13, 1971. In 1952, William Appleman Williams, in* American-Russian Relations, 1781 - 1947, *published by Rinehart and Company, devoted about twenty-five pages to a "revisionist" analysis of the years between the German-Soviet Pact and the Truman Doctrine.*

were offered, so it often sold at fifty cents in paper and $2.50, $2, and $1.50 in cloth. More than 50,000 copies were sold, including 10,000 in cloth, and the United Electrical Workers purchased and distributed almost half of the paperback copies. Beyond the dwindling left, however, the book received little attention and went largely unnoticed, unsold, un-reviewed, and unread. Because the book was often angry and lacked the veneer of scholarship, it was easily ignored by the academic community. Because the book broke with the conventional wisdom at a time when such challenges were unacceptable, the popular media comfortably disregarded it. We Can Be Friends, *like its author, was a casualty of the Cold War.*[18]

The major intellectual contribution of Marzani's book as a work of historical analysis is his detailed investigation of the origins of the Cold War. Restricted to published records, he rested his study primarily on about a dozen memoirs, biographies, and public reflections by policy-makers and their associates. These sources, as well as the daily press, the left-wing National Guardian, *and a handful of secondary studies, assisted Marzani in recognizing the pivotal importance, and challenging earlier interpretations, of such issues as the delayed second front in Europe, the meaning of Yalta, the "secret surrender" negotiations*

[18]*A portion of chapter VIII was first published as "How FDR's Policy Was Reversed,"* Monthly Review, *IV (September, 1952), 141-50. Curiously, the* Monthly Review *did not review the volume. Sales figures are based on Marzani's recollection.*

INTRODUCTION

in 1945 without the Soviets, the dispute over the composition of the Polish government, the abrupt cut-off of Lend-Lease to the Soviets in May, the quarrel over Argentina at the United Nations founding conference, the use of the atomic bomb against Japan and in subsequent diplomacy ("atomic diplomacy"), the connection between the Russian loan and German reparations, the Baruch plan for international control of atomic energy, the Truman Doctrine, the uses of "political" loans, the Czech coup, the Korean War, and European colonialism. In particular, Marzani focused on most of the issues in 1945 and 1946 that later "revisionist" historians would emphasize in their own analyses of the origins of the Cold War. Like them, he also stressed that no American policy-maker in the early years of the Cold War expected imminent Soviet aggression.[19]

[19] *For "revisionist" analyses on 1945-57, see: William A. Williams,* The Tragedy of American Diplomacy *(Cleveland, 1962, rev. ed.);* Barton J. Bernstein, ed., Politics and Policies of the Truman Administration *(Chicago, 1970);* Gar Alperovitz, Atomic Diplomacy *(New York, 1965) and* Cold War Essays *(Garden City, 1970);* Lloyd Gardner, Architects of Illusion *(Chicago, 1970);* David Horowitz, The Free World Colossus *(New York, 1965); and* John Bagguley, "The World War and the Cold War," *in* David Horowitz, ed., Containment and Revolution *(Boston, 1967), 76-124. Among the other related "revisionist" studies are:* Gabriel Kolko, The Politics of War, 1943-1945 *(New York, 1968);* Thomas G. Paterson, "The Abortive American Loan to Russia and the Origins of the Cold War," *Journal of* American History, *LVI (June, 1969), 70-92;* Walter LaFeber, America, Russia, and the Cold War, 1945-1966 *(New York, 1967); and* Lloyd Gardner, Economic Aspects of New Deal Diplomacy *(Madison, Wis., 1964), 292-329. For recent dissenting views, see: George Harring, "Lend-Lease to Russia and the Origins of the Cold War," *Journal of* American History, *LVI (June, 1969), 93-114;* Arthur Schlesinger, Jr., "Origins of the Cold War,"

INTRODUCTION

Marzani, like the Progressive party of Henry Wallace, concluded that Truman had reversed Roosevelt's policy of accommodation with the Soviet Union. The first confrontation was over Poland. Two weeks in the White House and the new President had tongue-lashed Vyacheslav Molotov, the Soviet Foreign Minister, telling him that the Soviets must live up to their agreements. Truman tried to impose his own interpretation of the Yalta agreement on Poland even though Admiral William Leahy, Roosevelt's military adviser and associate at Yalta, had told Truman that the agreement "was susceptible of two interpretations." To Roosevelt, Leahy had complained earlier, "this is so elastic that the Russians can stretch it all the way from Yalta to Washington without ever technically breaking it," to which Roosevelt had replied, "I know, Bill — I know it." "I did not believe that the dominating Soviet influence could be excluded from Poland," Leahy explained, "but I did think it was possible to give to the reorganized Polish government an external appearance of independence."[20]

Foreign Affairs, *XLVII (October, 1967), 22-51;* Herbert Feis, From Trust to Terror: The Onset of the Cold War, 1945-1950 *(New York, 1970);* Daniel M. Smith, *"The New Left the the Cold War,"* Denver Quarterly *IV (Winter, 1970), 78-88;* Adam Ulam, Expansion and Coexistence: The History of Soviet Foreign Policy, 1917-1967 *(New York, 1968) and "On Modern History: Re-reading the Cold War,"* Interplay Magazine, *III (March, 1969), 51-3; and* Charles S. Maier, *"Revisionism and the Interpretation of Cold War Origins,"* Perspectives in American History, *IV (1970), 313-50.*

[20] *Quoted from Marzani, p. 196. Emphasis added by Marzani.*

INTRODUCTION

Within six months the Grand Alliance, argues Marzani, had crumbled, with the American decision at San Francisco to ram through the seating of Argentina over Soviet objections and despite Roosevelt's earlier promises; and then with the practice of "atomic diplomacy," as Byrnes and Truman tried to use the threat of the bomb to push the Soviets out of Eastern Europe, an area FDR had conceded to the Soviets at Yalta. "The tragic impasse in American-Soviet relations had its chief original source in Byrnes' statement of August 18, 1945" attacking the Bulgarian elections and Soviet influence in Eastern Europe, concludes Marzani (quoting Frederic Schuman). The dropping of the bomb on Japan, contends Marzani (quoting P.M.S. Blackett), was "not so much the last military act of the second World War, as the first major operation of the Cold diplomatic war *with Russia. . . ." Marzani concludes: "Atomic Diplomacy started the Cold War."* Stimson had warned Byrnes against *"having this weapon rather ostentatiously on our hip."* Molotov charged Byrnes with (Byrnes reports) *"carrying an atom bomb in his pocket."* Contrary to the advice of Henry L. Stimson, outgoing Secretary of War, the administration did not move promptly *to private two-party negotiations for international control of atomic energy. After practicing "atomic diplomacy" and delaying ten months after Hiroshima, the United States finally unveiled its plan in the summer of 1946. Then it offered a program that was unacceptable to the Soviet Union because it*

21

*required access to her heartland, thereby opening it
to U.S. penetration, and also froze the American
nuclear monopoly. "The Baruch Plan was presented
merely as a maneuver in the Cold War diplomacy,"
Marzani concludes, again following Blackett. Stating his case bluntly, Marzani declares: "The Truman
Administration in full partnership with the leaders of
the Republican Party, started the Cold War.''*[21]

There is certainly considerable evidence that the
tactics of the Truman administration reversed Roosevelt's. Indeed, there is even evidence that Roosevelt at
Yalta had reluctantly accepted spheres of influence in
Eastern Europe and that Truman, armed with the
bomb and economic power, sought later to repudiate
the agreement and to "liberate" Eastern Europe.
What Marzani did not consider in appraising Roosevelt's strategy was why the President had concealed
even the fact of nuclear research from the Russians.
Perhaps FDR also hoped to use the weapon as a lever
to produce change in Soviet behavior? Also, why
didn't Roosevelt at Yalta offer the Soviets the loan
they had requested? Perhaps he was also hoping to
use the loan to move the Soviets out of Eastern
Europe. Put bluntly, Roosevelt's tactics of accommodation might well have given way to the tactics
that Truman followed after Alamogordo and Hiroshima, for both presidents shared the same vision
("ideology") of a world in which peace and pros-*

[21] *Quoted from Marzani, pp. 92-5, 99, and 60. Emphasis added by
Marzani.*

22

*perity could be guaranteed by expanding inter-
national trade, establishing economic multilateralism,
and extending political freedoms. Given the instru-
ments that could produce this world, would Roosevelt have refused to use them?*[22]

*These are tantalizing, unanswered — probably
unanswerable — questions. But a portion of Marzani's
analysis does not rely upon the answers to these
questions. He is on solid ground when he stresses that
Truman, a newcomer and a confirmed anti-
Communist, adopted the "Cold Warriors" (Byrnes,
Leahy, Forrestal, and Ambassador W. Averell Harriman) and followed — though at first only briefly, I
think — the tactics they proposed in dealing with the
Soviet Union. Truman did follow their advice briefly
on Poland and also on lend-lease, but ultimately he
yielded on Poland and reached an agreement with the
Soviet Union on this issue. Marzani is also effective in
reminding his readers of Truman's strong anti-
Communism. In 1941, when Germany attacked
Russia, Truman, then a senator, had advised: "If we
see that Germany is winning we ought to help Russia*

[22] *On the problem of continuity, see:* Williams, Tragedy, pp.
204-26; Alperovitz, Atomic Diplomacy; Gardner, "Liberals, Radicals
and the Cold War," (unpub. ms., 1967); and Bernstein, "American
Foreign Policy and the Origins of the Cold War," in Bernstein, ed.,
Politics and Policies, pp. 13-30; "FDR at the Helm," Progressive, *XXIV*
(December, 1970), pp. 41-2; and "The Cold War Reconsidered"
(unpub. ms., 1967). Also on FDR, see James MacGregor Burns,
Roosevelt: The Soldier of Freedom (New York, 1970), particularly for
a discussion of the second front, the atomic bomb, and the "secret"
surrender negotiations in 1945.

and if Russia is winning we ought to help Germany and that way let them kill as many as possible. . . ."[23]

It is difficult to square Marzani's analysis of Roosevelt as the accommodator and of Truman as the Cold Warrior with the author's assertion: "Foreign policy cannot be explained, fundamentally, by saying that some Presidents are 'good,' and other Presidents are 'bad.' The foreign policies a nation follows are a result of the internal pressures of its economy. . . ." Presumably, then, by Marzani's own admission, Truman's policies and tactics (Marzani does not distinguish) were what Roosevelt's would have been if he had not died. Marzani, like many on the left, stumbled on this basic problem and therefore sometimes fell into contradictions. Yet, had his book been directed at a scholarly audience, he might have dealt with this difficult problem by qualifying his generalizations, by discussing the differences between (long-run) goals and (short-run) tactics, and by analyzing the relationship between ideology and power and between individual actions and historical currents.[24]

Marzani also wavered uneasily between two theories of the Cold War: (1) it was the result of American imperialism; and (2) it was created to justify a large military budget. "The Cold War," he declares early in the book, "is the result of the

[23] Quoted from Marzani, p. 207.
[24] Marzani, p. 335. Chapter XV (329-39) was prepared by a friend but obviously had Marzani's endorsement. The friend ("Marvin") still prefers not to be identified any more fully.

24

internal needs of a big business economy. *It is an 'automatic pump-primer' which is deliberately manipulated, like 'turning a spigot,' by those interested. In big business thinking only the armaments resulting from the Cold War are saving us from chronic depression. . . ."* By this theory, great armaments would appear to be unnecessary for the conduct of foreign policy but conceived primarily to forestall depression at home. Militarism and the Cold War, then, were not a product of imperialism.[25]

Briefly, later on in the book, Marzani, influenced by Victor Perlo's American Imperialism *(1951)*, a clearly Marxist interpretation, offers what seems to be a rival interpretation:

> The goal of . . . the Cold War . . . is to make American Big Business the master of the world . . . .

> Imperialism reflects itself at home in a drive against labor; abroad in a drive for markets, for raw materials, for the export of protected capital, for the political domination of other countries to ensure economic penetration. Behind all these drives is the force and violence of the imperialists. . . .[26]

Later, in a belated return to this neglected theme, Marzani explains:

> Wall Street really regards the world as its oyster.

[25] Marzani, pp. 64-5.
[26] Marzani, pp. 107-10.

It captures foreign markets. . . . It builds plants in foreign countries, especially colonial countries, and makes super-profits from those workers' pitiful wages. It buys raw materials from backward areas at ridiculously low prices, and sells them manufactures at ridiculously high prices.

This is the basis of the Cold War. *The Soviet Union interferes with these Wall Street plans to rule the world. It stands as an example to the peoples of the world that they don't have to submit to the monopolists. . . . The Soviet Union is a real obstacle to the monopolists. The key to postwar history is the drive of monopolists to smash that obstacle, if necessary by war.*

Put simply, armaments, by this theory of imperialism, are required to strengthen the military in order to assist American economic expansion abroad — conceivably even despite (not because of) their cost, their impact upon the domestic economy, and the profits to arms-makers. Militarism, then, is essential to imperialism and the Cold War was the result of American imperialism. In theory it is possible to integrate these explanations of the Cold War and of militarism (for pump-priming and for imperialism) as Victor Perlo did. But because Marzani was writing for a non-academic audience, such distinctions may have seemed unnecessary and likely to over-burden his readers, thereby diverting attention from his central

26

theme: American responsibility for the Cold War.[27]

In his analysis of American responsibility for the Cold War, the Marshall Plan, surprisingly, was squeezed into a few pages. Marzani simply charged that it was devised to halt Communism in Western Europe, particularly in France and Italy, and to capture European markets for the United States. He cited some of the sketchy available evidence that some American labor leaders were disappointed by the limited achievements of the plan but he failed to note, and perhaps to understand, that European prosperity, according to policy-makers, was an essential condition for world peace and prosperity. Like many left critics of foreign policy during the Fair Deal, he did not understand that policy-makers of both the Roosevelt and Truman administrations truly believed that American freedoms rested upon prosperity and that depression would destroy liberty. Perhaps because he shared important portions of the American "ideology," he could not critically reassess it. Both policy-makers and Marzani were operating within a common framework of Rooseveltian internationalism. Where they differed, in part, however,

---

[27] *Marzani, pp. 336-7. Emphasis added. My own analysis indicates that few major businessmen, aside from those in the aircraft industry, supported or sought large arms budgets before about 1950 for reasons other than their belief that great military strength was essential to the nation's foreign policy. Between late 1945 and late 1948, inflation — not recession — was the immediate economic danger, and as a result the recession was only belatedly recognized in the spring of 1949. See Bernstein, "Economic Policy and Military Budgets" (unpub. ms., 1965).*

was that Marzani stressed the need for reform at home in order to avert depression, while the policy-makers stressed the need for economic expansion abroad for the same purpose.[28]

Marzani also neglected another significant aspect of the Plan: it had brought many liberals, briefly disaffected by the Truman Doctrine, back into support of the administration's foreign policy and had persuaded many Americans of the beneficence of American foreign policy and ultimately of the impossibility of working with the Soviets. The Nation, for example, which had opposed the Truman Doctrine, welcomed the Marshall Plan, with its provisions for non-military aid and its invitation to the Soviets, as evidence that the United States is "going to make at least one more effort to prevent the development of two irreconcilable worlds." Marzani never explained (though he later claimed he understood) that the Plan was devised to be unacceptable to the Soviet Union because, among other things, it permitted the U.S. to gain access to secret data on the Soviet economy, gave the U.S. a veto over plans for economic reconstruction, tried to shift Eastern trade to the West, sought to maintain the East as primarily agricultural, aimed to pry the satellites out of the Soviet orbit, and even anticipated assistance from (not to) the Soviet Union. Un-

---

[28] *See Paterson, "The Quest for Peace and Prosperity: International Trade, Communism, and the Marshall Plan," in Bernstein, ed.,* Politics and Policies, *pp. 78-112.*

fortunately, critics on the left did not explain these conditions to the American people and thereby gain a wider audience for their analysis of the administration's foreign policy. However, they, Marzani included, clearly understood that the United States tried to use economic power to achieve political goals. For them, as well as for the President, the Truman Doctrine and the Marshall Plan were simply variations on the same theme — "two halves of the same walnut," as Truman later stated.[29]

Partly because Marzani was so distressed by the militarization of American foreign policy, he stressed the Truman Doctrine, rather than the Marshall Plan, in his analysis of the Cold War. The Truman Doctrine, launched by the President in an atmosphere of crisis, seemed better to fit Marzani's general thesis that Washington was creating a "war psychosis" and thereby converting a reluctant American public to fear and hate the Soviet Union. Unfortunately, his analysis of the transformation of American attitudes was too simple. He neglected the widespread American opposition to communism and the deep suspicions before the war, as well as the lurking suspicions during the war, of many aspects of Soviet Russia. It was these objections and suspicions that were converted into deep fears and hostility in the

[29] Nation, CLXIV (June 21, 1947), pp. 729-31. Truman, quoted in Joseph Jones, The Fifteen Weeks (New York, 1955), p. 233. On the plan, also see Paterson, "The Quest for Peace and Prosperity," pp. 92-5; and Charles Bohlen, The Transformation of American Foreign Policy (New York, 1969), pp. 90-92.

postwar years. But this process was neither inevitable nor predetermined. To explain the change, Marzani focused upon American policy makers and their efforts to convince the American press to interpret international issues along the lines of official Washington analyses. Because he independently studied the available sources, he was able to challenge the Cold War consensus and to see that much of the press had eschewed any critical function and had become a purveyor of dubious official interpretations. Had he recognized the depths of popular American anti-communism, however, he might better have understood the behavior of the press and the responsiveness of the American people to these interpretations.[30]

Marzani's analysis of the Korean War, while demolishing popular myths, also ran into difficulties. He was correct, it now appears, when he followed I. F. Stone and denied that the "Soviet Union, through North Korean troops, had started the war as an act of aggression against the West." But it does not follow, as he concluded, that "the United States, acting through the South Koreans, started the war in part to save Formosa" and Chiang. The Korean War, itself, is probably best understood as the most dramatic part of an extended civil war, involving frequent border skirmishes, in which both North and South had

[30] *See Paul Willen, "Who 'Collaborated' with Russia?"* Antioch Review *XIV (Fall, 1954), pp. 274-282; Melvin Small, draft-manuscript on wartime public opinion toward the Soviet Union.*

earlier initiated minor aggressive actions. In June, 1950, the North, acting independently of the Soviet Union and probably also of China, attacked the South with the expectation of unleashing a revolution. But expectations directed by ideology proved a poor guide, and the South did not revolt. The North, however, was not the only prisoner of ideological analysis. The Truman administration, also in bondage to an ideology that distorted events, concluded wrongly that the attack by the North was part of a Soviet conspiracy to create a "test case of aggression." The administration, as a result, foolishly embarked upon a bloody war in order to stop communism, maintain American credibility, and protect Europe and Asia.[31]

There are also other serious problems in Marzani's analysis – particularly of imperialism and of the Soviet Union. "If the colonial nations free themselves, imperialism will starve for profits," he concludes in We Can Be Friends. But he seems in the book, unlike in his earlier film, unaware sometimes that imperialism takes many forms and that colonialism, though the most obvious, is only one form of imperialism. Unequal terms of trade and the heavy

[31] Marzani, pp. 299-300; I.F. Stone, The Hidden History of the Korean War (New York, 1952). On the Korean War, also see: "The North Korean Labor Party's Factions," Jiya (May, 1967), translated in Selected Summaries of Japanese Magazines (June 26–July 3, 1967), pp. 8-11; Edward Friedman, "Problems in Dealing with an Irrational Power: America Declares War on China," in Friedman and Mark Selden, eds., America's Asia: Dissenting Essays on Asian-American Relations (New York, 1971), pp. 207-252.

31

flow of profits back to advanced industrial countries can maintain the imperialist economic relationship even after the overt political form has ended. Given the shortage of capital and the structure of investments in an underdeveloped nation, it is often subject to continuing economic domination by foreign corporations.[32]

On the subject of the Soviet Union, *We Can Be Friends often seems naïve. Consider, for example, this statement: "It is time that we saw the Soviet leaders as they really are, and the Soviet Union as it really is, a country whose government is owned by its people, and therefore is truly of, by and for the people." Like many others in the years immediately after the Korean War who worked on the left for peace between the United States and the Soviet Union, Marzani felt compelled to assault the American "conventional wisdom" of a bellicose, expansionist Soviet totalitarianism teetering on the brink of internal upheaval and to offer a counter-myth: a democratic Soviet polity with representative leaders responding to the needs and desires of the people. By offering such an unwarranted interpretation of the Soviet Union, he was subscribing to the view offered by the Stalinist left and presenting an analysis that Americans could and did promptly reject. In 1952, only some portions of the dwindling peace movement understood that it could admit the harshness of the Soviet state and society and still argue, logically and*

[32]*Marzani, p. 338; cf., p. 218.*

reasonably, that negotiations and agreements were still possible: they did not depend upon both nations having similar forms of government. Some years before, Walter Lippmann, in criticizing the assumptions of George Kennan's policy of containment, had effectively expressed the faith in diplomacy: "The history of diplomacy is the history of relations among rival powers, which did not enjoy political intimacy, and did not respond to appeals to common purposes. Nevertheless, there have been settlements. . . . For a diplomat to think that rival and unfriendly powers cannot be brought to a settlement is to forget what diplomacy is all about." [33]

Marzani also has difficulty with a problem that much of the American left never comfortably resolved: their belief that power was generally concentrated in an élite or class which dictated policy, yet their optimism that there was a real possibility for reform of foreign and domestic policy. In his own analysis, Marzani faces another serious problem: Was power in America held by a class or élite? If an élite, which élite? He sees Truman directed by Big Business, but he also speaks of the "military domination" of American foreign policy. In places, however, he means that military considerations or martial values dominate — sometimes, he implies, through civilian adoption. He asserts that the "influence of the

[33] *Marzani, p. 363 and also see pp. 369-70. For Lippmann, see his* The Cold War: A Study in U.S. Foreign Policy *(New York, 1947), p. 60.*

33

*military and reactionary politicians on foreign policy
is only the surface manifestation of the controlling
influence in American life, the influence of Big
Business — bankers, monopolists, industrialists and
financiers." His analysis also stresses the integration
of top military, political and business leaders, and he
implies that business was ascendant in that relationship. Later on, he focuses upon James Forrestal,
former partner of Dillon, Read and Secretary of
Defense, calling him the "most powerful influence in
postwar American foreign policy" and the architect
of the alliance between the corporation, government
and the armed forces — what Forrestal called a
"politico-military administration." In primitive form,
Marzani seems to be expressing the notions that C.
Wright Mills offered a few years later in* The Power
Elite *(1956).*[34]

*In one very significant way Marzani's analysis of
businessmen differs from that of Mills and of later
theorists who have attributed to corporate leaders a
sophisticated "ideology" known as corporate liberalism. Marzani and many of his contemporaries, as
veterans of the New Deal crusade against the
"economic royalists," saw businessmen as reactionaries, as opponents of all reform, as naked exploiters
of workingmen and particularly of minority groups.*

[34] *Marzani, pp. 102-10, 267-85. For the speeches by Welch and
Jordan, which Marzani quotes from Perlo, see Henry Wallace's
testimony of February 24, 1948, against the Marshall Plan. (U.S. House
of Representatives, Committee on Foreign Affairs, Foreign Policy for a
Postwar Recovery Program, 80 Congress, 1st Session, pp. 1585-7.)*

INTRODUCTION

Later analysts have emphasized the ability of corporate leaders to reform moderately in order to maintain power and thereby to co-opt potential support for the left; to integrate the labor movement as a junior partner in the economy of large-scale corporate capitalism; and to use government regulations to restrain competition and to rationalize the economy. Even the Taft-Hartley law — condemned by unions as a "slave labor" law — did not weaken the labor movement or reduce the workingman to penury. Indeed, the harsh rhetoric of those postwar years was often exaggerated. The difference between labor and management, and even the quarrels between labor and corporate leaders over power in the Korean War mobilization agencies, was not a dispute about fundamentals but a squabble between a dominant and a junior partner who had briefly fallen out.[35]

There is the danger, when examining this path-breaking volume almost a generation after its publication, of holding it to standards that few, if any, of the contemporary political tracts of the late 1940's and the early 50's could meet. In the final judgment, it must command our respect, not because it was always right in detail (often it was not) or because it was always consistent or convincing (it was not), but because it focused upon so many of the right issues,

[35] *On corporate liberalism and labor, see C. Wright Mills,* The New Men of Power *(New York, 1948); and Bernstein, "America in War and Peace: The Test of Liberalism," pp. 289-321.*

35

because it sought to alert Americans to serious dangers, because it challenged the Cold War consensus, because it offered an important, often astute, interpretation of recent history, and because it held out the hope of peace. None who read it seriously and examined carefully the argument and sources could comfortably believe that America had been innocent in 1945 or 1946, that Soviet expressions of fears about the West were simply forms of "neurotic" behavior (as George Kennan had suggested), or that the Cold War started as late as 1947. Nor, for that matter, could they be ignorant in 1952 of American support of French colonialism — as part of the strategy of global anti-Communism — in Indo-China.[36]

Unfortunately, few American students or scholars read We Can Be Friends, *and that failure is eloquent testimony to the poverty of critical thought in American education in the 1950's. By reviewing the recent history of American foreign policy nearly a generation ago, Carl Marzani taught a lesson that many Americans were not prepared to learn until the war in Vietnam compelled a re-examination of America, its social structure and political economy, its "ideology" and self-conceptions, and its history and myths.*

Barton J. Bernstein

June, 1971   *Urbana, Illinois*

[36] *On Kennan, see his telegram of February 22, 1946 in James Forrestal Papers, Princeton University; "Mr. X," "The Sources of Soviet Conduct," Foreign Affairs, XXV (July, 1947), pp. 566-582.*

ACKNOWLEDGMENTS

I wish to express my gratitude to Allen J. Matusow, Blanche W. Cook, Ronald Radosh, Thomas G. Paterson, Martin D. Sherwin, and Carl Marzani for their generous counsel.

Barton J. Bernstein

WE CAN BE FRIENDS

WE
CAN
BE
FRIENDS

Carl Marzani

"Today we are faced with the pre-eminent fact that, if civilization is to survive, we must cultivate the science of human relationships—the ability of all peoples, of all kinds, to live together and work together in the same world, at peace."

President Franklin D. Roosevelt

"President Roosevelt has died but his cause must live on. We shall support President Truman with all our forces and with all our will."

Premier Joseph Stalin

"The only deadly sin I know is cynicism."

Henry L. Stimson

foreword by Dr. W. E. B. DuBois
illustrated by Fred Wright

1952 Topical Books Publishers, New York

ALL RIGHTS RESERVED. NO PART OF THIS BOOK
IN EXCESS OF FIVE HUNDRED WORDS MAY BE
REPRODUCED IN ANY FORM WITHOUT PERMISSION
IN WRITING FROM THE PUBLISHERS

PRINTED IN U.S.A.

COPYRIGHT, 1952, TOPICAL BOOKS PUBLISHERS, NEW YORK

In memory of my father
who fought fascism—the destroyer of peace

ACKNOWLEDGEMENTS

In the United States of today, it is not safe to mention names in a book like this unless the individuals concerned work for progressive employers. So for those who helped from within **Time** and **Life,** much thanks. To John and Jane who did most of the research and much of the writing on chapters 1 and 16, my grateful thanks.

In research, Tabitha Petran, associate editor of the **National Guardian,** has been a tower of strength. Her tenacity, acumen and accuracy need no puny testimonials—her brilliant work on the **Guardian** speaks for itself.

To several people who have criticized the manuscript, particularly Paul Sweezy and Victor Perlo, my heartfelt thanks, and absolution of responsibility for any opinions expressed. The same in regard to the criticism of the national staff of the UE, as well as gratitude for understanding for distracted work under the provoking disruption of getting a book out—Bill knows what I mean.

Heartfelt thanks to labor's own cartoonist, Fred Wright, for the illustrations which cost him sleep, and to the nameless designer of the book and of the cover—the work done is visible in your hands.

To compositiors and printers that saw this book through, my deep gratitude. Aaron, Arthur, Laddie, Harry, Marvin, Vic—to stop naming is invidious, to keep listing impossible. Except for Murry —a friend. To Jane, Fanny and Len, much thanks for preparing the index. To Sally and Lillian, for an unstinting labor of love— love in return.

I should like to express thanks to Dr. W. E. B. DuBois for his understanding and warmth in reading the manuscript and writing a foreword under great pressure of time.

To Edith for everything, and Tony and Ricky for being quiet.

Above all, to Marcia and Marvin for work so inextricably woven into the whole as to be impossible to apportion. I can only say that without them the book would not have been done at all. Beginning with organizing the notes brought out of jail, right through to reading proof, there isn't a page in the book that must not salute their ability, devotion and deep sense of responsibility. Chapter 15 was wholly written by Marvin, all were re-drafted by him at least once, after a certain nameless and lovely couple had torn them apart. There are occasions when to utter thanks is to minimize the aid given, and this would certainly be the case here. I can only say I am happy such folks live and work in the progressive movement.

C. M.

CONTENTS

JUNE 27, 1952

DIRECTOR DENIES FEDERAL PRISONS CODDLED MARZANI

WASHINGTON, June 26 (AP).— Senator Homer Ferguson, Republican of Michigan, has accused Federal Prison Director James V. Bennett of coddling Carl Marzani, former State Department employe convicted of perjury.

But Mr. Bennett insisted "we did not coddle him at all."

The exchange was during closed-door hearings on a Justice Department money bill. The testimony was released Wednesday.

Marzani was convicted in 1948 of lying when he told a State Department superior he never had been connected with the Communist Party. He was sentenced to one to three years and began his term.

Mr. Bennett testified that Marzani was caught trying to smuggle a book out of the prison. The director said he then took this
to the Lewisburg, Pa., prison; canceled 150 days of time earned for good behavior, and made him ineligible for parole at the end of one year

so that he eventually served more than 2½ years.

Mr. Ferguson, however, insisted that Marzani was given several favors. Among these, he said, were the decision to imprison him at Lewisburg, described as a "favored spot," instead of sending him to the Atlanta, Ga., prison as originally planned; restoration of 100 of the 150 days of canceled good time; and the return to Marzani of some of the writings he worked on in prison.

The senator wanted to know if this was under pressure from the Communist newspaper, the Daily Worker, and a Marzani defense committee.

The director said he permitted the prisoner to remain at Lewisburg because he "made a very satisfactory adjustment there" and his wife
adj
fro
be
e
Mr
on
an

Le
to restore the 100 days of credits, the witness said.

> "This book is the most complete revelation of the conspiracy to involve this nation in a Third World War."
>
> **Dr. W. E. B. DuBois**

FOREWORD

I have spent this Sunday in reading Carl Marzani's book, **We Can Be Friends.** I am honored to be asked to write a foreword. It is the most complete revelation which has yet been written of the conspiracy to involve this nation in a Third World War with the Soviet Union as our chief opponent.

Carl Marzani is the man to produce this exposure of greed and duplicity. He grew up in a working class family in the poverty of a Pennsylvania mining district. His father was an Italian immigrant who escaped from Mussolini's Italy in 1923, after refusing to take a loyalty oath. Young Marzani worked for his schooling, fought against Franco in Spain and is a veteran of the Second World War. He is a graduate of Williams College in America and Oxford University in England. He once taught at New York University. He has travelled widely over Europe and Asia.

For years he was in government service in the State Department, the Office of Strategic Services and other intelligence agencies. He picked the targets for the Doolittle raid on Tokyo and served under top military leaders in the United States, England and Italy, functioning as assistant divisional chief in United States Intelligence agencies, under Roosevelt and Truman. His work and loyalty were checked in 1942 and 1943 by the FBI, the Civil Service Commission, the Office of Naval Intelligence, Army Intelligence, and the security branch of the Office of Strategic Services. He resigned voluntarily from government service in 1946 and immediately began to speak on the Cold War and to criticize foreign policy.

He made a film for the United Electrical Workers, "Deadline for Action," called the best educational film ever gotten out by a labor union. This film which was documented and named names was immediately criticized as "communistic" and attacked by the press and certain corporations mentioned in it. Within a few months Marzani was indicted for making a false statement in 1946 as to his alleged membership in the Communist Party in 1940. At his trial the Government used only professional witnesses, one of whom in a similar case was indicted for perjury and later went insane.

Marzani was not charged with sedition, treason or perjury, yet he was convicted and sentenced to a federal penitentiary for three years. The Court of Appeals threw out nine of the eleven counts. The other two counts were carried to the Supreme Court of the United States which divided four to four on the question. The menace to civil liberties was so clear that the court took the very unusual course of allowing a rehearing. Again the vote was a tie and Marzani went to prison, in what Congressman Sabath called "the latest sordid episode in the decline of human freedom in our beloved country."

Persecution did not stop here. Usually a three year sentence is eligible for parole within a year. Marzani was imprisoned in March, 1949 and denied parole in February, 1950 and June, 1950, despite good conduct, a job waiting and a family in need. In contrast, Congressman Parnell Thomas, sentenced for theft, was paroled within a month of eligibility. Thousands of persons pled for Marzani's parole, including Albert Einstein, General Donovan, former chief of the Office of Strategic Services; Thomas Mann, Lowell Thomas, Alexander Meikeljohn and a dozen university professors. But no parole was ever granted and the typescript of three books which Marzani started to write while in jail, including this one, were confiscated and one was never returned.

The unquestioned desire of the American people for peace can be translated into action only by basic knowledge of how the present crisis has come about and how Roosevelt's peace policy became the Cold War. This book brings the reader undisputed proof of Truman's apostacy to the New Deal; of Churchill's machiavellian plans against the Soviet Union and of the sinister roles of Forrestal, Harriman, Dulles, Byrnes and Vandenberg, and of the murderous conspiracy which started the Korean War. These facts must be known and **We Can Be Friends** has spread the truth on the record.

W. E. B. DuBois
August 17, 1952.

The Rebirth of German Industry

It Is Still Too Early to Say Nation Has Gone Over Crest of the Economic Hill

By Sorin Crisaru

Nazis Return to Posts in Germany As Nation Approaches Sovereignty

Renewed Activity on Extreme Right Upsets Occupation Authorities—Dietrich, Former Press Chief, Gets Trade Journal Job

BONN DRIVE PUSHED TO FREE GENERALS

Adenauer Pressed to Urge Allies to Release Nazis He...
for West Ge...

By JACK R...

GERMANS MAP STEEL RISE

Western Zone Puts Output at 16,500,000 Tons Next Year

DUESSELDORF, Germany, May 13 (UP)—West German steel makers announced today that they hoped to hold a first post...
500,000...
million...

Bru...
that...
that...
need...
ity...

pres...
16,5...

Uni...

Nazi Terror Corps Plans A Reunion for Next Spring

By The Associated Press

HAMBURG, Germany, Nov. 3 —The "Waffen SS," Hitler's Elite Army Corps that acquired a reputation for terrorism in World War II, was summoned last night to hold its first post...
...se in Hamburg next...

RUHR STEEL FREED OF ALLIED CURBS

Limit on Production Removed and First Steps Are Taken to Dissolve Control Unit

By JACK RAYMOND

BONN, Germany, July 28 — A... Allied restrictions on West Ger... an steel production and capacit... ave been lifted and the first step... aken to liquidate the Interna... onal Authority for the Ruhr... which was created three years ag... a security measure again... erman military and economic... minance in Europe.
Sir Ivone Kirkpatri...
...months...

Germans View U.N. Steps at Koje As Similar to War Criminals' Acts

Feeling Is Widespread That Jailed Nazis Did Nothing Different Yet Were Punished— U. S. Is Considered Naive on Reds

By JACK RAYMOND

Special to The New York Times

BONN, Germany, June 5—Sto-ries out of Korea concerning inci-dents at the Koje prison camps have revived contentions in Ger-man political circles and in the German press that the United States has been naive about Com-munist fighting methods, and that if this were not the case the post-war trials of what the Germans persist in describing as the "so-called war criminals" in this coun-try would have had a different out-come.

Assertions of this nature have been made by influential Germans ever since the war in Korea start-ed, much to the consternation of Allied and particularly United States authorities. John J. McCloy, United States Hi...
public...

...camps as normal pr... the result that "hund... cent non-Communist... to die under the m... cumstances," but U... guards at Koje tu... of arms, tear ga... cars against the pri...
"In Nuremberg th... meant a death sentenc... declared.
United States au... feel that statements o... which are not isola... been made throughou... many, are a sly atten... the actions of the Ge... were condemned as wa... These authorities say the...

Collins Sees Germany As Dependable Ally

By the United Press

Gen. J. Lawton Collins, who fought against Germany in two wars, assured the Senate yester-day that West Germany would be an abable and dependable ally of the free world in case of war with Russia.

The Army Chief of Staff ap-peared before... eign Relations... urge speedy rati... new German peac... a companion ag... ing North Atlant... guarantees to Ge...
"I fought ag... vice." Collins s... ble fighters. The... ...efinite consider... ...nse of Western...

...ever seen, including tough... soldiers who can live in the... open. He would say the same o... Greece, he added.
"The French army today," Collins said, "has plenty of fight in it and they have demonstrat...

...power... at the... ...ay ahead o... defeat)... what the... The...

1952

INTRODUCTION

Franklin Delano Roosevelt died on April 12, 1945.

When Roosevelt died, hundreds of millions of people throughout the world sorrowed.

At Allied Headquarters in Caserta, Italy, a GI on sentry duty looked at the headline in **Stars and Stripes**. He was slowly shaking his head as I came in.

"It shouldn't have happened to us," he said simply.

He was right; it shouldn't have.

The GI's feelings were shared in every country of the world, in the farthest corners of the earth. In England, America, Russia, in Attu and in Malta, in Kamchatka and in Paris the masses of the people felt a great loss.

Instinctively they felt uneasy for the future. They were aware, however dimly, that powerful reactionary forces had been implacably fighting Roosevelt and the New Deal and that Roosevelt's death would be their opportunity.

Today in 1952 we see around us a world dominated by fear. A tremendous armaments race is taking place including dreaded atomic and bacteriological weapons. In Korea a frightful, inconclusive, unnecessary slaughter goes on day after day. A state of explosive tension exists known journalistically as the COLD WAR. The question persistently arises: How did the Cold War start?

President Truman says, it's all Russia's fault. Stalin wants to dominate the world, spread Communism, build an empire; the Russians played President Roosevelt for a sucker, got a lot of concessions from him, gave nothing in return and all along were going to double-cross his friendship.

9

Truman says he carried out all collective decisions to the letter, but the Russians broke their word. He claims the 1947 Truman Doctrine (the official name for the Cold War) was adopted after two years of patience with Soviet aggressiveness, and just showed that he was being realistic whereas Roosevelt had been naive.

This analysis has become compulsory in America. Democrats, Republicans and Dixiecrats all agree on it. The American Federation of Labor and the National Association of Manufacturers agree on it. John Rankin and Ralph Bunche agree on it. Eisenhower and Stevenson, the banker Harriman, the lawyer Dulles, the gambler Costello all agree on it. The press and radio have made this analysis an article of faith. To challenge it is to be un-American.

One wonders, is it really so simple?

Was President Roosevelt such a fool?

Did the Soviet Union start the Cold War?

I don't believe it. I say Truman's analysis is contrary to fact—and I find myself in good company, including Roosevelt's Undersecretay of State, Sumner Welles. Welles is a most conservative and most authoritative diplomat and he says of the Cold War that "the blame for the present disaster should be shared by the United States."

The son of Franklin Delano Roosevelt has spoken more sharply. Says Elliot Roosevelt that "it was the United States and Britain who first shook the mailed fist, who first abrogated the collective decisions." And stung by the bitterness at the betrayal of his father's work he asserts that "a small group of willful men in London and Washington are anxious to create and foster an atmosphere of war hatred against the Russians."

This is a strong and serious charge. I believe it's true. I believe it's true because when I tried to expose the State

Department's atomic bomb policy I was sent to jail on a pretext so flimsy that the Supreme Court of the United States twice deadlocked on the case, four to four. Four justices of the U. S. Supreme Court said the law was wrong—but I went to jail leaving a wife and two small children behind. Thirty months I spent in the Federal penitentiaries, almost a thousand days.

A thousand days is a lot of time. Trying to put this time to good advantage, I sought the evidence on how the Cold War started. I found great difficulty in getting the evidence because all my reading was censored.

In our United States, in the Union founded by Jefferson, preserved by Lincoln, and strengthened by Roosevelt, I, a political prisoner, couldn't get the books I wanted. Progressive books and liberal publications like the **N. Y. Daily Compass** and the **Monthly Review** were stopped. Even conservative books were prohibited if the title contained that fearful word **USSR—the Union of Soviet Socialist Republics.**

In such a situation the only books I could get on foreign policy were conservative books; the only newspapers, conservative newspapers. But so drastic was the change from Roosevelt's policy, that despite the suppression, censorship and prison bars I was struck by a glaring fact: these sources provided the essential proofs that the United States started the Cold War.

After I got out, I was able to draw on progressive sources, like the **National Guardian,** but most of the evidence in this book is from conservative sources. Much of it comes from the men who made policy on foreign affairs, often in their own words. Their words may represent opinions or facts. Opinions are not proof, but facts are the basis of proof. To prove an argument both facts and logic are necessary. Logic shows the causal connection between ideas, or between facts and ideas. For example:

11

If the alternative to war is negotiations (an idea); and a nation refuses to negotiate (a fact), then that nation envisages war (a logical conclusion).

In this book, both facts and logic are used. There is also substantial use of quotations and it is important to realize why and how they are used. First, the quotations establish facts. Admiral Leahy calls his book **I Was There**, and he was "there" at Yalta. When he reports what Roosevelt said about the Polish agreement, we may take it as a fact.

Sometimes a person is quoted because he is an expert in the field and his judgement can be accepted with confidence. In other cases opinions are quoted, not as a proof of what I say but to show that responsible and authoritative sources share my views.

A large group of quotations comes from public men who started the Cold War and support it—Forrestal, Dulles, Byrnes, Vandenberg, Truman, Leahy, Harriman. This category includes most newspapers and magazines. All of these sources are usually untrustworthy and biased, but they sometimes slip and reveal the truth. This is particularly the case in diaries like the **Forrestal Diaries** which were not meant for publication; or in the writings of Cold War leaders who want to prove they were anti-Soviet a long time ago; or in a magazine like **Fortune** which tells things to big business executives that newspapers don't tell the average American; or in a magazine like the **U. S. News and World Report** which says things openly and bluntly so that even the busiest, or dullest, businessman can understand immediately the real meaning of some State Department policy. Note also that when **Fortune** reports that the Soviet Union is ahead of us in jet plane technology, it can be believed, because it usually tries its best to put the Soviet Union in a bad light.

In some cases these slips and revelations are made by

men who support the Cold War in some respects but not in others. In the process of the argument they let out many relevant facts. Former Undersecretary of State Welles or Secretary of War Stimson are in this category. Some of these men in 1945 were against the Cold War and revealed many significant facts.

I must strongly emphasize that I do not accept their formulations or expressions. Some quotes are offensive in terminology but they are given as a whole to show the full thought of the person involved.Otherwise someone might believe I handled quotations the way the movie ads do. Reviewer John Doe of the **N. Y. Daily Blah,** after seeing the latest Hollywood release, "The Glamorous Stool-pigeon," writes: "The Glamorous Stool-pigeon, the greatest flop in show business since the days of the nickelodeon, is an outstanding example of film-making bad taste, as well as a colossal insult to the intelligence of the American people."

Thus the reviewer. The movie ads read:

THE GLAMOROUS STOOL-PIGEON
"greatest in show business since the days of the nickelodeon, an outstanding example of film-making. . . . Colossal. . . ."
John Doe, N. Y. Daily Blah

I leave such methods to the "free enterprise" boys. While the quotes have been chosen to develop this inquiry into the Cold War, at the same time I have been extremely careful not to misrepresent the position of the person quoted. I do not ask the reader to accept this statement on faith. I suggest a simple test. One of the books used is Sherwood's **Roosevelt and Hopkins,** which is a rich mine of facts. It is available in a 25c pocketbook edition and is well worth reading. Buy it, check any quote against it, and decide for yourself whether the quotes I have used are accurate and whether they do fairly represent the particular point being made. There are page references given in the footnotes and the reader can apply this test to any book, magazine or newspaper quoted.

I read many books in jail and so may consider jail instructive. It was instructive as well in terms of real life incidents. One of these is relevant to this book. I was in the same jail, the same cell-block, with ex-Congressman J. Parnell Thomas. Thomas had been head of the un-American "Committee on un-American Activities," one of the most powerful organs in instituting the witch-hunt hysteria in post-war America. I got to know Thomas and have some insight into his mind.

In the same jails were three other men who were sentenced for "contempt" of Congress as represented by J. Parnell Thomas. These men, Dr. Jacob Auslander of the Joint Anti-Fascist Committee, Ring Lardner Jr. and Lester Cole of the Hollywood Ten, were in jail because they refused to knuckle under Thomas.

There was an inescapable symbolism between Thomas and Auslander, between the New Jersey political hack, cowardly, vulgar, ignorant; and Auslander, the Vienna-born physician, courageous, cultured, trained, a healer with wisdom and compassion. Which truly represents America, the hysteria maker or the hysteria fighter?

Thomas is a cipher, a tool in the hands of the men he worked for. I say that he and his superiors, the "group of willful men" Roosevelt's son attacked, deliberately created a war hysteria. I believe that Roosevelt's policy of a peaceful and friendly world was perverted into the Truman Doctrine of an armed and fearful world. Between these two policies lies an abyss—an abyss of suffering and despair as the mutilated, scorched bodies in Korea can testify. I CHARGE A PLAN FOR COLD-BLOODED AGGRESSION.

This is a serious charge. It should not, it must not, be made or accepted without the most convincing evidence. For

14

three years I have been collecting it and I present it here for judgment in the form of answers to these questions:

1. Who started the Cold War?
2. How was Roosevelt's peace policy perverted into the Truman Doctrine?
3. What are the results of the Truman Doctrine?
4. What is the road back to American-Soviet friendship?

There is no mystery about the road back to friendship—it starts with negotiations. To negotiate, nations needn't be friends, just as workers and employers needn't be friends in order to bargain collectively.

Read and judge. Accept nothing, test everything. Decide for yourself what the truth is and then SPEAK UP AND ACT FOR PEACE. We must speak up, for time is running short. We, you and I, must speak for the living—and for the dead.

Carl Marzani

Danbury Jail, 1949-50
Lewisburg Penitentiary, 1950-51
New York City, 1952.

N.Y. Times
Dec. 7 1941.

PART I

'THREAT OF WAR' FRAUD

". . . the momentum of pro-Soviet feeling . . . had continued too heavily after the armistice. This made it difficult for the Administration to carry out the stiffer diplomatic policy required now. For this reason, a campaign was worked up. . . ."

C. Sulzberger, **N.Y. Times,**
March 21, 1946

"War scares are easy to create. . . ."

U.S. News and World Report,
February 17, 1951

EARLY in 1952 Winston Churchill visited America and held a press conference on his arrival. Big headlines in American newspapers proclaimed startling and welcome news: Churchill thought the danger of war had diminished. For the first time in years Churchill spoke of a "solid" outlook for peace, and gave it as his considered opinion that the Soviet Union did not want war. [1]

Coming from such an anti-Soviet leader who had been predicting war, this was indeed worth headlines.

Two weeks later, once more there were headlines: the Soviet Union does not plan war. Again, a prominent anti-Soviet leader was the source of the welcome news. This time it was Herbert Hoover, at this writing our only living ex-President. On a nation-wide radio and TV hookup Hoover said:

"There is in Europe today no such public alarm as has been fanned

1 N.Y. Times, January 6, 1952

19

up in the United States. None of those nations has declared emergencies or taken measures comparable with ours. **They do not propagandize war fears or war psychosis such as we get out of Washington.** Not one European country conducts such exercises in protection from bombs as we have had in New York.

"I recently made an inquiry from European sources as to why they calculate this risk of invasion as so much less than does Washington. The sum of this inquiry was that there was little public belief that there was risk of a Russian invasion in the near future." [2] (emphasis added)

Why should these statements make headlines?

One reason is obvious: the world is afraid of war. It is a divided world in which a tremendous armaments race is taking place, including dreaded atomic and bacteriological weapons. A state of explosive tension exists with armed colonial struggles in progress throughout the world, with civil war going on, with economic warfare on the largest scale, with propaganda warfare that never ceases. This state of tension has been tagged the COLD WAR by American newspapers.

Cold War seems to include such shooting wars as Korea, Indo-China, Malaya, in fact, everything short of global atomic war. Since people desperately want to avoid global war, news favorable to peace is welcomed by the American people.

But there have been many peace statements which have not made the headlines or even the inside pages of the daily press. Newspaper editors are hard-boiled, they only make headlines of striking, different or unusual events. Why should they consider newsworthy Churchill's and Hoover's opinions that there was little risk of Soviet aggression? Why should **this** statement, by **these** men, be news?

The reason is revealing: what they said was **directly opposed** to the official Washington position. Washington has been hammering on the theme that the Soviet Union is pre-

2 Ibid., January 28, 1952

paring aggressive war. Washington says that the present world tension, the Cold War, is the result of Soviet aggressive moves. Washington says that the Soviet Union started the Cold War as part of a scheme to extend its power by military force.

Again and again President Truman has made that point. "America," says Truman, is trying to keep the peace "in the face of a concerted campaign of threats of sabotage and outright aggression directed by the Soviet Union," a Soviet Union which is "ready and willing to try to extend its power by military conquest." [3] (emphasis added)

Hoover, on the contrary, implies this is not true. He charges Washington with propagandizing war fears, not only with words but with deeds. Not one European country, he points out, has exercises in bomb protection such as those conducted in New York. The result has been a national "war psychosis."

Herbert Hoover's description is accurate. A sharp observer of American life, columnist Walter Lippman, bears him out:

"A mood of quiet desperation has taken hold of great masses of our people. They have come to feel that they and their children are no longer free men—no longer free in the American sense of being able to make their own lives. They see themselves at the disposal of a huge undirected government buffeted about by senseless forces. . . . We are shaken and badly unnerved. Is it really because we think that Russia is so powerful and that we are so helpless? I am sure it is not. We are afraid of something else. In this century one war has led to another. We have never been able to prevent the war that was coming." [4]

We see around us a nation in semi-hysteria: dog-tags on children, airplane spotters on twenty-four hour duty, cities stockpiling pipes for emergency repairs on water mains, roads marked for quick evacuation, buildings designated as air raid shelters, air raid drills everywhere, in streets, in

3 Speech at West Point, N. Y. Times, July 21, 1952
4 N. Y. Herald Tribune, December 17, 1951

21

stores, in schools where children are made to hide under desks. In this atmosphere, we try to raise children. In this atmosphere the author's five-year-old son falls asleep asking, "Mommy, do bombs hurt?"

One looks around and wonders, is all this really necessary? Is war inevitable? Is there no peaceful alternative? Does the Soviet Union really want war?

For years progressive-minded observers have said that American-Soviet friendship is possible, that the Soviet Union neither needs nor desires war. These statements have been dismissed as pro-Soviet propaganda. But Hoover and Churchill cannot be dismissed. Their well known anti-Soviet sentiments only make their opinions more newsworthy. Peace is big news.

But an even bigger news story is hidden in Hoover's statement, hinted at in the word "propagandize." For Hoover is hinting at the greatest postwar scandal in America, namely that the Administration deliberately created a "war psychosis" with no foundation in fact!

If this is true, it means that Washington has **not** been expecting Soviet military aggression, that Washington does **not** believe the Soviets are deliberately planning war. To put it bluntly, certain government officials have deliberately deceived the American people.

HAS WASHINGTON MISLED THE COUNTRY

A key witness has left proofs showing that the Administration has constantly misled the people on the question of Soviet military intentions. The witness is James V. Forrestal, late Secretary of Defense; the proofs are his diaries. So important was their content that when Forrestal plunged to his death at Bethesda Naval Hospital in 1949, his diaries were sent to the White House for safe custody. Parts of these secret diaries have since been published, proving with chapter and verse that Washington did not believe the Soviet Union was planning war.

The Secretary of Defense himself did not believe it. As early as June 10, 1946, Forrestal wrote that it was his opinion that the Russians "would not move this summer—in fact at any time." [5] (emphasis added)

Forrestal was not alone in this belief. His diaries are sprinkled with similar statements. General Clay, Military Governor of Germany at that time, ". . . expressed it as his view that the Russians did not want a war. . . ." (July 16, 1946); General Eisenhower "gave it as his view that the Russians would not take steps leading to immediate war" (August 21, 1946); Averell Harriman "said that he did not believe the Russians would provoke war in the near future. . . ." (October 15, 1946) [6]

The Forrestal Diaries go through to 1949 and the estimate of Soviet intentions remains the same. On August 3, 1948, for example, the U. S. Ambassador to the Soviet Union, General Bedell Smith, presented a report to the War Council. (Before becoming Ambassador, General Smith had been Eisenhower's Chief-of-Staff). From this report the War Council, notes Forrestal, "gained the impression the Russians do not want war." On November 13, 1948, General Clay "gave it as his view that we were unduly apprehensive about the Russians," and, says Forrestal, "is confident that they (the Russians) do not want a war. . . ." [7]

The men quoted by Forrestal were top government officials, making judgements in the process of creating policy. These were not off-the-cuff press statements but calculated opinions expressed in the closed circles of high policy makers. These men were not guessing. They had intelligence services at their disposal supplying them with such basic facts as Soviet industrial activity and potential; [8] they received daily

5 Walter Millis, (editor), The Forrestal Diaries, New York, 1951, p. 171
6 Ibid, p. 182, p. 195, p. 212
7 Forrestal Diaries, pp. 469, 527
8 One estimate of war preparedness are armament budgets. The United Nations estimates that the U. S. arms budget for 1951 is higher than any other government in the world. UN estimates U. S. budget as capable of

reports from American military and diplomatic sources and from European agents.

The observations of the generals and the diplomats are not available to the public, but there are hints here and there of what these men reported. What did they report on Soviet intentions?

DID OUR DIPLOMATS EXPECT SOVIET AGGRESSIVE WAR?

As the formerly secret Forrestal diaries show, Ambassadors to Russia Harriman and Smith, reporting in 1946 and 1948, didn't believe the Soviet Union wanted war. In 1950 George F. Kennan, now Ambassador to Russia, wrote that "it is hardly likely that the Russians are now charting an early military onslaught on the Western World. . . ." [9]

Kennan's predecessor as Ambassador to Moscow was Admiral Alan G. Kirk, former commander of the U. S. Naval Forces in the Normandy invasion. As Ambassador to the Soviet Union, it was Kirk's business to determine Soviet intentions and as former head of Naval Intelligence (1931) he was presumably an expert on judging whether a nation is preparing for war. In December, 1950, it was reported that Admiral Kirk:

". . . sees no signs in Moscow that Russia expects war now. . . . Currently Admiral Kirk detects none of the tell-tale signs of war that the experts watch for. For example, Soviet Army units are remaining at peacetime strength. No over-age classes are being called up. No extraordinary movements of troops or supplies have been detected. There is no drive in Russia to build bomb shelters or to restrict civilian consumption of critical materials. There is no shifting of labor away from peacetime to wartime industries." [10]

buying 11,400,000 man-years of industrial labor; Russia's budget as buying 10,200,000 man-years. Comparing these armament budgets in proportion to population, the U. S is spending 1½ times as much as the USSR; in proportion to total area, 3 times as much

9 Reader's Digest, March, 1950
10 U. S. News and World Report—Since 1951 Admiral Kirk has changed his job. He now helps create the "war psychosis" Hoover talked about. He is chairman of the American Committee for the Liberation of Peoples of Russia, Inc. The moving spirits of this group are such notorious anti-Sovieteers as Eugene Lyons and Isaac Don Levine

That makes four American Ambassadors in a row who didn't expect Soviet aggression. Other American diplomats serving in Europe must have reported the same thing. There is a hint to this effect by a veteran correspondent, William Stoneman, who cabled home this dispatch in 1951:

"American diplomats serving behind the Iron Curtain appear to have agreed among themselves during a meeting in Paris, that Soviet or Soviet satellite aggression this year—or in the predictable future—is definitely unlikely.

"They are reported to feel that only a 'bad miscue' by the United States, such as **an American attack on Communist China could precipitate a Russian attack in Europe.**" 11 (emphasis added)

It is obvious that American diplomats in Europe gave Washington a good estimate of Soviet intentions. The Soviet Union had no idea of starting a war: the Soviet Union **has not started a war.**

What about our military men? Did they expect trouble?

DID OUR GENERALS EXPECT SOVIET AGGRESSIVE WAR?

The answer again seems to be no. We have seen in Forrestal's diaries that Generals Eisenhower, Smith and Clay are on record within the government as not expecting Soviet aggressive war. General Clay said so in 1946, in 1948 and again publicly in 1951 at a speech at the Hotel Waldorf-Astoria in New York City when he again pointed out the obvious, that if the Soviet Union had been planning to attack she would have done so long ago. 12

The Forrestal diaries end in 1949. Since then enough has come out to show that military men have not been expecting trouble. A year after Admiral Kirk's observations in 1950, his opinions were confirmed by the highest military chiefs in Europe. The chiefs of the North Atlantic Treaty Organi-

11 Chicago Tribune, February 7, 1951
12 Speech before Grocery Manufacturers Assn., November 14, 1951

zation (NATO) made a military report to the NATO Council, meeting in Rome. According to correspondent Benjamin Welles, the report stated that the armed forces of the Soviet Union and its allies had **not** increased since the end of World War II, "nor are there . . . any serious indications that the Soviet Union is preparing for hostilities." [13]

At this same meeting, General Gruenther, who was Eisenhower's Chief of Staff, pointed out that Soviet intentions could be gauged by her industrial production, which was not geared to all-out war. [14] By 1952 General Gruenther was even more explicit. Returning to the United Staees to make a report to Congress, he stated flatly:

"I don't think that war is imminent now and I don't think it's ever going to come. In my mind, there isn't going to be any war." [15]

These reports are from the top military men in Europe, the admirals and generals who were serving under Eisenhower. It is their business to expect and prepare for war. By training and profession they are suspicious of potential enemies, in this case the Soviet Union. Yet they all say that the Soviet Union is not planning to start a war.

What about the Europeans? They are supposed to be living under the shadow of "aggression": are they worried about the Soviet Union?

DO EUROPEANS BELIEVE IN SOVIET PLANS FOR WAR?

This question is vital to the peoples of Europe since their countries would be the battlegrounds of a third World War. Literally, this is a life and death question in Europe. We can expect them to be very realistic about the danger of Soviet aggression. In fact, since they are so close to the Soviet Union we should expect them to be even more fearful of aggression than the United States. But this is not so.

13 N. Y. Times. November 23, 1951
14 N. Y. Times. November 27, 1951, byline of Arnaldo Cortesi
15 Chicago Tribune, March 13, 1952

Exactly the reverse is true. The most responsible Europeans do not fear Soviet aggression. Ernie Hill, correspondent for the Chicago Daily News, reports that:

"The people of Europe remain pretty well unconvinced that Russia plans aggressive warfare. They contend that Russia could have swept over Europe at any time in the last six years. . . . The word used most frequently to describe Washington policy is 'hysteria.' The contrast between the American attitude toward Russia and that of Europe is shocking to anyone coming here from the U.S.[16] (emphasis added)

Herbert Hoover, in the speech already quoted gave eight reasons why Europeans did not believe in Soviet aggression. The first reason confirms fully Ernie Hill's dispatch quoted above. According to Hoover, informed European observers

". . . said that the Russian ground armies could have overrun Europe in a two months' campaign any time in the past five years and can no doubt do it during several years to come. That they have not done so seems proof to these observers that the Kremlin realizes several difficulties in making a Red world out of the West."[17]

In England both the right and the left seem to agree on this point. Said one of the leaders of the British Conservative Party, Foreign Secretary Anthony Eden:

"I do not believe that the Soviet leaders are eager to face the chaos and destruction which would result from a full-scale conflict with the West. . . ."[18]

A British Labor Party political scientist, the late Harold J. Laski, wrote:

"From what I have seen myself of Stalin, I do not believe he is either an expansionist or a warmonger. On the contrary, I doubt that there is anyone alive who knows better than he does that Russia's first need is peace."[19] (emphasis added)

In Germany, Pastor Niemoller, now a Bishop, said after

16 Chicago Daily News, October 26, 1951
17 N. Y. Times, January 28, 1952
18 Silver Lecture, Columbia University, January 11, 1952
19 N. Y. Daily Compass, December 28, 1949

a visit to Moscow that he found "little or no talk of war in Russia."[20] Another visitor to Moscow, French correspondent Michel Gordey of the conservative **France Soir** wrote after his visit in 1950 that nothing suggested "preparation in he USSR for mobilization or military aggression." On the contrary, "the Soviet people of the present time are working with all their might to rebuild their ruins," and are in no way prepared, "psychologically, physically, or morally," for "aggressive war".[21]

The prevalent opinion in Europe has been summed up by one of the most authoritative political analysts in Europe, Monsieur Maurice Beuve-Mery, who writes under the pen name of **Serius** in the Paper paper, **Le Monde.** This newspaper is roughly equivalent to the **New York Times,** and close to official government sources. **Serius** writes:

"While it is impossible to deny, without blindness or disingenuousness, that the Soviet Union seizes any occasion to increase the number of its supporters and its world influence, it is equally necessary to point out that she did not attack Greece after the defeats of General Markos, nor Berlin at the time of the airlift, nor Iran whose northern border has remained wide open, nor Czechoslovakia where the game was already won, nor Yugoslavia despite its spectacular secession. Even in Korea it is infinitely probable that nothing would have happened if the Americans had not, two years previously, deserted the post while leaving a free hand to Syngman Rhee and his blustering. Like the famous Gribouille, the Europeans seem likely through the very fear of war to throw themselves in its path."[22]

These opinions of Europeans are so widespread and openly stated that Washington has been informed of them a thousandfold. There is no doubt both from the Forrestal diaries of 1946-1949 and from the unbroken series of reports since then that official Washington had a good idea of Soviet intentions and **never** believed its own horror tales of Soviet military aggression. In deliberately creating a "war psy-

20 N.Y. Times, February 20, 1952
21 Michel Gordey, Visa to Moscow, New York, 1952, pp. 408-409
22 Le Monde, June 11, 1952

chosis" as Hoover put it, official Washington has been waging psychological warfare against us, the American people. War scares have been manufactured to frighten the American people. How? Why?

CREATING WAR SCARES

Newspapers still remain the major medium of information in modern society. Radio, movies and television have great popularity and great impact, but for the sustained and detailed spreading of ideas the daily paper still holds top rank.

In the creation of "war psychosis" newspapers have been willing tools. They have not only printed at great lengths the statements of those opposed to the Soviet Union while burying in obscure corners anything favorable to the USSR, but they have printed rumors and malicious gossip as if they were facts. We are speaking here not of the cheap, sensational press, but of reputable newspapers such as the **New York Times** and the **New York Herald Tribune.** Where reporters have tried to expose the fraudulent nature of these war scares, they soon found that their services were not needed. On occasion, the more cynical or the more courageous of the editors will blurt out the truth, and we read such statements as "War scares are easy to create," [23], "Grim warnings from the Pentagon are largely propaganda" [24] and the editor of the **Arizona Daily Star** warns "We are being shouted into a catastrophic war by the opinion makers of our country." [25]

The immediate reason for the war scares was to undermine the goodwill and friendship of the American people towards the Soviet Union. This was done deliberately as attested by the leading foreign correspondent of the **New York Times,** Cyrus Sulzberger, who wrote early in 1946 that

23 U. S. News and World Report, February 17, 1951
24 Wall Street Journal, March 17 1951
25 Letter to N. Y. Times, October 31, 1951

in the opinion of American diplomats:

". . . the momentum of pro-Soviet feeling worked up during the war to support the Grand Alliance had continued too heavily after the armistice. This made it difficult for the Administration to carry out the stiffer diplomatic policy required now. For this reason, these observers believe, a campaign was worked up to obtain a better psychological balance of public opinion. . . . "26

In other words, the feeling of friendship for Russia which President Roosevelt had fostered was to be undermined. Why?

Why was a hate campaign necessary? What kind of "stiffer diplomatic policy" is it that requires a hate campaign against an ally? Here already we see a first indirect hint as to who started the Cold War. This question will be fully discussed later; at this point it is important to see how a hate campaign in international relations gets organized by the government without the people knowing it. How is it done?

The State Department issues anonymous alarming communiques, newspapers run big headlines, editorials are written, commentators wave the flag. The technique was analyzed by Congressman Howard Buffett of Nebraska on a specific occasion: a 1948 administration request for a tremendous armaments appropriation.

In a letter to his constituents, Buffett tells how in the spring of 1948, in order to obtain Congressional approval of this program, the rumor was passed around that "we will be at war with Russia in 30 days." At the same time, a few Congressmen in an off-the-record talk with Admiral Hillenkoeter were told exactly the opposite. According to Buffett, the Admiral, who was then Chief of the Central Intelligence Agency, "declared that signs of offensive war by Russia in the foreseeable future were completely lacking." 27

It is worth noting that Congressman Buffett didn't tell

26 N. Y. Times, March 21, 1946
27 Statement of Cong. Howard H. Buffett, Washington Report, Sept. 13, 1951

this incident to the American people until 1951, although he had known about it for three years. It is also worth noting that men like Herbert Hoover said nothing year after year while the "war psychosis" was being developed. It is also worth noting that certain Big Business leaders are beginning to expose the true nature of the war scares. Why is the truth coming out **now**, and not two, three, four years ago?

WHY IS THE TRUTH COMING OUT?

The very business magazines which helped spread the war scares are now exposing them. How can such a situation occur?

If the war program has been profitable to General Electric Company, as it undoubtedly has, why should its Chairman of the Board of Directors, Philip Reed, go out of his way to slow it down? Why should he say that the peak of the re-armament program "is too high and it comes too soon?"

Yet this is what he said:

"It is my own carefully considered view that the peak of the re-armament program as presently projected is **too high and it comes too soon** . . . we who are not a part of the military (which always tends to overstate its requirements) and we who are not members of national legislative bodies (which the record shows are much more afraid of the political consequences of voting against huge military appropriations than of risking another wave of inflation) —we must speak up and express our views. . . ."[28] (emphasis added)

Philip D. Reed is in the top rank of American Big Business. His company, General Electric, is a Morgan company and the Morgan group is the most powerful single influence in American Big Business. When Reed speaks, he represents financial power.

In effect, Philip Reed was taking this occasion to warn his fellow monopolists that the entire re-armament program was moving too fast. The reason that Reed gives reflects the

28 N. Y. Times, December 5, 1951

DAILY NEWS
NEW YORK'S PICTURE NEWSPAPER

Tel. MUrray Hill 2-1234

Thursday, December 6, 1951

Published daily, except Sunday by News Syndicate Co. Inc., $29 № 42d St., Borough of Manhattan, New York City, N. Y. Daily mail subscription rates: U. S. and Poss. Daily and Sunday, $15.00 a year: Daily, Daily and Sunday News, U. S. $15.00 one year. Canada, $18.00 a year; Daily, $5 Daily and Sunday; $11.52 one year. Armed Forces Special Rates: Daily editor and secretary, Richard W. Clarke. President and general managers F. M. Flynn, executive

MEMBER OF THE ASSOCIATED PRESS
The Associated Press is entitled exclusively to the use for republication of all the local news printed in this newspaper, as well as all AP news dispatches.

TOO MUCH TOO SOON?

"Too little, too late" was a fre... year or more of war after Pearl H... was true.

As the nation now struggles ... munism...

among...

that may...

accompli...

Phi...

chairma...

out lou...

said so...

before...

of Mar...

Th...

tion is...

munis...

ng on a run...

oduction tar...

to 50 or 55...

y time soo...

aredness p...

Philip D. Reed

G. E. HEAD WARNS ON DEFENSE COST

Tells World Manufactures
Program Must Be Slowed to
Avoid Economic Trouble

By RUSSELL PORTER

Philip D. Reed, chairman ...
General Electric Company...
yesterday for reducing th...
try's peak defense product...
in 1953 from $65,000,000,000...
000,000,000 or $55,000,000,0...
for allowing two to fou...
nore than now planned...
lete the rearmament prog...
dvocated similar changes f...
ountries in the North
Treaty Organization.

Speaking at the first
ional Conference of M...
rs at the Pierre...
warned that
conce...
all...

Hoover Asks Recall of Army In Europe, Restudy of 'Risk'

Former President Herbert Hoover urged yesterday that the United States withdraw all its ground forces from Europe except those needed to protect our air bases outside the North Atlantic Treaty Organization nations.

The provision of ground armies that might be needed to oppose the Russians should be Europe's own problem, Mr. Hoover declared in a speech that was carried on the nation-wide radio and television networks of the Columbia Broadcasting System. He spoke at 1:30 P. M. from New York.

DEEP BUDGET CUTS URGED IN CONGRESS

Douglas Asks 7 Billion Slash

Military Target Date Now 1955
By Marquis Childs

Washington, Jan. 21—In the final discussion on the size of the military budget, it got down, as so often in the past, to balancing the danger of Communist attack 'from without against the threat to the economy within. When the showdown came, it was President Truman who spoke the fateful words and took on himself the responsibility for a fundamental alteration in the basic plan of the Joint Chiefs of Staff.

The change moves the target date for combat readiness from 1954 to 1955. Until now all calculations have been based on the assumption that the period of greatest danger would come in '54.

As viewed by military planners on the basis of all intelligence estimates, the Russian stockpile of atomic bombs will be much closer both in size and in kind to that of the U. S. then. At the same time, the defenses of western Europe will not have been brought to such a point that ...
armies could be ke...
Thus the tempta...
be greatest th...
The str...
It wa...
to...

NEW YORK POST, MONDAY, JANUARY 21, 1952   20

the press fall into line. We are beginning to find editorials warning about "depression and political demoralization" [35] resulting from our military expenditures and warnings that

"War preparations, U.S. style, aimed at some imaginary war that **Russian will not fight unless attacked,** is geared to yield disaster to all. . . ." [36] (emphasis added)

The same magazine said flatly:

"Russia is not going to start a war with the United States." [37]

With this truth, the entire basis of the Cold War falls away. With this truth we can begin our search for the basic question of contemporary foreign policy: who started the Cold War?

WHO STARTED THE COLD WAR?

It is official Washington doctrine that the Soviet Union started the Cold War but, against a background of fabricated stories, one can question the statements by Acheson, Dulles, Harriman, and dozens of other spokesmen who tell us that the Soviet Union started the Cold War. Why should we believe them?

Sumner Welles and Elliott Roosevelt don't believe them. FDR's Under-secretary of State and FDR's son are important witnesses. It is worth stating their opinions.

Elliott Roosevelt stated:

". . . it was the United States and Great Britain who **first** shook the mailed first, who **first** abrogated the collective decisions.
"And it should be noted too, that in the world shakedown that followed the end of the shooting, we vacated the vitally important role of operating as mediator between Great Britain and the Soviet Union, the only two nations whose security interests clash today. Rather than arbitrating those differences, as Father had always been careful to do, we chose sides; worse than that, we did not simply line up **beside** Britain, we lined up **in back** of her." [38] (emphasis in the original)

35 Detroit News, October 10, 1951
36 U. S. News and World Report, November 2, 1951
37 Ibid., February 1, 1952
38 Elliott Roosevelt, As He Saw It, New York, 1946, pp. 254-255

Elliott Roosevelt wrote this in 1946 as the Cold War was just starting. At about the same time, Sumner Welles wrote:

". . . it has become the tendency in the Western world to place the entire blame for the tragic collapse in peacemaking at the door of the Soviet government. It would seem to me far more realistic to admit that **the blame for the present disaster should be shared by the government of the United States.**"[39] (emphasis added)

Welles is not alone in disbelieving Washington.

The industrialist, Robert R. Young, in 1947 flatly disagreed that the Soviet Union had started the Cold War. He wrote:

". . . Russia showed not the remotest sign of aggression . . prior to our interest in her border states Poland and Manchuria coincident with gratuitious and undiplomatic insults. **Every move she made has been a counter-move.**"[40] (emphasis added)

Young maintains the USSR has been on the defensive, countering American policies. Professor Harry Elmer Barnes, historian and sociologist, thinks Russia has been remarkably restrained. He writes:

". . . many of the American policies affecting Russia, especially President Truman's Greco-Turkish policy, have been such as would have brought a declaration of war by this country if Russia had applied similar policies towards American interests."[41]

A prominent midwest industrialist, J. F. Lincoln, supports the historian's argument. At the end of 1951 he wrote:

" . . We would not have allowed even any small part of our present aggression to have been done by Russia anywhere in the Western Hemisphere without fighting them immediately, yet we expect that the communist world is going to accept our attacks and threats lying down. Under our present leadership we are attacking China and Russia, our recent allies, and arming our

39 Sumner Welles, Where Are We Heading, New York & London, 1946, p. 110
40 Saturday Review of Literature, March 8, 1947
41 Quoted by Jerome Davis, Peace, War and You, New York, 1952, p. 90. The most recent book on the issue of peace by a Quaker of wisdom and experience
42 Letter to Cleveland Plain Dealer, October 7, 1951

enemies, Japan and Germany, whom we fought to the death only six years ago." [42]

Remembering Washington's deception, as shown in **The Forrestal Diaries,** we would do well to take an extra long and hard look at the evidence. The evidence on the beginning of the Cold War will be found in the following chapters.

Our leaders deceived us in claiming the Soviet Union was planning military aggression. Are they also deceiving us when they say that it was the Soviet Union that started the Cold War?

The core of the evidence is American policy on the atom bomb. Its importance is self-evident. Failure to reach an agreement on its control was the signal for the present armaments race. It is in some ways the simplest issue because the alternatives were clear cut. These alternatives have been analyzed by one of the leading Americans of our generation, an American who thought deeply about the subject and set his thoughts down for President Truman. His name: Henry L. Stimson, Secretary of State under President Herbert Hoover, and Secretary of War under Presidents William Howard Taft, Franklin D. Roosevelt and Harry S. Truman. It is his analysis which is presented in evidence in the next chapter.

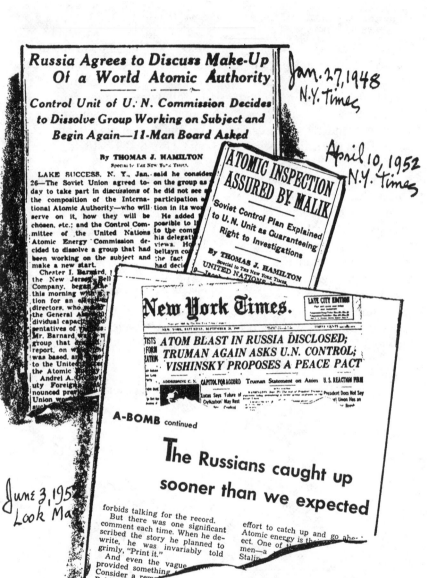

Russia Agrees to Discuss Make-Up Of a World Atomic Authority

Control Unit of U. N. Commission Decides to Dissolve Group Working on Subject and Begin Again—11-Man Board Asked

By THOMAS J. HAMILTON
Special to The New York Times.

LAKE SUCCESS, N. Y., Jan. 26—The Soviet Union agreed today to take part in discussions of the composition of the International Atomic Authority—who will serve on it, how they will be chosen, etc.; and the Control Committee of the United Nations Atomic Energy Commission decided to dissolve a group that had been working on the subject and make a new start.

Chester I. Barnard, the New Jersey Bell Company, began this morning with tion for an directors, who the General dividual capaci pentatives of Mr. Barnard, group that report, on was based. to the Unite the Atomic

Andrei A. uty Foreig nounced pr Union w such

said he consider on the group as he did not see participation tion in its wo

He added possible to l to the comp his delegat views. Ho beltsyn co the fact had decid

Jan. 27, 1948 N.Y. Times

ATOMIC INSPECTION ASSURED BY MALIK

Soviet Control Plan Explained to U. N. Unit as Guaranteeing Right to Investigations

By THOMAS J. HAMILTON
Special to The New York Times.

UNITED NATIONS

April 10, 1952 N.Y. Times

New York Times.

LATE CITY EDITION

ATOM BLAST IN RUSSIA DISCLOSED; TRUMAN AGAIN ASKS U.N. CONTROL; VISHINSKY PROPOSES A PEACE PACT

CAPITOL FOR ACCORD — Truman Statement on Atom — U. S. REACTION FIRM

Lucas Says Future of Civilization May Rest

President Does Not Say Union Has an

A-BOMB continued

The Russians caught up sooner than we expected

June 3, 195 Look Ma

forbids talking for the record.
But there was one significant comment each time. When he described the story he planned to write, he was invariably told grimly, "Print it."
And even the vague provided something Consider a rem Rabi

effort to catch up and go ahe ect. One of th men—a Stalin

ATOM BOMB MONOPOLY

CHAPTER 2

"The years before any possible power can . . . attack us with weapons of mass destruction are our years of opportunity."
Sec'y. of Defense, James V. Forrestal
December 8, 1947

". . . it will be five or ten years before they (Russians) could count on manufacture of it (the bomb) . . ."
General Walter B. Smith
September 24, 1948

"We have evidence that within recent weeks an atomic explosion occurred in the U. S. S. R."
President Harry S. Truman
September 24, 1949

THERE is a document in existence in the United States on the subject of American-Soviet relations which is dynamite. It is rare in foreign affairs that one single document could be so dangerous to a government, but this document is. It is a memorandum written especially for President Truman by his Secretary of War. It was long a top secret document which has become known only through a peculiar set of circumstances.

The importance of this document cannot be overestimated. Reactionaries have long realized its significance and have tried desperately to bury it and have people forget it. No mention is ever made of it, and two books, both important, **were deliberately distorted by omission** in order to cover it up. The two books were **The Forrestal Diaries** and **Mr. President** (excerpts from President Truman's diaries to a considerable extent). The distortion is a matter of objective proof as will be shown soon.

The document in question is a memorandum on atomic policy in respect to Russia, written on September 11,1945, nine days after the formal Japanese surrender. The elements of cold war were just coming together and this memorandum is crucial evidence on who is responsible for the Cold War.

Before quoting the memorandum in full a few words about Mr. Stimson are in order. He was at this time at the climax of a career unequalled in the United States outside of the Presidency itself. Between 1911 and 1945, he had been a Cabinet member under four administrations, both Republican and Democratic, either as Secretary of State or Secretary of War.

He was a corporation lawyer by profession, a Republican in politics, an expert on foreign affairs. On atomic energy he was probably the highest government authority on the subject with the exception of President Roosevelt himself.

From the beginning of the atomic program, Stimson was on the controlling committee that directed policy, and from 1943 onward he was directly responsible to the President for the administration of the entire undertaking. Stimson was also senior advisor to FDR on the military employment of atomic energy.

Stimson was in favor of dropping the atom bomb on Japan, and in keeping the bomb a secret. Then he changed his mind, not all at once, but slowly. He tells the story in his memoirs of how he thought about the problem of American monopoly of the bomb. The more he thought through the implications of American monopoly control, the more he began to wonder.

Returning from Potsdam, he went off to the Adirondacks for three weeks to wrestle with the problem. "In the quiet of the Adirondacks," say his memoirs, "he thought again about the atom and Russia. Twice McCloy came from Washington to talk with him, and at the other end of the secret telephone were Harrison and Bundy. . . ." [1]

The implication is clear that McCloy, Harrison and Bundy were Stimson's advisers. All three are top business men: John J. McCloy, corporation lawyer, ex-President of the World Bank, director of the Union Pacific Railroad, partner of the powerful Wall Street firm of Milbank, Tweed, Hope, Hadley & McCloy; George L. Harrison, Governor of the New York Federal Reserve Bank, President of the New York Life Insurance Company, director of many big companies; Harvey H. Bundy, corporation lawyer, member of the exclusive firm of Choate, Hall and Stewart, Assistant Secretary of War under Hoover.

They are as shrewd, hard-headed and conservative as Stimson himself, who on many issues, such as labor, was even reactionary. Forrestal reports that Stimson in 1946

" . . . expressed deep misgivings about the labor situation in the country and said that such 'conspiracy' against the public interest would have to be dealt with. . . . He said there were adequate precedents both in our own law and in old English common law to deal with such conspiracy." [2]

That these men, from the world of big business, should have decided that the United States must not try to keep an atom bomb monopoly, is powerful testimony to the fact that such a monopoly was not in the best interests of the United States. As a result of their discussions, Stimson modified his previous stand. Say the memoirs:

" . . . as he pondered a world of atomic competition, Stimson modified his earlier opinion and on September 11 he sent to the President a memorandum **urging immediate and direct negotiations with the Russians. . . .**" [3] (emphasis added)

1 Henry L. Stimson and McGeorge Bundy, **On Active Service in Peace and War**, New York, 1947, p. 641. (This is a different Bundy from the H. H. Bundy mentioned above)
2 **Forrestal Diaries**, p. 200
3 Stimson, **On Active Service**, p. 641

Stimson's memorandum is so carefully considered and so carefully worded that it should not be summarized. Moreover, it is a key document in the history of the Cold War. Here it is in full: [4]

The President,
The White House.

MEMORANDUM FOR THE PRESIDENT
11 September 1945

Subject: Proposed Action for Control of Atomic Bombs.

"The advent of the atomic bomb has stimulated great military and probably even greater political interest throughout the civilized world. In a world atmosphere already extremely sensitive to power, the introduction of this weapon has profoundly affected political considerations in all sections of the globe.

"In many quarters it has been interpreted as a substantial offset to the growth of Russian influence on the continent. We can be certain that the Soviet Government has sensed this tendency and the temptation will be strong for the Soviet political and military leaders to acquire this weapon in the shortest possible time. Britain in effect already has the status of a partner with us in the development of this weapon. Accordingly, unless the Soviets are voluntarily invited into the partnership upon a basis of co-operation and trust, we are going to maintain the Anglo-Saxon bloc over against the Soviet in the possession of this weapon. Such a condition will almost certainly stimulate feverish activity on the part of the Soviet toward the development of this bomb in what will in effect be a secret armament race of a rather desperate character. There is evidence to indicate that such activity may have already commenced.

"If we feel, as I assume we must, that civilization demands that some day we shall arrive at a satisfactory international arrangement respecting the control of this new force, the question then is how long we can afford to enjoy our momentary superiority in the hope of achieving our immediate peace council objectives.

"Whether Russia gets control of the necessary secrets of production in a minimum of say four years or a maximum of twenty years is not nearly as important to the world and civilization as to make sure that when they do get it they are willing and co-operative partners among the peace-loving nations of the world. It is true if we approach them now, as I would propose, we may be

4 Ibid., pp. 642-646

gambling on their good faith and risk their getting into production of bombs a little sooner than they would otherwise.

"To put the matter concisely, I consider the problem of our satisfactory relations with Russia as not merely connected with but as virtually dominated by the problems of the atomic bomb. Except for the problem of the control of that bomb, those relations, while vitally important, might not be immediately pressing. The establishment of relations of mutual confidence between her and us could afford to await the slow progress of time. But with the discovery of the bomb, they became immediately emergent. **Those relations may be perhaps irretrievably embittered by the way in which we approach the solution of the bomb with Russia. For if we fail to approach them now and merely continue to negotiate with them, having this weapon rather ostentatiously on our hip, their suspicions and their distrust of our purposes and motives will increase.** (the emphasis is Stimson's) [5] It will inspire them to greater efforts in an all-out effort to solve the problem. If the solution is achieved in that spirit, it is much less likely that we will ever get the kind of covenant we may desperately need in the future. This risk is, I believe, greater than the other, inasmuch as our objective must be to get the best kind of international bargain we can—one that has some chance of being kept and saving civilization not for five or for twenty years, but forever.

"The chief lesson I have learned in a long life is that the only way you can make a man trustworthy is to trust him; and the surest way to make him untrustworthy is to distrust him and show your distrust.

"If the atomic bomb were merely another though more devastating military weapon to be assimilated into our pattern of international relations, it would be one thing. We could then follow the old custom of secrecy and nationalistic military superiority relying on international caution to prescribe the future use of the weapon as we did with gas. But I think the bomb instead constitutes merely a first step in a new control by man over the forces of nature too revolutionary and dangerous to fit into the old concepts. I think it really caps the climax of the race between man's growing technical power for destructiveness and his psychological power of self-control and group control—his moral power. If so, our method of approach to the Russians is a question of the most vital importance in the evolution of human progress.

"Since the crux of the problem is Russia, any contemplated action

5 The emphasis was not in the original memo, but was added by Stimson when his memoirs were written in 1947. (Bundy, who wrote the book only followed Stimson's opinions). At that time Stimson considered this passage and one more, also emphasized, to be the heart of the memorandum

leading to the control of this weapon should be primarily directed to Russia. It is my judgment that the Soviet would be more apt to respond sincerely to a direct and forthright approach made by the United States on this subject than would be the case if the approach were made as a part of a general international scheme, or if the approach were made after a succession of express or implied threats or near threats in our peace negotiations.

"My idea of an approach to the Soviets would be a direct proposal after discussion with the British that we would be prepared in effect to enter an arrangement with the Russians, the general purpose of which would be to control and limit the use of the atomic bomb as an instrument of war and so far as possible to direct and encourage the development of atomic power for peaceful and humanitarian purposes. Such an approach might more specifically lead to the proposal that we would stop work on the further improvement in, or manufacture of, the bomb as a military weapon, provided the Russians and the British would agree to do likewise. It might also provide that we would be willing to impound what bombs we now have in the United States provided the Russians and the British would agree with us that in no event will they or we use a bomb as an instrument of war unless all three Governments agree to that use. We might also consider including in the arrangement a covenant with the U.K. and the Soviets providing for the exchange of benefits of future developments whereby atomic energy may be applied on a mutually satisfactory basis for commercial or humanitarian purposes.

"I would make such an approach just as soon as our immediate political considerations make it appropriate.

"**I emphasize perhaps beyond all other considerations the importance of taking this action with Russia as a proposal of the United States—backed by Great Britain but peculiarly the proposal of the United States. Action of any international group of nations, including many small nations who have not demonstrated their potential power or responsibility in this war would not, in my opinion, be taken seriously by the Soviets.** (emphasis is Stimson's) [6] The loose debates which would surround such proposal, if put before a conference of nations, would provoke but scant favor from the Soviet. As I say, I think this is the most important point in the program.

"After the nations which have won this war have agreed to it, there will be ample time to introduce France and China into the covenants and finally to incorporate the agreement into the scheme of the United Nations. The use of this bomb has been accepted by

6 The memoirs say that Stimson considered this the most important passage in the memorandum

the world as the result of the initiative and productive capacity of the United States, and I think this factor is a most potent lever toward having our proposals accepted by the Soviets, whereas I am most skeptical of obtaining any tangible results by way of any international debate. I urge this method as the most realistic means of accomplishing this vitally important step in the history of the world.

"Henry L. Stimson
"Secretary of War."

Such is the memorandum.

It is based on a basic fact of life and on a policy.

The basic fact of life is that as a result of World War II, the United States and the Soviet Union have emerged as the two superpowers. **There cannot be a world war without these two as opponents.** This does not mean that the rest of the world is negligible or unimportant—far from it. What it does mean is that the controlling decision of war and peace rests today with these two nations. If the U. S. and the U. S. S. R. are friends, there cannot be a war. If they are enemies, war is a constant possibility.

The policy on which Stimson's memo is based is President Roosevelt's policy of expanding the areas of agreement and reducing the areas of conflict by negotiation and compromise. As FDR told Congress, on his return from the Yalta conference, March 1, 1945:

". . . the conference was a successful effort by the three leading nations to find a common ground for peace. . . . I am confident that the Congress and the American people will accept the results of this conference as the beginnings of a permanent structure of peace. . . ."

FDR's policy toward the Soviet Union was "to find a common ground for peace." This was the public policy of our government until the day of his death, April 12, 1945. Stimson's memorandum rests squarely on this policy and, so do his warnings. When Truman rejected Stimson's suggestions and disregarded Stimson's warnings, he was reversing Roosevelt's policy. This is why his memorandum is such political dynamite.

A—Stimson begins by pointing out that some people are looking at the bomb as an instrument of power politics, something to "balance" Soviet influence; something, in other words, with which to threaten the USSR. He points out that the Soviets are aware of this, and the result can only be a "secret armaments race of a rather desperate character." This is exactly what has taken place.

B—Stimson next warns that "if we fail to approach them [the Soviets] now and merely continue to negotiate with them, **having this weapon rather ostentatiously on our hip,** their suspicions and their distrust of our purpose and motives will increase." The Soviets will race to get the bomb, and then we will find it more difficult to get the kind of agreement we "may desperately need in the future." Our relations with Russia may be "irretrievably embittered." This is strong language—but doesn't it describe the Cold War? Doesn't this warning sound prophetic in the light of the Cold War of today?

C—Finally, Stimson points out, in a paragraph of remarkably long-range view, that the bomb "constitutes merely a first step in a new control by man over the forces of nature too revolutionary and dangerous to fit into the old concepts," and he gives a warning as grave and sober as it is carefully considered, ". . . our method of approach to the Russians is a question of the most vital importance in the evolution of human progress."

This approach must be "direct and forthright" Stimson warns, or it would not be "taken seriously by the Soviets."

How seriously did Truman take Stimson's warnings and suggestions?

Truman disregarded everyone of Stimson's urgent suggestions. Not only that: **he did exactly the opposite.** The consequences have been precisely what Stimson predicted, a dreaded atomic armaments race which can only end in disaster for everyone. It is little wonder that books like **The**

Forrestal Diaries and **Mr. President** distort facts and mislead the people about Stimson's ideas. To prove this charge of distortion, Stimson's predictions and proposals must be seen in sharp focus.

THE CONTENTS OF THE STIMSON MEMORANDUM

The predictions of Stimson have all come true. This is quite remarkable even if we consider that he was an expert on foreign affairs and atomic problems. For some of his predictions are truly amazing. For example, he said that the Soviet Union might possibly make an atom bomb "in a minimum of say four years. . . ." Almost four years to the day from the date of Stimson's memo, President Truman announced that "an atomic explosion" had occurred in the USSR "within recent weeks!" (Date of announcement, September 24, 1949. Date of memo, September 11, 1945)

The writer doesn't want to ascribe supernatural powers to Stimson. He was making an estimate, from a minimum of four years to a maximum of twenty. But that his minimum estimate should have turned out so close to reality is a tribute to his thorough knowledge of atomic production. Compare Stimson's minimum estimate with that of General Walter Bedell Smith, Ambassador to Moscow, who as late as September 24, 1948 told Secretary Forrestal:

"**The Russians cannot possibly have the industrial competence** to produce the atomic bomb now, and it will be 5 or even 10 years before they could count on manufacture of it in quantity. They may well have the 'notebook' know-how, but not the industrial complex to translate that knowledge into concrete weapons." [7] (emphasis added)

The underestimation of Soviet industrial strength by men like General Smith is directly related to their arrogant nationalistic feelings of U. S. superiority. This underestimation

[7] Forrestal Diaries, p. 496. General Smith's statement that the Russians may have had the "know-how," and that only an adequate "industrial complex" was necessary undermines the entire premise of atomic spy scares. For the full story of this, including John Foster Dulles' opinion on the subject, see the appendix at the end of this book

lay at the bottom of Forrestal's strategic thinking as revealed in his diaries:

"As long as we can outproduce the world, we can control the sea **and can strike inland with the atomic bomb,** we can assume certain risks otherwise unacceptable. . . . The years before any possible power can achieve the capability effectively to attack us with weapons of mass destruction are **our years of opportunity. . . ."** 8 (emphasis added)

As Secretary of Defense, Forrestal had a powerful influence on Truman. If Truman had paid attention to the predictions and proposals of Henry L. Stimson, the world situation today would be much less dangerous.

What were Stimson's precise proposals?

Here they are, itemized from the memo.

1—In our negotiations with the Soviet Union, we must avoid "express or implied threats or near threats" based on our possession of the bomb.

2—**We** should make a **direct** approach to the USSR. He specifically warns that it should **not** be of an international group nature. He states most emphatically that any group approach would show the Soviets the Americans were not serious. The approach should be an invitation to the Soviets to participate in the partnership on a "basis of co-operation and trust."

3—We should negotiate an agreement to outlaw the atomic bomb as an instrument of war.

4—We should offer to "stop work on the further improvement in or manufacture of the bomb as a military weapon, provided the Russians and the British would agree to do likewise." We should be willing to "impound what bombs we now have in the United States" provided that the Soviets agree to outlaw the bomb.

5—We should exchange benefits of atomic energy with the USSR for commercial and humanitarian purposes.

8 Forrestal Diaries, p. 351

These were the Stimson proposals. What did Truman do? He got tough with the Soviets, proposed an international commission, has so far refused to outlaw the bomb, did not stop work on making bombs (on the contrary) and, of course, there has been no exchange of atomic energy. **On every count, exactly the reverse.**

THE SIGNIFICANCE OF THE STIMSON MEMORANDUM

This book seeks to determine the origins of the cold war. The significance of the Stimson memorandum for this purpose is tremendous. Given the memorandum, Truman and his advisers cannot plead ignorance. The initiative was in America's hands and Stimson warned what would happen if we took a certain road. Truman took the road.

A wrong approach, warned Stimson, might "irretrievably embitter" Soviet-American relations. What was the wrong approach? Stimson said the wrong approach was through an international commission. A United Nations commission, for example, would be wrong.

What's wrong with a UN Commission on atomic energy?

Offhand it seems only right and democratic for the UN to deal with atomic problems. The reality about the UN however is that the United States dominates it. This was apparent in 1945 when the first dramatic proof of U. S. domination was shown on the question of admitting Argentina.

Arthur Krock, chief political correspondent of the **New York Times** wrote that "the U. S. is the leader of an irresistible conference bloc" which was like the "steamroller of a national convention." [9]

Further details of the U. S. domination of the UN will be given in a later chapter but it was clear to the Soviet Union, as it was clear to Krock, that the U. S. did have a steamroller within the UN. Any proposal on atomic energy

9 N. Y. Times, May 2, 1945

by a UN Commission would be very apt to be identical with the United States proposal. This is in fact what did happen later.

If there were no prior discussion between the U. S. and the Soviet Union, Russia would inevitably reject the idea of a commission. Without prior direct discussion the Soviet Union would feel that the U. S. wasn't really interested in reaching agreement.

That is why Stimson wrote:

"... if the approach were made a part of a general international scheme ... including many small nations who have not demonstrated ... responsibility in the war [it] would not, in my opinion, be taken seriously by the Soviets. ..."

In 1947 Stimson said this was the most important point of all, yet Truman deliberately rejected a direct approach to the Soviet Union. He met with the Prime Ministers of Canada and Great Britain and on November 15, 1945 they announced that "... at the earliest practicable date a commission should be set up under the United Nations Organization to prepare recommendations. ..." [10]

Here it was, clear and unmistakable, a conscious, deliberate rejection of the very point which Stimson had emphasized and re-emphasized: action must be taken **directly** with the USSR, **not** by commissions, committees or what not.

Truman's proposals seemed to enhance the UN. Actually, as results have shown, the proposals were a roadblock.

Stimson was in favor of the UN. He wanted it to work, and he knew a United Nations could only work if it was based on Roosevelt's basic concept: Big Three Unity. Stimson wanted to strengthen the UN. That is why he clearly said, **after** a basic agreement was reached in direct Soviet-American negotiations the entire problem could be taken up in detail by the UN and incorporated into its structure.

10 N. Y. Times, November 16, 1945

This was the way of Teheran and Yalta. Big Three unity as the basis of lasting peace, as the start of the United Nations. This was Roosevelt's way, and to cover up its rejection, Stimson's position must be hidden and distorted.

Let the reader go back and re-read Stimson's memorandum, study his argument, see how logically, how sharply, how cleverly he reaches his main point—direct negotiations, not unilateral decisions. In the face of Stimson's recommendation, which was supported by many other experts including atomic scientists, it cannot be said that American policy makers did not know exactly what they were doing. Stimson's memo is a damning, unanswerable indictment of Truman's foreign policy. That is why it has been so thoroughly hushed up.

COVERING UP STIMSON'S POSITION

The two outstanding instances are **The Forrestal Diaries** and **Mr. President.**

"The Forrestal Diaries," published in October 1951, were censored to eliminate all references to the Stimson memorandum.

Walter Millis, the editor of the Diaries, states in the foreword that

". . . a rather large portion was condensed, paraphrased or in some instances omitted entirely on the ground that it might materially embarrass the current conduct of international relations, and that its publication would therefore not be in the national interest." Mr. Millis claims that "here there was no sinister suppression."

Now here are the facts.

On September 21, 1945, a Cabinet meeting was held, the last one Stimson attended since he was resigning on that day. In view of what happened at this meeting, it is probably one of the most momentous in the entire history of the United States. Forrestal kept notes and made comments in his diary on the meeting. Walter Millis gives a **condensation** of what Forrestal wrote down.

Millis says that this meeting was concerned exclusively with a discussion of the atomic bomb, and "was clearly fundamental in the formulation of American policy on this new and dread subject."

President Truman presented the question of what should be "the policy of this government in making available information in our possession to other nations. . . ." Millis then writes, "Beginning with Mr. Stimson, the President went round the table."

Millis never reports what Stimson said. Instead he jumps right into a report of what Wallace said and does so in such a manner as to give the definite impression that Wallace, then Secretary of Commerce, was the only one who wished to follow a policy of co-operation with the Soviet Union. There is a bitter attack on Wallace by Forrestal, who insisted on keeping the so-called "secret" and who insisted on sole control of atomic energy by the U. S.

Millis goes on to say:

". . . the underlying attitude of **nearly all** seemed closely in accord with Forrestal's contributions. . . ." [11] (emphasis added)

The impression is deliberately created that only Wallace was in disagreement. This impression is not true since we know that Mr. Stimson's views were even stronger than Wallace's, had been carefully formulated and put in writing. In this regard, Millis definitely leads the reader astray, writing:

". . . it is clear that ideas had not yet fully crystallized. . . ." [12]

In Stimson's case this simply isn't so. The memorandum cannot be blinked away.

The fact is, not only had Stimson formulated his ideas, but also he had presented them to the President. At this fateful Cabinet meeting, he again presented his opinions and

11 **Forrestal Diaries, p. 95**
12 **Ibid, p. 95**

fought vigorously for them. This is precisely what we should expect him to do on so grave a matter. That he did so, is explicitly stated on page 646 of his memoirs, which read:

". . . These opinions, **which he urgently expressed again to the President and the Cabinet on the day of his retirement,** were the ones with which Stimson left office. . . ." (emphasis added)

Wallace's recollection of the Cabinet meeting has been made public, in the following words:

"Secretary Stimson had stated in **Cabinet meeting on Sept. 21, 1945, that other nations would almost certainly have the bomb by 1950.** I believed him. . . .
"Our high policy makers, knowing nothing about science, thought we had a secret which we could use as a peacetime weapon in international affairs.
"They did not ask what would happen to our foreign policy when two countries had the bomb." [13] (emphasis added)

In **The Forrestal Diaries** Wallace is used as a straw man to cover up Stimson's position for the simple reason that Wallace could be attacked and dismissed as a New Dealer, but Stimson could not. Truman used the same technique in the book **Mr. President.** It is done more subtly, but the misleading is there as the reader can judge by himself.

TRUMAN OBSCURES STIMSON'S POSITION

Mr. President is a book written by a newspaperman, William Hillman, but Truman is explicitly a partner in the book. He gave special interviews to Hillman, made available his diaries, notes and private papers. The book says that its purpose is to present Truman as he sees himself.

Truman tries to show himself as a peace-loving, peace-seeking President. A large part of the book is a justification of his foreign policy, how he has striven to avert war and has been patient under the provocation of the USSR. In view of what we have seen in the chapter, that Washington has deliberately created a "war psychosis," Truman's self-portrait doesn't correspond completely with reality.

13 Speech before Prairie Club in Des Moines, Iowa, April 29, 1950

Furthermore, in view of the fact that Truman knows he rejected Stimson's memorandum, his treatment of Stimson is significant. Examining the book **Mr. President**, a striking fact emerges. The only mention of Stimson in the entire book, is a reference to Stimson's support of the North Atlantic Organization in 1949 and 1950. [14] The unwary reader gets the impression that Stimson has been in full accord with Truman's handling of foreign policy, which isn't true, given Stimson's position in 1945. As late as 1947, discussing Truman's course of action, Stimson "did not believe that this course represented precisely the **policy and method** he had in mind" in 1945 [15] (emphasis added).The omission of Stimson's position in 1945, obscures the truth.

This omission gains further significance by the way it is done. Here are the facts. The book has a section, Part Three, entitled **Diaries, Private Memoranda, Papers.** This section is the heart of the book, and received the greatest publicity, because it contains a whole series of entries from Truman's diary. The first entry is on the day he entered the White House, April 12, 1945.

Then follows a whole series of entries for each month through April, May, June, July, August and September, right up to September 20, 1945, the day before the crucial Cabinet meeting. Abruptly, with the very next line, **a whole year is jumped** to an entry of September, 1946. And what is this entry? **An attack on Mr. X, who has been generally taken to be Mr. Wallace.** [16]

14 William Hillman, **Mr. President**, New York, 1952, p. 55
15 Stimson, **On Active Service**, p. 647. Mr. Stimson's position on atomic control had not changed between 1945 and 1947. His attitude on other aspects of foreign policy had, however. It is not relevant here, but it is sufficiently important to be examined in Appendix I at the end of this book
16 **Mr. President**, p. 128.—Practically all the newspapers have mentioned Mr. Wallace in connection with the identity of Mr. X. Wallace himself sent a wire to Mr. Truman asking if Mr. X referred to him. Mr. Truman didn't answer. The entry said that Mr. X wanted to "disband our armed forces, give Russia our atomic secrets and trust a bunch of adventurers in the Kremlin Politbureau." By vulgarizing a policy of co-operation with the Soviet Union, Mr. Truman seeks to discredit it.

The Cabinet meeting is omitted entirely. This is very strange indeed when one considers its importance. Also there were certain colorful and historical details about that fateful day. It was Mr. Stimson's birthday, he was resigning after a long and honorable career in public life, and he was given an impressive farewell at the Pentagon. Surely Truman's sentimentality and sense of history must have been stirred.

Furthermore, why skip a year in order to put in an entry which is an attack on a policy of cooperation with the USSR? It almost seems as if Truman, in the very process of burying Stimson's proposals, is trying to justify himself. The bitterness of the attack gives one a sense that Truman is uneasy. If the analysis of this chapter is correct, Truman ought to feel uneasy. It is a heavy responsibility to have disregarded Stimson's memorandum.

The Cabinet meeting of September 21, 1945, shaped our atomic policy. Say **The Forrestal Diaries,** "The idea of submitting the matter for adjustment under the machinery of the United Nations became basic to subsequent American policy." [17] Millis gives Forrestal major credit for this result, which was made public by Truman on November 15. Taken together with Secretary of State Byrnes toughness at the London Conference, November, 1945, it was apparent to the Soviet Union (as Stimson had warned), that the American proposals were not serious. Nevertheless, the Soviet Union did not close the door. She agreed at the Moscow Conference to set up a UN Atomic Energy Commission which was done by resolution of the UN Assembly, January 24, 1946.

In March, 1946, the Acheson-Lilienthal report was made public, and on June 6, 1946, Bernard M. Baruch presented the American plan for atomic control to the UN. It became

17 Forrestal Diaries, p. 96

known as the Baruch Plan. The provisions of the Plan were unacceptable to the Soviet Union.

Furthermore, **the Baruch Plan was intended to be unacceptable,** which means that it was presented in bad faith. The proof is in the record.

WAS THE BARUCH PLAN PROPOSED IN BAD FAITH?

The heart of the Baruch Plan was that an international commission should have ownership of all major atomic installations and should decide where such installations would be built. It was to be run by majority vote without control of the Security Council of the UN. In other words the veto would not apply. For the Soviet Union to surrender its sovereignty to a U. S.-dominated commission was inconceivable, and even members of the Acheson-Lilienthal Committee objected. Mr. Chester I. Barnard, a member of the Committee, has spilled the beans. "Mr. Lilienthal and I," he has written, "**personally begged Mr. Baruch not to introduce the veto problem . . . .**" [18] (emphasis added)

Mr. Baruch knew exactly what he was doing. The veto question alone would guarantee rejection by the Soviet Union.

The Baruch Plan left no door open for compromise. Even had the Soviet Union accepted the Plan, the United States would not agree to the abolition of the atom bomb, or even to stop making bombs as Stimson had urged as a quid-pro-quo. The U. S. reserved complete liberty of action.

The Acheson-Lilienthal report made this clear.

"The significant fact is that at all times during the transitional period such facilities—stockpiles of bombs and plants to produce [fissionable] material—will continue to be located within the U. S. Thus should there be a breakdown in the plan during the transition, **we shall be in a favorable position with regard to atomic weapons.**" [19] (emphasis added)

18 Dartmouth Alumni Magazine, February, 1948. Mr. Barnard was President of the N. J. Bell Telephone Co.
19 U. S. Department of State, A Report on the International Control of Atomic Energy, Washington, 1946

In other words the effect of the Baruch Plan would be to strengthen the U. S. atomic position in relation to the Soviet Union. This is also the conclusion reached by one of the foremost international experts on atomic energy, Professor P. M. S. Blackett. Professor Blackett is a Nobel prize-winner and was a member of the official Advisory Committee on Atomic Energy for the British Government. He writes:

". . . the putting into operation of the Baruch Plan would undoubtedly have led to **an immediate reduction of Russian military strength** relative to America, **uncompensated by any clear reciprocal gain.** It is certain that the early stages of the operation of the Baruch Plan would be definitely detrimental to immediate Soviet security. . . ."[20] (emphasis added)

This is fine from the point of view of American military advantage, but why should Baruch expect the Soviet Union to accept it? The answer of course is that he didn't.

One more item of the Baruch Plan was so clearly unacceptable to the Soviet Union as to prove that Baruch so designed his Plan as to guarantee rejection.

The first step in the Plan was the carrying out of a world-wide survey for raw materials of atomic energy. Says Professor Blackett:

"The operation of such an unlimited survey in the USSR would have given the UN inspectors—and hence the American Chiefs of Staff—a fairly **complete target map** of the USSR."[21]

The importance of a target map in relation to strategic bombing is simply tremendous. Its significance is fully appreciated by anyone who has worked in the field of strategic bombing. In this connection, a personal note by the writer may be forgiven.

The writer of this book served during the war as assistant Division Chief in the Office of Strategic Services. This was

20 P. M. S. Blackett, Fear, War and the Bomb, New York & Toronto, 1948, pp. 152-53. This book is one of the best contributions to the problem of atomic control.
21 Ibid, p. 152

an independent intelligence agency responsible only to President Roosevelt and the Joint Chiefs of Staff. It had very broad functions ranging from parachuting aid to the French Resistance Movement to making estimates of German casualties. The writer spent a large part of his time on military problems of all kinds, logistics, enemy capabilities, army organization, general staff controls, new weapons evaluation such as radar and rockets, propaganda and economic warfare.

Strategic bombing was one of the military problems with which the writer was connected. He headed a team of experts who picked the targets for the famous Doolittle raid on Japan in 1942, and he personally picked the targets in Tokyo, Yawata and Yokohama. In 1944 he supervised the making of a book on target selection, **Strategic Air Objectives,** which became one of the texts in the armed forces. In 1945-46 the writer helped prepare the reports of the U. S. Strategic Bombing Survey.

The most important single factor in strategic bombing is the location of the target. This is so obvious that to point it out seems silly. Yet it is often overlooked. One of the Soviet Union's important defensive measures has been the secrecy on the location of their armaments plants. Even location of general industrial areas is of great military significance, and Soviet secrecy paid off as the Nazi Generals have testified. Said their top commander, Field Marshal Von Runstedt, about the invasion of Russia:

"I realized soon after the attack was begun that everything that had been written about Russia was nonsense."

"The maps we were given were all wrong. The roads that were marked nice and red and thick on a map turned out to be tracks, and what were tracks on the map became first class roads. Even railways which were to be used by us simply didn't exist. Or a map would indicate that there was nothing in the area and **suddenly**

22 Shulman, **Defeat in the West,** p. 66; quoted in **Fear, War and the Bomb,** p. 153

we would be confronted with an American-type town with factory buildings and all the rest of it." 22 (emphasis added)

The Soviet Union has carefully guarded the location of its armaments plants. This is one reason why foreign diplomats and military attaches are restricted in their travels around the Soviet Union. 23 To expect the Soviet Union to hand over "a fairly complete target map of the USSR" to a U. S.-dominated survey is sheer nonsense and Baruch knew it.

It is clear that the Baruch proposals would be unacceptable to the Soviet Union. Furthermore the Baruch Plan was based on a series of wrong estimates both of the Soviet Union's capabilities and of the nature of atomic problems. This is the conclusion of Stephen White, assistant managing editor of **Look** magazine, who has followed atomic developments closely. He writes that the Baruch Plan:

". . . was a plan based for the most part on misconceptions and mistakes. . . .

"The Baruch Plan assumed that uranium was scarce. It is abundant.

"The Baruch Plan assumed that atom bombs were extremely difficult to make. They are relatively easy to make.

"The Baruch Plan assumed that atom bombs would be made in relatively small quantities. They are being made wholesale.

"The Baruch Plan assumed that the United States **had a monopoly of atomic know-how.** . . . But the monopoly has long since vanished and with it a good deal of America's bargaining power." 24 (emphasis added)

There is no reason on earth why the Soviet Union should have accepted such a plan. She didn't.

A HOAX ON THE AMERICAN PEOPLE

In March 1947, Forrestal wrote in his diary that the United Nations could not handle the problem of atomic

---

23 The publication of the diary of Major General Robert W. Grow (U. S. Military Attache in Moscow) shows that he was busy looking for targets. Washington Post, March 6, 1952. Otis and Voegeler admitted in the American press that they were interested in new industrial plants
24 Look, June 8, 1952
25 Forrestal Diaries, pp. 258-259

energy. [25] This underlines the insincerity of the American proposals. If the UN couldn't handle the problem, why did Truman use that organization for the American control proposals?

Given what Forrestal, Stimson and Barnard have written, the only answer is that we knew beforehand that our proposals would be unacceptable, and that the Baruch Plan was presented merely as a manoeuver in the Cold War diplomacy. Professor Blackett confirms this analysis, writing:

"In the long run, the Baruch plan . . . must be considered historically as an astute move and a very considerable victory for American diplomacy. For so great was the success with which this **specious** plan was put across in most countries as a wise and generous measure, that it became possible to brand the Soviet Union, by her rejection of it, as the sole obstacle to world peace." [26] (emphasis added)

From Mr. Truman's standpoint, all well and good. But who was being misled by this act of bad faith? Not the Soviet Union certainly. Soviet leaders knew what was going on.

The primary victim of this "astute move" was the American people. We were made to believe that the Soviet Union was against peace and atomic control. We were made to believe the Soviet Union wanted war. **The elaborate hoax of the Baruch Plan was directed in the first place against the American people.** It became an important ingredient in the creation of the "war psychosis" that Herbert Hoover had spoken about.

Looking back to late 1945 and 1946 the pattern of hysteria-making becomes clear. At every turn, the United States made impossible proposals to the USSR, backed by the threat of the atom bomb. When the Soviet Union made counter-proposals, the United States refused to consider them, ac-

---

26 Blackett, Fear, War and the Bomb, p. 158. Professor Blackett goes on to explain why the plan was "specious." The Baruch Plan would have failed even if all its supporters had been sincere in their intentions, because it attempted the impossible task of devising an international control scheme whose primary objective was to provide one nation, the U.S., with a nearly perfect assurance that its atomic monopoly would be preserved

cused the Soviet Union of bad faith and of planning aggressive war. In this manner the American people were driven by fear, war scares were whipped up and the "war psychosis" developed.

Our relations with the Soviet Union entered into a blind alley. Since the Truman Administration had been forewarned by Stimson, this situation must have been foreseen. Some strange implications arise. First, war scares are manufactured to offset popular American friendship for the Soviet Union in order, says Sulzberger, to have a basis for stiffer bargaining. Then the door to bargaining is deliberately closed. It turns out that war scares are only one ingredient of the Cold War and we must seek deeper reasons for the war scares than the simple strengthening of our diplomatic poker hand.

Why has Washington created a "war psychosis"?

COLD WAR —
FROZEN WAGES

".. . it has taken greater and greater defense expenditures just to hold business on
an even keel. . . ."
Journal of Commerce,
July 14, 1952

"War scares are easy to create and are
nearly sure fire producers of money for
more arms. . . ."
U. S. News and World Report,
February 17, 1950

"American business might be forced to
turn to some form of disguised Fascistic
dictatorship."
H. W. Prentis, Security Review Board,
Atomic Energy Commission

CHAPTER 3

A CALCULATED policy of war hysteria
has brought America to the verge of disaster. Disaster is
not too strong a word to use for the present situation. Says
Henry Ford II:

"There are two obvious places we could go. One is to war. The
other is broke." [1]

And Charles E. Wilson, President of General Motors,
quotes approvingly an editorial of the **Detroit News:**

"Either it [our country] willl be beggared by the cost of military
upkeep . . . or . . . we will take the road to war, **even as Hitler
did."** [2] (emphasis added)

1 U. S. News & World Report, January 25, 1952
2 Speech before Society for Advancement of Management, October 10, 1951

63

A policy which can be compared to Hitler's by a Big Businessman like Wilson is obviously not a good policy. Hitler's policy resulted in a smashed Germany; the present situation in the world is very dangerous to America.

How could political leaders in America have followed a policy so disastrous to the nation. What are they thinking about:

"Government planners figure they have found the magic formula for almost endless good times. They are now beginning to wonder if there may not be something to perpetual motion after all. . . . **Cold War** is the catalyst. Cold War is an automatic pump-primer. Turn a spigot, and the public clamors for more arms spending. Turn another, the clamor ceases. Truman confidence, cockiness is based on this 'Truman Formula.' **Truman era** of good times, the President is told, can run much beyond 1952. Cold war **demands,** if fully exploited, are almost limitless."[3] (emphasis in the original)

This is a clear, if shameless, explanation of what is behind the Cold War. But no one should think that the Democrats have a monopoly on cynicism. Here is what the Republicans are thinking as given in their big business paper, the **Journal of Commerce:**

"The nomination of Dwight D. Eisenhower eliminates most of the uncertainty over the future course of defense and foreign aid expenditures. . . . The assurance of a continued high level of defense expenditures under present conditions cannot be overestimated because **the whole economy pivots around it.**
"Actually nothing short of the present gigantic defense program could have successfully filled **the 'air pocket' in the civilian sector** of the economy . . . it has taken greater and greater defense expenditures just to hold business on an even keel."[4] (emphasis added)

These statements from business publications reveal the reasons for the Cold War. The Cold War is the result of the **internal needs of a big business economy.** It is an "automatic pump-primer" which is deliberately manipulated, like "turning a spigot," by those interested.

3 U. S. News & World Report, May 26, 1950
4 Journal of Commerce, July 14, 1952

In big business thinking only the armaments resulting from the Cold War are saving us from a chronic depression by filling the "air-pocket" in the civilian economy. Such thinking exposes the true nature of the Cold War, for what is this "air-pocket" business talks about?

"AIR POCKETS" AND PAY ENVELOPES

The "air-pocket" of big business double talk means the empty space in the pockets of the American people—workers, farmers, teachers, professionals. It is their lack of purchasing power in comparison to our tremendously expanded production.

Since 1939 our industrial production has doubled. [5] A flood of goods and materials covered the postwar market. What is this "market?"

Primarily it is the people, millions and millions of workers, farmers and so on, whose average purchasing power did not go up, but in fact **went down.** Government statistics show that spendable income per person was at its highest in 1944 ($1,487 a year) and has been below that every single year since—as low as $1,379 in 1949. [6]

In other words, while production expanded, purchasing power contracted. The average person has been going steadily into debt. Total consumer credit (debts) which amounted to five billion in 1944, stood at 20.6 billions in 1951. [7] The rise in consumer credit is a storm signal of depression: the figure in 1929 was 6.2 billions.

The people go into debt, the well-to-do save the money. [8] The goods pile up on shelves and in warehouses, factories begin to shut down. If the government does not intervene, a depression occurs as in the 1930's. The American people

5 Midyear Economic Report of the President, July, 1952, p. 2
6 Ibid., p. 149. The figure for 1951 was $1,458
7 Ibid., p. 165. Fifty per cent of the lowest income families in the country are in debt, according to the Federal Reserve Bulletin, September, 1951
8 The wealthiest 20% of all families have 93% of liquid savings, Federal Reserve Bulletin, September, 1951

rightly fear a depression. Big Business tries to exploit this fear by saying that only armaments and a war economy can prevent a depression. They try to hide the real alternative to the Cold War economy, a peaceful program for the people's needs. Such a program was set forth by President Franklin D. Roosevelt in his "Economic Bill of Rights," January 11, 1944.

ROOSEVELT'S POSTWAR PROGRAM

Foreign policy and domestic policies are closely tied together and determine each other in many ways. As Hitler so clearly showed, an aggressive foreign policy means a drive against the people at home. Opposing Hitler, President Roosevelt was keenly aware of the connection between foreign and domestic policies and presented the alternatives to Fascism in both fields. Alongside his foreign policy of postwar friendship and peace, Roosevelt projected a policy of economic wellbeing at home.

Roosevelt's way to fill the "air pocket" was not armaments but a higher standard of living for the people. He set forth his program in detail in a Message to Congress, January 11, 1944. While the war was still raging he looked forward to the peace and said:

"We have accepted, so to speak, a second Bill of Rights under which a new basis of security and prosperity can be established for all—regardless of station, race, or creed.
"Among these are:
"The right to a useful and remunerative job in the industries or shops or farms or mines of the nation;
"The right to earn enough to provide adequate food and clothing and recreation;
"The right of every farmer to raise and sell his products at a return which will give him and his family a decent living;
"The right of every business man, large and small, to trade in an atmosphere of freedom from unfair competition and domination by monopolies at home and abroad;
"The right of every family to a decent home;
"The right to adequate medical care and the opportunity to achieve and enjoy good health;

"The right to adequate protection from the economic fears of old age, sickness, accident and unemployment;

"The right to a good education.

"All of these rights spell security. And after this war is won we must be prepared to move forward in the implementation of these rights, to new goals of human happiness and well-being." [9]

Roosevelt was "prepared to move forward."

Reactionaries knew what that meant—the mobilization of the political and economic power of the American people. They remembered the heyday of the New Deal, the labor unions organizing the mass-production industries, the intellectual ferment in the schools, the political activities in the communities, the fearless discussion of social problems and social changes. Reaction remembered the way culture became a weapon of the people, the way writers and artists spoke out and helped the people's fight in every area of our national life.

The New Deal had been dreadful enough for the reactionaries. The postwar New Deal looked even worse. For reaction knew, as Roosevelt knew, that the pre-war New Deal hadn't solved America's problems. By 1940 although production was back at the 1929 level, there were still 8 million people unemployed in America by official count. In the postwar period, to keep everyone at work, wages would have to go up, working hours would have to go down, profits would have to be reasonable. This is what Roosevelt meant by "moving forward."

The Roosevelt postwar program was very clear: progressive policies at home and peace abroad. As FDR said at the time, "unless there is security here at home there cannot be lasting peace in the world." [10]

The postwar program of the reactionaries has been equally clear: Cold War abroad and an anti-people drive at home. This has meant an attack on our standard of living, an attack

9 N. Y. Times, January 12, 1944
10 N. Y. Times, January 12, 1944

on our civil liberties, an attack on our labor unions. Behind all this is the drive for profits. The profiteering by big corporations in postwar America surpasses anything known in our generation.

UNCONTROLLED PROFITEERING

The golden year of American business used to be considered 1929. In that year corporate profits before taxes were 9.8 billion dollars. That's a lot of money. Yet during World War II, corporate profits were twice as much, averaging over 22 billion dollars profits every year of the war. Even this was only a beginning. After the war, corporate profits before taxes jumped up to 29 billions a year average!

The Korean War blew the lid off. In two years of war the average was 43 billion dollars of profits. [11] This is **four and a half times** the peak year of 1929 profits. In just one year, profits were greater than the U. S. national income for 1932, greater, that is, than **all** the income of **all** the people in the United States.

Even after taxes profits have been enormous. The average for all corporations during the war was 10 billion dollars a year **net**, in the postwar period 18 billion a year **net**, and since Korea 20 billion dollars a year **net**.

The profiteering on the Korean "police action" is revealing. Said the American Federation of Labor, through its broadcast by Frank Edwards:

". . . as soon as the conflict in Korea began, the profiteers started jacking up prices. Months dragged by. The public got promises but no protection. Profiteers stacked up enormous profits. In the last three months of 1950, corporation profits jumped 60% above the first three months of last year. Buying power shriveled steadily and workers' savings vanished." [12]

11 All profits figures from Table B-32, Midyear Economic Report of the President, July, 1952. These are profits before taxes. Companies argue this is not fair, since they don't keep all the profits. But the worker points out that profits before taxes is what the companies make on him through frozen wages and high prices. Furthermore, wages are always reckoned before taxes.
12 Quoted by Jerome Davis, Peace, War and You, p. 135

In the first eight months of 1950 corporate profits were 8% above 1949. In the last four months of 1950 the profits jumped to 45% above 1949. Dividends paid out were 20% above 1949—eight billion dollars in four months. [13]

Single large corporations showed incredible increases. General Motors, for example, had profits in 1950 which were the **greatest of any corporation, anywhere in the world, of any time in corporate history**—834 million dollars after taxes. This is a gain of almost 500% over 1939. General Motors has three billion dollars of defense contracts on its books.

War contracts have been a powerful lever in further concentrating financial power in the hands of large corporations. In the year following the Korean War, 50 corporations got 64% of all war contracts. [14] In comparison, in World War II, 50 corporations had received 57.6% of war contracts. [15]

The reverse of this picture is the declining share of small business in war contracts, from 24½% in 1950 to 21% in 1951 to 18½% in 1952. [16]

It is no wonder that business publications fear what they call an "outbreak of peace" [17] which will "take a lot of steam out of the markets,' [18] or that a United Nations report warns that a cut in armaments would "involve a serious risk of recession." [19]

It is a sober, frightening fact that war is healthy for the monopoly corporations of America.

It is also a sober fact that what is healthy for the monopolists causes bitter suffering to labor and the people generally.

From the end of 1945 to the end of 1951 total profits were

13 Letter, National City Bank, April, 1951
14 Study of Monopoly Power, House Judiciary, 82d Congress, 1951, p. 1056
15 U. S. Senate Report, Doc. No. 206, 1946, p. 30
16 Wall Street Journal, January 7, 1952
17 U. S. News & World Report, April 18, 1952
18 Journal of Commerce, October 10, 1951
19 Report to Economic and Social Council, UN, January, 1952

202 billions before taxes, an average of 34 billion dollars a year. These profits have come from only one place: the people of the United States.

THE COST TO LABOR AND THE PEOPLE

The people pay as citizens through high taxes which go for war contracts.

The people pay as consumers through high prices.

The people pay as producers through speed-up and frozen wages.

The impact of taxes is known in every household in America. The average worker pays a total tax burden of $1,095 a year or 31% of his entire income. This tax burden for the average worker is 32 times heavier than it was in 1939. Furthermore, he gets less for his own needs from these high taxes than he did from lower taxes in 1939. [20]

The impact of inflation and high prices is also well known. The value of the food dollar has gone down from 100 cents in 1939 to 32 cents today in terms of what it will buy in actual groceries. [21]

The impact on wages is less well known. While profits doubled between 1944 and 1951, real wages in manufacturing declined by 15%. [22]

It is little wonder that the consumption of food has declined throughout the United States. There is a 5% drop in per capita consumption since 1946; consumption of essential foods has dropped even more: [23]

Per Capita Decline in Consumption, 1946 to 1951

Meat	10.0%	Fresh Vegetables	7.4%
Milk Products	6.6%	Wheat Flour	14.7%
Butter	7.6%	Coffee	17.6%
Fresh Fruit	13.9%		

20 **What We Need,** Publication No. 227, United Electrical, Radio and Machine Workers of America (UE), chart opposite page 13
21 **Ibid.,** chart opposite page 8
22 **UE Steward,** December, 1951, monthly publication of the UERMWA (UE)
23 U. S. Statistical Abstract, 1951, p. 86, 916. **National Food Situation,** U. S. Dept. of Agriculture, January-March, 1952

The contrast between the tremendous rise in the profits of the employers, and the decline in the standard of living of their employees is a revealing commentary on who benefits from the Cold War. This contrast has become particularly sharp since the onset of the Korean war because of the political control of wages.

THE WAGE FREEZE

The control of wages, known as the Wage Freeze, is performed by a so-called Wage Stabilization Board set up under the Defense Production Act of 1950 and 1952. This board (WSB) has tied wages to the Consumers' Price Index of the Bureau of Labor Statistics. This index presumably shows the rise and fall of the cost of living. If the index goes up, wages go up; if it goes down, wages go down. This seems fair except for the fact that the BLS index operates against the workers by minimizing the rise in their cost of living. Says a union publication:

"BLS left out of its index the less expensive food, clothing, used cars, etc., which workers buy and which have increased most in price, and based its index on the more expensive things which workers can't afford and which have increased least in price. BLS did not include in its living cost index a single item of taxes, which have become in recent years one of the heaviest drains on a worker's income." [24]

As a result of the Wage Freeze, manufacturers' profits per worker have increased in two years as much as in the previous ten years. The following table shows this clearly: [25]

Profits Before Taxes per Employee in Manufacturing

1939	Pre War	$ 410
1944	World War II	933
1949	Pre Korea	1,116
1951	Korean War	1,796

24 UE Steward, December, 1951, issued by the United Electrical, Radio and Machine Workers of America (UE). This union has taken the lead in analyzing the BLS index. The union maintains its own cost of living index and its own index of unemployment

25 Based on **Survey of Current Business**, special issue on "National Income," 1951

Some labor leaders who are fully aware of these facts and heartily against what they represent, have nevertheless gone along with the Wage Stabilization Board for fear of being called "unpatriotic." These labor leaders have themselves fallen victims to the "war psychosis" Herbert Hoover talked about. At the same time, the "patriotic" business leaders have been using the war emergency to weaken and cripple the unions.

"PATRIOTIC" UNION-BUSTERS

On September 20, 1950 a meeting took place in New York City at the stately University Club. The meeting comprised 14 men including Charles E. Wilson, then head of GE who **within three months** went into the government to execute the plan agreed to in this meeting. Partial reports of the meeting have appeared in a national magazine, Henry Luce's **Architectural Forum.**

The basic idea discussed at this meeting was the moving of plants into non-unionized areas, a program now known as the "decentralization" program. Workers have a more descriptive name—the "runaway plant" program. Despite careful editing the **Architectural Forum** reveals that one of the basic aims of the program is to weaken labor. The magazine reports there was unanimous agreement that:

". . . the new industrial plants recently built and to be built will save manpower, and therefore money, through increased mechanization of materials handling. They will be smaller plants to further increase efficiency and **to offset the growing power of labor."** [26] (emphasis added)

Charles E. Wilson showed concretely what was meant. He said GE was putting back into production five idle plants used during World War II. "In these five plants," he explained, "there are 3000 or 3500 people. They are not major plants. In fact, **we are all through with those big plants re-**

26 CIO News, December 31, 1951
27 Architectural Forum, special issue, September 30, 1950

quiring 20,000-40,000 employees." [27] (emphasis added)

The program is simple. Move your plant to a non-union, low-wage area. This has a twofold effect. First, lower wages mean higher profits. Second, unemployment in the union area weakens the unions so that they can be crippled. This is exactly what has happened to the Textile Workers Union, CIO, which has been mercilessly attacked despite the fact that its president, Emil Rieve, went along completely with the Wage Freeze.

Ordinarily, to move a plant costs money. But the Defense Production Act authorized what amounts to government subsidies in the name of defense. "Certificates of necessity" are issued carrying high tax amortization so that the plant is paid for out of untaxed profits. Charles E. Wilson, present at the meeting, became the Defense Mobilizer who issued these certificates. **In nine months** he issued 15 billion dollars worth, **more than in the entire five years** of World War II.

Union men call the Defense Production Act, the **Profits** Production Act.

There was one possible flaw in the program: unions might go after the plant, organize it, and raise wages. But this too was taken care of. Under the regulations of the Wage Stabilization Board, a low wage area must remain low wage. Wages cannot increase above the prevailing rate. The Wage Freeze has been an essential condition for the success of the "runaway plant" program. This union-busting, profiteering scheme has been made possible by the government, paid by the government and protected by the government.

The use of the Wage Freeze and of the "runaway plant" program to undermine the unions economically has been accompanied by a parallel drive to use anti-labor laws to cripple unions. The most damaging law has been the Taft-Hartley Act, which completely undermined the Wagner Act of the New Deal. It is worth recalling that Taft-Hartley was passed in 1947, the same year the Truman Doctrine and the Marshall Plan were announced.

The Taft-Hartley Act was passed under cover of red-baiting. One provision of the law required non-communist affidavits from union officials to qualify the union before the NLRB. For some time employers pretended that the attack was only against "left" unions. But by 1952 this pretense was discarded. Said one corporation executive:

"Certainly in the present defense period, the various anti-Communist or right-wing unions are at least neck and neck with any left-wing union in their threatened or actual interruption of critical defense production in our own atomic, steel, electronics and aircraft plants." [28]

The words are those of L. G. Boulware, vice-president of General Electric Company, and one of the brain trusters of the attack on labor. Big Business was ready to move on a broad front against all unions.

THE ANTI-LABOR DRIVE

On April 16, 1952, nearly 150 of the nation's top industrialists met in Washington, D. C. Sponsors of the meeting were the National Association of Manufacturers and the Chambers of Commerce. [29] The session was closed. Some facts, however, leaked out. It was revealed that Charles Wilson, ex-President of GE and ex-Defense Mobilizer, had been put in charge of a tremendous anti-labor campaign. The purpose of this campaign was made known by **Newsweek**, a weekly magazine of Big Business. Its ace brain-truster, Henry Hazlitt, wrote on April 21:

"Either we must make it legally possible once more for a strike to be broken or we yield completely to constantly mounting union demands. There is no alternative. . . ."

Soon after, Wilson himself testified in secret session, May 2, 1952, before the Senate Banking Committee. Syndicated columnist Robert Allen revealed that Wilson had recom-

28 Boulware's press statement, May 20, 1952
29 Washington Post, April 17, 1952

mended an end to industry-wide bargaining. Within a few months the head of the NAM, William J. Grede, demanded that the government "outlaw industry-wide bargaining." [30]

A return to a single plant union which employers can dominate means a return to the company union of the 20's. It means wiping out all the gains of the New Deal. A powerful anti-labor drive is in full swing and its major weapon has been the red-baiting hysteria of the Cold War. A typical sample of red-baiting and false patriotism was a full page ad in the **Wall Street Journal,** April 9, 1952, attacking the AFL and CIO presidents:

". . . Green, Murray and other such piously anti-Communist leaders [are] actually playing, unintentionally we hope, Russia's game by striking or threatening to strike. . . ."

All unions must knuckle under, says Big Business. The anti-labor drive of the employers merges into the general attack against civil liberties so apparent in our country. What is not so apparent is that Big Business master-minded this general attack, seeking complete thought control in America.

THOUGHT CONTROL

The current attack on American freedoms has been master-minded by the Chamber of Commerce. The proof is in their own documents, **Reports on Communism,** five of which have been issued by the Chamber for use by their employer-members. [31] Since 1946 these reports have blueprinted the government's actions to destroy basic American freedoms.

In 1946 the Chamber of Commerce suggested the loyalty purge in the government—carried out a year later in President Truman's loyalty order.

In January, 1947, the Chamber of Commerce proposed that the Department of Justice publish "a certified list of Communist-controlled front organizations. . . ." The Justice Department did publish such lists—which were incorporated

30 N. Y. Mirror, July 28, 1952
31 I. F. Stone, in the N. Y. Compass, March 13, 1952, analyzed these reports

by Congress in the McCarran Act establishing concentration camps in America.

The 1947 report also called for investigations by Congressional Committees into foreign policies "which appear to be more pro-Soviet than pro-American," and particularly "into the influences which entered into such important decisions as the Potsdam agreement, the Argentine policy and the China policy."

Since that time, through McCarthy and McCarran, men like Professors Lattimore and Fairbanks, John Carter Vincent and many others have been harassed and browbeaten for hostility to Chiang Kai-shek.

That same year the Chamber of Commerce issued another report suggesting Congress "modify the Wagner Act so that employers can work more effectively in opposing Communists within the labor movement." In June, 1947, Congress passed the Taft-Hartley Law.

In 1948 the Big Business groups called for "community action" to bar Communists as teachers, radio commentators, librarians, social workers, book reviewers, etc. This was followed by loyalty oath probes in the state universities and colleges, blacklists in the entertainment industry, and state laws such as the Ober Law in Maryland, the Fineberg Law in New York and many others. They have been characterized by Supreme Court Justice Hugo Black as "rapidly multiplying legislative enactments which make it dangerous to think or say anything. . . ." [32]

In 1952 the Chamber of Commerce issued a fifth report which broadened the attack on civil liberties. Besides Communists, all liberals are under fire as "fellow-travelers," as "dupes," and as "those who engage in pro-Communist activities" such as the CIO fight against the Smith Act.

"The danger," says the Chamber, comes from "ostensibly non-Communist individuals and organizations," such as the

32 N. Y. Times, March 4, 1952

CIO and the Americans for Democratic Action (ADA). The Chamber suggests ADA is part of a Communist plot, asking, "Is it merely a coincidence that we have thousands of so-called 'liberals' who are fighting the Communist battle?" [33]

In this report, the Chamber of Commerce develops a new line against labor: outlaw strikes. The argument starts with an obvious fact:

"Many workers are restive under wage stabilization and similar control measures." Naturally; speed-up and low wages make workers fighting mad. Maybe mad enough to strike. The bosses call such action "sabotage." Says the report: ". . . We can expect continuous sabotage, in the guise of economic issues. . . ."

But the bosses have a cure: fascism. The advice of the report is that employers should, ". . . keep very close watch on worker morale and attitudes. . . ."

This was the achievement of Hitler, a complete watch over every worker in Germany. In America, as in Germany, red-baiting paves the way to concentration camps, destruction of unionism, and ultimate disaster to the entire nation.

GOVERNMENT JOINS BUSINESS

Employers operating within the government are carrying through the line of the Chamber of Commerce. This is the most dangerous post-war development in the United States. At hearings before a Senate sub-committee, John D. Small, former vice-president of Emerson Radio and now head of the Munitions Board said legislation was being prepared to fire workers "who may engage in sabotage, or other willful activities intended to disrupt the national defense program."

As already pointed out the Chamber of Commerce calls strikes "sabotage." Secretary of Labor Tobin, at the same hearings, sharpened the point, speaking of ". . . strikes which, while ostensibly for good trade union objectives, are designed

33 N. Y. Compass, March 13, 1952

to disrupt the defense program. . . ." [34]

Automatically, all strikes are "subversive" since they "disrupt" production. The full flowering of this fascist approach was seen in recent attacks on CIO and other unions. A full page ad of McGraw Hill, publishers of Business Week, on March 31, 1952 branded as "subversive" the union shop, "out of a decent regard for those ideals of our country which we are now fighting in Korea to protect. . . ."

The **Akron Beacon Journal** editorialized against the Rubber Workers, CIO:

"Actually a union doesn't need to be Communist-dominated or to be led by Communists in order to constitute a potential danger to industrial security." [35]

Any union, say the bosses, is a danger to industrial security. This was Hitler's conclusion.

A sinister aspect of the anti-labor drive is the role of the Federal Bureau of Investigation under J. Edgar Hoover. The FBI chief is no novice to anti-labor schemes. He was the man who conducted the infamous "Palmer Raids" of the early 20's. Today, under his leadership, the FBI is moving directly into the trade unions to wreck them.

The FBI was caught in the act in December 1951, trying to wreck the International Longshoremen's and Warehousemen's Union which is led by Harry Bridges. First the union's regional director in Hawaii, Jack Hall, was indicted. Then a union official was approached by the FBI with offers to drop the indictment if Hall would lead an anti-Bridges faction within the union.

Unknown to the FBI agents, the room had been wired for sound. The entire conversation was recorded on tape by the union, proving beyond question that the FBI is today in the union-busting racket. [36] The only difference between the FBI

34 Hearings, Senate Committee on Labor and Public Welfare, March 18, 1952
35 Quoted in UE Steward, May, 1952
36 Transcript or disc recording available from the ILWU, 150 Golden Gate Avenue, San Francisco, Calif.

men and the goons of the thirties is that taxpayers are paying the salaries instead of businessmen.

The deterioration of civil liberties in contemporary America is frightening. A single incident highlights this deterioration. In Madison, Wisconsin, on a Fourth of July, a reporter went around to collect signatures to a petition. He asked 212 people, and 211 refused on the grounds of fear or that the petition was subversive. The petition was made up of paragraphs from the **Declaration of Independence!** Only one person in 200 dared to sign!

THE ROAD TO FASCISM

There are political prisoners by the dozens in the jails of America today, men and women who have committed no other crime than to speak or teach beliefs about social problems. The indictments under the Smith Act stated the crime as "conspiracy to teach" the overthrowing of the government by force and violence.

The rights of the Negro people, always a sensitive barometer in our democracy have been subjected to increasing attack as the Cold War developed since 1945. An index of Negro rights is Negro employment, and the character of that employment. The percentage of Negro employment within all male employment fell from 9.8% in 1944 to 8.3% in 1950, a drop of fifteen per cent. In the professions and semi-professions the drop is even sharper, being as high as 21 per cent. [36a] The reason is given by a representative of the Michigan State Unemployment Compensation Commission who reported that while in 1945 employers who specified "white only" were 35% of the total in 1949 this figure had jumped to 50% and by 1950 it was up to 80 per cent. [36b]

36a UE Fights for FEPC, UE Publication No. 229
36b Quoted in **We Charge Genocide**, a petition to the United Nations by a group of Americans, Negro and white, seeking relief from the crime of genocide against the Negro people. It is a powerful, documented book, published by the Civil Rights Congress, New York, 1951. A paper edition is on sale in bookstores and many unions

The censorship of information, direct and indirect has reached such alarming proportions that so conservative a man as Arthur Krock of the **N. Y. Times** is forced to protest.

"In the name of 'security' public servants and their activities are being more and more secluded. . . .
"Implicit in all this is an attempt to keep from the public facts that are omitted or distorted. . . ." [37]

In the words of Justice Douglas, a "silence of fear" is spreading over America. More and more observers point to the deadly parallel between our country today and Hitler Germany. Writes State Senator Chester E. Dempsey of Wisconsin:

"'We used to wonder at the servility of the patient Germans under the propaganda of Herr Hitler and Dr. Goebbels. We are now worse than the Germans ever were. We have complete thought control. . . ." [38]

Thought control at home should make us suspicious of our foreign policies. It cannot be emphasized too often that foreign policies and domestic policies are closely related. The same Congress that passed the anti-labor Taft-Hartley Act approved the Truman Doctrine. [38a]

The connection between foreign and domestic policy was sharply indicated by Roosevelt. His policy of postwar friendship abroad was tied in with his policy of postwar economic progress at home. Big Business sees the connection very well—that's why it wants enmity abroad to get reaction at home. This line was projected openly by an authoritative spokesman of American business, Charles E. Wilson while he was still head of General Electric Company. Said Wilson in 1946:

". . . the problems of the United States can be captiously summed

37 N. Y. Times, April 18, 1952
38 Letter to Madison Capitol Times quoted in Natl. Guardian, Nov. 28, 1951
38a A key factor in the current thought control is the role of the Supreme Court which has abetted the undermining of civil liberties. It should never be forgotten that it was Truman's appointments of Vinson, Clark and Minton which swung the scales in favor of reaction.

up in two words: Russia abroad and Labor at home." [39]

Big Business' solution is fascism. As far back as 1938 an ex-president of the National Association of Manufacturers said out loud what many were thinking. Said H. W. Prentis:

"American business might be forced to turn to some form of disguised Fascistic dictatorship." [40]

Fifteen years ago men like Prentis were held back by an alert people under progressive leadership. Today the people are confused, the two major political parties are under the control of men like Prentis. Prentis is still around, a director of the NAM, director of a Mellon Bank, chairman of the Board of Armstrong Cork Company. Does anyone doubt what he is thinking today?

The Cold War is tailored to suit reactionaries like Prentis. Isn't it probable then that they had it made to order? Isn't it probable that American reactionaries started the Cold War?

39 Speech to Economics Club of Chicago, October 10, 1946
40 N. Y. Times, November 29, 1938

BACK TO AN OLD ROOST

1941

I AM PROTECTING EUROPE FROM BOLSHEVISM

Fitzpatrick in The St. Louis Post-Dispatch

1946

NEW YORK **Tribune** LATE CITY EDITION

WEDNESDAY, MARCH 6, 1946

Churchill Urges Anglo-U.S. Military Pact,

re Not Speaking to America and Britain From a Missouri Rostrum

Churchill Asserts Russia Aims at an 'Indefinite Expansion' of Its Power

Wants World Police To Be Set Up Quickly

Truman Applauds as He Warns Against Giving U.N.O. Atom Bomb Now

Text of Churchill speech— Page 16

By Bert Andrews

FULTON Mo March 5—Winston Churchill, in an address in which he voiced all his fears of Soviet Russia's intentions toward the rest of the world, declared today that peace can be assured only by reaching "now, in 1946—this year 1946—a good understanding on all points with Russia under the general authority of the United Nations Organization.

He gave a grim warning to the world and Great Britain unequivocally on the importance of reaching agreement until all nations willing to allow it affiliated in a permanent alliance Russia is not...

THE WORLD AS A WALL ST. OYSTER

CHAPTER 4

"The British were perfectly willing for the United States to have a war with Russia at any time. . . ."
Franklin D. Roosevelt, March, 1945.

"I said that frankly . . . he [Churchill] was now expressing the doctrine which Hitler and Goebbels had been proclaiming and reiterating for the past four years."
Joseph E. Davies to Churchill, May, 1945

"We (the U. S.) must assume the responsibility of the majority stockholder in this corporation known as the world."
Leo D. Welch, treasurer, Standard Oil of New Jersey, November 12, 1946.

ON MARCH 5, 1946, Winston Churchill made a speech at Fulton, Missouri, calling for an Anglo-American military alliance in defense of "Western civilization." This theme is not new to Churchill. It had been the main theme of Hitler's Minister of Propaganda, Dr. Josef Goebbels. Churchill in his speech was even brazen enough to use the phrase, "the iron curtain," a phrase invented and popularized by the Nazi Goebbels.

What made Churchill's speech particularly shocking was the fact that on the platform with him were President Truman, Admiral Leahy and other high U. S. officials. When the reaction in America was unfavorable, Truman promptly disavowed the speech, saying he hadn't seen it beforehand. But political observers know that a President doesn't sponsor a speech if he doesn't have an idea of its content, and Truman later admitted that he did know what Churchill would say.

This admission is important because it is clear, looking back, that Churchill's speech at Fulton may be considered the formal declaration of the Cold War against the Soviet Union.

It would be easy and convenient to blame Churchill for the Cold War. But it wouldn't be true. The British Empire at this time was nearly bankrupt and about to borrow billions and billions from the U. S. No one who borrows money tells the banker what to do. The banker calls the tune, and the powerful American financial interests speaking through banker Forrestal, banker Harriman and banker Dulles, were formulating American foreign policy. But Churchill was useful.

Churchill had the know-how of an old imperialist. Britain had accumulated through long experience a vast knowledge on how to rule imperialistically. Churchill could act, and did act, as the ideologist and the strategist for the Cold War. Moreover, Churchill was the best reactionary propagandist in the world. Since at this time the American people still were friendly towards the Soviet Union, Churchill could say things in an "individual" capacity that U. S. administration officials could not say openly. He was, as it were, a convenient "front man" for American reaction. This role Churchill welcomed.

CHURCHILL'S ROLE
Churchill had always been a bitter, irreconcilable enemy of Socialism and the Soviet Union. The necessities of a war of survival forced England to be an ally of the Soviet Union, but Churchill never wavered in his personal enmity. Through-

out the war, he had his eyes fixed on the postwar period and kept up a steady stream of anti-Soviet propaganda directed at strategic points. Two of his favorite targets were the press and American military men.

For example, he told a journalist, Miss Virginia Cowles, the day after D-Day in Normandy (June 6, 1944):

"When this war is over England will need every ally she can get to protect herself against Russia. I'm sick of these parlor pinks, always criticizing the internal regimes of countries . . . Spain is ready to make her peace with Britain and I am ready to accept it; the Italian monarchy is friendly to Britain and I would like to see it preserved." [1]

Into American generals Churchill pounds the inevitability of war with Russia. According to Lt. General Brereton, Churchill used to invite senior American commanders to dinner at his home during World War II, and hold "interesting conversations" on "the Russian situation and its future possibilities and Anglo-American relations." [2] General "Hap" Arnold, Commanding General of the U. S. Army Air Forces, who attended one of these private dinners, tells us more about Churchill's table talk. Churchill told him that "Russia is like an amoral crocodile, lurking in the depths, waiting for whatever prey comes along." [3] Churchill then went on to some fancy warmongering:

"Churchill came out with a sincere statement. . . . he said he still feared the Russians and warned us (the American generals) of the period of twenty years hence. He said they bred like flies: that we, the United States and Britain, were far too conservative in handling the Russians on an even basis." [4]

The date of this little gem is December 7, 1943, which in itself shows how honest Churchill was in his Fulton speech when he implied that the Soviet Union had not returned Allied friendship once the war was over.

1 Virginia Cowles, No Cause for Alarm, New York, 1949, p. 77
2 Lewis M. Brereton, The Brereton Diaries, New York, 1946, p. 249
3 H. H. Arnold, Global Mission, New York, 1949, p. 230
4 Ibid., p. 474

The real content of Churchill's ideas was exposed by Joseph E. Davies, former American Ambassador to the Soviet Union and friend of President Roosevelt. Davies told Churchill to his face in May, 1945:

"I said that frankly, as I had listened to him [Churchill] inveigh so violently against the threat of Soviet domination and the spread of Communism in Europe, and disclose such a lack of confidence in the professions of good faith by Soviet leadership, I had wondered whether he, the Prime Minister, was now willing to declare to the world that he and Britain had made a mistake in not supporting Hitler, for as I understand him, **he was now expressing the doctrine which Hitler and Goebbels had been proclaiming and reiterating for the past four years."** 5 (emphasis added)

To Churchill the Cold War seemed necessary to save the British Empire, which was threatened from the left and from the right. On the left were the colonial liberation movements rising powerfully in Asia, Africa and the Near East.

On the right, American economic might had already taken huge bites out of the British wealth in every part of the world. American monopolists, before Lend-Lease was given, had stripped England of many valuable assets, like the markets in Argentina and a share in the oil of Iraq in exchange for guns and planes. After the war, the process of stripping England continued. 6 One way in which America could cut into British markets in Africa and in Asia was by pushing for colonial independence as in the case of India.

By setting the U. S. and the USSR against each other, Churchill felt that the British Empire would survive. America would need British help in waging the Cold War; she would give loans and leave the Empire alone. There is little doubt that Soviet-American friction and enmity were basic goals of

5 William D. Leahy, I Was There, New York, 1950, p. 378
6 An interesting glimpse of stripping England is shown by a Baruch-Forrestal talk, where Baruch "expressed a strong disinclination to continue American aid unless we had more facts and figures to base judgment. He believes both the British and the French have assets which they have not yet disclosed. . . ." Forrestal Diaries, p. 311

British diplomacy. Certain clear-sighted Americans understood this as shown by a conversation that Forrestal had with Harry Hopkins on British policy:

"Harry said that he was skeptical about Churchill, at least in the particular of Anglo-American-Russian relationship; that he thought it was of vital importance that we not be maneuvered into a position where Great Britain had us lined up with them as a bloc against Russia to implement England's European policy." [7]

That's worth re-reading. It's exactly what happened after Roosevelt's death.

Roosevelt shared Hopkins' opinion. He is quoted in Forrestal's diaries as follows:

"The President indicated considerable difficulties with British relations. In a semi-jocular manner of speaking, he stated that the British were perfectly willing for the **United States to have a war with Russia** at any time and that, in his opinion, to follow the British program would be to proceed to that end." [8] (emphasis added)

It avails little to call FDR's remarks semi-jocular. There is more truth in that half-joke than in a library of serious volumes. The plain fact is that Roosevelt was well aware of Churchill's game. His remark constitutes both an exposure and a warning against this policy, a year before Churchill came out in the open at Fulton.

But if the voice was Churchill's, the hand was Truman's. Behind the declaration of the Cold War was the power of the atom bomb. As we have seen in Chapter 2, it was Truman, who had based our foreign policy on our atomic monopoly.

Atomic diplomacy has been the chief instrument of the Cold War, and the use of atomic diplomacy is a clear cut test of who started the Cold War.

ATOMIC DIPLOMACY BY THE UNITED STATES

The United States was the first country to produce atom bombs, the first country to use them, and, for several years,

7 Forrestal Diaries, p. 58
8 Forrestal Diaries, pp. 36-37

the only country to have them. What the United States did with this monopoly provides a perfect and dramatic test of United States intentions. United States atomic policy provides a type of test which is almost unique in politics, because **one country, and one country alone, had the full control over the atomic decisions.** It is the nearest thing to a controlled experiment in a physical laboratory where cause and effect can be objectively observed. Rarely in world politics is there such a clear connection.

The initiative in atomic policy was **entirely** up to the United States. What we did was a test of **our** intentions, **our** attitudes, **our** judgments as to how to deal with the USSR.

Stimson had written in his memorandum:

"The chief lesson I have learned in a long life is that the only way you can make a man trustworthy is to trust him; and the surest way to make him untrustworthy is to distrust him and show your distrust." [9]

Mr. Truman's policies proclaimed to the world that we didn't trust the Soviet Union and that the way to deal with Russia was not through developing friendly relations but through the implied threats of force. Truman deliberately rejected the **only** atom bomb policy that was consistent with a policy of peaceful co-existence with the USSR. The decision is clear proof that Truman consciously adopted, **in 1945,** a policy that was an essential part of the Cold War.

ATOMIC BLACKMAIL

Truman saw the bomb as a way to coerce the Russians. He said as much as he awaited the news of the first atomic bomb test. According to Jonathan Daniels, he said:

"If it explodes, as I think it will, **I'll certanly have a hammer** on those boys [the Russians]" [10] (emphasis added)

9 See Stimson memorandum, Chapter 2
10 Jonathan Daniels, The Man of Independence, New York and Philadelphia, 1950, p. 266

Truman said this at the Potsdam Conference which ended on August 1, 1945. The atom bomb was dropped on Hiroshima on August 6, 1945. Thereafter, American foreign policy was based on the threat inherent in our having a monopoly of the bomb. So obvious was our policy that Byrnes (then Secretary of State) attempted hypocritical disclaimers. He wrote that:

"As I said in Charleston on November 16, 1945 the suggestion that we might use the atomic bomb 'as a diplomatic or military threat against any nation' is not only untrue in fact but is a wholly unwarranted reflection upon the American government and people." [11]

Byrnes' words of denials are worthless when measured against the facts of American atomic policy. An atom bomb was dropped on Hiroshima; an atom bomb was dropped on Nagasaki. Many distinguished Europeans, including a British Nobel prize winner, have charged that the bomb was dropped primarily for its effect **not on Japan but on the Soviet Union** in two important respects. One, to force a Japanese surrender before the USSR came into the Far Eastern war, and two, to show **under war conditions** the power of the bomb. Only in this way could a policy of intimidation be effective.

If these charges are true, dropping the bomb would be an indication that in August of 1945 the U. S. government was beginning the Cold War. In fact, Hiroshima would be the first overt act of the Cold War. What does the evidence say?

WAS HIROSHIMA THE FIRST OVERT ACT OF THE COLD WAR?

From a military standpoint, there is fairly general agreement that the dropping of the bomb was unnecessary. Japan knew she was defeated. In early July an exchange of messages took place between Japanese Foreign Minister Togo and Japanese Ambassador to the U. S., Sato. Togo wanted to negotiate peace with the U. S. through Russia. Sato's final

11 Byrnes, **Speaking Frankly**, p. 275

message stated that "Japan was thoroughly and completely defeated and that the only course open was quick and definite action recognizing such fact. . . ." [12]

The important thing about these exchanges is that the **American government was listening in to the Japanese conversation!** We had broken the Japanese code and knew exactly what they were thinking. Even Forrestal in May, 1947, wrote that he doubted the strategic soundness of dropping the atom bomb because we knew the Japanese position was hopeless. [13]

From a political standpoint, the dropping of the bomb was harmful. The atomic scientists who developed the bomb were vigorously opposed to its use on Japan. These scientists had thought long and deeply about the problems of atomic warfare and its implications and had appointed a committee to present their views to the Secretary of War. Accordingly, a month before the test of the bomb in New Mexico, a committee of seven scientists, headed by Professor James Franck, submitted a report.

This report has become known as the **Franck Report,** and its main purpose was to advise against use of the bomb on Japan. Its arguments are remarkably clear-sighted, particularly when we remember that it was written in June, 1945. It says:

"Russia, and even allied nations which bear less mistrust of our ways and intentions, as well as neutral countries, may be deeply shocked by this step. **It may be very difficult to persuade the world that a nation** which was capable of secretly preparing and releasing a new weapon as indiscriminate as the rocket bomb and a thousand times more destructive, **is to be trusted.** . . . A demonstration of the new weapon might be made, before the eyes of the United States on a desert or a barren island. . . . **We believe these considerations make the use of nuclear bombs** in an early attack against Japan **inadvisable."** [14] (emphasis added)

12 Forrestal Diaries, pp. 74-77. Incidentally, the Soviet Union behaved as a loyal ally, turning down the Japanese and immediately notifying use of their approach
13 Ibid.. r. 277
14 Bulletin of Atomic Scientists, May, 1946

90

The report specifically warned that if the U. S. did use the bomb, she would "precipitate the race for armaments, and prejudice the possibility of reaching an international agreement on the future control of such weapons." [15]

Politically and militarily there were no reasons to drop the bomb.

Morally, the use of the bomb was indefensible.

Why then did we drop the bomb?

Why did we deliberately, in a few minutes, condemn hundreds of thousands of human beings to a cruel, unnecessary death?

The answer was given by Secretary of State Byrnes in a conversation with Forrestal. Right after the bomb was successfully tested, on July 28, Forrestal records in his diary that "Byrnes said he was most **anxious to get the Japanese affair over with before the Russians got in. . . .**"[16] (emphasis added)

This was spelled out by Norman Cousins and Thomas K. Finletter in an article in 1946. Finletter later became Truman's Secretary for Air. The article said, that in dropping the bomb, **"the purpose was to knock out Japan before Russia came in**—or at least before Russia could make anything other than a token of participation prior to a Japanese collapse:

". . . **unless we came out of the war with a decisive balance of power over Russia,** we would be in no position to checkmate Russian expansion." [17] (emphasis added)

There it is, laid on the line by people who know.

The anti-Soviet implications of the use of the atom bomb in Japan have been thoroughly analyzed by Professor P. M. S. Blackett, one of the world's most distinguished physicists, Nobel prize winner in 1948, Professor of Physics at

15 Ibid., quoted by Blackett, who adds, "To reinforce the effect of the Commission's report, a petition along similar lines signed by 64 scientists . . . was sent to President Truman"
16 Forrestal Diaries, p. 78
17 Saturday Review of Literature, June 15, 1946

Manchester University, England. Professor Blackett was a leader in early atomic research and served on the official Advisory Committee on Atomic Energy for the British government. Professor Blackett, after a thorough analysis, says soberly:

"The dropping of the atomic bombs was not so much the last military act of the second World War, as the **first major operation of the cold diplomatic war** with Russia now in progress." [18] (emphasis added)

This conclusion stands as a damning indictment of Truman's atomic power politics.

THE IMPORTANCE OF A DATE

If Hiroshima was the first overt act of the Cold War, then subsequent events in American-Soviet relations should reflect the increasing tension.

Hiroshima was in August. In September the first international conference after the advent of the bomb took place, the Conference of Foreign Ministers meeting in London.

Byrnes reports the Conference in his book, **Speaking Frankly**, [19] a title as misleading as most of the content of the book. The book is frank in the sense of being anti-Soviet, but not frank in the sense of telling the whole truth or even a substantial portion of the truth. There isn't a hint in the book that the United States was tough and belligerent; there isn't a hint that maybe the Soviet Union did have a

18 Blackett, Fear, War and the Bomb, p. 139
19 James F. Byrnes, Speaking Frankly, New York and London, 1947. Byrnes' book marks a turning point in writings of American foreign policy by policy makers. Men like Stimson, Hull, Leahy, Stettinius, Sherwood (on Hopkins), while defending their position, tried to present the issues involved. Even such a markedly anti-Soviet book as The Strange Alliance, by Gen. John R. Deane, gives a sense of the complex problems involved. The more recent books by Byrnes, Dulles, Generals Clay and Smith, Millis (on Forrestal), deliberately present only the American point of view in the most vulgarized manner. They cover up facts, obscure issues, reduce complex problems to an idiot's tale of cops and robbers. Only someone with plenty of time to spare can trace the truth hidden in the mass of self-serving verbiage
These books themselves, have been important tools in the campaign of vilification and hysteria directed against the Soviet Union and the resultant "war psychosis"

case on some points. In the book there is just one side to every question—Byrnes' side.

Byrnes insists that the United States was friendly at London in September 1945, and never used atomic diplomacy. Why was Byrnes so insistent that the U. S. was friendly and not using pressure?

Because if atomic diplomacy was being used it proves that the Cold War was well underway by then and that the Soviet Union could not be responsible for it since she had no bombs. Fixing the date of the Cold War's beginnings thus becomes a key factor in fixing the responsibility for it.

The supporters of the Cold War have been very conscious of the importance of the date as to when the Cold War began. Senator Douglas of Illinois, one of the worst Cold War-mongers in Congress, specifically presents the argument:

"Truman, like Roosevelt, was willing to cooperate with the Russians so long as they would co-operate. But when it became clear in early 1946 that they were resolved to treat us as enemies, he had no recourse but to oppose the Soviet attempt at aggression." [20] (emphasis added)

Truman himself makes this argument, only pushing the date to 1947, so as to make it seem that the U. S. adopted a "tough" policy with the proclamation of the Truman Doctrine as an answer to Soviet aggression. Says Truman of himself:

"I tried for more than two years to reach an understanding with them [the Russians] . . ." [21]

And this position has become official Washington doctrine. For example, the dean of Washington correspondents, Arthur Krock writes:

". . . After the first two years of his Presidency, **during which he dealt with Soviet Russia on the basis of President Roosevelt's illusion** that the Kremlin would be a co-operative post-war partner in

20 N. Y. Times, February 19, 1950
21 Hillman, Mr. President, p. 223

making a durable and just peace, Mr. Truman turned to the doctrine of overbalancing force. . . ." [22] (emphasis added)

This fairy tale of a meek, patient U. S. falls to the ground if Byrnes was "tough" at London in September 1945. Sumner Welles completely exposes Byrnes, saying that the London meeting was "one of the most disastrous international conferences of modern times," [23] in large part because "Secretary Byrnes adopted a position of intransigence." [24]

Welles is a trained diplomat, precise in his use of words. "Intransigence" is a strong word, it means not only a refusal to negotiate, but it implies an unreasoning attitude, an arrogant "or else" attitude. Soviet Foreign Minister Molotov, who dealt with Byrnes at the meeting, put his finger on the reason for Byrnes' intransigence, namely, the atom bomb monopoly.

Molotov used a phrase very similar to one used by Stimson. Stimson had warned against "having this weapon rather ostentatiously on our hip." Molotov charged Byrnes, to his face, that Byrnes "was carrying an atom bomb in his pocket." [25] The phrase is complacently reported by Byrnes.

Clearly everything was not sweetness and light in September of 1945. Moreover, since the Potsdam Conference (which ended August 1st) was conducted on a give-and-take basis, the change to a tough policy must have taken place soon after. The atom bomb was dropped on August 6. Atomic diplomacy was underway.

Byrnes' attitude fits in completely with what Truman said at Potsdam when the bomb exploded, with what Tru-

22 N. Y. Times, Sept. 25, 1950. It may be noted in passing that Roosevelt's "illusion" gave us a happier and safer America than Truman's "realism."
23 Sumner Welles, Where Are We Heading, p. 67. Mr. Welles was one of the few top experts who continued to write somewhat objectively during the Cold War
24 Ibid., p. 380. A more recent example of Byrnes' intransigence is his action as Governor of South Carolina. He proposes to amend the State Constitution to sanction defiance of the U. S. Supreme Court. Byrnes' proposal permits the Legislature to abolish the public school system, if the Supreme Court rules against segregated schools for Negroes
25 Byrnes, Speaking Frankly, p. 266-267

man decided on Hiroshima, with what Truman did on atomic policy—the Baruch Plan instead of the Stimson approach.

ATOMIC DIPLOMACY STARTED THE COLD WAR

Evidence on when the Cold War started comes from several dissimilar but authoritative sources. One of them is Admiral Leahy, who says flatly that at Potsdam "one factor was to change a lot of ideas, including my own . . . the atom bomb." Leahy also unequivocally says that Potsdam "was the beginning of the 'Cold War.' " [26]

An eminent historian considers August 1945, as the beginning of the Cold War. Professor Frederick L. Schuman, Professor of Government at Williams College, is probably the foremost non-Communist authority in the United States on international affairs, particularly with regard to the Soviet Union. He says:

"The tragic impasse in American-Soviet relations [the cold war] had its chief original source in Byrnes' statement of August 18, 1945. . . . " [27]

Thirdly, there is corroboration from an unexpected source: the Republican partner in the building of Truman's foreign policy, John Foster Dulles.

Dulles is one of the most dour anti-Sovieteers in America. He has an unsavory history. His law firm of Sullivan and Cromwell was the outstanding cloak of respectability for the Nazis before the war, acting as their counsel in the U. S. Republican advisor to Byrnes, architect of the Japanese treaty, adviser to Dewey and Eisenhower, he fancies himself as the next Secretary of State. This shrewd reactionary tries to bolster the Truman date of 1947, but he slips unwittingly and confirms the period given in this book, beginning in August 1945, and ending with Churchill's Fulton speech in March 1946.

26 Leahy, I Was There, p. 429
27 Frederick L. Schuman, The Devil and Jimmy Byrnes, New York, 1948, p 7
The Byrnes statement attacked the Bulgarian election, took a crack at Poland, and said the United States wouldn't countenance the elections

Dulles gives the same argument as Truman, that the Soviet Union behaved so aggressively that by the spring of 1947 America had to get tough. He writes:

"Soviet tactics were so flagrantly threatening that they involved an overreaching. They slapped our faces until we waked up from our postwar daze. Awakening was, however, a gradual process, and it took the Moscow meeting of the Council of Foreign Ministers [March-April, 1947] and its attendant circumstances to arouse the leaders and the people to the fact that the peril was great and called for positive policies of large scope." [28]

Dulles is here referring to the military aid to Greece and Turkey which Truman announced on March 12, 1947 when he set forth the Truman Doctrine.

However, Dulles elsewhere in his book slips up. He refers to the London Conference of **September 1945,** as the time when ". . . our postwar policy of 'no appeasement' was born." [29]

This is doubletalk for cold war. Later in the book he slips up again, this time even more clearly. He begins a sentence, saying: "After nearly five years of 'cold' war. . . . [30]

The "five years" is a truly revealing slip: Dulles is writing **in 1950.**

The elements of the Cold War came together soon after Potsdam in August 1945. The Cold War was brought out in the open at Fulton in March 1946 and was declared official U. S. policy with the Truman Doctrine. Some of the shrewder supporters of the Cold War recognize that the facts speak for themselves and that the beginning of the Cold War in August-September 1945 cannot be denied. They therefore use the cunning argument that the Soviet Union started the Cold War even before the death of Roosevelt. Byrnes for example, says:

"Before President Roosevelt's death, in fact, even before his return

28 John Foster Dulles, **War or Peace,** New York, 1950, p. 101
29 Ibid., p. 30
30 Ibid., p. 140

from Yalta, difficulties had arisen with the Soviet Union. . . ."[31]

If this were true, it would clear Truman, Byrnes, Forrestal, Dulles and the rest of any responsibility for the Cold War. They could say they were just meeting hostility with hostility. No one could accuse them of changing FDR's foreign policy. For Roosevelt, according to this argument, had changed it himself before he died.

It's a clever argument. The only trouble with it is that it isn't true.

DID FDR CHANGE IN HIS FRIENDSHIP TO THE USSR?

The entire argument of Byrnes rests on a single message written by FDR one hour before he died. It was advice to Churchill who was going to make a speech in Parliament referring to the Soviet Union. Wrote FDR to Churchill:

"I would minimize the general Soviet problem as much as possible because these problems, in one form or another, seem to arise every day and most of them straighten out as in the case of the Bern meeting.
"We must be firm, however, and our course thus far is correct."[32]

Says Byrnes:

". . . these messages **dispose of the legend** that our relations with the Soviet Union began to deteriorate only after his death."[33] (emphasis added)

Unfortunately for Mr. Byrnes, the messages of FDR show exactly the opposite of the Cold War policy. When FDR says "our course is correct," he means the course of friendship and cooperation. Professor Schuman, in a review of Byrnes' book, writes:

"Mr. Byrnes disproves his own point because he does not understand the course. Franklin D. Roosevelt's course was to treat the Soviet Union as an equal, to minimize frictions, and to adjust differences by discussion and compromise—all of which was diametri-

31 Byrnes, Speaking Frankly, p. 49
32 Ibid., p. 59.
33 Ibid., p. 59

97

cally opposite to the course of President Truman. . . ."[34]

But there is even more powerful proof that FDR had not changed his policy from people who saw him daily. Mrs. Roosevelt, for example, mentions that while there were disagreements after Yalta, her husband thought "that he, Stalin, and Churchill, having fought the war together, had gained enough understanding and respect for each other to be able to work things out." [35]

Grace Tully, FDR's secretary, writes similarly about FDR's attitude toward the Soviets. She writes that while Roosevelt had reservations:

"On the whole, however, he did indicate a feeling that compromise in wartime, for the sake of the mutual effort, might pay off in the postwar period."
"That they haven't may prove that Mr. Roosevelt was wrong; or it may indicate simply that **others have failed to accomplish what he might have accomplished.**" [36] (emphasis added)

And Sumner Welles, FDR's Under Secretary of State, who saw him constantly writes:

". . . the possibility of cooperation, which is now, (in 1946) tragically enough, becoming every day more remote, constituted the very basis of the foreign policy carried on by President Roosevelt **until the day of his death.**" [37] (emphasis added)

Finally there is Harry Hopkins' testimony. Hopkins was closer to FDR than any other man in the administration. After Roosevelt's death he went to Moscow on a special mission for President Truman. He would have known if either Roosevelt or Stalin had changed their minds about cooperation. Hopkins found no such change, but he did say there was a group in America who didn't want to cooperate with Russia. This, he said, would be disaster. Hopkins wrote, in August 1945:

34 Schuman, Devil and Jimmy Byrnes, p. 10
35 Eleanor Roosevelt, This I Remember, New York, 1949, p. 341
36 Grace Tully, FDR, My Boss, New York, 1949, p. 269
37 Welles, Where Are We Heading?, p. 102

"We know or believe that Russia's interests, so far as we can anticipate them, do not afford an opportunity for a major difference with us in foreign affairs. . . . I believe they not only have no wish to fight with us, but are determined to take their place in world affairs in an international organization, **and above all, they want to maintain friendly relations with us.**

"The Soviet Union is made up of a hundred and eighty million hard working, proud people. They are not an uncivilized people. They are a tenacious, determined people who think and act.just like you and I do. Our Russian policy must not be dictated by **people who have already made up their minds** there is no possibility of working with Russia and **that our interests are bound to conflict and ultimately lead to war.** From my point of view, **this is an untenable position and can but lead to disaster.**" [38] (emphasis added)

No, President Roosevelt did not change his mind about co-operation. His course remained consistent to the end—a course of friendship and co-operation with the Soviet Union.

It was after his death that a change did take place, the change to a policy of friction, tension, hostility, a policy of Cold War.

WHO STARTED THE COLD WAR?

The Truman Administration, in full partnership with the leaders of the Republican Party, started the Cold War. A small clique of reactionaries sharply reversed the peace policy of President Roosevelt. The change was noted by Sumner Welles who writes:

"The fruits of the Roosevelt policy became apparent at Teheran and Yalta. Then **suddenly,** the **direction of American policy passed to other hands.** The dire change this brought in Soviet-American relations was apparent to every objective observer present at the meeting at Potsdam.

"Naturally, the Soviet government knew that President Truman was beset by conflicting advice as to the methods he should adopt in his dealings with it. It was fully aware that one **group of advisers,** who decried what they termed the 'appeasement of Russia' policy of Franklin Roosevelt, was asserting that **strong-arm tactics** constituted the only means of achieving success." [39] (emphasis added)

38 Robert E. Sherwood, Roosevelt and Hopkins, New York, 1948, pp. 922-923
39 Welles, Where Are We Heading?, pp. 375-376

Who were these advisers who urged "strong-arm tactics"?

Two men may be taken as typical, one a Republican, the other a Democrat, John Foster Dulles and W. Averell Harriman. The first wrote the foreign policy plank for Eisenhower at the 1952 Republican Party Convention, the second was a candidate for the Presidential nomination at the 1952 Democratic Party Convention.

John Foster Dulles is one of the most astute reactionaries in America. President Roosevelt would never have anything to do with him, but soon after FDR's death he moved in. Wrote correspondent William Shirer at the time:

" . . . Mr. Truman and Mr. Byrnes, green as they are in foreign politics, have taken over so many ideas of Mr. Dulles, especially in regard to Russia. . . . One cannot but have reservations about an authority [Dulles] who right up to the outbreak of war saw no danger to America in the Nazi-Fascist conspiracy but who now presumes to see the imminent danger of a clash with Russia. . . ."[40]

Shirer could have been much sharper. Dulles has been one of the specialists in international fascism. His law firm, Sullivan and Cromwell is the general counsel for the New York Schroeder Bank which is closely tied to the Schroeder Bank in London and the Schroeder Bank in Cologne, Germany. The Schroeder Bank was one of the main supporters of Hitler. **Time Magazine** in July 1939 called it "an economic booster of the Rome-Berlin Axis."[41] A Dulles partner sits on the board of directors of the Bank.

Dulles himself was chosen to represent all the New York Banks when he went to Berlin in 1933 and made a deal that gave Hitler's government one billion dollars and established the credit Hitler needed for his re-armament program.

While Dulles worked the Republican side of the street, Averell Harriman worked the Democratic side. The juxtaposition of these two men, both bankers, both anti-Soviet, both influencing the government, yet working in different

40 N. Y. Herald Tribune, June 9, 1946
41 Richard Sasuly, I. G. Farben, New York, 1947, p. 187

parties for the same purpose is one more ironical example of the way the two-party system usually works. As President Roosevelt once said, the Democratic and Republican parties usually represent the difference between Tweedle-dee and Tweedle-dum.

Harriman was a salesman of the Cold War. He was consistently anti-Soviet on every issue throughout the war. Whether it was Lend-Lease, the question of credits versus loans, the question of reparations or the question of the UN at San Francisco, Harriman was always there to support men like Dulles in their anti-Soviet policies. Basic to Harriman's attitude was an undisguised contempt for the Soviet Union. According to Alfred Friendly, Director of Information for ECA who worked with Harriman, this 'democrat' "considers the Kremlin leaders—and the Russians as a whole —to be barbarians." [41a]

The best expression of Harriman's attitude to the USSR, as well as of his own mentality is in a statement made to Forrestal at Potsdam, July 1945. Says Forrestal:

"Averell was very gloomy about the influx of Russia into Europe. . . . He said **the greatest crime of Hitler** was that his actions had **resulted in opening the gates of Eastern Europe to Asia. . . .**" [42] (emphasis added)

That's quite a statement. The greatest crime of Hitler was not that he had unleashed a global war in which some 20 million soldiers and 50 million civilians, were killed.

The greatest crime of Hitler was not that in seven years he had reduced a cultured, modern nation to a state of medievalism, that he had placed a million Germans in concentration camps, nor that he had made of Europe a prison of nations.

The greatest crime of Hitler was not that he had killed **six million** Jews in gas chambers and crematoria in one of the most coldly calculated evil massacres of recorded history.

41a N. Y. Times, July 2, 1950
42 Forrestal Diaries, p. 79

No the greatest crime of Hitler was—that he had lost! This is the logic of Harriman's remark. It is so shocking that one can hardly believe that he meant it.

Harriman and Dulles are a fair example of Truman's civilian advisers but there is another influence in the American government today which must not be overlooked—the influence of the military men. The sword of the Pentagon lies heavily on the delicate scales of diplomacy.

THE MILITARY IN AMERICAN POLICY

Military domination of foreign policy is utterly alien to American traditions and government structure. Yet it is a universally acknowledged fact by those in the know. Dulles, for example, writes as follows:

"During the past five years the military viewpoint has predominated, for better or worse, in a good many instances. . . .
"Now the **State Department is** in many respects **subordinated** to the National Security Council **in the field of foreign affairs.** The National Security Council during most of the period under review has been predominantly military in character. . . ." [43] (emphasis added)

Correspondent Howard K. Smith also draws attention to the National Security Council:

"At the end of 1947 American foreign policy . . . came pretty tightly under the control of a body called the National Security Council. . . . It began life modestly, stockpiling strategic raw materials and surveying the nation's resources for war. It has gradually grown into **the supreme power shaping American policies.** It was no longer odd that General Clay, the American commander in Germany, on returning home in the summer of 1948 should make his report not to the Cabinet but to this Council." (emphasis added)

Smith goes on to quote Sumner Welles:

"No emergency," says Welles, "can justify the control of this country's foreign policy by a council which reaches its decisions from a military standpoint. . . ." [44]

And Walter Lippman delicately conveys the same idea,

43 John Foster Dulles, War or Peace, New York, 1950, pp. 235-236
44 Howard K. Smith, The State of Europe, New York, 1949, p. 96

102

saying that there has developed in the Pentagon "a very good and a rather serious imitation of what in any other country but this free-wheeling democracy would be militarism—namely the **military control of foreign policy. . . .**"[45] (emphasis added)

By 1952 the dominant position of the military in American foreign policy was being openly proclaimed. Newspaper columnist Marquis Childs wrote that "military men are usurping the functions of civilians"[45a] and Secretary of Army Frank Pace in a speech to West Point cadets spelled out what this means. The military officer of today, he said, must learn "to be a technician, a negotiator, an attache, an administrator, a military governor, a scientist, or a superintendent of production."[45b] This is the language of militaristic empire-building. The speech included the basic appeal to the pocketbook. "For those who succeed," said Pace, "there should be rewards commensurate in recompense and responsibility" and this will "be the case in the **new** army." (emphasis added) A U. S. army to run the world is "new" indeed, new to American political theory and American traditions.

In contrast to the military domination of America's foreign policy it may be well to consider the Soviet Union. Dulles has to acknowledge the truth from his personal experience. He writes:

"The leaders of the Soviet Union are civilians whose judgment is controlling as against military judgment.
". . . The Soviet government has always made the military a subordinate department.
"During five years . . . I have attended ten major international conferences averaging about two months in duration. . . . I have sat across the table from leading Soviet personalities such as Molotov, Vishinsky, and Gromyko I have never felt that they were overawed by military advice, or that their strategy or tactics were dominated by military considerations."[46]

45 N. Y. Herald Tribune, June 20, 1950
45a Washington Post, April 2, 1952
45b N. Y. Times, May 21, 1952
46 Dulles, War or Peace, pp. 234-235

Americans might well wish that the same could be said of Mr. Truman. Instead, admits Dulles ruefully on the same page:

"In our own case, the military have been more obvious partners in postwar policy making."

The influence of the military and reactionary politicians on foreign policy is only the surface manifestation of the controlling influence in American life, the influence of Big Business—bankers, monopolists, industrialists and financiers.

These men have moved into government, consciously and deliberately, as shown by a statement made in 1946 by one of them, the treasurer of Standard Oil (N. J.) who said:

"As our country has begun to develop its overall postwar foreign policy, private enterprise must begin to evolve its foreign policy, starting with the most important contribution it can make—'men in government.' " [47]

THE CONTROL CENTER OF REACTION

There has taken place since the war a most dangerous development for American democracy. This is the integration of top military, political and business reactionaries into a powerful control center of Big Business. The most trusted men of reaction move at will from government to business to the armed forces and back again.

General Eisenhower is the most dramatic example. From General of the U. S. Army to President of Columbia University, [48] back to General in charge of European War preparations, and now back as a potential Republican President.

General Clay leaves Germany and becomes president of Continental Can Co. McCloy, a corporation lawyer, takes his place in Germany. Draper, an investment banker in Forrestal's firm, becomes a general in charge of Germany's

47 Victor Perlo, American Imperialism, New York, 1951, p. 131
48 The presidency of Columbia University is a Big Business managerial job, rather than an education position. The trustees of Columbia are dominated by the Morgan interests and represent one of the highest concentrations of Big Business anywhere in America

economic comeback. General Marshall becomes Secretary of State; General Smith and Admiral Kirk become ambassadors to Russia; Admiral Moreell becomes President of Jones and Laughlin Steel Co.; Investment banker Lovett becomes Undersecretary of State and the Defense Secretary. Banker Harriman and banker-lawyer Dulles become foreign policy-makers and Byrnes leaves the State Department to become a director of Newmont Mining Co., a Morgan controlled company.

Executive vice-president Huggins of Westinghouse becomes Ass't Secretary for Air, Wilson of GE becomes War Mobilizer, banker Souers becomes an Admiral in charge of Central Intelligence, Admiral Halsey becomes an executive of Int'l Tel. and Tel. On the side, he goes into business with ex-Secretary of State Stettinius and makes a million dollars on a "surplus" tanker deal. In the wings is the Maritime Commission, of which an Admiral is the head. General Doolittle becomes vice-president of Shell Union Oil Company, General Nelson, vice-president of N. Y. Life Insurance Co., and d'Olier, president of Prudential Insurance Co., becomes a General.

So blatant has this control of Big Business become that even Truman's own supporters object. The **New York Post** writes that "The representatives of Big Business have taken over all the key posts in the defense program with a speed and thoroughness unequalled in history. [49]

Republican Senator Homer E. Capehart, defending his party against the charge of Big Business domination, accused the Democratic administration of giving in to Big Business. He lists 150 top businessmen in government and their connections—running 175 inches of fine type and 6 pages of the Congressional Record of May 20, 1952.

The Cabinet of President Truman has been so loaded with top businessmen that it seems like a sub-station of Wall

49 New York Post (articles in 1951 entitled Washington Gold Rush)

Street. Here is a partial list of financiers, industrialists and corporation lawyers who are or have been in the top levels of the cabinet agencies during the Truman Administration:

Sec'y of Defense	James V. Forrestal	Pres., Dillon, Reed & Co., Invest. Banker
	Louis Johnson	Corporation Lawyer
	Robert C. Lovett	Partner, Brown Bros. Harriman & Co., Invest. Banker
Sec'y of Navy	Francis P. Mathews	Chairman of Bd., Securities Accept. Corp.
Sec'y of Army	Wm. H. Draper, Jr.	Pres., Dillon, Reed & Co.
Sec'y of Air	Stuart Symington	until 1945, Pres. and Chmn. Bd., Emerson Elec. Mfg. Co., St. Louis
	Thos. K. Finletter	Wall St. Corporation Lawyer
Under Sec'y of Air	J. A. McCone	Pres., Calif. Shipbuilding Corp.
Ass't Sec'y of Air	E. W. Higgins	V. P., Westinghouse Electric Int'l Co.
Sec'y of State	Dean Acheson	Corporation Lawyer
Ass't Sec'y of State	G. W. Perkins	V. P., Merck & Co.
Spec. Ambassador	John Foster Dulles	Corporation Lawyer
Sec'y of Treasury	John W. Snyder	V. P., First Nat'l Bank of St. Louis
Mutual Security Dir.	W. Averell Harriman	Partner, Brown Bros. Harriman & Co.

Examples can be multiplied, literally by the hundreds. They give a clear picture of a coalescing control center for reaction for which Forrestal found a fancy phrase. He called it a "politico-military administration." Forrestal should know. He was organizer and center of the organization, an organization formed consciously for one purpose—the domination of the world by U. S. Big Business. This purpose has been openly proclaimed by monopoly strategists.

BIG BUSINESS AND WORLD DOMINATION

Leo D. Welch is as big a Big Businessman as one can find. He is treasurer of the Standard Oil Company of New Jersey, the grandmother of all the Standard Oil companies in various states, and the most powerful American oil company in the international oil combines.

Through Welch's hands since World War II has passed a billion dollars worth of foreign investments—and he has already received back nearly a billion in profits. Welch is tops in Big Business and he has openly proclaimed its goal. He says:

"Our foreign policy will be more concerned with the safety and stability of our foreign investments in the future than ever before. **The proper respect for capital abroad is just as important as re-spect for our political principles. . . .**"[50](emphasis added)

Welch is speaking in November 1946, right after Truman made the decision to use the atom bomb as a diplomatic threat. The goal of the atomic diplomacy, the goal of the Cold War, is to make American Big Business the master of the world. Welch says this in so many words:

"As the largest producer, the largest source of capital, and the biggest contributor to the global mechanism, we must set the pace and assume the responsibility of **the majority stockholder in this corporation known as the world.** . . . Nor is this for a given **term of office. This is a permanent obligation.**"[51] (emphasis added)

Hitler was more modest. He spoke of a thousand year Reich: Welch speaks of permanent rule by Wall Street. Welch speaks in the double talk of the financier, "majority stockholder in this corporation known as the world." There is an older, more precise term for Welch's goal: imperialism.

The **Washington Post** doesn't hesitate to use the term, as it discusses the problems facing America's outward drive. Its 1952 New Year editorial said that "the hard core of fact about **our imperialism** remains the same," namely, "we are still faced with the dilemma of giving up what has been gained in Korea or of maintaining troops indefinitely on that precarious spot." [52] (emphasis added)

In a later editorial, the **Washington Post** points out what we Americans must face as good imperialists. It says:

50 Speech at the National Trade Convention, November 12, 1946. Quoted in Victor Perlo's American Imperialism, p. 129
51 Ibid
52 Washington Post, January 1, 1952

"A great power to be worthy of the title must get into the habit of sitting on bayonets. This is how the British kept the nineteenth century tolerably quiet." [53]

This is very explicit—and also well known. The Americans made a revolution against this sort of thing in 1776.

While abroad American imperialism means napalm bombs and atom bombs, at home it means a militaristic state of the most drastic type. This has been pointed out in no uncertain terms by another spokesman of Big Business, Virgil Jordan, who told the Investment Bankers Association of New York that the United States was the new rising empire, inheritor of the British Empire. Jordan spoke as President of the National Industrial Conference Board, an offshoot of the National Association of Manufacturers. After glorifying American imperialism, Jordan spelled out what it meant:

"Imperialism . . .implies an enormous task of expanding and maintaining a **vast organization of manpower,** machines and equipment, not merely for national defense, but for effective and continuous exercise of international authority in the maintenance of law and order." [55] (emphasis added)

In the same speech he goes on to describe what this militarism and imperialism mean in our daily lives.

". . . our imperial responsibilities . . . must rest on the solid and broad base of **internal unity** and domestic prosperity, which will imply intelligent and courageous reconstruction of our own economic and political life after the immediate war effort is over." [56]

In Jordan's language "internal unity" and "courageous reconstruction" mean the thought control program of the Chamber of Commerce which has been exposed in Chapter 3.

Imperialism reflects itself at home in a drive against labor; abroad in a drive for markets, for raw materials, for the export of protected capital, for the political domination of other countries to ensure economic penetration. Behind all

53 Washington Post, July 10, 1952
55 Speech before Investment Bankers Association, N. Y., December 10, 1940, quoted in Perlo, **American Imperialism,** p. 131
56 Ibid

these drives is the force and violence of the imperialists: jails at home, napalm bombs abroad.

American imperialism has been compared to racketeering by a General who had to do the dirty work for many years. Major General Smedley D. Butler, who was head of the United States Marine Corps, has described his work in unforgettable language:

"There isn't a trick in the racketeering bag that the military gang is blind to. It has its "finger men" (to point out enemies), its "muscle men" (to destroy enemies), its "brain guys" (to plan war preparations), and a "Big Boss" (supernationalistic capitalism). "It may seem odd for me, a military man, to adopt such a comparison. Truthfulness compels me to do so. I spent 33 years and 4 months in active service as a member of our country's most agile military force—the Marine Corps. I served in all commissioned ranks from second lieutenant to Major General. And during that period I spent most of my time being a high class muscle man for Big Business, for Wall Street and for the bankers. In short, I was a racketeer, a gangster for capitalism.

"Thus I helped make Mexico and especially Tampico, safe for American oil interests in 1914. I helped make Haiti and Cuba a decent place for the National City Bank boys to collect revenues in. I helped in the raping of half a dozen Central American republics for the benefit of Wall Street. The record of racketeering is long. I helped purify Nicaragua for the international banking house of Brown Brothers in 1909-12. I brought light to the Dominican Republic for American sugar interests in 1916. In China in 1927 I helped see to it that the Standard Oil went its way unmolested.

"During those years, I had, as the boys in the back room would say, a swell racket. I was rewarded with honors, medals and promotion. Looking back on it, I feel that I might have given Al Capone a few hints. The best he could do was to operate his racket in three city districts. I operated on three continents." [56a]

American Imperialism is a real and menacing threat to the peace of the world. It should be studied, and no better book on the subject is available than **American Imperialism** by Victor Perlo. This book cannot be too highly recom-

56a Common Sense, November, 1935, quoted in Davis, Peace, War and You, pp. 67-68
57 Perlo's American Imperialism is now available in an inexpensive paper edition on sale in bookstores and many unions.

mended. It is a must for every thinking man and woman in America today. [57]

WE THE LIVING

When Baruch presented his plan on atomic energy to the UN, he said the choice was between "the quick and the dead." He didn't say which side he was on.

American imperialism means death.

We the living can halt these reactionaries. We can stop the Cold War and return to Roosevelt's policy of peace and friendship with all nations. But to do so we must be clear as to what happened, how and why it happened. We must know and understand each step by which Roosevelt's policy of peace was perverted into Truman's doctrine of war. The next part of the book deals with this question.

For the American people this knowledge is literally a matter of life or death. Knowledge is life. The alternative is atomic vaporization.

111

BACKGROUND OF SUSPICION

CHAPTER 5

"Congress has not declared war against the Russian government. . . . (Yet) we have an army in Russia."
Senator William Borah, 1919

"Were they (the Allies) at war with Russia? Certainly not; but they shot Soviet Russians on sight."
Winston Churchill, 1924

"The agreements of Munich confirmed the conviction of the Soviet government that the Western powers strove to keep Germany from the west only by turning her to the east."
Sumner Welles, 1946

THE LACK of knowledge in the United States about the Soviet Union is truly amazing. A survey on this subject, made by Princeton University and reported in the **Saturday Evening Post,** disclosed that:

". . . In our adult population of about 90,000,000 there are 63,000,000 of us who think that 'abolition of private ownership' in Russia means that all goods are held in common. Two out of three Americans don't know that Russians can privately own homes, furniture, cars, and so on, and that farmers till individual plots. The same inquiry disclosed that about 64% of adult Americans don't know that wages are not equal in Russia, but differential; 83% don't know that most Russians are **not** members of the Communist Party. Seven out of nine Americans don't know that Russia pro-

113

duced most of the war materials used by the Red Army and . . .
thirty-eight million Americans of voting age don't know at all
what kind of government Russia has."[1] (emphasis in original)

Anti-Soviet spokesmen exploit this lack of knowledge.
They have tried to create a picture of a mysterious, unknowable land and a government whose actions are unpredictable, secretive and even irrational. Churchill has called Soviet policy "a riddle wrapped in an enigma" and George F. Kennan, one of the State Department's leading authorities on the USSR and our present (1952) Ambassador to Russia writes that "at the bottom of the Kremlin's **neurotic view of world affairs** is the traditional and **instinctive** Russian sense of insecurity. . . ."[2] (emphasis added)

If Kennan's statement is correct, if Soviet fears and suspicions are neurotic—without foundation in fact or in reason —then stable relations with Russia are inherently impossible. The chances for peace are very slim.[3]

But Kennan is one of the makers of the Cold War. We would do well to examine his statements with care. For if Soviet fears are justified, then the responsibility is also ours to behave in such a way as to create mutual trust.

Let us look briefly at the record of Western-Soviet relations between the two wars and then judge for ourselves: how "neurotic" are Soviet suspicions?

BACKGROUND FOR SUSPICIONS: THE INTERWAR YEARS

War is nothing new to the Soviet Union—whether hot war or cold war.

The Soviet Union was born in the midst of a hot war. At its birth, she was invaded **without a declaration of war** by fourteen countries, including all the major powers, England,

1 Edgar Snow, "Why We Don't Understand Russia," **Saturday Evening Post,** February 15, 1947
2 The Forrestal Diaries, p. 136
3 Kennan puts the chances as "far greater" than a thousand-to-one. N.Y. Times, February 17, 1952. How much greater he doesn't say but that thousand-to-one reflects a level of "hope" which is very close to despair

114

France, Germany, Italy, Japan and the United States. The excuse for the invasion was to keep Russia fighting against Germany—actually, the invasion went on after the Kaiser and Germany were beaten. The United States participated in the invasion together with Japan. There are many Americans who do not know that the United States illegally invaded Siberia in 1918-1919. They do not know because the story has been thoroughly hushed up. Yet at the time, powerful voices spoke up against our intervention. Senator William Borah spoke on the floor of the Senate, September 5, 1919:

"Mr. President, we are not at war with Russia; Congress has not declared war against the Russian government or the Russian people. The people of the United States do not desire to be at war with the Russian people. **We have an army in Russia;** we are furnishing munitions and supplies to other armed forces in that country. . . . **There is neither legal nor moral justification** for sacrificing these lives. It is in violation of the plain principles of free government." [4] (emphasis added)

The entire story of the American invasion has been told in detail by the American who commanded it, General William S. Graves, in his forthright and courageous book, **America's Siberian Adventure.** The book, published in 1931, was promptly buried by press and schools.

Major General William S. Graves, commander of the 8th Division, turned out to be a man of integrity and deep democratic tradition. When he arrived in Siberia he found all his ideas were wrong. The "wild" Bolsheviks were peasants and factory workers fighting to defend themselves and their country from the gentry and the landlords who had called in the foreign armies to put down the people. The White Guards, as the enemies of the people called themselves, were vicious, brutal and worthless. General Graves was soon disgusted with their brutality.

Moreover, Japan had double-crossed the U. S. on a joint

4 Quoted in **High Treason**, by Albert E. Kahn, New York, 1950, p. 6

agreement to send in 7,000 troops each into Siberia. The Japanese actually sent in 70,000. So General Graves quietly began to hamper the Japanese and Russian White Guards and tacitly to support the Soviet Union. General Graves remained until the day of his death during the Second World War, a warm admirer and a staunch friend of the Soviet Union.

General Graves' conduct was not typical. Other commanders behaved with cold ferocity. British troops shot Communists on sight. In Baku 26 Soviet leaders out of 27 were shot in one batch by the British. The 27th was not recognized and managed to escape. His name—A. I. Mikoyan, today Soviet Minister for Trade and a member of the Politbureau. [5]

Winston Churchill, the organizer and inspirer of the Allied intervention in Russia has given a revealing word-picture of those years. In a mood of cynical "humor" he writes:

"Were they [the Allies] at war with Russia? Certainly not; but they shot Soviet Russians on sight. They stood as invaders on Russian soil. They armed the enemies of the Soviet Government. They blockaded the ports and sank its battleships. **They earnestly desired and schemed its downfall.** But war—shocking! Interference—shame. It was, they repeated, a matter of indifference to them how Russians settled their own affairs. They were impartial —bang! [6] (emphasis added)

Intervention was hardly a joke, however, to the Soviet people and the Soviet leaders. The two and a half years of intervention and civil war were responsible for the death through battle, starvation and disease of some 7,000,000 men, women and children plus material losses estimated at some 60 billion dollars. No reparations of course were ever paid by the fourteen invading countries.

The intervention was defeated primarily through the ten-

---

5 Walter Duranty, Stalin & Co., The Politbureau, New York, 1949, pp. 34-35
6 Winston Churchill, The World Crisis, the Aftermath, quoted in Kahn's High Treason, p. 6

acity and strength of the Soviet people, who were helped in the struggles by the more conscious workers of other countries. In England "Hands Off Russia" Committees were organized and workers refused to load munitions ships. In Archangel, North Russia, there were mutinies in both the British and the French armies, and in the Black Sea, Andre Marty led a mutiny in the French Navy.

The Allied governments were **forced** to withdraw. The impact of their intervention on Soviet-Allied relations has been pointed out by the eminent historian, Professor Frederick L. Schuman. He writes:

"The injuries inflicted upon Russia by the Western democracies between 1918 and 1921 not only exposed innocent millions to hideous suffering but disfigured the whole face of world politics for decades to come." [7]

And on the same page Professor Schuman shows why:

"No more fatal decision has ever been reached at Washington, London and Paris, **for its enduring effects** so **poisoned** the atmosphere of **Soviet-Allied relations** as . . . even to jeopardize unity among the United Nations in the wake of a costly common victory. Deep wounds leave ugly scars." (emphasis added)

COLD WAR IN THE 20's

Japan was the last nation to leave the Soviet Union, evacuating Vladivostok in 1922. The Hot War became a Cold War. The Locarno Treaty of 1925 brought Germany into a Western European grouping whose chief significance was its anti-Soviet orientation. Anti-Soviet governments were installed and supported in the nations bounding Russia, forming the so-called "cordon sanitaire"—the isolation of an "infected" district. There was constant economic warfare. The Soviet Union was never able to obtain long-term credits, though her international credit standing was first class.

There followed a series of assassinations, raids and

7 Frederick L. Schuman, **Soviet Politics At Home and Abroad**, New York, 1946, p. 149

provocations. In 1923 the Soviet Minister to Rome was murdered while in Switzerland. In 1927 in two separate areas of China, controlled by two different warlords, the two Soviet embassies in those areas were raided on the same day. The suspicion that someone had nudged the warlords was strengthened when the Russian trade offices in London were raided by the British government within a month of the Chinese raids. In June 1927 the Soviet Minister to Poland was assassinated in Warsaw. [8]

During this entire period the United States refused to recognize the Soviet government. Soviet-British diplomatic relations were broken off and it appeared so likely that war was being planned against the Soviet Union that there were anti-war workers' demonstrations in several countries.

HOT WAR IN THE 30's

In 1933 Hitler came into power in Germany with a declared program of war against the Soviet Union. In his book **Mein Kampf,** Hitler had made it very clear that his projected military expansion of Germany would be directed at the Ukraine. Wrote Hitler in Mein Kampf:

"**We stop the endless German movement to the south and west, and turn our gaze toward the land in the east.**... If we speak of soil in Europe today, we can primarily have in mind only **Russia** and her vassal border states.[9] (emphasis in original)

On the other side of the World, Japan had made her intentions clear, in the famous **Tanaka Memorandum,** written by Premier Tanaka to the Emperor of Japan.

"In order to conquer China, we must first conquer Manchuria and Mongolia. . . . It seems that the inevitability of crossing swords

8 The murderer of the Soviet Ambassador was admitted in 1952 into the United States on a special visa and with a special waiving of the law against criminals. The Congress of the United States formally took action to let the man into our country at the very time that deportations are sought for leading trade unionists such as Jim Lustig of the United Electrical, Radio and Machine Workers of America (UE), Harry Bridges of the International Longshoremen's and Warehousemen's Union, and many other progressive foreign-born Americans
9 Adolf Hitler, Mein Kampf, Boston, 1943, p. 654

with Russia on the fields of Mongolia . . . is part of our program of national development. . . . Sooner or later we shall have to fight against Soviet Russia. . . . One day we shall have to fight against America." [10]

Against these plans of aggressive war, Stalin issued a weighty warning in 1934:

"Some bourgeois politicians think that war should be organized against the USSR. . . . One such war against the USSR was waged already, if you remember, 15 years ago. As is well known, the universally esteemed Churchill clothed this war in a poetic formula— 'the march of fourteen States.' . . . You know how it ended. . . . It can hardly be doubted that a second war against the USSR will lead to complete defeat of the aggressors, to revolution in a number of countries in Europe and Asia. . . ." [11]

The Fascist states did not heed Stalin's warning. In swift succession, Italy attacked Abbysinia, Germany seized Austria, Germany and Italy intervened in Spain, and Japan attacked Manchuria. Then, in 1937, after developing Manchurian strategic railways, Japan moved directly against the Soviet Union.

It is not generally realized that from 1937 to 1939 there were a series of armed conflicts between the Soviet Union and Japan, in some cases involving several army divisions equipped with tanks, planes and artillery. In one campaign, for example, the Japanese lost 600 planes, 144 artillery pieces and 8 tanks. [12] This was hot war, though on a small scale. In every case, the Soviet Union won the battles but prudently refrained from expanding hostilities.

WESTERN COUNTRIES PREFERRED FASCISM

In the thirties the main enemies of the Soviet Union seemed to be Nazi Germany and Japan. Help given to these countries was indirectly a hostile act toward the Soviet Un-

10 Memorandum of Premier Tanaka to the Emperor of Japan, smuggled out and first printed in **The China Critic,** September 24, 1931. Quoted in Schuman's **Soviet Politics,** p. 243
11 Report to the 17th Congress, January 26, 1934. Quoted in Schuman's **Soviet Politics,** p. 245
12 For details of the fighting see Schuman, **Soviet Politics,** p. 252

ion and, in fact, much of this help was motivated by anti-Soviet plans. This is particularly true of the aid given Hitler by powerful American banking groups such as the group of New York banks that sent John Foster Dulles to Berlin to re-establish Hitler's credit, as already described in Chapter 4.

Powerful business groups in every country supported the Axis powers, often against their own national interests. This was true in France, it was true in England, it was true in the United States. The case of the United States and Japan is particularly instructive because President Roosevelt was aware of the Japanese threat to the United States, and was trying to meet it. Yet during the late thirties, when Japan attacked China, American financial interests aided Japan while the Soviet Union aided China. The United States sent oil and scrap iron to the aggressor; the Soviet Union sent planes and artillery to the victim. General Claire Chennault, a long time supporter of Chiang Kai-shek, and bitter enemy of the Soviet Union, was an eyewitness and he writes:

"Soon after the Japanese attacked at Shanghai the Chinese sent an official call for help to all the major powers. Only Russia responded. . . .
"The Russians had no love for the Generalissimo" (Chiang) . . . "but didn't pause to play partisan politics. . . .
"The Russians sent four fighter and two bomber squadrons completely staffed and equipped to fight the Japs in China. . . .
"The Russians gave China a twenty-million-dollar credit, about 400 combat planes in addition to the Russian squadrons, and anti-aircraft artillery. Russians set up flying and artillery schools for the Chinese and opened an overland supply route. . . . Although little publicized, **this road actually carried more war material into China than the famous Burma road** . . . **From the outbreak of war in the summer of 1937 to the end of 1942, the bulk of China's foreign aid was Russian. . . .**" [13] (emphasis added)

The unremitting hostility of the Western countries toward the Soviet Union is the key to the world history in the 1930's. The basis of this hostility was a class basis, the hatred of the employers' governments for a workers' government. This is

13 Claire Chennault, Way of a Fighter, New York, 1949, pp. 61-62

admitted by a conservative diplomat. Writes Sumner Welles:

"In those pre-war years, **great financial and commercial interests** of the Western democracies, **including many in the United States,** were firm in the belief that war between the Soviet Union and Hitlerite Germany could only be favorable to their own interests. They maintained that Russia would necessarily be defeated, and with this defeat Communism would be destroyed." [14] (emphasis added)

Against the drive to war and the pro-fascist policies of the Western countries, the Soviet Union led a titanic struggle for collective security. The Soviet spokesman, Maxim Litvinov, stirred the conscience of the world with his impassioned struggles within the League of Nations. Sumner Welles, at the time FDR's Undersecretary of State, writes:

"Litvinov became the foremost prophet of the basic principles underlying the Covenant of the League of Nations.
". . . as one looks back today, that same Maxim Litvinov must be rceognized as the only outstanding European statesman who was consistently right during the years between the wars. It was Litvinov's constant appeal that 'peace is indivisible' . . . he strove with all his great ability to make the League work. **It should never be forgotten that the Soviet Union did not desert the League. It was the great powers** which dominated the League in its later years that deserted the Soviet Union." [15] (emphasis added)

The record speaks for itself: the Soviet Union sought to achieve collective security, and thereby peace; the Western powers sabotaged collective security and thereby insured war. The reason, as Sumner Welles pointed out, was hatred of the Soviet Union.

It isn't necessary to study the policies of all countries during this period. A good idea of the times is given by the record of the two most powerful influences in European affairs in the thirties; the Vatican and the British Foreign Office. Both are world-wide organizations with great economic and political power, threatened by the rise of Socialism. Therefore, both were bitterly anti-Soviet.

14 Sumner Welles, **The Time for Decision,** New York and London, 1946, p. 32
15 Ibid., p. 31

121

The policies of the Vatican and Britain not only played a leading, perhaps a decisive, role in the events culminating in World War II, but they have since played an important role in the development of the Cold War. While the importance of the British Foreign Office is obvious, the importance of the Vatican is only fully realized when one thinks not only of its enormous influence in Europe but its great political influence (officially and unofficially) in the United States.

THE VATICAN AS A WORLD POWER

In dealing with the Vatican, it must be strongly emphasized, the writer is not dealing with Catholicism as a religion. He is dealing with the Vatican as a world power. This is not a routine disclaimer. There are many outstanding Catholics who were clear-eyed enemies of Fascism. For example, it is well-known that the entire Catholic hierarchy of the Basque region was against Franco during the Spanish Civil War. Perhaps the noblest of the Catholic anti-fascists was a prelate at the very top of the world Catholic hierarchy, the Cardinal Primate of Catalonia, Spain. His name, Cardinal Vidal y Barraquer.

Cardinal Vidal y Barraquer, together with the Bishop of Victoria, opposed Franco from the very first. When Franco, with the aid of German and Italian Fascist armies won the Civil War in Spain, the Cardinal left Spain forever. He continued all his Catholic duties and prerogatives, participating in the election of the present Pope, Pius XII, but steadfastly refused to return to Spain despite great pressure from the Vatican. Cardinal Vidal y Barraquer died in Switzerland in 1944, in self-imposed exile. The inscription on his tomb, composed by himself, reads: [16]

**DIED IN EXILE BECAUSE HE DID NOT WISH
TO LIVE UNDER INIQUITY**

[16] Julio Alvarez del Vayo, The Last Optimist, New York, 1950, p. 319. Del Vayo, Foreign Minister of the Spanish Republic, gives a moving account of Negrin, Prime Minister of the Spanish Republic, visiting the Cardinal's tomb to place some flowers in tribute.

Today many Catholic Priests fight for peace. Abbe Boulier was a delegate from France to several World Peace Congresses. Father Andrea Caciero was a delegate from Italy. A Catholic Bishop of France, Monseigneur Ancel, said that in case of a preventive war against Russia "Catholics have a plain duty to disobey the Government." He added:

"Promoters of preventive war are war criminals and any Catholic who wishes the Americans to engage in a preventive war against Russia flagrantly violates the Sixth Commandment." [17]

These Priests and hundreds like them, behaving in the true spirit of their beliefs, deserve honor from all, Catholics and non-Catholics alike. In no way therefore is any criticism aimed at Catholics or at the Vatican as the center of a world religion. Criticism is aimed at the Vatican as a world power engaged in world politics.

Officially, the Vatican is a State. It has institutions similar to that of any other world power, excepting armies. But the Vatican exercises over countries which do have armies such as Spain, Portugal and Italy, a powerful and often decisive influence. The power of the Vatican in Europe is shown by one simple fact: from Berlin westward all of Europe is a solid Catholic bloc, with clerical political parties in control and with clerical politicians in the top government position. One of the obstacles to German unity lies precisely in this fact. While in West Germany alone the Catholic Church is predominant, East Germany is predominantly Protestant. and in a united Germany the Protestant majority in the East and the Protestant minority in the West would together constitute a majority of the entire nation. A Protestant Germany would be less under the influence of the Vatican. [17a]

Like any world power, the Vatican has a chief, (the

17 Catholic Worker, February, 1952. Monseigneur Ancel is Auxiliary Bishop of Lyon
17a "Western minded Catholics would rather keep a divided Germany for the present, with the Catholic Adenauer in control," Ferdinand Kuhn, Washington Post, April 12, 1952

Pope), a Cabinet, (the College of Cardinals), a Foreign Office (The Papal Secretary of State), official ambassadors (Apostolic Nuncios and Legates), a powerful broadcasting station, an official newspaper (the **Osservatore Romano**), a foreign policy of unparalleled tenacity, continuity and consistency, complete with all the paraphernalia of diplomatic pouches, diplomatic passports and foreign treaties (the various concordats).

In Europe, the distinction between the Vatican as a religious center and the Vatican as a political power is taken for granted. In Catholic countries like France and Italy, political leaders who are themselves Catholics often fight the Church on domestic and international issues. So commonplace is this situation that it even has a name: anti-clericalism.

FASCISM AND VATICAN'S FOREIGN POLICY

The most striking commentary on the Vatican's policies was made by the Catholic Foreign Minister of Poland, Colonel Josef Beck. Beck himself was a semi-fascist, pro-Nazi politician, but in 1940 after Poland's defeat he said:

"One of those mainly responsible for the tragedy of my country is the Vatican. Too late do I realize we have pursued a foreign policy for the Catholic Church's own ends. We should have followed a policy of friendship with Soviet Russia, and not one of support of Hitler." [18]

This is quite an admission from a man who followed the Vatican's suggestions while a member of a government which was one of the most vicious and reactionary in Europe.

Unfortunately, it is a fact that no government has ever been too despotic for the Vatican, provided it was anti-communist. The Vatican supported Japan in its hour of danger by establishing diplomatic relations with that country in **March 1942, three months after Pearl Harbor.** As soon as Japan was defeated, the Vatican shifted its support to Chiang

18 Avro Manhattan, **The Vatican in World Politics,** New York, 1949, p. 277

Kai-shek, establishing diplomatic relations with Chiang in July 1946.

The clearest case of Vatican support of reactionary governments based on anti-communism are those of Fascist Italy and Nazi Germany. Taking each in turn, we can follow Vatican policy from the statements of high-ranking prelates, Bishops, Archbishops, Cardinals and the Pope himself.

THE VATICAN AND FASCIST ITALY

The support of Mussolini by the Vatican was unqualified. The late Pope, Pius XI, actually said, December 1926, "Mussolini is the man sent by Providence." [19] Cardinal Merry del Val, in the same year, said that Mussolini was "visibly protected by God." [20] By September 1932, Fascism seemed the only sound type of government to the hierarchy. Said Cardinal Gasparri:

"The Fascist Government of Italy is the only exception to the political anarchy of government, parliaments, and schools the world over. . . . Mussolini is the man who first saw clearly in the present world chaos. He is now endeavoring to place the heavy government machinery on its right track, namely to have it work in accordance with the moral laws of God." [21] (emphasis added)

Acording to the Cardinal, the U. S. Government sits in "political anarchy." Only Mussolini governed in accordance with the "moral laws of God." These moral laws seemingly included the unprovoked attack on Ethiopia in 1935. This attack was fully supported by the Church. Said Cardinal Schuster, "The Italian flag is at the moment bringing in triumph the Cross of Christ in Ethiopia." [22] And after that unhappy country had been defeated, the Pope himself said he was partaking in:

". . . the triumphant joy of an entire great and good people over a peace [i. e., the conquest] which, it is hoped and intended, will be

19 Ibid., P. 115
20 Ibid., p. 115
21 Ibid., p. 120
22 Ibid, p. 123

125

an effective contribution to the true peace in Europe and the world." (Speech of May 12, 1936) [23]

By this definition, "true peace in Europe" meant Fascist conquest. The next year, 1936 Mussolini and Hitler extended the "true peace" by helping Franco's rebellion against the legally elected Republican Government of Spain. As the Civil War progressed, all restraint was abandoned by the Church. Said an Order of the Day of 60 Archbishops in 1938 about Mussolini:

"The clergy of Italy are invoking on your person, on your work as a creator of the Empire, and of the Fascist regime, the blessing of the Lord. Duce, the priests of Christ give honor to you and swear their allegiance to you." [24]

In 1930 Pope Pius XI died, and Cardinal Pacelli who had been directing Vatican foreign policy as the Papal Secretary of State, became the present (1952) Pope under the name of Pius XII. The attitude of the Vatican towards Fascism did not change even though World War II had begun.

Two days after Italy invaded Greece the Pope blessed two hundred Italian officers in uniform, representing the army, and told them it was most gratifying to bless men "who serve the beloved Fatherland with fealty and love." [25] In February he blessed a mixed delegation of German and Italian pilots, in uniform.

THE VATICAN AND NAZISM

Many Americans do not realize that the Vatican supported Hitler because they have read of the persecution of the Catholics by the Nazis. The persecution was real enough, for, as in the case of Spain, tens of thousands of Catholics fought Nazism.

But for the top hierarchy, it was a different story. Subtly, but unmistakably, the Church backed Hitler. The key men who helped Hitler to power were all Catholics (Bruening,

23 Ibid, p 124
24 Manhattan, Vatican in World Politics, p. 128
25 Ibid., p. 128

Groener, von Schleicher, von Papen). The leader of the Catholic Centre Party, Monseigneur Kaas had this to say, after speaking with the Pope:

"Hitler knows well how to guide the ship. . . . It matters little who rules so long as order is maintained. The history of the last few years has well proven in Germany that the democratic parliamentary system was incapable." [26]

Cardinal Faulhaber, in supporting Hitler, also openly endorsed Hitler's totalitarian philosophy. He said:

"In the liberal epoch it was proclaimed that the individual had the right to live his own life as he chose; today the masters of power (i. e. Hitler) invite the individuals to subordinate themselves to the general interests. We declare ourselves partisans of the doctrine and **we rejoice in this change of mentality.**" [27] (emphasis added)

In the summer of 1934 there was the famous "Blood Purge" which included the murder of such Catholic leaders as von Schliecher. Neither the Vatican nor the German Hierarchy said a single word of protest.

In the next four years, Hitler and the Catholic Church were involved in a running fight over the Catholic Press. The Church kept reminding Hitler that it, also, wished to fight Bolshevism.

The Conference of German Bishops at Fulda issued a pastoral letter on August 20, 1936 to be read in all Catholic Churches which declared:

".. . . the danger from Bolshevism in many other countries demands peace, union with and complete support of Hitler and the Nazi regime within Germany—but (this was made impossible by) the suppression of the **Catholic Press, whose main task is to prepare the German people for a final fight against Boshevism.**" [28] (emphasis added)

The Catholic Church never made any secret of its great political goal: a crusade against Soviet Russia. As a price

26 Ibid, p. 175
27. Ibid., p. 175
28 Ibid, p. 206

of that crusade, the Church was willing to support Hitler even though Hitler was bent on undermining the Church. [29]

In 1937 Cardinal Faulhaber declared:

"All the civilized world, but especially the Catholic nations, must unite into a Holy Crusade against atheist Russia, and crush Bolshevism wherever it may be found." [30]

In 1938 the Bavarian Bishops complained:

"How long will the State continue to reject the co-operation of the Church and of her religious Orders in carrying out the German national task of today: the fight against Communism?" [31]

The Church finally got its wish. When the war on Russia came, the German Bishops were emphatic:

"A victory over Bolshevism would be equivalent to the triumph of the teachings of Jesus over that of the infidels." [32]

The war, however, developed contrary to Vatican expectations. After the Battle of Stalingrad the Vatican saw that a Nazi victory was impossible. Immediately, it initiated repeated attempts for a peace that would save the Axis governments and limit Soviet victories. Goebbels, Nazi Minister of Propaganda reported on March 3, 1943:

". . . I learn that the Pope intends to enter upon negotiations with us. He would like to get into contact with us and would even be willing to send incognito to Germany one of the cardinals with whom he is intimate." [33]

The Nazis, less far-sighted than the Pope, turned the idea down at that time. They thought they could still win.

Such has been the role of the Vatican in support of Fascism. The Soviet Union can hardly be considered "neurotic" in its suspicions of pro-Catholic governments. As for non-Catholic governments, England provides a good test of whether Soviet suspicions of the West are justified.

29. Ibid., p. 206
30 Ibid, p. 205
31 Ibid, p. 206
32 Ibid, p. 207
33 Louis P. Lochner, The Goebbels Diaries, New York, 1948, p. 271

The British Foreign Office, like the Vatican, was animated by a deep and bitter hatred of the Soviet Union. The pattern set by Winston Churchill in the intervention of 1918-19, remained the guiding principle for the Foreign Office: destroy the USSR.

BRITAIN AGAINST THE USSR

Following this policy, the British Foreign Office gambled on strengthening Mussolini's and Hitler's armies for their loudly advertised war against Russia. Even when British imperial interests were threatened, the British Foreign Office let the Fascists carry on. Mussolini's conquest of Ethiopia was dangerous to the British Empire. Britain did nothing. In the Spanish Civil War, Fascist submarines sank dozens of British cargo ships. Britain did nothing. Like the Vatican in Germany and Italy, Britain accepted a loss of prestige rather than undermine Hitler or Mussolini. In 1937 Churchill and Chamberlain were sure Hitler would deliver what he had promised for six years: a Nazi assault on the Soviet Union. Therefore Chamberlain, Prime Minister of Britain, gave Hitler a free hand in the "Cold War" of the thirties, culminating in the infamous betrayal of Munich. At Munich Czechoslovakia was handed over to Hitler by her two "allies," Britain and France. The meaning of Munich has been given by Sumner Welles, who from within the State Department, had inside knowledge of what took place. He writes:

"The agreements of Munich confirmed the convictions of the Soviet government that the Western powers strove to keep Germany from the west only by turning her to the east.' [34]

Munich was a calculated step to enable Hitler to strike against Russia. Every effort is made today by reactionaries to hide this fact and to minimize Munich. When Chamberlain died, Churchill said that "he had acted with perfect sincerity," as a true "English worthy." Shrewd apologies for

[34] Welles, Times for Decision, p. 322

Munich have become a mark of political respectability, to be found in the most unexpected places. In a book on literature, Professor Highet of Columbia University throws this in:

"Alfred (King of England) negotiated peace with the Danes in 878. This was really a Munich settlement made to hold off invaders for a breathing space. . . ." [35]

Munich was not a breathing space. It was an act of incitement to Nazi war against the USSR. The essence of appeasement **was not fear, but complicity**—a tacit complicity but very real and undeviating. The immediate victim of Munich was Czechoslovakia, but the ultimate corpse was to be the Soviet Union. Just as today Indo-China, Korea, Burma are the immediate battlegrounds, but the ultimate American targets are the USSR and China.

The inner meaning of appeasement is of great importance today. Reactionaries shout "appeasement" wherever there is any move for negotiations with the Soviet Union. Negotiation and a give and take attitude is not "appeasing." Appeasement means giving your opponent strength with no return. As in the case of Chamberlain, it means being in agreement with your enemy.

After Munich, the Soviet Union was a presumably isolated, easy prey. She watched the constant aid which England gave Hitler. In March 1939, Hitler took the rest of Czechoslovakia and marched into Prague. The obliging Bank of England illegally turned over the gold of the Czech government to Germany.

Despite all this appeasement by England, the Soviet Union as late as March 1939, tried to achieve a collective pact against aggression, and suggested a conference to England. Chamberlain replied that the idea was "premature."

35 Gilbert Highet, **The Classical Tradition**, New York and London, 1949, p. 39. Professor Highet is a Britisher who used to teach at Oxford University in the middle thirties. In those days he was allergic to politics

The Soviet Union issued weighty warnings. At the 18th Congress of the Bolshevik Party, March 1939, speaker after speaker warned Britain. [36] Said Manuilsky:

"The plan of the British reactionary bourgeoisie is to sacrifice the small States of southeastern Europe to German Fascism so as to direct Germany eastward—against the USSR. . . .
"But the British reactionary bourgeoisie are digging their own graves with their predatory plans . . . they are paving the way for the collapse not only of Fascism, but of the entire capitalist system."

Said Molotov:

" . . No enemy can now break down our Soviet Union. . . . Whomever our frank warnings do not suffice, will get to know this at the appropriate hour. . . ."

Said Stalin on March 10, 1939:

". . . England and France, have rejected the policy of collective resistance to the aggressors, and have taken up a position of nonintervention. . . .
". . . the policy of non-intervention means conniving at aggression.
"Far be it from me to moralize on the policy of non-intervention, to talk of treason, treachery and so on. It would be naive to preach morals to people who recognize no human morality. . . . It must be remarked, however, that the big and dangerous political game started by the supporters of the policy of non-intervention may end in a serious fiasco for them. . . ."

Finally, Stalin gave a solemn warning, still applicable to this day:

"In case of war, the rear and front of our army, by reason of their homogeneity and inherent unity, will be stronger than those of any other country, a fact which people beyond our borders who love military conflicts would do well to remember."

The Soviet Union then took another meaningful step. France and Britain had rejected and were rejecting the policy of collective security. Soviet Foreign Minister Litvinov had fought for years for this policy and his name had become synonymous with it. He was now relieved of his duties,

36 18th Congress speeches quoted in Schuman's Soviet Politics, p. 346, 353, 359-361

a warning that the Soviet Union was re-evaluating its policy. Britain paid no attention although every foreign office and the world was aware that Germany was angling for an alliance. Cordell Hull, who was then our Secretary of State, says as much in his Memoirs:

"The prospect of a German-Russian pact had long been in our minds. As early as November 30, 1938, our legation in Bucharest had informed us that Germany had offered secretly a non-aggression pact to Russia. We gave due significance to the replacement on May 3, 1939, of Foreign Commisar Maxim Litvinov. . . .
"In July and August, 1939, Ambassador Laurence Steinhardt in Moscow sent us a series of cables concerning the negotiations between Berlin and Moscow. . . .
"Berlin's announcement five days later that the German-Russian accord had been reached did not surprise us." [37]

But Prime Minister Chamberlain, sure of a Nazi war against Russia, continued on his blind path to destruction in a way that infuriated more alert men like Churchill and Lloyd George. Churchill, who had backed Hitler, now realized the danger and said in May 1939, to Chamberlain:

"If you are ready to be an ally of Russia in time of war, . . . why should you shrink from becoming an ally to Russia now, when you may by that very fact prevent the breaking out of war? I cannot understand all these refinements of diplomacy and delay. . . ." [38] (emphasis added)

Lloyd George, Prime Minister of England in World War I, lashed out against Chamberlain on July 29, 1939:

"Negotiations have been going on for four months with Russia and no one knows how things stand today. You are dealing with the greatest military power in the world; you are asking them to come to your help; you are not negotiating terms with an enemy but with a friendly people whose aid you want. Mr. Chamberlain negotiated directly with Hitler. He went to Germany to see him. He and Lord Halifax made visits to Rome. They went to Rome, drank Mussolini's health, shook his hand, and told him what a fine fellow he was. But whom have they sent to Russia? They have not even sent the lowest in rank of a Cabinet officer; they have sent a clerk

37 Cordell Hull, The Memoirs of Cordell Hull, New York, 1948, p. 655-657
38 Speech in House of Commons, Debate of May 19, 1939

132

in the Foreign Office. It is an insult." [39]

Lloyd George is here referring to a political mission of the Foreign Office. There was also a British military mission which had been suggested by the Soviet Union. The mission left England in a slow boat and took six days to reach Moscow, **seventeen days** after the suggestion had first been made. It would have taken one day by air, the way Chamberlain had travelled to see Hitler. When the mission arrived, "they had no authority to agree to anything of importance." [40] England wasn't interested in an alliance. A shrewd political observer, I. Deutscher, has characterized Chamberlain's treatment of the Soviet Union as follows:

"If Stalin intended an alliance [with England] the way he was treated might almost have been calculated to make him abandon his intention. If his objective was, on the contrary, to come to terms with Hitler, and he negotiated with the western powers in order to obtain a moral alibi and to be able to blame the British and the French for the abortion of the great and long-heralded anti-Nazi coalition, then the British and the French provided him with that alibi, gratuitously and with baffling zeal." [41]

There is nothing baffling about Chamberlain's policy. He simply expected Hitler to fight the Soviet Union first. The Soviet Union drew its own conclusions from British actions, and took the necessary measures. On August 29, 1939, the German-Soviet Non-Aggression Pact was signed.

THE GERMAN-SOVIET NON-AGGRESSION PACT

The German-Soviet Pact is brought up again and again in contemporary discussions. Munich is forgotten, and the Soviet Union is accused of having joined Hitler in starting a World War. This is anti-Soviet propaganda of the worst type.

Leading historians in Britain and America have analyzed the events leading up to the Pact. Three very thorough

39 Quoted in D. N. Pritt, The State Department and the Cold War, New York, 1948, p. 54. Pritt is a British lawyer and former Member of Parliament who has specialized in foreign affairs.
40 Ibid., p. 55. The details of the negotiations are given by Pritt in this book
41 Isaac Deutscher, Stalin, A Political Biography, New York and London, 1949, p. 434

books on the subject were written by the Englishman, L. B. Namier, **Diplomatic Prelude,** and by the American, F. L. Schuman, **Europe at Eve** and **Soviet Politics at Home and Abroad.** Writes Schuman in summation:

"The constant misrepresentations of the Nazi-Soviet Pact as an 'alliance' and the distortions of its meaning by Dallin and other anti-Soviet publicists cannot alter this judgment among those concerned with facts. . . . Chamberlain's policy of fostering a German-Soviet war with the Western Powers neutral was a failure. . . . Stalin's policy of self-protection against the Tory-Nazi threat was a success. . . ."[42]

In retrospect, the Pact was more than a success. It was probably the most brilliant stroke of Soviet diplomacy since the inception of the USSR. Its military and economic advantages were obvious: it gave the Soviet Union a broad buffer belt in territory, and twenty added months of production. Both these advantages have been minimized by critics, the first on the ground that German armies covered the territory in a few days, and the second on the ground that Hitler by the defeat of France and the integration of European industries gained more in relative production. These criticisms are invalid.

The strategic importance of a buffer territory is to minimize the elements of surprise as to the time and and the direction of the attack. Without it, Leningrad probably would have fallen. As it was, the city just barely managed to hold on.

As to the second point, that Hitler also could produce, the answer is that he didn't need to. Hitler had plenty of weapons in 1939. The Soviet Union, on the other hand, needed weapons badly, and twenty months of extra production meant reserves which made a lot of difference at Stalingrad.

However, towering over all these advantages were the political and diplomatic advantages. The Pact smashed Chamberlain's policy. The incredible disregard of France

42 Schuman's **Soviet Politics,** p. 379

and England towards the Soviet Union as shown at Munich was in part due to the fact that they assumed the USSR had no choice but to support them. The Pact was a rude disillusionment.

Furthermore, Hitler had been supported in his aggression on the expectation that he would fight Russia. The moment Hitler indicated that he might not fight the USSR, England and France had to oppose him before he became stronger. They could watch with complacency his increase in strength so long as they believed it was directed at the USSR, but they could not tolerate such increase when it was directed at them. Thus the Pact forced them to reverse their policy. **It wasn't the British guarantee to protect Poland against attack which was the motive behind the declaration of war; it was the double-cross on Hitler's part. After all, for the governments that betrayed Czechoslovakia, there would have been no difficulty about Poland, if Hitler had kept on going East.**

Finally, the effect of the Pact, by showing that the Soviet Union did have freedom of action, was to give depth and reality to the Anglo-American-Soviet coalition when it was finally achieved. Both Churchill and Roosevelt were acutely aware that the Soviet Union always had the possibility of a separate peace, if there were any dishonest dealings on our side.

Many of the facts outlined above were known at the time. Yet the moment the Pact was signed a tremendous campaign of slander was launched against the Soviet Union. The most shameful propaganda and distortion was put out. The plain sober fact, of course, was that the Soviet Union had broken no treaties, betrayed no allies. After a long, unbroken series of rebuffs, she made the best of a rotten world situation pregnant with danger to herself. As Professor Schuman said, "Anglo-French policy gave Stalin and Molotov no viable alternative to the course they finally adopted." [43]

Chamberlain's appeasement policy had proved itself a dismal failure and a boomerang. The Nazis instead of attacking the USSR attacked Poland and the West on September 1, 1939. Were the appeasers convinced that they were wrong? Not at all. They were too blinded by their hatred of the Soviet Union. Their first reaction was to blame the outbreak of war with Germany on someone else. There is a startling illustration of this in the Forrestal Diaries. In an entry dated December 1945, Forrestal reports a conversation with Joseph P. Kennedy (who was U. S. Ambassador to Great Britain in 1939) as follows:

"Kennedy's view: That Hitler would have fought Russia without any later conflict with England if it had not been for Bullitt's [William C. Bullitt, then Ambassador to France] urging on Roosevelt in the summer of 1939 that the Germans must be faced down about Poland; **neither the French nor the British would have made Poland a cause of war** if it had not been for the constant needling from Washington. Bullitt, he said, kept telling Roosevelt that the Germans wouldn't fight, Kennedy that they would, and that they would overrun Europe. **Chamberlain, he says, stated that America and the world Jews had forced England into the war.**" [44] (emphasis added)

Chamberlain, that "English worthy," here reveals himself as an anti-Semite. That sentence could have come directly from a speech of Hitler. It also shows that the appeasers didn't want to fight over Poland. This, for them, was the wrong war.

They tried hard to rectify their "mistake". This was the period of what was called the "phony" war, when the governments of Britain and France tried hard to switch the war to one against the Soviet Union. Their efforts were completely exposed during the Soviet-Finnish War.

Finland had been a part of Czarist Russia before 1917. Its upper class of Swedish descent who had supported the

43 Schuman, Soviet Politics, p. 380
44 Forrestal Diaries, pp. 122-123

Czar included one Marshal Mannerheim, who had achieved high rank as a Czarist general.

THE SOVIET-FINNISH WAR

After the Bolshevik Revolution Finland was immediately given her independence with no strings attached. Lenin as Soviet Premier and Stalin as Commissar of Nationalities signed the decree. The Finnish people decided they would have a Republic and elected their own government, a non-Communist government slightly to the left.

International reaction promptly moved in to smash this people's government. Although Germany, France and England were still fighting each other in France, they co-operated in Finland. German troops from the Baltic, under German General van der Golz, advanced northward to meet British and French troops. Co-ordinating their work was none other than the Czarist General Mannerheim. By 1918 the job had been done for Mannerheim by German and British troops. He then proceeded to the title given him by workers, "Mannerheim the Butcher." In cold blood, by his orders, "some 15,000 men, women and children were slaughtered," and in addition "73,915 Red rebels, including 46,000 women, were prisoners of war."

These quotations are taken from the **Encyclopedia Brittanica,** 1929 edition,volume 9, page 254, under the title FINLAND. Later editions of the encyclopedia have censored these figures that reveal Mannerheim as a valiant warrior against women, once foreign troops had beaten the men for him.

Mannerheim and a Fascist clique ruled Finland between the two wars, veering between England and Germany, but always anti-Soviet. Huge airfields were built, a powerful military line (the Mannerheim Line) was built near Leningrad, and the Finnish General Staff kept in touch with both the British and the Nazi General Staffs.

In 1939, while the war in the west occupied Germany,

137

the Soviet Union moved to close possible avenues of attack by the Germans. Leningrad was within artillery range of the Finnish frontier. The Soviet Union proposed the frontier be moved away a few miles and offered in exchange ten times as much territory to the north. Finland refused and the result was the Soviet-Finnish War.

Immediately the performance of 1917 was repeated. The enemies on the Western Front co-operated to help a fellow-reactionary government in the East. England and France on one side, Germany and Italy on the other, all sent great amounts of war material to Mannerheim. Both France and England prepared to intervene. They sent 280 planes, 586 artillery pieces, 5,100 machine guns, 250,000 grenades, over a million shells, plus aerial bombs, ambulances, uniforms, shoes and all kinds of war material. [45]

They also prepared armies of intervention. England prepared an army of 50,000 men to attack the Soviet Union from the north; France an army of half a million men in Syria under General Weygand to hit the Soviet Union from the south. [46]

Meanwhile, as so often before, a tremendous propaganda campaign took place against the Soviet Union. Newspapers which had defended Hitler and Chamberlain, Mussolini and Franco, Dolfuss and Hirohito, now thundered against the USSR. Ex-President Herbert Hoover, whose name in America was a symbol of reaction, became head of Finnish War Relief. The Vatican, which had been silent over the bombing of Ethiopia, the slaughter of Badajoz and Guernica, and the literal rape of Nanking—the Vatican suddenly found its moral indignation and blasted the Soviet Union.

The League of Nations was galvanized into action. It had created commissions that spent futile months and

45 Schuman, Soviet Politics, p. 389
46 The estimate is by Pierre Cot, Minister of Aviation in the Blum Government, at present a deputy in the French Assembly. See his book, Triumph of Treason, Chicago, New York, 1944, p. 201

months splitting hairs over Manchuria, Ethiopia, Spain and Czechoslovakia: now in a matter of days it expelled the Soviet Union. This was the only expulsion from the League in its entire existence—including a decade of the most blatant Fascist aggression. Says Professor Schuman:

"In view of the past, Soviet expulsion was a futile act of hypocrisy. In the light of the future, it was an act of folly." [47]

The American government did its share of propaganda. Roosevelt, for example, sharply attacked the USSR and its war with Finland in the famous White House lawn speech to the American Youth Congress as it stood in the rain.

The smashing of the Mannerheim Line by the Soviet Army put an end to the war and, for the moment, to the intrigues of the Allies to switch the war eastward.

It is worth noting in passing that within a few months both France and England were in desperate need of the planes and equipment they had sent to Finland. France, moreover, was in desperate need of army divisions. Her defeat was in part due to the lack of reserve divisions. Churchill tells the story of asking the French Commander-in-Chief what his strategic reserve was. Gamelin replied— "Aucune" (there is none). The troops for the strategic reserve were in Syria. [48]

GROUNDS FOR SUSPICION

Allied armies and planes ready to strike at the Soviet Union are substantial grounds for suspicion. Moreover, since the Soviet actions were directed against Germany, the concern of the Allies only confirmed the USSR that the Allies wanted to switch the war.

That the Soviet moves were directed against Germany was clear to all governments. Secretary of State Hull tells how the Finnish war showed that Stalin didn't trust Hitler and he "could sympathize with Russia's efforts to protect

47 Schuman, Soviet Politics, p. 389
48 Churchill, Their Finest Hour, Boston, 1949, p. 46

herself" [49]; he also reports that American Ambassador Steinhardt thought the Finnish war was begun and ended for Russia to be free to meet a German threat in the Balkans [50]; and Undersecretary of State Welles states that soon after the Finnish war he suggested a modification of the embargo on Russia, so that in the **spring of 1940** the U. S. began sending machine tools to the USSR. [51] Also in 1940 Hull writes that he and Roosevelt had agreed to let the Soviet Union build a battleship in America. [52]

In view of all this, allied public attacks against the Soviet Union looked very suspicious. There were many other indications of attempts to switch the war. The Vatican, for example, was very busy endeavoring to stop the war in the west on Hitler's terms. In December 1939, the Pope put out a peace plan. In January 1940, the Vatican attacked the Soviet Union's behavior in Poland, passing lightly over Hitler's actions.

Meanwhile the French appeasers were working through the Vatican. Says Avro Manhattan, "The Nuncio (Papal Ambassador) in Paris had assured the Pope that if Germany should steer the war to the East, France would not move." In March 1940, the Italian Fascist ambassador reported that Petain had told the Papal Nuncio to inform His Holiness "that there were good reasons to hope that the bloodshed between France and Germany could be avoided." This was communicated to Hitler who wanted to know "with certainty how far the French could really go in carrying out their intentions." Von Ribbenthrop, Hitler's Foreign Minister, went to Rome after many interviews with the Papal Nuncio, as reported by William Shirer in **Berlin Diary.** Ribbentrop had a meeting with the Pope at which no one else was allowed to be present and the following day Hitler sent a telegram to

49 Hull, Memoirs, p. 701
50 Ibid., p. 706
51 Welles, Time for Decision, p. 170
52 Hull, Memoirs, p. 743

the Pope congratulating him personally on the first anniversary of his election to the Papacy. [53] Though all these manouevers finally came to nothing, Europe buzzed with rumors.

This brief survey covers twenty years. It shows a series of hot and cold wars to which the Soviet Union was incessantly submitted. From the day of her birth the USSR has been subjected to attacks in word and in deed ranging from the most desperate military warfare to political isolation. Soviet leaders like Stalin and Molotov have lived through the entire nerve-racking era in high positions of responsibility. They knew the facts, they knew the reality of the danger. Their suspicions of the Western countries, far from being "neurotic," were based, and are based, on very real events. They expected war, did their utmost to prevent it, and when it came they met the test with courage and calm.

On June 22, 1941 Hitler invaded the Soviet Union on a 3000 mile front with an initial striking force the most powerful in all human history.

How "neurotic" was the Soviet sense of insecurity?

53 Most of these facts came to light in the Nurenberg trials. They are given in greater detail in Manhattan's The Vatican in World Politics, p. 196 ff.

WARTIME MISTRUST

CHAPTER 6

"Inform Mr. Stalin that we expect the formation of a second front this year."
Roosevelt to Molotov, White House, May 30, 1942

"One dreads to think what would happen if the English and the Americans were suddenly to attempt a landing."
Goebbels to Goering, March, 1943

"Those who oppose invasion are trying to arrange this matter so that Britain and America hold the leg for Stalin to skin the deer. . . . Stalin won't have much of an opinion of people who have done that. . . ."
Henry L. Stimson, May, 1943

AT DAWN on Sunday, June 22, 1941 Hitler's armies invaded the USSR. In the afternoon of the same day, Churchill broadcast to the world:

"At 4 o'clock this morning Hitler attacked and invaded Russia. All his usual formalities of perfidy were observed with scrupulous technique. . . .

"Hitler is a monster of wickedness, insatiable in his lust for blood and plunder. . . . The terrible military machine which we and the rest of the civilized world so foolishly, so supinely, so insensately allowed the Nazi gangsters to build up year by year from almost nothing; this machine cannot stand idle lest it rust and fall to pieces. It must be in continual motion, grinding up human lives. . . .

"So now this bloodthirsty guttersnipe must launch his mechanized armies upon new fields of slaughter, pillage and devastation. . . .

"We have but one aim and one single irrevocable purpose. We are resolved to destroy Hitler and every vestige of the Nazi regime. . . .

"Any man or State who fights against nazism will have our aid.

143

Any man or State who marches with Hitler is our foe. . . . That is our policy and our declaration.

"It follows, therefore, that we shall give whatever help we can to Russia and to the Russian people. We shall appeal to all our friends and Allies in every part of the world to take the same course and pursue it as we shall, faithfully and steadfastly to the end.

"We have offered to the Government of Soviet Russia any technical or economic assistance which is in our power. . . ."

Thus Churchill. Aid with no strings attached. He was promptly backed by President Roosevelt and American Lend-Lease was open to the Soviet Union.

This was an auspicious beginning. Most Americans and Englishmen accepted Churchill's offer at face value as a spontaneous, generous, warm-hearted measure.

But the Soviet leaders knew Churchill. They hadn't forgotten, they couldn't forget the intervention and the hot and cold wars to which the Soviet Union had been subjected through the interwar years. Nor could they forget who had built up Hitler and the reason—the policy of the men of Munich to unleash aggressive war eastward. Churchill could talk about allowing Hitler's war machine to be built "so foolishly, so supinely, so insensately" as if it had been a foible of a stupid Chamberlain, but the Soviet leaders knew that the war machine had been built up intelligently, aggressively and with plenty of sense—anti-Soviet sense. Churchill's cover-up of Munich as a "foolish" policy might work on the man in the street. But the Soviet leaders knew, and they knew that Churchill knew.

No, Churchill hadn't changed. To him, the alliance and the help he offered the Soviet Union were obvious acts of self-protection and power politics. Soviet leaders accepted them on the same basis.

AREAS OF MISTRUST

Reactionaries have used the Soviet mistrust of England and America as proof that the Soviet Union has evil intentions against us. They try to create a picture of utmost friendliness and honesty on our part and dislike and hatred on the part of the Soviet Union. This misleading picture is a powerful propaganda weapon of the anti-Sovieteers.

The reasons for the prewar Soviet mistrust of Britain and the other Western countries were indicated in the previous chapter. During World War II the mistrust and friction continued.

A major reason for the persistence of this mistrust during the war was the question of the opening of a Second Front. The U. S. and Britain had pledged to the Soviet Union that they would open a Second Front in 1942—and then broke the pledge. The pledge was unequivocal; the breaking of it deliberate. The proof is given in this chapter, but first it should be clear that the Second Front was only the most serious instance of friction among the wartime allies. Literally thousands of trouble-making incidents took place.

Take the case of Finland for example. Finland was the fighting ally of Hitler from June 1941 until the very end of the war; and Churchill had said "who marches with Hitler is our foe." Yet the British tried hard not to declare war on Finland whose conservative government they approved. Churchill, in the third volume of his war history gives details of the arguments he had with the Soviet Union on the subject. The Soviet leaders were both angry and suspicious of British reluctance. Churchill maintains in his book that he was reluctant to declare war because he wanted to get an unspoken agreement with the Finns whereby Finland would quietly sit out the war and not fight for Hitler. Stalin finally agreed to make the try, but Finland refused. Churchill had no choice left but to declare war. The Soviets could see that Churchill's reluctance to declare war was motivated by reactionary political and ideological considerations.

As for the United States, it never declared war on Finland. It **didn't even break off diplomatic relations until after the Normandy invasion in June 1944.** Throughout the war until Normandy, the Finnish legation remained functioning

145

in Washington as a listening post and center of intrigue for the Nazis. In fact, individuals friendly with members of the Finnish Legation in Washington were not even barred from working in American intelligence agencies. In the wartime intelligence agency, the Office of Strategic Services, the writer worked next door to such an individual, a man incidentally, with a known fascist record, having fought with both Franco in Spain and Mannerheim in Finland.

The Russians looked with little favor upon a U. S. security policy which permitted Hitler's ally to maintain a listening post here in the midst of a merciless war of survival. The subject of security was an important source of friction between the Americans and the Russians. The United States resented Soviet reluctance to give information; the Soviets were loath to rely on the primitive American security.

There were security leaks by the United States that verged on betrayal. One hair-raising illustration was committed by the Chief of Staff himself, General Marshall in an "off-the-record" Washington press conference. A newspaperman present tells how the General

". . . disclosed to a lot of pop-eyed correspondents the allied battle order in the West, our own and the Russians'. He cheerfully conceded that if the Russians knew their disposition had been disclosed to us **they might do almost anything short of quit the war.**" [1] (emphasis added)

A nation's Order of Battle is **the** key military secret in wartime. It gives the number, type and location of divisions at the front, and from these facts the enemy can easily figure out the country's war plans and strategy. Even to give out our own Order of Battle was risky. But to give the Russian Order of Battle to a group of newspapermen, some of them anti-Soviet, in a town full of anti-Soviet Americans and a functioning Finnish legation was inexcusable. It indicated a kind of arrongance on the part of the Americans, as if this

1 Lyle C. Wilson in Dateline Washington, an anthology of experiences by Washington newspapermen. New York, 1949, p. 189

country was above our allies.

This attitude was sufficiently widespread to affect officers at every level, who behaved in such a manner as to strengthen Soviet mistrust. One rather dramatic incident, created by members of the Office of Strategic Services, was told to the writer by the men involved and has to do with a raid made by Americans into a Soviet occupied city.

The city was Bucharest, capital of Rumania. The Russians took the city in the fall of 1944 after prolonged bitter fighting by the retreating German armies. Meanwhile our air forces had been bombing the Romanian oil fields with some particularly long range raids over Ploesti.

The Air Force wanted to know the results of the raids as shown by enemy statistics. Instead of asking the Russians for the information, a lieutenant in the OSS mission in Italy got the idea of flying into Bucharest without telling the Russsians beforehand and simply seizing the documents. Approval was given by the highest Air Force and OSS authorities and a mission set out in a U. S. bomber. They landed in Bucharest two days after its fall, expecting to have to talk their way out of trouble with the Soviet command. It happened instead that the Soviet combat troops had already left the city in pursuit of the Nazis and that the supporting Soviet troops and military government had not yet arrived. For twenty-four hours, as it were, Bucharest was our meat. The OSS mission took nearly two tons of documents and came back to Italy.

The Soviet authorities were not warned of the mission. The very timing of our arrival in a temporarily unoccupied city must have seemed to them the result of an elaborate espionage network. The sheer discourtesy of the act which constituted a serious diplomatic affront, was enough to convince the Soviets that Americans were up to no good.

Imagine how we would have felt if a Soviet mission had dropped into Paris right after we had taken it, seized a couple of tons of important documents and took off. Imagine the editorials in American newspapers, the indignation of radio commentators.

The Bucharest incident was kept quiet, but many others of a similar character have been made public. Here are a couple related by General Deane:

"In one case, a plane was forced down in Poland because of insufficient fuel to return to Italy. It was undamaged, and the crew was hospitably received at the airfield where they landed. The Russian commandant refueled the plane but told the crew they could not depart until clearance had been obtained from Moscow. The pilot asked permission for himself and his crew to go to the plane and get some clothes. This was granted, and when they were aboard they slammed the doors, started the engine and departed. In another case, a Pole friendly to the London regime was dressed in an American uniform and taken from one part of Poland to another on an American plane then on its way out of the country." [2]

But the most outstanding instance of American effrontery toward the Russians was the so-called Bern incident which resulted in a sharp exchange of messages between Roosevelt and Stalin. Here, the Americans who were themselves so lax on security, used security as an excuse to exclude the Soviet Union from important military negotiations.

THE BERN INCIDENT

In February 1945 certain Nazi leaders approached the allies secretly with a view of surrender on the Italian front. Secret negotiations took place in Bern, Switzerland. The Soviet Union was excluded from these negotiations on the grounds of security. This excuse was a little hollow because the Soviet Union had already been told of the negotiations. The real reason is given by General John Deane head of the American military mission in Moscow who had recommended exclusion of the Soviet Union.

"While the Bern incident caused a severe strain in our relations with the Soviet Union . . . it did serve a useful purpose. **Regardless of the merits of the case**, it marked a distinct turn in the attitude

[2] John R. Deane, The Strange Alliance, New York, 1946, p. 293

of the United States toward the Soviet Union and gave notice that we were not to be pushed around. . . ."[3] (emphasis added)

This statement is worth examining. When Deane says, "regardless of the merits of the case," he is saying that even if the Russians were right, he was glad we had a fight with them to show them they couldn't push us around. But the point is, that if the Russians were right, we would be pushing them around. General Deane, with his attitude, was not looking for trouble; he was creating it.

Were the Russians right in insisting that they be present at the surrender negotiations? The answer is an unqualified yes. The negotiations dealt not with a single battle like Stalingrad or a single sector of a separate front like Tunisia. By 1945 there was strategically only **one German front** in three huge sectors, Western, Southern, Eastern—all directly connected and interdependent. What was involved in the Bern meeting was the beginning of the end, the surrender of the southern sector and the collapse of the whole front. Obviously the Soviets were directly concerned with the negotiations. Even the combined Chiefs of Staff saw "some justification in the Soviet demands."[4]

But there was an even more fundamental political problem of unity. The German General Staff was desperately trying to split the allies by separating the war into two parts, east and west. They planned to surrender in the west, keep fighting on the east and perhaps salvage something other than total defeat. The Nazi Himmler approached the Swedish government with an offer to the western powers to surrender all German forces on the west.[5]

The Soviets feared a separate deal. Stalin sent a message to Roosevelt making the accusation. FDR replied that no such

3 Deane, Strange Alliance, p. 165. Deane's glee at the thought that the U.S. might be taking an anti-Soviet line was premature. Roosevelt had no intention of adopting such a policy as the outcome of the Bern incident showed. There was not, as yet, a "distinct turn in our policy"
4 Deane, Strange Alliance, p. 164
5 Ibid., p. 166

deal was intended. Stalin replied that he didn't believe it; perhaps the Army was not keeping Roosevelt informed. FDR countered with a scorching cable of anger at Soviet mistrust and Stalin sent back a placating answer saying he had never doubted the President's honesty. Meanwhile the negotiations had been broken off by the Nazis and the whole incident blew over.

President Roosevelt specifically stated that the Bern incident was not important. According to Leahy, the President said that he was:

". . . anxious to minimize this unfortunate episode in our relations with Russia. In the last cable message he ever sent he told Ambassador Harriman on April 12, the day of his death, 'It is my desire to consider the Bern misunderstanding a minor incident.' " [6]

Despite this clear expression of FDR, reactionaries like Byrnes and others have used the Bern incident as an illustration of Soviet arrogance and bad faith, whereas, if anything, it showed our arrogance.

Overshadowing all the many incidents, great and small, through which distrust flourished, was the great controversy of World War II, namely the question of the Second Front. On this the record is clear. A Second Front in 1942 was pledged by President Roosevelt. The pledge was broken. The how and the why of that broken pledge are of the greatest importance.

WHY THE SECOND FRONT WAS PLEDGED

When Hitler invaded the Soviet Union it was taken for granted by both the British and American governments that Soviet resistance would be brief. The American Army Staffs actually expected Hitler to take Moscow in six weeks. This was the official estimate of the U. S. Army Intelligence, G-2 under Major-General Strong. [7] The United States even sent

6 Leahy, I Was There, p. 336
7 Stimson, On Active Service, p. 383: "It was the estimate of the War Department Intelligence Officers . . . that the campaign could last only one to three months"

a military commission to Iran to take over the remnants of the Red Army after they had been defeated. [7a]

At the time, England was very weak and fearful of invasion. She saw Hitler's campaign in the East as a breathing spell during which she could build up her strength. The longer Hitler was tied up in Russia, the greater England's chances to get stronger. Therefore any help to the Soviet Union was of great value to England and would lengthen that breathing spell given by the invasion of Russia.

The successful defense of Moscow in December 1941 did not change the opinion of allied leaders. They still expected the Soviet Union to be defeated only now the breathing spell was much longer, America was in the war, and the allies were stronger. Strong enough, they felt, to land in Europe while Hitler was still entangled in Russia. **The decision to open a second front in 1942 was made on the basis of a probable Soviet collapse.** We had to land in Europe before Hitler could shift his huge army from East to West. This interpretation is confirmed by General H. H. Arnold, wartime head of the U. S. Air Force. Speaking of the period early in 1942 he writes:

"Repeatedly, the President stated that we must establish a front somewhere in Western Europe, where 'we can actually fight the German ground forces face to face as soon as possible'—this not only to pull some of the German juggernaut off the hard-pressed Russians but **to insure that the Russian stand would not be wasted . . . by reason of our own delay.** If Hitler got another chance to turn on one enemy at a time, he might still win." [8] (emphasis added)

The implication in this quotation is clear. Roosevelt feared that the Russians would be defeated, and then Hitler would turn on the west. Therefore it was to **our strategic interest** to establish a second front. The following statement of General Arnold's proves the point:

7a Davis, **Peace War and You,** p. 86. Davis was in Iran at the time, and was told about this by American officers
8 Arnold, **Global Mission,** p. 302

"At the beginning of 1942 it certainly looked as if the Allies were losing the war. The U. S. Chiefs of Staff were afraid that unless we pressed hard for a cross-Channel invasion we would **never get it at all.**" [9] (emphasis added)

With this in mind, the decision to open a Second Front by a cross-Channel invasion in 1942 was taken in April and a definite commitment made to Molotov in May. Churchill in his memoirs maintains he never made a formal commitment. As we shall see this is a lawyer's truth to cover a deception. Churchill promised to "prepare" a Second Front in such language that even FDR was misled.

The American commitment was formal and without loopholes. It was made at the White House, May 30, 1942, by President Roosevelt to Molotov when the Soviet Foreign Minister came to Washington. Molotov specifically asked whether a second front would be established in 1942 and the answer was yes. The details of the conversation have been recorded by Professor Cross, the American interpreter for Mr. Roosevelt. Here is the record:

"Mr. Molotov therefore put this question frankly: could we [the western allies] undertake such offensive action as would drive off 40 German divisions. . . . He requested a straight answer.
"The President then put to General Marshall the query whether developments were clear enough so that we could say to Mr. Stalin that we are preparing a second front. 'Yes,' replied the General. **The President then authorized Mr. Molotov to inform Mr. Stalin that we expect the formation of a second front this year.**" [10] (emphasis added)

Two days later, Monday June 1, 1942 at a farewell conference before Molotov left Washington, Molotov again, to avoid any misunderstanding raised the question formally. Here is Professor Cross' record:

"Mr. Molotov also noted that he had another question to present. . . . 'What answer,' he asked, 'shall I take back to London and Moscow on the general question that has been raised? What is the

9 Arnold, Global Mission, p. 304
10 Robert E. Sherwood, Roosevelt and Hopkins, New York, 1948, p. 563

President's answer with respect to the second front?'
"To this direct question the President answered that . . . we expected to establish a second front." [11]

The pledge was made public in the official communique on Molotov's visit, June 11, 1942:

"In the course of the conversations full understanding was reached with regard to the urgent tasks of creating a Second Front in Europe in 1942."

President Roosevelt was fully aware of the nature of the pledge he had given. Writes an English historian concerning Roosevelt:

"For the next two years the assurance he had given lay uneasily on his conscience and left him at a moral disadvantage in his dealings with Stalin." [12]

In view of the present Cold War, an important point can be made here. The Soviet Union is constantly accused of not keeping its word. Acheson, John Foster Dulles, Churchill, Truman, all the anti-Soviet politicians say that the Soviet Union's promises are worthless because they break their pledges.

It is a simple matter of fact that the first major instance of a broken promise during the war came from the American side. We gave our pledge for a Second Front freely; we broke it and broke it on a matter of life and death for the Soviet peoples. The controversy over the Second Front was to poison relations for a long time.

WAS A SECOND FRONT POSSIBLE?

The British rejected **Sledgehammer** (code word for the 1942 cross-channel invasion) on July 22, 1942, against American pressure. Eisenhower's reaction at the time was interesting for the reason behind his disappointment. Says his aide, Butcher:

"Ike thought that Wednesday, July 22, 1942, could well go down as

11 Sherwood, Roosevelt and Hopkins, pp. 574-575
12 Chester Wilmot, The Struggle for Europe, New York, 1952, p. 105

153

the 'blackest day in history,' **particularly if Russia is defeated** in the big Boche drive now so alarmingly under way." [13] (emphasis added)

Since the war, an attempt has been made to minimize the importance of the Second Front issue since it is so damaging to Western protestations of how upright and honest we are as compared to the Soviets. Many military leaders including Eisenhower have come out and said that the Second Front in 1942 was unrealistic. However it is a fact that at the time, General Marshall and General Eisenhower did think the Second Front was feasible. It is also a fact that the German General Staff was fearful of it. A few top military men, writing after the war, still consider 1942 a missed opportunity.

General Arnold, the U. S. wartime air chief, writing in 1949 says that perhaps it was all for the best that the second front was deferred, but adds, "Nevertheless, in early 1942 the situation seemed to offer a golden opportunity for such a bold stroke." [14]

The British Lieutenant General Martel argues that in 1942 the Germans had less troops for the defense of France than in 1944. Martel, interestingly enough, used the same phrase as Arnold. He writes that "here (in 1942) was our golden opportunity, but the landing craft were not there." [15]

A "golden opportunity" is no exaggeration when one considers the German situation. The highest military German authority, Field Marshall von Runstedt, told the British military historian Liddell Hart the details about his situation in France:

"I had over 3,000 miles of coastline to cover from the Italian frontier in the south to the German frontier in the north, and only 60 divisions with which to defend it. Most of them were low-grade

13 Harry C. Butcher, My Three Years with Eisenhower, New York, 1946, p. 29
14 Arnold, Global Mission, p. 304
15 Lt. General Martel, The Russian Outlook, quoted by Deutscher, Stalin, a Political Biography, p. 479

154

divisions, and some of them were skeletons." Adds Liddell Hart, "That was an impossible proposition." [16]

Through early 1943 the "golden opportunity" remained, as the Germans reeled back from Stalingrad and occupied all of France. Said von Runstedt:

"I expected an invasion in 1943 . . . for I thought you would take early advantage of this extensive stretching of the German forces in the West." [17]

And Goebbels, after a long talk with Goering analyzing the war situation in March 1943, wrote in his diary:

"He [Goering] is also somewhat worried about our having pretty much stripped the West in order to bring things to a standstill in the East. **One dreads to think what would happen if the English and the Americans were suddenly to attempt a landing.**" [18] (emphasis added)

The shortage of landing craft, which General Martel mentions, and which Churchill made his central point when he talked to Stalin in August 1942 was certainly a fact. But the American military planners knew all about it. They knew exactly the amount of landing craft available and they thought it was enough. The man who made the plans for the invasion was none other than General Eisenhower, then head of the War Plans Division. His plans had been approved by the Joint Chiefs of Staff including General Marshall, General Arnold and Admiral King. Stimson himself wrote formally to President Roosevelt on March 27, 1942, in specific answer to British criticisms based on the landing craft shortage:

". . . you should lean with all your strength on the ruthless re-arrangement of shipping allotments and the preparation of landing gear . . . aimed at a definite date of completion not later than September. The rate of construction of a number of landing barges should not be allowed to lose the crisis of the World War." [19]

The "ruthless re-arrangement" Stimson talks about refers

16 B. H. Liddell Hart, The German Generals Talk, New York, 1944, p. 228
17 Liddell Hart, German Generals Talk, p. 229
18 Goebbels' Diaries, p. 262
19 Stimson, On Active Service, pp. 417-418

to the Navy's hoarding of landing barges for the Pacific. An idea of the Navy's hoarding can be gathered from one comparison. On May 1, 1944, the U. S. Navy controlled 31,123 landing craft of which only **eight percent** (2,493) was allotted to the Normandy invasion by the U. S.

More important, however, is the fact that the number of landing craft depends on many other facts of which two are crucial. The first fact is, how big is the initial assault? Five divisions, ten, twenty? The more soldiers, the more landing craft. In 1944 everything had to be on a huge scale because for **two years the Germans had been fortifying the coasts and training new divisions.**

Secondly, the number of landing craft depends on whether a harbor can be captured at the very start. Then soldiers don't hit the beaches; they land directly from transports. In 1942 the ports were not as fortified as in 1944. A harbor could have been captured as the experience of Dieppe shows.

Dieppe is a harbor on the coast of France which was raided in 1942 by allied troops who suffered a bloody defeat. This defeat was constantly used by Churchill during the war to show that its was impossible to seize a port. Churchill's opinion has become standard history by now. Yet the facts show that Churchill, as usual, twists events to suit himself. Dieppe probably could have been taken.

This statement is made on the basis of a thorough study of the Dieppe Raid made by the writer. In line of duty, during the war, the writer examined the plans for the raid, the orders for execution during the raid and finally staff evaluations after the raid. [20]

The raid on Dieppe turned out to be a massacre because of a change of plans. The original plans drawn up by Combined Operations (the Commandos) called for a **flank** attack on the town, landing on the coast on both sides of the town and taking it from the rear. This plan was rejected by the

Canadian General McNaughton who was put in command of the operation. He substituted a **frontal** attack, coming in directly from the sea, despite the fact that the harbor was known to be heavily defended on the seaward side.

As a result, Canadian troops in the frontal attack were massacred, with over three thousand casualties. The original plan in all probability would have been successful.

These considerations about the second front have been presented not as proof, but as indications that Soviet expectations for a cross-channel invasion in 1942 was based on reality. The proof that the Second Front was possible can be simply stated: Marshall and Eisenhower were prepared to carry it into effect.

BREAKING THE PLEDGE: CHURCHILL DOUBLE-CROSSES FDR.

The reason why the American pledge was broken is clear cut: Churchill said no to a cross-channel invason in 1942. Churchill's power to veto the operation was very real since the invasion of the continent would have to be launched from the British Isles.

But Churchill was too subtle a man to face FDR with a bare denial. He suggested an alternative, the North Africa invasion. That this idea was of British origin is testified by General Arnold:

". . . the first mention of the North African invasion, came during the visit of Churchill's to Washington, just after Pearl Harbor . . ." and Arnold explicitly mentioned its importance as ". . . an energetic British counter-measure to the zeal with which we of the American Chiefs of Staff urged a cross-channel invasion." 21

And Stimson reports that:

"Mr. Churchill and his advisers categorically refused to accept the notion of a cross-Channel invasion in 1942. Mr. Roosevelt categorically insisted that there must be some operation in 1942. The

20 Churchill in **Hinge of Fate** gives the impression that "no records were kept." Actually the documents comprise a thick book and reference to it is made in Eisenhower's **Crusade in Europe,** p. 493, note no. 8
21 Arnold, **Global Mission,** p. 304

only operation that satisfied both of these conditions was 'TORCH' (the invasion of North Africa)." [22]

The shift from a cross-channel invasion to the North African invasion was accomplished by Churchill with consummate ingenuity and considerable duplicity. It is quite a double-cross and he brags about it. He tells us himself that he agreed to the American proposal for a second front on April 14 with no intention of carrying it through, but instead with full intention of shifting the invasion to North Africa or to Norway. But he didn't even mention these alternatives at the time because he knew that to mention them would expose his previous agreement as insincere and deceitful. Writes Churchill:

". . . I had to work by influence and diplomacy in order to secure agreed and harmonious action with our cherished Ally, [the U. S.] without whose aid nothing but ruin faced the world. **I did not therefore open any of these alternatives at our meeting on the 14th.**" [23] (emphasis added)

What Churchill calls "influence and diplomacy" was making a pledge he didn't intend to keep.

The meeting of April 14, 1942 in London, consisted of Hopkins and Marshall for the Americans and, for the British, their Chiefs of Staff and the Defense Committee of the War Cabinet chaired by Churchill. Churchill's agreement to the American plans was so forthright that, writes Sherwood:

"Hopkins cabled exultantly to Roosevelt that the British Government had agreed to the main American proposal and Marshall cabled confirmation of this to the Secretary of War [Stimson]. . . . The British Government, Marshall said, now **intended to proceed immediately and energetically with all necessary preparations for the major operation.**" [24] (emphasis added)

And all along Churchill had no such intentions!

Yet it was on the basis of this agreement, that six weeks

22 Stimson, *On Active Service*, pp. 425-426
23 Winston S. Churchill, *The Hinge of Fate*, Boston, 1950, p. 324
24 Sherwood, *Roosevelt and Hopkins*, p. 538

158

later, Roosevelt gave America's pledge to Molotov for a second front in 1942. A week after Molotov had returned to Moscow, Churchill began to move. On June 9 Admiral Mountbatten dined with FDR and Hopkins in the White House and intimated that the British Chiefs of Staff were considering revision of the decision on the cross-channel invasion and suggesting the North African invasion instead. [25]

Secretary of War Stimson exposed the British game. In a letter to FDR he said:

". . . the British theory . . . is that Germany can be beaten by a series of attritions in northern Italy, in the eastern Mediterranean, in Greece, in the Balkans, in Rumania and other satellite countries. . . .

"To me, in the light of the postwar problems which we shall face, that attitude . . . seems terribly dangerous. We are pledged quite as clearly as Great Britain to the opening of a real second front. None of these methods of pinprick warfare **can be counted on by us to fool Stalin into the belief that we have kept that pledge."** [26] (emphasis added)

We may assume that Stalin wasn't fooled.

But the American and British people were. As always, the first victims of the deceptions and distortions of Western leaders are their own peoples. Churchill boasts of his deceit, yet the adulation and build-up of this man in the American press goes on and on. Leading universities such as Massachusetts Institute of Technology give him degrees and a platform for anti-Soviet propaganda. Nowhere is the corruption of the "leaders" of our society more clearly seen.

CHURCHILL'S GAME

In 1943 the Second Front was still not opened. As the months went by Churchill's game became obvious. An English historian has exposed it, saying that "the Prime Minister (Churchill) sought a plan of campaign," namely the invasion of the Balkans, "which would ensure that victory did not

25 Sherwood, Roosevelt and Hopkins, p. 590
26 Stimson, On Active Service, pp. 436-437

leave the democratic cause politically weaker." [27]

This is fancy double-talk for a British control of the Balkans similar to what they achieved in Greece where the "democratic" cause has been "strengthened" by a semi-Fascist regime put in power by British bayonets and maintained by American dollars.

The Balkan campaign is the reverse side of blocking the Second Front. Churchill is acutely conscious that his activities in this connection discredit his Fulton propaganda theme that we were friends to the USSR until Soviet "expansionism" led to the Cold War. Therefore, he has vehemently denied his opposition to a Second Front and his desire for a Balkan invasion.

In his memoirs, **The Second World War** of which five volumes have so far appeared, he hammers again and again at this point, bringing up every scrap of documents, however tiny, to prove his point. He writes:

"It has become a legend in America that I strove to prevent the cross-Channel enterprise called 'Overlord,' and that I tried vainly to lure the Allies into some mass invasion of the Balkans, or a large scale campaign in the Eastern Mediterranean, which would effectively kill it. Much of this nonsense has already in previous chapters been exposed and refuted. . . ." [28] (emphasis added)

Churchill, in this paragraph utters no falsehood; he just misleads. It's as difficult to catch him in on outright falsehood as to catch him in an outright truth. Trained in Parliament, he knows just the right word to use which gives the literal truth yet completely misleads the listener.

In the quotation just given, Churchill talks about a "mass" invasion of the Balkans and a "large-scale" operation in Eastern Mediterranean, and says he was against both. But "mass" and "large-scale" are conveniently vague terms. A study of his proposals, from his own book, shows inescapably that he tried his best to get a Balkan campaign.

27 Wilmot, Struggle for Europe, p. 130
28 Winston S. Churchill, Closing the Ring, Boston, 1951, p. 344

Even more important is Churchill's misleading statement on the second front. He says he didn't try to prevent "Overlord." Overlord was the code name for the cross-channel invasion of 1944, not that of 1942 which was called "Sledgehammer," nor that of 1943 which was called "Roundup" and both of which Churchill did prevent. The question of the Second Front has always been one of the precise time when it should take place so as to have an effect on the Eastern Front when it was needed. No one has ever accused Churchill of being against the Second Front at his own convenience in some indefinite future, when the Germans were ready to collapse. Eisenhower confirms this in so many words:

"I never at any time heard Mr. Churchill urge or suggest complete abandonment of the Overlord plan. His conviction, so far as I could interpret it, was that at some time in the indefinite future the Allies would have to cross the Channel. But he seemed to believe that the attack should be pushed elsewhere until the day came when the enemy would be forced to withdraw most of his troops from Northwest Europe, at which time the Allies could go in easily and safely." [29] (emphasis added)

Not only Eisenhower, but Marshall, Stimson, Hopkins, Deane, Hull, Forrestal and scores of other top leaders are on record against Churchill on this point. Hull specifically states that at Quebec in 1943 Churchill spoke against a cross-channel invasion and in favor of a Balkan invasion to prevent a "Soviet rush into the area" detrimental to "British and U. S. interests." [30] Forrestal says that Churchill brought "pressure" to bear for a Balkan invasion in a "desire to have American troops, jointly with the British, appear in those countries (the Balkans) as the conquerors of the Germans." [31] And General Deane after admitting that from a military point of view "there can be no doubt of the wisdom" of a Second Front also praises Churchill for his opposition to it, which "points to foresight on Churchill's part" even

29 Dwight D. Eisenhower, Crusade in Europe, New York, 1948, p. 199
30 Hull, Memoirs, p. 1231
31 Forrestal Diaries, p. 117

161

though a Balkan invasion "probably would have prolonged the war." [32]

Churchill can protest all he wants; the methods he used and boasts about invalidates his protestations. If all these American leaders received an identical impression from Churchill's words and deeds, Soviet leaders must have also come to the same conclusions. Churchill's policy was designed for the mutual exhaustion of Germany and the USSR, leaving the Western powers as unchallenged and unchallengeable arbitrators. This was precisely the policy of Munich, refined, sophisticated and brought up-to-date to fit changed conditions.

THE AMERICAN ROLE IN THE SECOND FRONT

President Roosevelt and his top advisers remained firm in their desire for a second front, first in 1942 and then in 1943. All evidence points to the fact that they honestly wished to win the war as quickly as possible and that a cross-channel invasion was the way to do it. It must be assumed that Soviet leaders were aware of this attitude and aware that it was Churchill who was the stumbling block. In fact, the American position was an important basis for the developing mutual confidence and respect that culminated in Yalta.

American policy-makers had deep and long-range reasons to be honest about crossing the channel. After Stalingrad it was clear that the Nazis would ultimately be defeated by the Soviet Union. Roosevelt and his advisers were deeply concerned that the victory should not be entirely a Soviet one. Stimson was worried about it and strongly opposed Churchill, admitting to a "certain sympathy with Russian suspicion of Western motives." [38] He told Roosevelt that the opponents of invasion

". . . are trying to arrange the matter so that Britain and America hold the leg for Stalin to skin the deer and I think that will be

32 Deane, Strange Alliance, p. 44
33 Stimson, On Active Service, p. 527

dangerous business for us at the end of the war. Stalin won't have much of an opinion of people who have done that and we will not be able to share much of the postwar world with him." [34]

Roosevelt, more far-sighted than Churchill, realized that it was to American interests to have a Second Front. But Churchill had his way. There was no Second Front for two years after it had been promised.

WERE THE SOVIETS UNDULY SUSPICIOUS?

Looking back over the long years of intervention, hot and cold wars, and the broken pledges, conflicts and recriminations of the Second World War, the amazing thing to an impartial observer is not that suspicion existed, but that it wasn't worse. In actual fact, the Soviet Union was not dogmatic in its wariness. Even such a basically anti-Soviet general as General Deane agrees to this. He tells how the Russians took considerable risks to show their friendship. For example, the American fliers who had been in the Doolittle Raid on Japan and had landed in Russia were allowed to "escape" from internment.

As the war went on hundreds of American fliers landed in Siberia after bombing Japan and were interned. This internment was required by international law, since the Soviet Union was not as yet at war with Japan. The fliers were allowed to "escape" with excellent transportation even though this violated Soviet neutrality towards Japan and Japan could have used this as a pretext for war. Writes General Deane:

"In the case of the internees, the Russian attitude was more generous than might reasonably have been expected." [35]

And again a little later:

34 Ibid., p. 527. In passing, it is interesting to note Stimson's way of speaking. He sounds like a monopoly lawyer with his talk of "sharing the postwar world." The peoples of the world don't want to be "shared." Indo-China doesn't want to be "shared" by France, nor Malaya by Britain, nor Iran by Standard Oil. The peoples of the world want to be free—free to develop their abilities, their knowledge, their natural resources
35 Deane, The Strange Alliance. p. 63

"The assistance given by the Russians in effectuating the prompt release of General Wainwright (from a Japanese prison camp in August, 1945) recalled their cooperative attitude in allowing American internees to escape from Tashkent. It was further evidence that Soviet officials are inclined to be cooperative when they are convinced that the Americans involved in a given situation are not actuated by any ulterior motives. . . ." [36] (emphasis added)

Soviet officials were friendly when they were not suspicious. This is the considered judgment of an American General who was in Moscow for a long time, and who, we must remember, had a strong dislike for the Soviet system and the Soviet government.

ROOSEVELT'S WARTIME POLICY

Roosevelt's policy was consciously aimed at creating conditions of friendship. Roosevelt recognized the legitimate Soviet suspicions and carefully avoided any act which would suggest an Anglo-American bloc. Stettinius and Sherwood in their books give many examples of Roosevelt's attitude. Roosevelt told Stettinius when the latter was Secretary of State that "too many Anglo-American meetings before Yalta" would not be desirable as suggesting "a combined front against them" (the Russians). Adds Stettinius:

"The President was always careful to keep the Russians informed of diplomatic negotiations between the British and our government. At the Teheran Conference, although the Prime Minister [Churchill] was quite irritated at the time, the President had declined to have lunch with him alone just before a plenary session. At Yalta, too, the President and the Prime Minister didnothold a private luncheon until five days after the Conference had been in session." [37]

Roosevelt also avoided a haggling attitude towards the Soviet Union. He fully appreciated the forthright way in which the Soviets fought in their own defense and the defense of a common cause. Therefore Roosevelt insisted that our contribution should be made freely. General Deane com-

36 Ibid., p. 283
37 Edward Stettinius. Roosevelt and the Russians, New York, 1949, p. 62

plains that he wanted to disapprove some particular Russian request during the war. The Russian spokesman implied that if Deane disapproved, they would go over his head to Washington, and get their request approved there. Deane then adds, bitterly: "The hell of it was, when I reflected on the attitude of the President, I was afraid he was right."[38]

Roosevelt's attitude, which Deane dislikes, was the attitude of a sincere ally and of a friend. Had this attitude been maintained there would be no Cold War today, no Korea, no threat of atomic annihilation.

It is imperative to show that Roosevelt's policy was and is a real alternative to the present course of events. This alternative of peace is not only possible, but consistent with the power and economic relationships between and within the great powers. It would be contrary to the purpose and spirit of this book to leave the reader with the impression that as a result of the events described above, the "Cold War" was inevitable. Such a view would logically lead to the conclusion that a global war is inevitable—which is contradicted by the experiences of history, by morality, and by common sense.

38 Deane, Strange Alliance, p. 98

165

NEW YORK HERALD TRIBUNE, FRIDAY

10

Roosevelt Report to Congress, Hails Yalta as

Says Big Three Cemented Unity On Political and War Problems

President Calls Era of Unilateral Actions Ended; Urges U. S. to Play World Role to Bar Another Conflict; Final Plans Set for Nazis' Defeat

Mar 2. 1945
N.Y. Herald-Trib

Three Days Before Death Roosevelt Wrote Plea to Accept Pact of 'Co-Equal Nations'

TALLAHASSEE, Fla., April 27 (A.P.)—Franklin D. Roosevelt, looking to the San Francisco Conference, expressed the hope that public opinion would recognize that "under our theory nations are co-equal and therefore any treaty must represent compromise."

This was disclosed in an unpublished letter read by Senator Pepper before a special meeting of the Legislature held as a memorial to the former President.

Written three days before Mr. Roosevelt's death, the letter was in reply to one from Mr. Pepper on the confirmation of Assistant Secretaries of State.

Dated April 9 at Warm Springs, Ga., the letter read:

"Yours of April ... sent to me ...

Apr. 28, 1945
N.Y. Times

ROOSEVELT'S POLICY OF PEACE

CHAPTER 7

"To Franklin Roosevelt a firm agreement with the Soviet Union was the indispensable foundation for peace in the future."
Sumner Welles, 1946

"After this war . . . we are going to have to export far more than ever before. . . . Russia is one of our largest potential customers."
Donald Nelson, 1943

FRANKLIN DELANO ROOSEVELT was elected President of the United States four times in a row. This fact can never be erased by his enemies no matter how much they rewrite history and the U. S. Constitution. Today a concentrated campaign of slander is taking place to wipe out the memory of Roosevelt, of the great progressive struggles of the American people in the thirties, and of American-Soviet collaboration during the war. Fearful that the American people will again march under progressive leaders, reactionaries in America are seeking to cut Roosevelt down to their own level. They cannot do it.

Roosevelt was President in the midst of the worst depression and the biggest war in United States history. Wars and depressions are today mankind's greatest scourge, worse than floods, droughts, epidemics, eruptions, tidal waves or any other evil tricks that Mother Nature ever played upon

167

defenseless man. Wars and depressions are man-made, and Roosevelt undertood that peace and prosperity can also be made by man. In the world today peace and prosperity can be possible on one basis and one basis alone—friendship between the U. S. and the USSR.

It was Roosevelt's supreme virtue that he saw this fact clearly, sharply, deeply and that he said so unequivocally. Writes Sumner Welles, his Undersecretary of State:

". . . I can without hesitation assert that . . . from the time when Hitler invaded Russia in June of 1941, the President regarded understanding and cooperation between Moscow and Washington as one of the indispensable foundations for American foreign policy." [1]

Roosevelt moved directly to achieve understanding. Roosevelt knew the historical background of Soviet international relations and therefore did not regard Soviet suspicions as "neurotic." On the contrary, since the acts of the Western countries had caused this mistrust in the first place, Roosevelt realized it was up to the U. S. to behave in such a way as to create belief in its good intentions.

Roosevelt was very specific about American behaviour. For example, the first head of the U. S. supply mission to Moscow during the war was General Faymonville. Says General John Deane:

"Faymonville had had instructions from the President that no strings were to be attached to our aid to Russia and that the program was not to be used as a lever to obtain information about and from the Russians. He carried out the President's instructions almost too literally, and it was over this point that a difficult conflict arose between him and the War and Navy Departments. . . ." [2] (emphasis added)

What Deane doesn't mention is that Army and Navy brasshats were against Faymonville because he was one of the few Regular Army officers who was sympathetic to the

1 Welles, Where Are We Heading, p. 102
2 Deane, Strange Alliance, p. 91

USSR and believed the Soviet Union would not be defeated. The brasshats preferred to rely for their information on Soviet matters on strongly anti-Soviet individuals such as the U. S. military attache in Moscow, Major Yeaton. About this gentleman, one small incident reported in Sherwood's book is sufficient to show his reliability:

"On October 10 [1941], Yeaton reported that he considered it possible that the 'end of Russian resistance is not far away.' . . . On October 11, Faymonville reported the view of the Soviet General Staff that adequate reserves could prevent the encirclement of Moscow. . . ."[3]

Moscow of course did not fall. Faymonville, the friend of the USSR, proved more objective and correct than the anti-SovietYeaton. Again and again this has been the case, and is still the case today.

Roosevelt made every effort to demonstrate to the Soviet Union that the U. S. was worthy of trust, and that we meant what we said. He fought hard for the cross-channel invasion; he placed no strings on Lend-Lease. Above all, Roosevelt was very strict and scrupulous about reciprocity—a technical word in international relations which implies a recognition of full equality between nations. Secretary of State Hull was always careful to notify the Soviets of any action he intended to take, and he has placed on record the fact that the USSR did the same.

On many occasions American thoughtfulness impressed the Soviets. For example while the Yalta Conference was goin on, Constantine Oumansky, Soviet Ambassador to Mexico, was killed in a plane crash. Roosevelt offered an American military plane to bring his ashes to Russia. Says Stettinius, "This offer was quickly accepted and it was a gesture the Russians seemed to appreciate deeply."

Or take this small incident at the Moscow Conference

3 Sherwood, Roosevelt and Hopkins, p. 395

when Hull said that he had attended many international conferences but in none had he found greater hospitality and consideration than that offered by the Soviet government, and especially by Mr. Molotov. Stalin was pleased and remarked, a trifle bluntly, that he hadn't expected to hear this comment.

President Roosevelt's policy of allaying Soviet mistrust was not a simple-minded politician's approach. Roosevelt's policy of friendship and cooperation rested on a hard-headed understanding of national security in the modern world. Writes Welles about FDR that:

". . . in the wider sense he saw that each [the U.S. and USSR] could achieve security only if it had the co-operation of the other. He told me in one of the final talks I had with him that he believed that **Stalin saw this fact as clearly as he did himself.** Neither the Soviet Union nor the United States could be safe unless each was confident that there was no reason for it to defend itself against the other. Each could prosper only if it could live in a safe and prosperous world. Each could progress only if the community of nations witnessed a universal rise in living standards."[4] (emphasis added)

The leaders of the Soviet Union were in complete agreement with FDR. Their devastated country and their suffering people needed one thing above all else, peace.

American-Soviet friendship in the post-war world would have assured peace, a peace of creative achievement. In this peaceful world, problems would still have existed, but these problems and conflicts would have been subject to negotiations, arbitrations and compromises. Roosevelt and Stalin were keenly aware of the problems, but both felt that they could be solved. It is indeed remarkable to see how close their views were.

ROOSEVELT AND STALIN

There is on record an exchange of views between Roose-

4 Welles, Where Are We Heading, pp. 36-37

velt and Stalin which reactionaries would pay dearly to suppress forever. Mrs. Roosevelt is the source for the following conversation between FDR and Stalin:

"My husband said, 'Do you think it will be possible for the United States and the USSR to see things in similar ways?' Mr. Stalin responded: 'You have come a long way in the United States from your original concept of government and its responsibilities and your original way of life. I think it is quite possible that we in the USSR, as our resources develop and people can have an easier life, will find ourselves growing nearer to some of your concepts and you may find yourselves accepting some of ours.' "5

Roosevelt agreed with Stalin on this score. He also thought America and the Soviet Union would become more nearly alike as time went by. Sumner Welles, who was close to him, reports that FDR once told him:

". . . that he believed that if the world could remain at peace the following phenomenon would probably take place. He regarded the American form of democracy as being at the opposite pole from the original form of Soviet Communism. In the years which had elapsed since the Soviet revolution of 1917, the Soviet system had advanced materially toward a modified form of state socialism. In the same way, the American policy since that time had progressed toward the ideal of true political and social justice. He believed that American democracy and Soviet Communism could never meet. But he told me that he did believe that if one took the figure 100 as representing the difference between American democracy and Soviet Communism in 1917, with the United States at 100 and the Soviet Union at 0, American democracy might eventually reach the figure of 60 and the Soviet system might reach the figure of 40. The gap between these two final figures it seemed to him would never lessen." 6

One may agree or disagree with Roosevelt's way of putting the relationship, but the significant thing about Roosevelt was that he did recognize that changes were inevitable and that the U. S. and the USSR could grow closer together in friendship and cooperation, particularly in foreign affairs.

Welles goes on to say:

5 Eleanor Roosevelt, This I Remember, p. 253
6 Welles, Where Are We Heading, p. 37

"He [Roosevelt] felt, therefore, that even though the internal systems of the two countries could never conceivably become identical, some progress toward approximation had already been made, and that this approximation made for a better understanding between the peoples of the two nations. . . ." [7]

Cooperation between America and the USSR was helped by the fact that as the war went on, Soviet and American leaders developed a mutual respect and friendship. For example, Vice-Admiral McIntire who was FDR's personal physician, noticed that Premier Stalin seemed to have a genuine respect for FDR. McIntire observed:

". . . I believed then, and still believe, that Stalin had a very real liking and respect for F. D. R. I watched many of their meetings, and as the two came together, the Marshal's eyes would lose their hard, shrewd, 'trading' look and take on warmth. If it was all an act, then he was a mighty good actor." [8]

Sumner Welles testifies that Soviet leaders came to believe in FDR's sincerity in his friendship for the Soviet Union. He writes:

"Soviet leaders, and Stalin in particular, had, as the result of many years of direct dealing with President Roosevelt, finally convinced themselves that the policy he pursued had no ulterior motives." [9]

On the American side, as we came to know and work with the Soviet leaders, we broke through the prejudice of years and began to realize that here were first rate men. Stalin in particular made a deep impression even on such staunch conservatives as Secretary of State Cordell Hull. Mr. Hull is an austere person, slow to praise. This is what he writes about Stalin.

"I had an impressive experience with Stalin as we parted. After the usual expressions of leave-taking, he shook hands with me and said, 'Goodbye' in Russian. Then after walking three or four steps away from me, he suddenly turned and walked back and

7 Ibid., p. 37
8 Ross T. McIntire, White House Physician, New York, 1946, p. 220
9 Welles, Where Are We Heading, p. 106

shook hands a second time to a rather protracted extent, but without saying a word. Then with serious demeanor, he turned and walked away. **I thought to myself that any American having Stalin's personality and approach might well reach high public office in my own country.**" [10] (emphasis added)

President Roosevelt made no bones about his liking for Stalin. After the two men had first met, FDR's son Elliott asked his father what kind of a man Stalin was. President Roosevelt answered:

"Oh . . . he's got a kind of massive rumble, talks deliberately, seems very confident, very sure of himself, moves slowly—altogether quite impressive, I'd say.
" 'You like him?'
"He [FDR] nodded an emphatic affirmative. . . ." [11]

A few days later, Roosevelt again confided to his son:

"He gets things done, that man [Stalin]. . . . Father spoke slowly and thoughtfully. 'It's a pleasure working with him. **There's nothing devious.** He outlines the subject he wants discussed, and he sticks to it.' " [12] (emphasis added)

This is a strikingly different picture than the one reactionaries in America have painted. Whom should Americans believe? Roosevelt who had worked with Stalin for peace, or those who have deceived the American people and who have deliberately created a "war psychosis"?

THE BASIS OF SOVIET-AMERICAN FRIENDSHIP

The fact that Soviet and American leaders came to know, like, and respect each other made friendly relations easier to achieve. But what made the friendship possible were the objective bases underlying American-Soviet relations which FDR recognized and made the foundations of his policy. These are as valid today as when FDR died.

There are no objective economic or geographic rivalries between the United States and the Soviet Union. The economies of the two countries are not competitive. Trade be-

10 Hull, Memoirs, p. 1311
11 Elliot Roosevelt, As He Saw It, p. 176
12 Ibid., p. 183

tween the two is not only possible, but greatly beneficial.

This obvious fact of life is accepted even by conservative businessmen. Donald Nelson, former head of Sears Roebuck and Co. and wartime chairman of the War Production Board, pointed out in 1943, the benefits of postwar trade when "we are going to have to export far more than ever before. . . . Russia is one of our largest potential customers."

Answering the reactionaries who argued that we shouldn't help Russia with credit, Nelson went on:

"If we benefit from it, why not? By helping Russia raise her living standards we could benefit in two ways. First, in trade. Second, because if we and Russia can do business together, we won't be so likely to have trouble. . . . We don't have to fear Russian industrial competition. We're fifty years ahead. The Soviets won't be able to compete with us for world markets for a long time to come, except perhaps in countries right next door to her . .. (but) whatever we might eventually lose to Russian competition would be offset many times over by what we would sell to Russia, and by the over-all increase in world trade." [13]

This kind of thinking seems much more sensible than a tremendous armaments race, cold wars, Koreas, atomic explosions and a fearful world.

From a geographic point of view there are no sources of friction between us and Russia. We have no boundaries to dispute, no territory that we want from one another. It is no accident that Tsarist Russia and the Republic of the United States got along together for well over a century despite very differing ideologies, political and economic systems.

None other than General Eisenhower has summarized the basis of American-Soviet friendship. Today he seems to have forgotten these words, written as late as 1948:

"In the past relations of America and Russia there was no cause to regard the future with pessimism. Historically, the two peoples had maintained an unbroken friendship that dated back to the

13 Albert Z. Carr, Truman, Stalin and Peace, New York, 1950, p. 15

birth of the United States as an independent Republic. Except for a short period, their diplomatic relations had been continuous. Both were free from the stigma of colonial empire building by force. The transfer between them of the rich Alaskan territory was an unmatched international episode, devoid of threat at the time and of any recrimination after the exchange. Twice they had been allies in war. Since 1941 they had been dependent each on the other for ultimate victory over the European Axis." [14]

President Franklin Delano Roosevelt knew that there was no basis for conflict in the national interests of the two countries. As Sumner Welles put it:

"He felt it was indispensable that both governments should realize that in the field of world affairs their respective courses could always be parallel and need never be antagonistic." [15]

It must be remembered that FDR, as one of his first acts as President in 1933, established diplomatic relations with the Soviet Union, ending 16 years of hostility.

Within the Soviet Union, Roosevelt's attitude was completely reciprocated. When Secretary of State Hull was in Moscow, he had long talks with Stalin who made it very plain that the USSR considered American-Soviet cooperation as essential to world peace. Hull writes:

The Marshal [Stalin] stressed the necessity for collaboration and co-operation between the U. S. and Russia in the most sympathetic manner. . . .
"I concluded that patience on the part of both countries, and especially of their leaders in key positions, would be necessary in dealing with a mistake made here and there, and **with intemperate individuals who would try to give trouble in both countries.**" [16] (emphasis added)

FDR's POLICY WAS SUCCESSFUL

Roosevelt's policy of friendship was a successful policy. Its success shows that peace in the world is possible. Welles has written that his policy "had established a far closer and far more understanding relationship between Moscow and

14 Eisenhower, **Crusade in Europe**, p. 457
15 Welles, **Where Are We Heading**, p. 38
16 Hull, **Memoirs**, p. 1310

Washington than had ever previously existed." [17]

The success of Roosevelt's policy is shown most clearly in the victorious prosecution of the war. Secretary of War Stimson wrote that "the Russians were magnificent allies. **They fought as they promised** and they made no separate peace." [18] (emphasis added)

Stimson pays tribute to Soviet fidelity to their promises. The Soviet Union powerfully helped the Western powers during the famous Ardennes offensive of the Nazis **when they didn't have to.** This fact has been completely buried by the American press and by Churchill. It was revealed in 1948 when the government of the USSR released the text of a correspondence between Stalin and Churchill at the time of the Ardennes offensive. The entire story has been summarized by an Englishman, a former Labor Member of Parliament and one of the leading lawyers in England today, the Honorable D. N. Pritt, K. C.

Writes Pritt:

". . . it is useful to remind oneself now and then of what the Soviet Union did in the war. I will allow myself one short incident, not so well-known as some.

"Towards the end of December, 1944, when most people confidently believed that no major offensive from the German side was any longer possible, the Nazis launched a formidable one in the Ardennes, broke through the front, and placed many of the American and British troops in Belgium in a difficult and even dangerous situation. Their ambition was to reach Antwerp; for a time it looked as if they would achieve it; and if they had done this they would have prolonged the war considerably and greatly increased the losses and hardship of the American and British armies and people.

"In this somewhat anxious position, Mr. Winston Churchill, who bears his share of the responsibility for having kept the Soviet peoples waiting—with incredible sacrifices—almost three years for the Second Front, turned naturally and properly to Stalin for help. On January 6, 1945, he sent a message to Stalin, which I may quote:

" 'The battle in the West is very heavy and, at any time, large

17 Welles, **Where Are We Heading,** p. 105
18 Stimson, **On Active Service,** p. 527

176

decisions may be called for from the Supreme Command. You know yourself from your own experience how very anxious the position is when a very broad front has to be defended after temporary loss of the initiative. It is General Eisenhower's great desire and need to know in outline what you plan to do, as this obviously affects all his and our major decisions. I shall be grateful if you can tell me whether we can count on a major Russian offensive on the Vistula front, or elsewhere, during January, with any other points you may care to mention.'

"Stalin replied on the following day, January 7:

" 'I received your message of January 6, 1945, in the evening of January 7. . . .

" 'It is very important to make use of our superiority over the Germans in artillery and air force. For this we need clear weather for the air force and an absence of low mists which prevent the artillery from conducting aimed fire. We are preparing an offensive, but at present the weather does not favor our offensive. However, in view of the position of our Allies on the Western front, Headquarters of the Supreme Command has decided to complete the preparations at a forced pace and, disregarding the weather, to launch wide-scale offensive operations against the Germans all along the Central front not later than the second half of January. You need not doubt but that we shall do everything that can possibly be done to render help to the glorious troops of our Allies.'

"In his reply to this message Mr. Churchill wrote to Stalin on January 9:

" 'I am most grateful to you for your thrilling message. May all good fortune rest upon your noble venture.'

"It is worth while just following out the results of this appeal of Mr. Churchill, and of the Soviet response to it, at this time when Mr. Churchill and others are feeding a campaign of hysterical abuse against the Soviet Union.

"The offensive against the Germans on the Soviet-Carpathian front, planned for January 20, was advanced to the 12th. On that day, a great offensive was launched by the Soviet forces on a wide front from the Baltic Sea to the Carpathians. One hundred and fifty Soviet divisions, supported by a large quantity of artillery and aircraft, broke through the German front and threw the German troops back many miles. Five or six days later, German troops on the Western front, among them the 5th and 6th Panzer Armies, had to be withdrawn from the front and transferred to the East to meet the attacking Soviet troops. The German offensive in the West was thus frustrated.

"On January 17, Mr. Churchill wrote to Stalin:

" 'On behalf of His Majesty's Government and from the bottom of my heart, I offer you our thanks and congratulations on the immense assault you have launched upon the Eastern Front.'

"The general public could not, of course, be told at the time of the arrangements that were being made for this Soviet offensive—that would have assisted the Nazis—but the results were communicated in a Soviet Order of the Day in February, 1945, in which, after an account of the great success of the Red Army offensive just mentioned, it was announced:

" 'The first consequence of the successes of our winter offensive was that they thwarted the Germans' winter offensive in the West, which aimed at the seizure of Belgium and Alsace, and enabled the armies of our Allies in their turn to launch an offensive against the Germans and thus link their offensive operations in the West with the offensive operations of the Red Army in the East.' " 19

It is worth emphasizing that only **three days** after Stalin's answer, and **five days** after Churchill's request, the Soviet Union launched a formidable offensive along a three thousand mile front. Military men know what a great achievement this was and at what cost. Furthermore this Soviet contribution was made without pressure for the Nazis couldn't possibly have won the war at that stage even if they had reached Antwerp. Hitler could not have inflicted a decisive defeat to the coalition, but he could have given the Allies in the West a severe set-back.

If the Soviet Union had not been straightforward to the utmost degree, it could have taken things easy, it could have let the Allies receive a serious setback and then marched forward to take all the glory and all the credit for itself. In view of Churchill's treacherous and double-dealing role on the Second Front, Soviet leaders had many grounds for dragging their feet. But they didn't. They fought honestly, loyally and beyond narrow nationalistic selfishness. No wonder Stimson wrote that they were "magnificent allies."

Furthermore, it should be noted that the Soviet Union never made propaganda hay out of this episode. The public in England and America were not informed by their governments and the Soviet Union said nothing. The Soviet Union

19 D. N. Pritt, The State Dept. and the Cold War, New York, 1948, pp. 24-26

spoke up only after the State Department pulled one of the most shameless propaganda stunts of the postwar period as part of the Cold War. The State Department published captured German documents on the Soviet Union in such a manner as to give a distorted and false picture of Soviet-German relations. It was only then that the Soviet Union published the Churchill-Stalin correspondence.

The Ardennes Offensive is only the clearest case of Soviet military cooperation. Eisenhower himself has testified, that when it became necessary, after January 1945, "he was kept fully informed at all times of the essentials of the Red Army's plans, particularly the timing of their offensives, their objectives, and the direction of their main efforts." [20]

General Deane himself, despite his animosity, admits that he received considerable cooperation from the Soviets. He summarizes his first year in Moscow by saying that:

". . . we had been continuously engaged in some co-operative venture, large or small, that required Russian good will for its successful accomplishment. First there had been our shuttle-bombing bases in the Ukraine, then the establishment of teletype communications, then the exchange of weather information, then the co-ordination of operations against Germany, and finally the hope of setting up an air force close to Japan in the Maritime Provinces." [21]

Outside of purely military cooperation, the Soviet Union took many steps to indicate her desire to have friendly relations with her allies.

The Soviet Union always informed the U. S. promptly of the Japanese peace feelers, and permitted the escape of U. S. airmen from Siberia when there was great danger that the Japanese might use this as an excuse to invade Siberia and force the USSR to fight on two fronts. At the Moscow conference during the war the Soviet Union agreed to the establishment of a post-war world organization in response to the

20 Deane, The Strange Alliance, p. 160
21 Ibid., p. 262

great importance attached to this by Roosevelt and Hull.

In December 1943, Roosevelt, Churchill and Stalin held a highly successful conference at Teheran, Iran. Stimson at a press conference at the time said that:

". . . the presence of Premier Stalin and of his companion at the conference, Marshal Voroshilov, has contributed mightily to the success of the conference. Marshal Stalin's power of lucid analysis and the fairness of his attitude contributed strongly to the solution of several long-standing problems." [22]

The Teheran Conference was primarily concerned with military affairs but it also dealt with some of the problems of the peace. Said the Joint Declaration:

". . . The common understanding which we have here reached guarantees that victory will be ours.

"And as to the peace, we are sure that our concord will make it an enduring peace. We recognize fully the supreme responsibility resting upon us and all the United Nations to make a peace that will command good will from the overwhelming masses of the peoples of the world and banish the scourge and terror of war for many generations.

"With our diplomatic advisers we have surveyed the problems of the future. . . .

"We came here with hope and determination. We leave here friends in fact, in spirit, and in purpose."

Signed at Teheran, Dec. 1, 1943, Roosevelt, Stalin, Churchill.

The unity apparent at Teheran was consolidated at the Yalta Conference which opened on Sunday, February 4, 1945. Yalta was the climax of Roosevelt's policy. At Yalta there was a firm agreement for a United Nations Organization including the time and place for the setting up of the UN. There was agreement on a wide range of problems and workable compromises on the question of Polish frontiers, Polish government, German reparations, liberated areas. There was a firm pledge by the Soviet government to enter the war against Japan three months after VE day, May 6, 1945, a pledge fulfilled to the letter when the Soviet Army marched

22 Stimson, On Active Service, p. 440

against Japan on August 6, 1945.

It was at this conference that Stalin sounded a prophetic warning:

"It is not so difficult to keep unity in time of war since there is a joint aim to defeat the common enemy which is clear to everyone. The difficult task will come after the war when diverse interests tend to divide the Allies. It is our duty to see that our relations in peacetime are as strong as they have been in war." 23 ·

The Yalta Conference met with an enthusiastic response from the people of America. Senator Barkley, Majority Leader, cabled to President Roosevelt:

"Accept my sincere felicitations upon the historic Joint Statement [of the Conference] released today. I had it read to the Senate immediately upon release and it made a profound impression. Senator White, Minority Leader, joined me in the expressions of commendation and satisfaction on the floor of the Senate. I regard it as one of the most important steps ever taken to promote peace and happiness in the world." 24

Harry Hopkins who was at the Conference told Sherwood:

"The Russians had proved that they could be reasonable and far-seeing and there wasn't any doubt in the minds of the President or any of us that we could live with them and get along with them peacefully for as far in the future as any of us could imagine." 25

Hopkins, as we shall see, never changed his mind.

Soviet friendliness continued unabated after the death of President Roosevelt, and gave many proofs of it. A particularly impressive demonstration is reported by General Deane. On August 13, 1945, Eisenhower arrived in Moscow for a victory celebration and parade, and was "recognized and wildly cheered by the Russian people who were lined up to participate in the parade." Stalin invited Deane, Harriman and Eisenhower to join him on the reviewing stand atop Lenin's tomb. Deane states:

"We were the first foreigners who had ever been invited to witness

23 Byrnes, Speaking Frankly, p. 44
24 Sherwood, Roosevelt and Hopkins, p. 870
25 Sherwood, Roosevelt and Hopkins, p. 870

a Soviet ceremony from atop Lenin's Tomb, and I was fully conscious of the honor even though I had attained it by sliding in on Eisenhower's coatails."

Afterward, they witnessed a soccer game.

"When the game ended and Eisenhower and [Soviet General] Zhukov rose to leave, the crowd gave them an ovation that grew larger and larger in volume. Finally Eisenhower, in a gesture of friendliness, threw his arm over Zhukov's shoulder, and Zhukov responded by embracing Eisenhower. With that, pandemonium broke loose. . . . There was nothing rehearsed about this and it had nothing to do with ideologies or political aspirations. It was a sincere demonstration by a representative cross-section of the Russian people of their affection for the American people as embodied in Eisenhower. It was heartwarming and reassuring to us Americans who were there." [26]

Soviet friendship was obvious to the most hardened reactionary. It was the fruit of FDR's foreign policy, a policy which aimed at a peaceful world, a policy welcomed by Soviet leaders and by the peoples of the world.

For the American people, a friendly post-war world would have meant the full use of our technical know-how in repairing the desolation and devastation in war torn areas, making the United States the welcome friend of French and Italians, Greeks and Ukrainians, Hindus and Chinese. There would have been no signs in other countries, as there are today, saying, AMERICANS, GO HOME!

Wealth would have been the perspective of every country, wealth not only in economic terms but the riches of political and cultural developments. The working together of such diverse systems and cultures as the English, the Chinese, the Soviet, the Hindu, the American and so on would have meant a cross-fertilization of ideas and institutions to everyone's benefit. There would have been, and there still can be, a great diversity of "mixed" economic systems between the two extremes of Soviet Communism and American Capitalism. It would have meant the development of new organiza-

26 Deane, **The Strange Alliance**, pp. 215, 217

Polish Issue Still Unsolved; Truman, Molotoff Confer

Russian, Eden and Stettinius Hold Repeated Meetings and Secretary Reports Often to White House— Soong at Night Session

By LANSING WARREN

The situation was complicated during the day by a memorandum presented by the Polish exiled government in London to the British and United States Governments ex-pressing regret at not being in-cluded to the United Nations con-...

Apr. 24, 1945
N.Y. Times

Hull's Policy On Argentina Seen Scrapped

U.S. Position at Parley Now Is for Hemispheric Unity, as Advocated by Welles

By John C. Metcalfe

SAN FRANCISCO, May 1.—The hard-hitting anti-Fascist policy of Cordell Hull, former Secretary of State, against the government of Argentina lay abandoned on the American diplomatic road tonight as the United Nations Conference on International Organization awaited arrival of the Buenos Aires delegation. In it the United States dele... Francisco h-... sphere...

May 2, 1945
N.Y. Times

tional forms, new political solutions. It would have entailed a frontal attack on racism whether Nazi or Japanese, the undermining of Fascist regimes such as those of Franco, Peron and Chiang-Kai-Shek. It would have meant widespread travel, mingling of people, learning of each others customs, history, attitudes—slowly but surely building to a complete world understanding.

The possibilities stagger the imagination—they are beyond our powers to predict. A billion Asians moving into the stage of world history, not through the bitter destructive fighting of the Chinese Revolution and the Korean upheaval but through the constructive channels of modern agricultural techniques, literacy spread through the mass medium of films and pictures, health on the basis of penicillin and water systems.

In such a world, plenty, not scarcity, would be the goal; co-operatives not cartels the rule; friendship not hostility, the norm. A world beautiful to behold—warm to inhabit. A world secure in a peace more stirring and glorious than any war could ever be.

It was a world within our reach as the result of FDR's foreign policy. It is a world we can still achieve—mankind free-wheeling in a world unafraid.

TRUMAN TALKS TOUGH

CHAPTER 8

"... *if the Russians did not wish to join us (at San Francisco) they could go to hell...* "

President Harry S. Truman,
April 23, 1945

"*FDR's appeasement of Russia is over....*"
Senator Arthur H. Vandenberg,
April 24, 1945

"*Our Russian policy must not be dictated by people who have already made up their minds that there is no possibility of working with Russia ... this is an untenable position and can but lead to disaster.*"
Harry Hopkins, August 1, 1945

THE YALTA CONFERENCE TOOK place in February, 1945. Two months later Roosevelt died and Truman became President. Within a week of Roosevelt's funeral, Truman had begun to reverse Roosevelt's foreign policy. Instead of American-Soviet co-operation, Truman established a "get tough" policy with Russia. Truman's flip-flop became apparent during a visit of Foreign Minister Molotov to the U. S. to attend the United Nations San Francisco Conference. The clear cut nature of Truman's reversal of FDR's policy is shown, as if in a mirror, by the reaction of Roosevelt's political enemies. Senator Arthur Vandenberg,

185

Republican leader, shifted from unhappiness at FDR's policy to joy at Truman's policy.

VANDENBERG'S SATISFACTION

Before Roosevelt died, Vandenberg had been totally against Yalta. He wrote privately immediately after Yalta:

". . . I want frankly to state my deep disappointment in respect to the Polish settlement. . . . I . . . **believe the 'Curzon Line'** [the Soviet-Polish frontier] **is indefensible.** . . . I feel that **the recognition of the Lublin government** in net effect **is unjustified.** . . ." [1] (emphasis added)

When Roosevelt died, Vandenberg could not conceal his political satisfaction. **On the next day,** he wrote in his diary about FDR's death:

"One thing it does is to wash the slate clean of whatever undisclosed commitments FDR has made to Stalin or Churchill. **This is all to the good.** The 'Big 3' no longer exists as a monopoly in respect to world destiny." [2] (emphasis added)

Big Three unity, the foundation stone of Roosevelt's policy had always been opposed by Vandenberg. He now saw his chance to smash it. Along with others, he went to work to undermine the wartime unity and succeeded thanks to Truman's help.

Truman reversed FDR's policy by adopting in its entirety Vandenberg's position. At the Truman-Molotov meeting the President's attitude was identical with Vandenberg, as revealed by the then Secretary of State Stettinius, who had been at the meeting. Reported Stettinius to Vandenberg:

"**If you** had been talking about Poland to Molotov, not even **you** could have made a stronger statement than Truman did." [3] (emphasis original)

And, Vandenberg added happily:
"FDR's appeasement of Russia is over. . . ."
What Vandenberg called "appeasement" was the policy

1 The Private Papers of Senator Vandenberg, Boston, 1952, pp. 148-150
2 Vandenberg, Private Papers, p. 167
3 Ibid., p. 176

of co-operation which had brought victory in a terrible war and held promise of a peaceful future. Roosevelt had died on April 12; Vandenberg wrote the above words on April 24, referring to Truman's meeting with Molotov on April 23. In eleven days Truman had begun to wreck FDR's foreign policy.

THE TRUMAN-MOLOTOV MEETING

President Truman's first meeting with Soviet Foreign Minister Molotov boded ill for future Soviet--American relations. Truman seems to have been in an aggressive mood. He had told Cabinet members, just before the meeting, that the Russians "could go to hell.' It is known that he charged Molotov with breaking the Yalta agreements and used very blunt language. Byrnes says that "it was not a very harmonious meeting and ended rather abruptly."

Washington gossip had it that Molotov had walked out on Truman. According to foreign correspondent Edgar A. Mowrer, Molotov had said, "No one has ever talked to me like this before."

What made Truman's attitude particularly boorish was that Molotov had been sent to America as a Soviet gesture of friendship to the United States on the occasion of Roosevelt's death. Harry Hopkins gives the following details:

"Stalin sent for Ambassador Harriman soon after he learned of President Roosevelt's death and told Harriman that he wanted to give some immediate assurance to the American people to indicate his, Stalin's, desire to continue on a co-operative basis with this country. Harriman promptly told him that the thing the American people would appreciate most would be to send Molotov to the San Francisco Conference." [4] (emphasis added))

Molotov was sent to San Francisco by the USSR: on the way to the conference he stopped in Washington to meet with the President. Truman knew that this visit was a good-will gesture, therefore his attack on the Soviet Union could

[4] Sherwood, Roosevelt and Hopkins, p. 883

only be interpreted by Molotov as a deliberate offense particularly because Truman's attack was without foundation in fact. Truman charged the Soviet Union with breaking the Yalta agreement on Poland. This was not·true, and Truman had been told so·by Admiral Leahy, who had been at Yalta. No wonder Molotov was indignant.

That Truman's action was deliberate is proven by the fact that he attacked Molotov against the advice of Stimson, Admiral Leahy and General Marshall. As in the case of atomic energy, where Truman chose the tough policy against the warning embodied in Stimson's memorandum, so on Poland, Leahy's testimony shows that Truman deliberately chose an anti-Soviet policy.

The inside story of Truman's reversal of FDR's policy is given by Admiral Leahy and by Senator Vandenberg whose private diaries have recently been published. It is a shameful story of surrender to the reactionary forces in America.

Vandenberg was jubilant when Stettinius told him the details of the Truman-Molotov interview. In his diary he gushes like an adolescent when he tells how Stettinius:

". . . immediately met our delegation and gave us a **thrilling** message. The new President [Truman] . . . has just sent a blunt message to Stalin including a general demand for Frisco cooperation. Stettinius said that Eden could scarcely believe his eyes when he saw a copy—and cheered loudly.
". . . This is the best news in months. F.D.R.'s appeasement of Russia is over. . . . Russia may withdraw. If it does, the conference **will proceed without Russia.** Now we are getting somewhere!"[5] (emphasis in the diary)

Vandenberg was certainly getting somewhere. No wonder he was "thrilled." And no wonder British Foreign Minister Eden cheered loudly. Vandenberg and others like him, through Truman, were agreeing with Churchill's ideas and reversing FDR's foreign policy. From this reversal to the armaments race and to Korea is a direct open road, a road

5 Vandenberg, Private Papers, pp. 175-176

which has meant death to hundreds of thousands of human beings and profits in scores of billions to American corporations. "Thrilling" is no word for it.

What was the agreement on Poland over which Truman attacked Molotov?

THE POLISH QUESTION

The Polish question is a classic example of something which seems very remote to the average American, yet at the same time is crucial not only in international affairs but also domestic politics. There is a large population of Polish descent in the United States, particularly in Michigan, which was Senator Vandenberg's state. This national group is organized in several associations and supports Polish language newspapers. Most of these associations and newspapers are controlled by extremely reactionary elements under the influence both of the Vatican and of the old Polish government. From the viewpoint of U. S. politics, the Polish question was made to order for Vandenberg to use against Roosevelt. The reactionary Poles' hatred of the Yalta decision could be used to attack the whole policy of U. S.-USSR friendship.

Before World War I, Poland was partitioned among Germany, Austria-Hungary and Tsarist Russia. As a result of the Russian Revolution, Poland, like Finland, received her freedom and independence. Under Article 87 of the Treaty of Versailles, the Allied Supreme Council drew a frontier between Russia and Poland based on existing populations. On one side the Poles were in the majority, on the other side they were in the minority. This frontier came to be known as the "Curzon line" after the British Foreign Secretary, Lord Curzon. In view of what happened in 1945 it must be strongly emphasized that the "Curzon Line" was drawn up by friends of the old Poland, particularly England and France, with American approval. The newly born Soviet Union had no say in the matter.

The reactionary Polish Government of Dictator Pilsudski refused to recognize this frontier. It launched an unprovoked war against the weak Soviet Union, which Poland almost lost. Promptly England and France came to her help and finally in 1921 the war was settled on a line well to the east of the Curzon Line. The Polish Government had taken by force large sections of Russian territory. So barefaced was this conquest that the United States refused at first to recognize the new boundary.

From 1921 until 1939 the Polish Government was one of the most reactionary governments in Europe, run by a clique of Colonels which brought Poland to ruin. Foreign Minister Josef Beck wrote the epitaph to his own policy and government: "We should have followed a policy of friendship with Soviet Russia and not one of support to Hitler."

Hitler double-crossed Poland and in two weeks Warsaw was surrounded, and all the Western provinces lost. To prevent Hitler's Army from reaching the Soviet borders, the Red Army marched. The final boundary between the Soviet Union and Nazi Germany was roughly the Curzon Line of 1919.

Reactionaries have since talked about Russia's "stab in the back," arguing that if the Soviet Union hadn't marched, Poland could have fought on. This is complete nonsense. Professor Schuman writes that by September 15, 1939, "the Polish Army and State had ceased to exist." This is the bare truth. **On the morning of September 17, the Polish Government had fled across the border to Rumania,** hours before the Red Army marched. As for the Polish Army, the correspondent of the **London Times** (a most conservative newspaper) telegraphed on that very day (September 17) that "The Polish front has collapsed completely. . . ." [6]

Churchill, who has since slandered the Soviet Army on this very issue, broadcast on October 1:

6 Quoted in Pritt, The State Department and the Cold War, p. 75

"... that the Russian armies should stand on this line [the Curzon Line] was clearly necessary for the safety of Russia against the Nazi menace." [7]

Again, it must be emphasized that the Soviet Union stood **on the Curzon Line, a frontier drawn up by England and France, Poland's friends,** as a fair and equitable border line. The Soviet Union made it unalterably clear from the beginning of their British alliance in 1941 that she would not again withdraw from the Curzon Line.

So clearly fair was the Soviet position, that it was Churchill himself who, at Teheran, suggested as Polish borders the Curzon Line on the East and the Oder Line on the West. It was Churchill too who first brought up the idea of giving to Poland territory then a part of Germany. In view of all the later slanders this point must be emphasized. Writes Churchill in his History:

"Personally I thought Poland might move westward. . . . Eden said that what Poland lost in the East she might gain in the West. Stalin replied that possibly she might, but he did not know. I then demonstrated with the help of three matches my idea of Poland moving westward." [8]

After further meetings and **a joint examination of maps** in regard to both the Curzon and the Oder Lines, Churchill goes on:

"I said I liked the picture, and that I would say to the Poles that if they did not accept it they would be foolish, and I would remind them that but for the Red Army they would have been utterly destroyed." [8a]

Such is the background at the time of Yalta.

THE YALTA AGREEMENT ON POLAND

The Polish frontiers agreed upon at Yalta in February, 1945, were substantially those agreed upon two years before at Teheran, December, 1943. This should dispose once and

7 Ibid., p. 79
8 Churchill, Closing the Ring, p. 362
8a Churchill, Closing the Ring, p. 396

for all of the myth that Roosevelt was "tired" and "ill" and "sold out Poland to the Russians" at Yalta. As a matter of fact at Yalta Roosevelt tried to modify the Curzon Line, so the Poles would get certain oil fields around the city of Lwow. Byrnes, who was present, records what happened:

"Marshall Stalin replied with an impassioned statement.
"'The Curzon Line is the line of Curzon and Clemenceau and of those Americans who took part in 1918 and 1919 in the conference which then took place,' Stalin declared. 'The Russians were not invited and did not take part. . . . Lenin was not in agreement with the Curzon Line. . . . Now some people want that we should be less Russian than Curzon was and Clemenceau was. You would drive us into shame. What will be said by the White Russians and the Ukrainians? They will say that Stalin and Molotov are far less reliable defenders of Russia than are Curzon and Clemenceau. I could not take such a position and return to Moscow with an open face.'
"At this point, Stalin stood at the conference table as he spoke. It was the only time during the entire conference that he exhibited his strong feelings in such a manner." [9]

The Curzon Line was adopted. Russia received her own territory back. Yet this is the Curzon Line which Senator Vandenberg found morally "indefensible."

On the Polish government a compromise was reached. There were at the time two Polish governments. One, in London, was the remnants of the pre-war reactionary government which had fled within three weeks of the Nazi invasion. It was a bitterly anti-Soviet government, utterly blind to the realities of the situation. Even Churchill despised them —they were so hopelessly incompetent. [10]

Even after it was clear that the Soviet Union was winning and that a Polish government could not be blindly anti-Soviet, the London group went on making incredible errors. As their bankrupt policy worsened their position, they blamed the Soviet Union for it. Perhaps the worst example of their reckless dealing with the lives of people is the story of the

9 Byrnes, Speaking Frankly, p. 30
10 Stanislaw Mikolajczyk, The Rape of Poland, N. Y. & Toronto, 1948, p. 98

Warsaw uprising.

At the end of July 1944, the Soviet Army under the Polish-born Marshal Rokossovsky was within twenty miles of Warsaw, on the opposite side of the Vistula River which skirts the city. On August 1st, the underground Polish fighters rose in arms against the Germans, expecting to win the city. Instead the Germans annihilated them in one of the worst butcheries of the war.

The London Polish Government immediately accused the Soviet Union of deliberately asking for the uprising with a promise of help, and then sitting back while the Germans wiped out the Polish underground.

The Polish underground itself has never supplied any proof that the Soviets asked for the insurrection. The leader of the underground, General Bor, who managed to come out alive and has since lectured in the U. S. has never produced any proof of the charge.

Premier Mikolajczyk, last head of the reactionary London Polish Government, with all the documents and facts at his disposal relies for proof only on a Soviet broadcast of July 29, 1944. This broadcast he publishes in full and demolishes his own argument. For the broadcast is not a signal for a general revolt but merely a call to sabotage the Nazis and defend Polish property against the retreating Germans. [11] It was a broadcast comparable to the allied broadcasts to French partisans during the invasion of France.

The writer of this book was in London at the time, and in all allied intelligence agencies it was taken for granted that the uprising had been ordered by the Polish General Bor as a result of a definite miscalculation of German military strength and will to hold on.

From a military standpoint the Soviet armies were greatly over-extended. The Germans brought up several armored divisions and sharply forced the Soviets back at several

11 Ibid. p. 69

points through sharp counter-attacks—this at a time when the Russians were supposed to be sitting idly while the uprising was suppressed. As a matter of military history, it took the Soviet Army **three months** to bring up supplies, cross the river and encircle the city. Warsaw did not fall until January 17, 1945—over three months after the end of the uprising.

Bor was a professional soldier and the vicious miscalulation was his responsibility. The decision he made was a political, not a military decision. Incidentally, Mikolajczyk says he didn't even know the insurrection had started; he was, on August 1st, on the way to North Africa in transit to Moscow for negotiations.

Stalin later told Hull that the insurrection was an "insane adventure." The London Polish Government gambled and lost the lives of thousands of people, demonstrating once and for all that it was callous and incompetent.

In striking contrast was the other Polish government, which had first been formed in the town of Lublin, Poland, and was therefore known as the Lublin Government. It had an army, a Polish Army Corps under the Polish General Berling, which had been formed on Soviet soil and had fought alongside with the Soviet Armies for thousands of miles. The leaders of the Lublin government were workers, farmers and professionals, the exact opposite of the London government. Some of these leaders were Communists, some Catholics, all were friendly to Russia.

The London Government was not recognized by the Soviet Union; the Lublin Government was not recognized by England and America. The question to be decided at Yalta was how to bring the two governments together into one which would be acceptable to everyone.

Byrnes says that this issue:

". . . . was one of the most serious issues of the entire conference. More time was spent on this subject than on any other. Because of the intensity of the argument, Mr. Roosevelt would assume a role more of an arbiter than of advocate although he, as well as Prime Minister Churchill, urged the establishment of a new Polish Government in Warsaw.

"The Soviet Union, on the other hand, wanted to continue the Lublin government. . . .

"Mr. Churchill eloquently painted the danger which arose from the continuing existence of two Polish governments. . . .

"Stalin displayed great earnestness in replying.

" 'For the Russian people, the question of Poland is . . . a question of security.'

"In every subsequent discussion the Soviet Government has used this argument to justify what it has done in Poland. . . ."[12]

Byrnes here implies that the Soviet argument is specious, but two years before he had himself agreed that the argument was valid, saying that he "was fully aware of (Soviet) special security interests" in Poland and Balkan countries.[13]

The Soviet Union was understandably distrustful of the London Poles. They were strongly anti-Soviet and had supported Hitler's foreign policy in the pre-war period, co-operating with Hitler in the dismemberment of Czecho-slovakia. Their policy had wrecked Poland. Once back in Poland these men would be sure to manoeuver in co-operation with England, if England chose to follow an anti-Soviet policy. This is not guesswork: Churchill specifically promised to support one of the London Poles, Mikolajczyk, in a phrase full of innuendoes. Urging the Pole to enter the new compromise government, Churchill said:

"I think," said Churchill, "you should use this last opportunity to get not only your foot but your leg in the door. . . . Above all you must go. You can count now on the support and influence of both the British and the Americans."[14] (emphasis added)

12 Byrnes, **Speaking Frankly**, pp. 31-32
13 Speech of October 31, 1945. Quoted by Corliss Lamont, **Monthly Review**, March, 1952
14 Mikolajczyk, The Rape of Poland, p. 118. The word "now" is of extraordinary significance. Churchill is speaking in June, 1945, that is after the death of Roosevelt. He could therefore promise the support of "both the British and the Americans." Had Roosevelt lived, Churchill could not have made this promise because FDR strongly disagreed with the Prime Minister on the issue of Poland. The Roosevelt-Churchill disagreement

Stalin was well aware of Churchill's enmity. Nevertheless at Yalta, after several days' discussion, Stalin agreed in the interests of unity that a few Polish representatives from London should be included in the new government. A joint declaration on Poland provided that:

"The Provisional government which is now functioning in Poland [the Lublin government] should therefore be reorganized on a broader democratic basis with the inclusion of democratic leaders from Poland itself and from Poles abroad [the London government]." [15]

This was a great concession by the Soviet Union. It must be remembered that **they didn't have to agree.** The Red Army was in occupation and no one was in a position to challenge them. As the then Secretary of State Stettinius has written:

"... As a result of the military situation, it was not a question of what Great Briain and the U. S. would permit Russia to do in Poland, but what the two countries could persuade the Soviet Union to accept. . . ." [16] (emphasis in original)

The agreement to take in reactionary London Poles who would inevitably run their political campaigns on an anti-Soviet basis is only one more evidence of the Soviet Union's genuine desire to co-operate.

The wording of the Yalta agreement meant beyond question a pro-Soviet government. This was recognized by all present. Writes Admiral Leahy:

"Personally, I did not believe that the dominating Soviet influence could be excluded from Poland, but I did think it was possible to give to the reorganized Polish Government an **external appearance of independence.**" [17] (emphasis added)

These four words are very important. First as to the word "independence." In the vocabulary of Leahy, Churchill and the rest, a nation is independent when it follows their

is set down in correspondence still marked secret, but its existence was revealed by Bert Andrews in the N. Y. Herald Tribune, May 17, 1945
15 Yalta Communique, February 11, 1945
16 Stettinius, Roosevelt and the Russians, p. 301
17 Leahy, I Was There, p. 352

policies, a "satellite" when it has pro-Soviet policies. If the British Army had entered Warsaw and the reactionary London government-in-exile had been brought back, then Poland would be "independent," just as Greece is "independent" with a Greek King put into power with British bayonets, or Transjordan is "independent" although British money pays its army and a British General is the Commander. In the same way Chiang Kai-shek's China was "independent" although for decades her cities and her rivers had been under the control of England, France and America. In the same way, Japan today is "independent" though an American Army is there by "treaty" empowered to intervene in domestic disputes.

All this is independence. But let China become Communist and she is no longer independent, but a satellite. Let Rumania throw out Standard Oil and she is no longer independent. Let Tunisia, or Egypt, or Indo-China seek to end imperialist influence and they are accused of playing Russia's game.

So much for the word, independence. Now for "external appearance." What Leahy meant by this was that although the new government would be pro-Soviet, a few London Poles (known to be anti-Soviet) were to obscure this basic fact. In this Leahy was reflecting Roosevelt's concern with domestic American politics.

President Roosevelt had a real problem in dealing domestically with the Catholic Church and its influence on various national groups in this country.

The concession of the Soviet Union enabled Roosevelt to meet the attacks of the Church, the reactionary Polish organizations, and such men as Senator Vandenberg.

For England too, the concession was important. The British had a legal dilemma of their own making. On one hand the British had guaranteed Polish territory as of 1939, which included Ukrainian land east of the Curzon Line. On the other hand Britain had allied herself with the USSR as of June, 1941, when Soviet territory included the same Ukrainian land east of the Curzon Line. In other words England had agreed with each of its allies that they had a right to that territory. It was a legal contradiction. Since it was difficult to challenge the Soviet claim on the basis of ethics, and impossible to do so on the basis of power, England would have to renege on her Polish guarantee. This would besmirch her "honor" as Churchill might put it. The inclusion of the London Poles, accepting the new frontiers, solved this problem for England.

But there was no question in anyone's mind that the Lublin government would be the core of the new government and that it would be pro-Soviet. Later, when Soviet policies in Poland began to be attacked, the Soviet Union felt quite properly that England and the U. S. were going back on their agreement. Harriman conceded this, when he cabled Roosevelt on April 6, 1945, that:

"It may be difficult for us to believe, but it still may be true that Stalin and Molotov considered at Yalta that by our willingness to accept a general wording of the declaration on Poland and liberated Europe, by our recognition of the need of the Red Army for security behind its lines, and of the predominant interest of Russia in Poland as a friendly neighbor and as a corridor to Germany, we understood and were ready to accept Soviet policies already known to us." [18]

It shouldn't have been at all "difficult for us to believe" that the Soviets felt that way. **Roosevelt knew, at Yalta, that this was the Soviet interpretation of the Polish agreement.** If this can be proved, then the Soviets did **not** violate the Yalta agreement, because both we and they knew that Yalta meant that a pro-Soviet government was to be permitted to arise in Poland.

As we have seen, the Yalta declaration provided that the Lublin government would be "reorganized." The Soviets in-

18 Forrestal Diaries, p. 40

sisted that "reorganized" meant additions to the existing Lublin government of some London leaders. The U. S. said it meant a new government. But at Yalta, when the communique was being written, Leahy said after reading it (according to his own account):

" 'Mr. President, this is so elastic that the Russians can stretch it all the way from Yalta to Washington without ever technically breaking it.'
"The President replied, 'I know Bill—I know it."
Added Leahy, "This 'settlement' of the entire Polish Government question appeared to me to be so loose that it could be interpreted in almost any way that pleased the Russians." [19] (emphasis added)

In the face of this evidence, no one can deny that the Soviet interpretation was known beforehand, and the communique written to fit it. To talk of Soviet betrayal of Yalta Truman saw Molotov. Just before he saw Molotov, Truman was not ignorant of the facts. Leahy himself told Truman that what had taken place in Poland was what he had expected at Yalta.

Leahy spoke to President Truman on the same day that Truman saw Molotov. Just before he saw Molotov, Truman had called a meeting at the White House. This was a fateful meeting, for at this meeting the "'get tough with Russia" policy showed that it had the upper hand within the American government. Some details of the meeting, given by Forrestal in guarded language, show that Stimson, Leahy and Marshall protested strongly against the new policy. Bohlen, a State Department official who was present, took notes which give sharper details. Both versions are given in the Forrestal Diaries, together with the comments of Walter Millis, the Editor:

"The Secretary of State," wrote Forrestal, "said that the Russians had receded from their agreement at Yalta with President Roosevelt on the Polish question." [20]

19 Leahy, I Was There, pp. 315-316
20 Forrestal Diaries, p. 49

199

Admiral Leahy disagreed. According to Bohlen:

"He [Leahy] thought the agreements were susceptible to 'two interpretations.' . . .21

Walter Millis, who as Editor of the Forretal Diaries read all the notes, including those that weren't printed, lets the cat out of the bag very neatly when he says:

"The comment of Admiral Leahy who had taken part in the Crimean [Yalta] Conference, comes a little unexpectedly. . . ."22

Indeed it does, for Leahy, conservative and anti-Communist though he was, told the truth at the meeting. According to Bohlen:

"Admiral Leahy said that he had left Yalta with the impression that the Soviet government had no intention of permitting a free government to operate in Poland, and that he would have been surprised had the Soviet government behaved any differently than it had."23

Of course, Leahy's idea of a "free government" is the Polish London government, such an unsavory bunch that Roosevelt had sent a message to Churchill warning him not to be "wedded to that group." 24

However, it is clear that as far as Leahy was concerned the Soviet interpretation was within the meaning of the Yalta agreement. There was no pledge broken by the Soviet Union, and the loose construction of the communique was deliberately written for the political convenience of Roosevelt to meet the attack of men such as Vandenberg.

At this fateful meeting, Leahy wasn't the only one to protest. According to Millis, "General Marshall was even more cautious" as he thought about the war in the Far East. But it was Stimson again, the conservative Republican, who argued for Roosevelt's policy. According to Bohlen's notes:

21 Ibid., p. 51
22 Ibid., p. 50
23 Ibid., p. 51
24 Hull, Memoirs, p. 1440

"He [Stimson] said he thought that the Russians perhaps were being more realistic than we were in regard to their own security." [25] (emphasis added)

And Forrestal hints at the fact that a new policy was being presented:

"The Secretary of War [Stimson] said that it was such a newly posed question so far as he was concerned that he hesitated . . . but . . . he hoped we would go slowly and avoid any open break. He said the Russians had carried out their military engagements quite faithfully and was sorry to see this one incident [the differing interpretations of Yalta over Poland] project a breach between the two countries." [26] (emphasis added)

Forrestal immediately jumped on this:

"I gave it as my view," wrote Forrestal in his diary, "that this was not an isolated incident but was one of a pattern of unilateral action on the part of Russia . . . and that I thought we might as well meet the issue now as later on."

"Ambassador Harriman expressed somewhat the same ideas. Admiral Leahy took the view, on the other hand, more or less the same as that of the Secretary of War. . . ." [27]

What is most interesting is that Leahy was on Truman's side about "getting tough" with Russia, but he disagreed on Poland as the issue because he knew the U. S. was wrong. Yet Leahy was very happy about the results. He writes:

"Truman's [strong] attitude in dealing with Molotov was more than pleasing to me. I believed it would have a beneficial effect on the Soviet outlook on the world." [28]

TRUMAN BACKS FORRESTAL

Truman's agreement with Harriman and Forrestal, who were the outstanding anti-Sovieteers in the government, shows clearly that he himself was deeply biased against Russia. Warned by General Marshall that it "would be a serious matter to risk a break," the President, according to Millis, "accepted the risk. . . . The strong view prevailed."

25 Forrestal Diaries, p. 50
26 Ibid., p. 49
27 Ibid., p. 49
28 Leahy, I Was There, p. 352

Warned that toughness on Poland might mean wrecking the UN Conference at San Francisco, Truman said, according to Bohlen:

"The President said . . . that he felt our agreements with the Soviet Union so far had been a one-way street and that he could not continue; it was now or never. He intended to go on with the plans for San Francisco and if the Russians did not wish to join us, they could go to hell. . . ."[29]

Truman's statement has all the seeds of the Cold War in it. It is worth examining.

To begin with, Yalta had not been a "one-way street." Stettinius, who as Secretary of State accompanied Roosevelt to Yalta, writes very sharply:

"The Yalta record . . . reveals that **the Soviet Union made more concessions to the United States and Great Britain than were made to the Soviet Union** by either the United States or Great Britain. On certain issues, of course, each of the three Great Powers modified its original position in order to reach agreement. Although it is sometimes alleged that there is something evil in compromise, actually, of course, compromise is necessary for progress as any sensible man knows. . . . We should not be led by our dislike and rightful rejection of appeasement in the Munich sense into an irrational and untenable refusal to compromise."[30] (emphasis added)

Harry Hopkins also specifically stated that the Soviet had made many concessions. During the Yalta discussion on German reparations he wrote and passed to Roosevelt a note saying:

"The Russians have given in so much at this conference that I don't think we should let them down. Let the British disagree if they want to. . . ."[31]

Roosevelt took the advice, indicating he agreed with Hopkins. As a matter of fact, President Roosevelt himself was very satisfied by Yalta. His physician, Admiral McIntire, reports that at the end of the conference he found

29 Forrestal Diaries, p. 50
30 Stettinius, Roosevelt and the Russians, p.6
31 Sherwood, Roosevelt and Hopkins, p. 861

Roosevelt in high spirits, and:

". . . it was with his old smile that he announced, 'I've got everything I came for, and not at too high a price.' "[32]

To talk of a "one-way street" is to talk the language of Harriman, Forrestal and Senator Vandenberg, the men who regarded Yalta as a calamity. Truman went along completely with their position. The diaries and private papers of Senator Vandenberg literally drool over the change of policy. His reaction to Roosevelt's death has already been quoted; his estimate of Truman made at the same time is also worth quoting:

"Can he [Truman] swing the job? Despite his limited capacities, I think he can."[33]

Truman certainly did, to Vandenberg's satisfaction. Behind Vandenberg was John Foster Dulles, one of the most sinister influences in American foreign affairs. Vandenberg says about Dulles:

"I think the most valuable man in our entire American setup has been John Foster Dulles. **Nominally just an 'advisor,' he has been at the core of every crisis.** . . . I do not know what we should have done without him. . . . He would make a very great Secretary of State."[34] (emphasis added)

Dulles, whose law firm represented the Nazi government, is shown here as the power behind the scenes of American foreign policy. Soon he was to be brought out into the open, particularly in framing the Japanese "peace" treaty. Such a man would never have been tolerated in a major policy making position by President Roosevelt.

That American foreign policy should suit Dulles is the clearest proof that our foreign policy was sharply reversed, literally within a couple of weeks of Roosevelt's death. Actually, so abrupt was this shift that one may wonder how it could have happened so quickly. After all, the death of one

32 McIntire, **White House Physician,** p. 221
33 Vandenberg, **Private Papers,** p. 165
34 Ibid., p. 215

man, however important, should not have such drastic effects on a nation's foreign policy. A foreign policy is shaped by more basic forces than the personality of any one individual. How could the shift have happened?

THE ENEMY WITHIN THE GATES

Roosevelt's policy of peace and co-operation could be reversed so abruptly because the anti-Sovieteers were in positions of power **within** the Administration. For the sake of unity. Roosevelt had given hostages to reaction. As he put it, "Dr. Win-The-War" had replaced "Dr. New-Deal."

Roosevelt's cabinet and war administration was composed of men of sharply different social views. On one side were people like Hull, Hopkins, Ickes, Morgenthau, Wallace and Perkins, and, on foreign affairs, Stimson and Marshall. On the other side were Harriman, Byrnes, Leahy, Forrestal and the powerful influence of the Vatican. The second group was never reconciled to peace with the Soviet Union. Their anti-Soviet position was well known and Roosevelt men were conscious of their influence. Says Carr, for example, referring to the summer of 1943:

". . . high officials in Washington and London did not conceal in private talks their expectation of trouble with Russia after the war. Roosevelt's insistence on 'unconditional surrender' by Germany was considered a mistake by this group. It was evident that they preferred not to destroy Germany's military power, since they expected that eventually it would again be directed eastward." [35]

Harry Hopkins, who had been Roosevelt's most trusted adviser, warned the nation just before he died:

"Our Russian policy must not be dictated by people who have already made up their minds there is no possibility of working with Russians and that our interests are bound to conflict and ultimately lead to war. From my point of view, this is an untenable position and can but lead to disaster." [36]

[35] Carr, Truman, Stalin and Peace, p. 14. During the war, Carr was a top-level adviser to Donald Nelson, chief of WPB
[36] Sherwood, Roosevelt and Hopkins, p. 923

Roosevelt was strong enough to control the opposition within his administration and to fight the opposition outside. Roosevelt's strength was directly due to the fact that he represented the aspirations of the American people. Furthermore, objective conditions in the first two years of the war forced the anti-Sovieteers to go along with FDR's policy. While it looked as if Germany would beat Russia, these people were willing to aid Russia.

The world-shaking Soviet victory at Stalingrad, when the encircled Nazi Army finally surrendered in January 1943, was not only the turning point of World War II, but also a turning point in the thinking of the anti-Soviet group. Deane makes no bones about it, spelling out the thinking of reactionaries in detail:

"With respect to Russian aid, however, I always felt that their mission (Hopkins and his men) was carried out with a zeal which approached fanaticism. Their enthusiasm became so ingrained that it could not be tempered when conditions indicated that a change in policy was desirable. In the early days of the program their attitude was not only understandable but essential. Russia had her back to the wall, and the news indicated that it was problematical if she could remain in the war. It is not necessary to go into the disastrous effect that Russian capitulation would have had on the Allied effort. And it was right tha we should give Russia every material and moral support of which were capable. However, when the tide finally turned at Stalingrad and a Russian offensive started which ended only at Berlin, a new situation was created." 37 (emphasis added)

Even after Stalingrad some anti-Sovieteers were still restrained by their belief that the USSR might ease up on its offensive and leave the Allies to face the German in the West. Secondly, Russia's help was needed against Japan.

After Yalta, however, both of these factors became less important. The Soviet Army was on its way to Berlin, the Japanese Empire was being strangled through bombings and naval power. The Joint Chiefs of Staff decided that Soviet

37 Deane, The Strange Alliance, p. 90

aid would not be essential. Again Deane obligingly spells out the details:

"I was elated by these decisions [of not needing Soviet help]. . . . The fear of a separate peace had long since been removed by Russian military successes, and now the fear of jeopardizing some co-operative venture with Russia was removed because there was no longer any in which we were interested." [38]

Significantly, Deane adds that therefore "our policy could be revised."

Roosevelt's death was an unexpected opportunity for the anti-Sovieteers. As Vandenberg said, "One thing it does is to wash the slate clean . . . this is all to the good." It enabled Dulles, Vandenberg and the rest to move in.

Vandenberg's private diaries and papers give a step by step account of how the shift was accomplished. After seven years it still makes dramatic reading. Before Roosevelt's death we find Vandenberg unhappy, uneasy, frustrated, looking for some way to undermine Yalta. He wrote in a letter, March 7, 1945:

"I could get no greater personal satisfaction out of anything more than from joining—aye, in leading—a public denunciation of Yalta. . . . But . . . I am forced from the circumstances to believe that **we cannot get results** by trying to totally combat decisions which are supported by our own American Administration and by the British Parliament. . . . **We must find some other way.** . . . I must primarily work . . . through the Frisco Conference and not in a public campaign of denunciation. . . ." [39] (emphasis added)

Five weeks later Roosevelt died. Within two weeks, Truman attacked Molotov, and Vandenberg wrote, "This is the best news in months." Within three months, Vandenberg could boast of complete victory. On July 27, 1945, he wrote in a letter:

"The price of this unity [Republican and Democratic unity] was a **complete reversal** of the Administration's appeasement and

38 Ibid., pp. 265-266
39 Vandenberg, Private Papers, pp. 155-156

surrender attitudes at Yalta. **Some day we shall overtake Yalta itself.** That is what the Republican contribution . . . has been." [40] (emphasis added)

Vandenberg and company played a shrewd game. But it would not have succeeded without Truman's whole-hearted co-operation. It was Truman who went against Stimson, Leahy and Marshall on the Molotov interview. It was Truman who backed Forrestal against Stimson in the question of atomic policy. It was Truman who turned the peace into a Cold War.

In 1941, when Hitler attacked Russia, the then Senator Truman said:

"If we see that Germany is winning we ought to help Russia and if Russia is winning we ought to help Germany and that way let them kill as many as possible although I don't want to see Hitler victorious under any circumstances." [41]

Four years later, the same Truman as President, said "the Russians could go to hell." His anti-Soviet bias has not changed. He had been and remained one of those men whom Hopkins had feared would lead to a world disaster.

40 Ibid., p. 314. Both letters were written to the same man, Frank Januszewski, owner of the **Polish Daily News,** in Detroit, a most reactionary paper which reflected both the Vatican and the London government-in-exile
41 N. Y. **Times,** June 24, 1941

A British paratrooper firing fr

Dec. 21, 1944
N.Y. Times

SCOBIE TO ATTACK ELAS TROOPS TODAY

Continued From Page 1

away from danger wherever it is indicated.

No offensive action on an appreciable scale has been undertaken by either side in the last twenty-four hours. Sniping continued, but there has been distinctly less of it in most areas since the British troops consolidated the previously cleared stretches of urban and suburban territory and as an ever-increasing number of men called up for the National Guard becomes available for duty.

It was revealed today that Sunday night's attack on the Royal Air Force billets and headquarters at Kiffisia was launched by about 1,000 rebels against a much smaller force, mostly non-combatant personnel occupying the compound, which includes two large fashionable hotels, the Cecil and the Pentelli. The rebel forces, using mortars as well as a variety of automatic weapons, included women and children with grenades. The hotels finally were dynamited.

A British armored column sent out from Athens did not arrive in time to scatter the rebel host before it overran the beleaguered RAF personnel, many of whom, however, were eventually brought out to safety.

Rhallis Is Recaptured

Jean Rhallis, President

BRITISH 'CORRECT' BYRNES

Deny Agreement With Russia to Split Spheres of Influence

LONDON, Oct. 16 (AP)—The British Foreign Office today declared "incorrect" a statement attributed to James F. Byrnes that Great Britain and Russia agreed in 1944 to set up spheres of influence placing Greece in the British orbit and Rumania in the Soviet realm.

A Foreign Office spokesman said the former United States Secretary of State made the statement in his book, "Frankly Speaking."

"It is true, however, that there was some discussion in 1944 between the big powers as to how best pressure could be brought to bear on the enemy," the spokesman added. "As a result it was agreed that, militarily, it would be best for Britain to operate in and from Greece, leaving Rumania to the Russians. At best the discussions could be said to have ended in an agreement for coordinating military strategy."

Oct. 17, 1947
N.Y. Times

OPERATION 'RENEGE'

"A complete diplomatic rupture with Russia, with war not far off, was then privately predicted by certain Washington officials—one of them, at least, on the White House staff."

Albert Z. Carr, as of May 1945

"Despite the fact that they were simple people, the Russians should not be regarded as fools, which was a mistake the West frequently made, nor were they blind and could quite well see what was going on before their eyes."

Stalin to Hopkins, May 27, 1945

TRUMAN'S ATTITUDE IN HIS MEET-ing with Molotov was ominous enough, but worse followed at the San Francisco Conference setting up the United Nations. The President's "get tough" policy was a green light for Senator Vandenberg who, with Dulles at his elbow, practically made policy for the American delegation. The Vandenberg influence was well known to Washington insiders. The **Washington Times-Herald** said that "it is the hand of Vandenberg that is generally discerned in U. S. moves on Conference chessboard." [1] And dealing with this period two years later, newspaper columnist Tris Coffin wrote, "After Roosevelt's death Vandenberg dominated all foreign policy decisions." [2]

The Truman-Vandenberg-Dulles policy was a masterpiece

1 Vandenberg, **Private Papers**, p. 182
2 Tris Coffin, **Missouri Compromise**, Boston, 1947, p. 264

of hypocrisy. We first accused the Soviet Union of breaking the Yalta agreement (which, as we have seen, the anti-Soviet Leahy said wasn't so), and then we proceeded to break one of our specific Yalta pledges on a matter of grave importance—the admission of Argentina to the UN. The proof of our bad faith is given by Cordell Hull, Secretary of State in four Roosevelt Cabinets.

Hull makes the third conservative witness against Truman's policies. There was Stimson on atomic energy, Admiral Leahy on the Polish question and now Hull on the United Nations.

RENEGING ON A PLEDGE

It had been agreed at Yalta that Argentina, with its pro-Nazi government which was even then giving refuge to Nazis (the war was still on), would not be admitted to the United Nations. This agreement was unequivocal, and Roosevelt himself had made the promise to Stalin. According to Hopkins:

". . . he [Hopkins] had heard President Roosevelt at the Yalta Conference in February promise Marshal Stalin twice that he would not support such action [admission] on behalf of the Argentine Government." 3 (emphasis in the original)

Despite this solemn promise the American delegation at San Francisco supported the admission of Argentina. Molotov suggested a postponement of the question, saying:

"Up to now all invitations to this Conference have been approved unanimously by the four sponsoring governments which hold an equal position here. . . .
"The Soviet delegation suggests that the question of inviting Argentina to the conference be postponed for a few days for further study.
"This is the only request made by the Soviet delegation." (emphasis added)

This put the issue on a simple basis, a true test of whether bloc voting had been organized.

3 Hull, Memoirs, p. 1408

Secretary of State Stettinius followed the new Truman "tough" policy. He spoke against the Soviet request for postponement and won by a vote of 28 to 7. Argentina was admitted.

The significance of the U. S. action was clear to all observers. The conservative **N. Y. Herald Tribune** in a news story said openly that "the hard-hitting anti-fascist policy of Cordell Hull had been "abandoned," and that the U. S. had "built a steamroller" against the Soviet Union.[4] This, we must remember is Truman's policy, **less than three weeks after the death of Roosevelt.** It was a shocking policy opposed by nearly all the European countries as columnist Walter Lippmann pointed out the next day.

Except Holland, "not one single liberated European country supported us" when Stettinius "to the astonishment and dismay of every experienced observer" demanded a "showdown." Further, Lippmann hinted at the U. S. control of the U. N., "which will be dominated by the American Republics with the help of British votes" and warned that we "had adopted a line of conduct which, **if it becomes our regular line, will have the most disastrous consequences.**"[5] (emphasis added)

Even stronger language was used by ex-Secretary of State Cordell Hull. Hull was furious. He had not been consulted on such a major shift of policy although he was a member of the U. S. delegation and its senior adviser. Unfortunately he was in a hospital in the East and could not block the Vandenberg policy. However, he called Stettinius on the phone and delivered a scorching blast at such breaking our word. Hull said that "**irreparable** harm had been done" in admitting Argentina.[6] (emphasis added)

Hull was a cautious, precise speaker. "Irreparable" is a

4 N. Y. Herald Tribune, May 2, 1945
5 N. Y. Herald Tribune, May 3, 1945
6 Hull, Memoirs, p. 1722

strong term: Hull did not use it lightly. He adds:

"I also said to Stettinius that if the American delegation were not careful we should get Russia into such a state of mind that she might decide that the United Nations organization was not going to furnish adequate security to her in the future." [7]

These are terribly prophetic words by FDR's Secretary of State. Hull was fully conscious that the U. S. had broken a specific pledge in a manner that compounded our bad faith, and cast doubt on the value of our pledged word. As Stalin later told Hopkins, "the action of the Conference and the attitude of the United States had raised the question of the value of agreements between the three major powers." [8]

The admission of Argentina was the first open indication that our foreign policy was being formed by the most reactionary forces in America. Argentina had opposed us throughout the war and a democratic United States would justifiably oppose the pro-Nazi Argentine government which had actually harmed the U. S. militarily as Hull shows in a detailed chapter. [9]

The admission of Argentina was the first instance of a broken Yalta agreement. This is a fact. While American accusations against the Soviet Union were on a matter of interpretation of agreements, on the question of Argentina the commitment was specific. The admission of Argentina was not only the first step in smashing the Yalta agreements, it was also the first step in the development of Dulles' strategy to use the United Nations as a cover and an instrument to break the Yalta agreements—what Vandenberg called, "overtaking Yalta." The admission of Argentina was the first step toward wrecking Big Three unity—the greatest roadblock to reaction all over the world.

THE MEANING OF BIG THREE UNITY

The unity of the three major powers had won the war.

7 Ibid., p. 1722
8 Sherwood, Roosevelt and Hopkins, p. 893
9 Hull, Memoirs, p. 1403

Only such unity could win the peace. Roosevelt and Hull made this unity the cornerstone of the United Nations. Without this unity, the United Nations wouldn't work, for a very simple reason. The United States would dominate the UN. **The U. S. would always get a majority on an anti-Soviet basis.** Because of its political and economic domination over Latin American and other nations, the U. S. was sure of twenty Latin American votes plus the Philippines and Liberia. Together with Britain and British influence countries the Anglo-American bloc had 35 sure votes out of some 50-odd countries irrespective of the merits of the issue, plus an assured majority on the Security Council.

In contrast the Soviet Union could only count on itself in the Security Council and less than ten votes in the Assembly. As Hull clearly pointed out, the Soviet Union could hardly accept such a situation.

An Anglo-American UN would simply be a screen for anti-Soviet attacks. The Soviets wanted no part of it, and Stalin at Yalta was very explicit about it. He reminded Churchill and Roosevelt of the fact that the League of Nations had been used against the Soviet Union, and only the Soviet Union.

The USSR had been the only country expelled from the League [10], and as Stalin pointed out England and France at that time "had mobilized world opinion against her (Russia), even going so far as to speak of it as a crusade." [11]

At the same time, the Soviet Union welcomed a mechanism for compromises and for reducing world tensions. [12] A United Nations organization based on Big Three unity would be such a mechanism and Soviet leaders showed their trust in Roosevelt's good faith by accepting almost entirely the American scheme of organization.

10 See Chapter 5
11 Stettinius, Roosevelt and the Russians, p. 149
12 Ibid., p 150

Tremendous readjustments are necessary after global war. Some nations which were great powers may completely disappear as did the old Austro-Hungarian Empire after World War I. New nations arise—Czechoslovakia in 1918, Israel in 1948. Trade gets shifted, raw materials are grabbed, markets seized. What one nation gains, another nation loses.

PROBLEMS FOR THE UN

During World War II the United States took over German markets in South America. It took over the oil of Saudi Arabia and part of the oil in the Near East at the expense of the British; it took over British investments in Argentina, Dutch investments in the Near East and full control of the Belgian Congo's uranium.

But this grabbing process in modern times can be very dangerous. Peoples resent being exploited. So an Iran, an Egypt, or an India, or an Indo-China may fight back and in the world today, once a war starts anywhere, it can easily become a world war. Hull was aware of the explosive nature of colonialism, writing:

"We felt that unless dependent peoples were assisted toward ultimate self-government . . . they would provide kernels of conflict." [13]

This was a serious problem for the United Natons. It was clear then and very clear today, that the UN is constantly faced with the problem of national liberation movements, as in Tunisia, Indo-China, Indonesia and so forth. These countries would come forward before the UN to demand justice and freedom. Either the UN would be antagonistic to these liberation movements, in which case it would be functioning as an oppressive "unholy alliance" and the USSR, India, China would object; or the UN would be sympathetic, i.e., support colonies towards self-determination. The latter policy would assure the opposition of the

[13] Hull, Memoirs, pp. 1477-1478

colonial powers of France, Holland, Belgium, Britain and certain dominions.

Hull had a continuing sharp struggle with Eden on this point of colonial independence, beginning with the First Quebec Conference in August, 1942. Says Hull:

"He [Eden] pointed out that under the British Empire system there were varying degrees of self-government running from the Dominions . . . to backward areas **that were never likely to have their own government.** He added that Australia and New Zealand also had colonial possessions that they would be unwilling to remove from their supervisory jurisdiction." [14] (emphasis added)

Despite Eden's "irremovable objection" to the word independence, Hull persevered and with the support of the USSR finally had the word written in the UN Charter. English opposition went underground, as it were, but remained. It was not to be minimized.

This political conflict on colonialism reflected basic economic antagonisms. Colonial areas are profitable to the owning country. The rubber and tin of Malaya sold to America at British controlled prices are a primary source of dollars for Britain. American businessmen might like to see Malaya free if they would get tin and rubber much more cheaply.

Furthermore, the British Empire has a very tight tariff system, known as the Imperial Preference System, or the Ottawa agreements. American businessmen would like to break that system down in order to sell their goods abroad. [15] America with its huge productive resources would gain from free trade and Britain would suffer.

Equally as grave as the conflicts of colonialism were the conflicts between the socialist and the capitalist sections of the world. At the end of the war, Rumania, for example, took control over her oil fields. Corrupt pre-war governments had allowed these oil fields to be taken over by for-

14 Hull, Memoirs, p. 1237
15 At the same time American business has in the United States one of the highest tariff systems in the world

eign capital. Now when the Rumanian government took them back, the English, French and American capitalists did not like it at all.

Even in non-socialist countries, nationalization of major industries seemed the only solution. Take the problem of the Ruhr in Germany. The Ruhr is the great steel-making area which has been the material basis of German aggression. The Ruhr steel magnates were important backers of Hitler. If the German people nationalized the Ruhr, American capitalists could be expected to object.

The examples could be multiplied endlessly. Everywhere, economic conflicts existed. Closely related were the political conflicts of security. The United States as a world power might consider itself to be concerned with any changes anywhere in the world. We insisted, for example, that we should have a voice in the control of the Dardenelles and of the Danube River. With equal justice the Soviet Union, as a world power, could demand a voice in the control of the Suez Canal, and logically, the Panama Canal. Can anyone imagine what Congress would say to this?

Even with good-will and a friendly approach there would have been great friction in the United Nations. Yet there were three major reasons for optimism. A functioning UN based on Big Three unity would strengthen peace all over the world and lessen the urgency of strategic bases for each nations' own security. Secondly, the tremendous production facilities of the United States, greatly increased as a result of the war, would have been available to help devastated areas back on their feet. American grants or loans would have been powerful levers to induce England and France to give more freedom to their colonial peoples.

Thirdly, the smaller nations in a functioning UN would be a stabilizing and moderating influence. If the U. S. and the USSR are facing each other in a gigantic struggle, small nations are forced to take sides. Every issue becomes one of prestige and there is little independence of choice for small nations. In a functioning UN, smaller nations would have a more independent role and serve as a fluid group of arbiters.

At the same time, the United Nations organization recognized the fact of power and sovereignty. The United States would have never agreed to surrender its power of decisions on major issues. The USSR and other nations would not have done so either. Hence the veto, the right to say no to any action which a big power thought harmful to itself.

The veto was a safeguard in case the Big Three unity was broken. It was as much a demand of the U. S. as of the USSR. Without the veto power, no American Congress would ever have approved of the UN. Today, when the United States has a majority in the UN, it is Russia which constantly uses the veto for its own protection. In the future, if socialist nations form a majority, it may well be the U. S. which will constantly use the veto. On the other hand, if the world can return to the Roosevelt concept of Big Three unity, the veto's importance will diminish.

POWER POLITICS IN THE UN

Americans dislike the very words "power politics," as if there is something immoral about the idea. They dislike such components of power politics as "spheres of influence" and "balance of power." Yet, as a sovereign nation, we have always used our power. The Monroe Doctrine was and is power politics. It served notice on European nations that we would use our power to keep them out of Latin America. The Spanish-American War was power politics. The U. S. obtained paramount influence on Cuba, essential to U. S. security in the Caribbean, and the Philippines, a base of expansion in the Pacific.

During the Second World War we took over from the British more of the Caribbean area, and from Japan all its Pacific islands. Our share of influence covers Japan itself,

217

where we have permanent military bases.

Hull was aware of the inconsistencies of our foreign policy. [16] In 1945 the United States was the primary mover of the Act of Chapultepec, signed in Mexico by the Latin American countries, which in effect gave the U. S. the right to intervene militarily in those countries. Hull opposed the Act because "once we had agreed to this new position on intervention," we couldn't very well oppose Soviet influence in Eastern Europe. [17] Hull realized that we couldn't oppose Soviet arguments that control of the Black Sea is essential to her security while at the same time we grabbed the Japanese Pacific islands on grounds of U. S. security. Says Hull:

"I opposed the view of our Joint Chiefs of Staff that the Pacific Islands we would take from Japan should become United States property." [18]

Hull lost. Today the U. S. not only has all these islands but military control of Japan as well.

But Hull, when the chips were down, acted unilaterally to secure American imperialistic interests. The most noteworthy example is Saudi Arabia, where Hull himself backed American oil companies to get concessions and urged the construction of American Air Force bases in Saudi Arabia. This was done.

Hull's actions are the very heart of power politics. He was establishing an American "sphere of influence" in Saudi Arabia, that is to say an area where American interests and American control were paramount. The approach suited Churchill fine. The British had a "sphere of influence" in the Mediterranean and the Near East which they would never willingly give up and Hull's actions removed the basis for possible American objections. Also it gave Churchill an opening to negotiate with the Soviet Union on a straight

16 Hull, Memoirs, p. 1467
17 Ibid., p. 1467
18 Ibid., p. 1466

basis of power politics.

Power politics and "spheres of influence" are not pleasing concepts to Americans. War, however, is much worse. Capitalism exists and it has military power; socialism exists and it has military power. If the peace is to be maintained the world must be so organized as to have room for both. When an area of conflict develops, a compromise must be found.

The British wanted to keep the Mediterranean under their control. This control was threatened by Soviet victories in the Balkans and the resistance movements in the liberated countries. A left wing government, in Greece particularly, might resist British influence. Churchill therefore sought an agreement whereby England would retain its influence in Greece. To this end, in May, 1944, he visited Moscow and suggested a series of agreements on the Balkans.

THE AGREEMENTS ON THE BALKANS

The Balkan agreements initiated by Churchill and accepted by Stalin and Roosevelt were basic to Big Three unity. They were the real target of Dulles, Vandenberg, Forrestal and the rest of the reactionaries. These Balkan agreements were the basis of Yalta, and the real issues behind the Argentina vote.

The Balkan agreements basically were security agreements. They were designed to assure the Soviet Union of friendly governments on her borders, and to assure the British Empire of friendly governments on her imperial lines of communications. In May, 1944, Churchill suggested to Stalin that they reach an agreement whereby England would have paramount influence in Greece and the Soviet Union would have paramount influence in Poland and Rumania.

Stalin immediately asked whether the U. S. had been consulted and when Churchill said no, [19] **Stalin insisted that**

19 All the details, facts and quotations on the agreements are taken from Hull's Memoirs, p. 1451 to p. 1459

FDR be informed. Stalin's insistence shows his concern that nothing be done except by mutual agreement of the three allies. As a result, the British government laid the proposals before the American government.

Hull argued against the agreement as representing "power politics" and "spheres of influence." Churchill pointed out that decisions had to be made since military developments were forcing them. Soviet armies would soon enter the Balkans; the British Navy would soon control the Mediterranean.

Hull was not in a strong position to argue since he had already gone along with the British on many an important occasion. For example, he had supported the Polish London government-in-exile, although reluctantly. He had granted the Poles a yearly subsidy of 12½ million dollars from 1942 onwards. Also he had already agreed on a Control Commission for Italy which was Anglo-American under British leadership, while the Soviet Union would only have an observer on it with no power. Since the Mediterranean was an Anglo-American military area this was understandable—on the premise of a "sphere of influence." In the same manner, Eastern Europe was a Soviet military area.

Roosevelt agreed with Churchill and accepted the Balkan agreement for a three month period "for military purposes only." However, as Churchill was well aware, such actions are irreversible.

In October of 1944 Churchill was again in Moscow and the agreement was spelled out. England was to have paramount influence in Greece, and the Soviet Union in Poland. In Rumania, Bulgaria and Hungary, English influence was restricted to 25 percent and in Yugoslavia, 50 percent. Both sides were fully aware of what was implied. According to Byrnes, they agreed that:

". . . if the British found it necessary to take military action to quell internal disorders in Greece, the Soviets would not interfere.

In return, the British would recognize the rights of the Soviets to take the lead in maintaining order in Rumania." [20]

That this agreement existed is beyond question. Byrnes himself has double-riveted his statement as a result of a curious incident. When Byrnes' book appeared in 1947 an anonymous British Foreign Office spokesman declared on October 16, 1947, that the above quotation (concerning the agreement) was "incorrect." Byrnes immediatley struck back:

"Evidently the Foreign Office spokesman is not informed. My statement was based on a message from Prime Minister Churchill to President Roosevelt, dated March 8, 1945, in the first paragraph of which, after deploring Soviet actions in Rumania, Mr. Churchill said, 'We have been hampered in our protests against these developments by the fact that, in order to have the freedom to save Greece, Eden and I at Moscow in October recognized that Russia should have a largely preponderant voice in Rumania and Bulgaria while we took the lead in Greece. **Stalin adhered very strictly to this understanding.** . . .'" [21] (emphasis added)

It is important to realize the vast difference between the results of British and Soviet influence. British influence in Greece meant that **British troops shot down** Greek fighters, restored the pre-war corrupt government, including quislings and fascists, and maintained a system of government which gave the people of Greece poverty, misery and illiteracy. Soviet influence in Eastern Europe meant that the peoples settled accounts with their quislings and fascists without interference from reactionaries in the West, that honest governments were formed which are developing industries, wiping out illiteracy and generally modernizing the various countries. The difference between the British and the Soviets is illustrated by a striking fact: in no country of Eastern Europe has the Red Army behaved as the British Army did in Greece.

20 Byrnes, Speaking Frankly, p. 53
21 N. Y. Times, October 18, 1947, quoted by Schuman, The Devil and Jimmy Byrnes

However, leaving these questions aside, the revelant point to the argument of this book is the fact that there were **agreements on the Balkans which America had accepted,** and under those agreements whatever happened in Rumania, or Bulgaria, or Poland was none of our business. If the Soviet Military Government in Rumania talked harshly to the King of Rumania, that was none of our business. If the government of Poland jailed the fascist supporters of Mikolajczyk, that was none of our business. When Byrnes, or Forrestal or Truman said that these acts violated the Yalta agreement, this was simply not so. In May 1945, only one Yalta agreement had been broken—the agreement not to admit Argentina to the United Nations.

THE MEANING OF THE ARGENTINE ADMISSION

The vote on Argentina was of crucial importance as a warning that America was reneging on her agreements. By itself, the admission of Argentina was not of world-shaking importance. The U. S. could argue, and did argue, that the U. S. was going along with the unanimous desire of the Latin American countries. The Soviet Union understood such considerations of diplomatic necessities and Molotov didn't say he wouldn't accept the admission. All he asked was a postponement of the vote, obviously to discuss it with the U. S. As Stalin said to Hopkins, he did not understand "why Argentina could not have been asked to wait three months or so before joining the world organization." [22]

When the United States contemptuously rejected the request of a friendly ally for a brief postponement, there was only one possible interpretation on the action. The Truman administration was not interested in unity and friendly cooperation. Molotov now knew what Vandenberg had written in his diary the day of Roosevelt's death—Big Three unity had ceased to exist.

22 Sherwood, **Roosevelt and Hopkins**, p. 893

Taken together with Truman's attack on Molotov, the action of the United States at San Francisco showed the Soviet Union that we no longer intended to abide by the Yalta agreements, since Argentina's exclusion had been agreed upon at Yalta. **But the heart of the Yalta agreement was the security of the border states of the Soviet Union.** No one has ever questioned the importance of this question to the Soviet Union. Secretaries of State Byrnes and Acheson have both repeatedly agreed with the Soviet view that its security requires friendly border states. [23] Even such a conservative Catholic as Edward J. Flynn, the political Democratic boss, has recognized this. As late as 1947 he wrote:

". . . we must realize that it is a very normal reaction for Russia to seek to have sympathetic governments on her borders. This is a course with which we cannot wholly disagree. Our Army and Navy today are insisting that we should have control of various islands in the Pacific in order to protect our Pacific shoreline." [24]

The Soviet Union's fear that the United States intended to go back on the Yalta agreements on Poland and the Eastern European countries was pointed up by the open hostility which Ambassador Harriman was showing over the Polish question. At San Francisco, Harriman was holding "off-the record" press conferences to build up attacks on the Soviet Union in press conferences. On May 1, 1945, he said in so many words:

"I have come to the conclusion that on long range policies there is an **irreconcilable** difference between the United States and Great Britain on the one hand—and Russia on the other." [25] (emphasis added)

These remarks were off-the-record, that is they couldn't be printed, but everyone in San Francisco knew about them, including the Russians. And if the Soviet Union had not been convinced of American animosity by the Truman-Molo-

23 See Chapter 8, p. 195
24 Edward J. Flynn, You're The Boss, New York, 1947, p. 203
25 Henry Wallace, Prairie Club Speech, Des Moines, Iowa, April 29, 1950

tov interview, by the vote on Argentina, by the influence of Dulles and Vandenberg and by the remarks of Harriman, we took another drastic step, is if to dramatize the point.

On May 12, 1945, the head of the Foreign Economic Administration, Leo T. Crowley, stopped Lend-Lease shipments to the Soviet Union without warning, although the USSR was scheduled to join in the war against Japan within three months. Albert Z. Carr, a special assistant to Truman at the time, tells the story in detail, trying to excuse Truman. Carr says that the decision to stop Lend-Lease was taken by Crowley without consulting the President. Yet as far as is known, Crowley was not even reprimanded, let alone fired. The action was done and its seriousness cannot be overestimated. Carr quotes the **N. Y. Times** in a special dispatch from Washington:

"To this city's shrewd and cynical observers . . . the Soviet Union was being deprived of goods until it entered the war against Japan. . . . The histories of this generation may be unable to weigh the influences and the factors that 'went into the reduction of Lend-Lease aid to the Soviet Union.' "

"Between these careful lines one could read the perception that a **powerful section of official opinion** in Washington was **eager to give maximum provocation to the Kremlin. . .**"[26] (emphasis added)

Carr, working inside the White House spoke as an eyewitness when he revealed this shocking fact and its cause:

"A complete diplomatic rupture with the Soviets, **with war not far off,** was then privately predicted to certain Washington officials—one of them, at least, on the White House Staff."[27]

This, it must be remembered was within a month of Roosevelt's death and while America was still at war with Japan.

The Soviet Union was not blind to these developments. As Stalin told Hopkins bluntly:

"Despite the fact that they were simple people, the Russians should not be regarded as fools, which was a mistake the West frequently

26 Carr, Truman, Stalin and Peace, p. 61
27 Carr, Truman, Stalin and Peace, p. 62

made, nor were they blind and could quite well see what was going on before their eyes." 28

Faced with a hostile United States, the Soviet Union moved swiftly to restrict the powers of the United Nations. Stalin had already warned Churchill that a world organization could not be used as a major propaganda platform against the Soviet Union, just as the League of Nations had been used to mobilize world opinion against the USSR. To prevent an Anglo-American majority from utilizing the agenda for propaganda purposes, Molotov insisted on the veto applying to the agenda. In opposition, England and the U. S. insisted that the United Nations had the right to discuss any question by majority vote and therefore the veto should not apply.

The Soviet Union refused to enter the trap. The Anglo-American coalition insisted. A deadlock resulted, and Molotov went back to Moscow. It seemed as if the United Nations would not even get started because of American-Soviet tensions—and this within less than a month of Roosevelt's death.

It looked as if Dulles and Vandenberg had won.

28 Sherwood, Roosevelt and Hopkins, p. 894

RELATIONS WITH RUSSIA SEEM NOW ON UPGRADE

Plans for Berlin Control Commission And Polish Talks Indicate That Cooperation Is Progressing

OTHER ISSUES FOR BIG THREE

By EDWIN L. JAMES

Relations of the United States Government with the Russian Government have taken a distinct turn for the better. And that appears to date from the visit of Harry L. Hopkins to Moscow as special representative of President Truman. The news that American troops will start next week to withdraw from positions where the end of the war in Europe left them to the east of the Russians' western occupation limit comes along at about the same time that assurances are given that the Joint Control Commission in Berlin is soon to come into being. In the same week it was arranged for a resumption of the talks in Moscow for the widening of the present Polish Cabinet, with leaders of the Polish parties participating. And, of course, there is the announcement that the Big Three are to meet in the vicinity of Berlin in July.

These developments, coming as the San Francisco Conference is on the last lap of the completion of a charter for the United Nations, present a much brighter international picture than existed even a month ago. That is not to say that all pending issues with Moscow have been settled, but that some of mate interests not only in those countries but in Hungary. Bulgaria, Austria and Czechoslovakia. There are indications that the Russians are preparing to recognize this interest with respect to Austria and Czechoslovakia, and it would be no surprise if at their coming meeting the B[ig Three]

REACTION HESITATES

"Sometimes when I hear these whisperings [against Russia] I wonder whether Goebbels is really dead as he deserves to be, or has only emigrated to the U. S."
Harold L. Ickes, June 26, 1945

"What we must do now is not to make the world safe for democracy but make the world safe for the U. S.
James F. Byrnes, July 1945

"To use our Air Force successfully we must have bases located around the world."
General H. H. Arnold, July 1945

WHEN Molotov went home, the reactionaries suddenly began to get worried. They had recklessly pursued a "get tough" policy without seriously weighing the consequences. They had taken it for granted that if the Soviet Union withdrew, they would be very happy. Vandenberg had written in his diary at this time, April 24, 1945:

"Russia may withdraw. If it does, the conference **will proceed without Russia.** Now we are getting somewhere!" [1]

Likewise, on the previous day, Truman had been very blithe about the Soviet Union's absence at San Francisco:

". . . if the Russians did not wish to join us, they could go to hell. . . ." [2]

1 Vandenberg, **Private Papers,** p. 176
2 Forrestal **Diaries,** p. 50

This glib, irresponsible attitude sounded fine in the abstract. But when Molotov went home, the reactionaries suddenly realized they had gone too far and too fast. If the San Francisco Conference failed, and the facts came to light, they would be held responsible by the American people and by world opinion.

Within the Cabinet were Ickes, Wallace, Stimson. They might express publicly what they were saying privately. Stimson for example was writing in his diary for April 23, 1945:

"Contrary to what I thought was the wise course, they [State Department officials] have not settled the problems . . . by wise negotiations before this public meeting in San Francisco . . . to me, it seems that they might make trouble between us and Russia. . . . I have very great anxiety. . . ." [3]

Many newspapers, alarmed by the Argentina case, spoke uneasily. The **Washington Post** attacked Stettinius and his associates as "bush league diplomats," and Secretary of Interior Ickes, at a dinner for the anti-fascist writer, Thomas Mann, attacked

" . . . the efforts to thwart peace . . . by fomenting fear and hate of the great nation, Russia. Sometimes when I hear these whisperings, I wonder if Goebbels is really dead, as he deserves to be, or has only emigrated to the U.S." [4]

However, the most important factor in the situation was that a great majority of the American people felt admiration and friendship for the Soviet Union. An editorial in the New York **Herald Tribune** early in that year gives a good picture of basic American attitudes.

"There are no greater enthusiasts for 'Uncle Joe's boys' than our troops on the Roer and in the Ardennes. . . .
"Here is one aspect of international relations too often overlooked by the theorists. 'Uncle Joe's boys' may inspire alarm in some sections of the armchair brigade, but to the man in the street they

3 Stimson, On Active Service, p. 610
4 N. Y. Herald Tribune, June 26, 1945

are 'ours,' and to the fighting soldier they are heroes. The men in the foxholes have been made passionately aware of the fact that this is one war in one world, that each fights for all and all for each, and that getting the big job done is far more important than any question of who does it. Afterwards, no doubt, the politicians and publicists will get to work to destroy such foolish notions, but it may be that fighting men and ordinary people will remember 'Uncle Joe's boys' and will still believe that great nations which were so desperately dependent on each other in war can hang together even in peace." [5]

In the brief period since Roosevelt's death, popular attitudes towards the Soviet Union hadn't changed. The USSR was still our great ally, and the Red Army a subject of warm praise. As late as June 25, the **Herald Tribune** could editorialize about the Red Army:

"It has, in fact, proved an 'army of liberation' for Europe and half the world in the vital sense that without the Red Army and the illimitable sacrifices with which the Russian people supported and sustained it, liberation from the brutal blight of Nazism would have been all but impossible. . . .
"As Marshal Zhukov dedicates it now to a 'period of peaceful development,' all must be glad that there is this strong and stable force arrayed upon the side of order and human welfare." [6]

It was clear that the majority of the American people were holding fast to Roosevelt's policy of friendship and cooperation. Even Forrestal's biographer admits this in his usual backhanded way:

". . . the country was not yet in the mood to face up to the basic issues of Soviet relations already apparent to Forrestal and Harriman." [7]

What this means in plain English is that the American people had not yet been poisoned by distortions. The average man in the street would have been horrified and angry had he known what was going on in Washington and San Francisco. A breakdown of the San Francisco Conference might

5 Ibid., January 26, 1945
6 N. Y. Herald Tribune, June 25, 1945
7 Forrestal Diaries, p. 58

expose the Cold War makers, Dulles, Harriman, Vandenberg, Forrestal and the rest. They had pushed so hard that if the truth came out, they would be very vulnerable.

It was therefore of the greatest importance to these men that the Conference should not fail. The very reactionaries who had wantonly attacked the Soviet Union now found it necessary to slow down, and to try to convince the USSR that the American government would continue Roosevelt's policies. In view of Truman's words, Stettinius' acts and Harriman's press conferences, this was a hard job. It was at this point that the reactionaries got a bright idea—to send Hopkins to Moscow on a goodwill mission. Hopkins was a friend of Roosevelt, a friend of the Soviet Union. He could convince the Soviet leaders. Hopkins' Mission was conceived by reactionaries as a cover up operation.

THE TWO-FACED POLICY

Truman has since given the impression that it was his idea to send Hopkins to Moscow; actually the idea came from two State Department anti-Sovieteers, Harriman (then ambassador to the Soviet Union) and Bohlen. Sherwood reveals the truth:

". . . less than a week after V-E day, it seemed that the San Francisco Conference was going on the rocks. Molotov and Eden were both headed for home. Harriman and Bohlen were on an airplane flying eastward . . . with a sense of despair in their hearts. They asked each other whether there was any conceivable way of saving the situation. . . . Bohlen suggested the possibility that President Truman might send Hopkins to Moscow. . . . Harriman was enthusiastic about the suggestion. . . ." [8]

When Harriman saw Hopkins, and asked him if he would go, Hopkins immediately agreed although he was very ill. Hopkins was very disturbed about the turn of events in American-Soviet relations, and he knew who was responsible for these cold war tactics. This is shown by the fact that

8 Sherwood, Roosevelt and Hopkins, p. 885

when he did go to Moscow, he sent his dispatches directly to the President and apparently arranged it so that Forrestal couldn't get them. Forrestal was furious. He told his friend McCloy:

"I said I did not like that procedure. . . . I said I suspected that it was at Harry's (Hopkins) own instigation that this restraint was made. . . ." [9]

Therefore, when Hopkins agreed to go, it may be assumed that he knew what Harriman was up to. Furthermore, he had few illusions about Truman's liberalism, for his reaction to Harriman's proposal was "the despondent conviction that Truman would never agree to send him on this mission." [10]

But Hopkins was wrong; Truman did send him and out of the Hopkins Mission grew the agreement for Potsdam which was the last thing reactionaries wanted. In other words, Harriman's idea boomeranged for a short period.

THE HOPKINS MISSION

Hopkins arrived in Moscow on May 25, just six weeks after the death of Roosevelt. The Hopkins-Stalin talks covered six meetings over a period of ten days. The details are given in Sherwood's book, in twenty-five solid pages which are well worth reading for the light they throw on this problem: how Truman scuttled Roosevelt's policy.

The meetings were made more dramatic by the presence of Ambassador Harriman, one of the men responsible for the Cold War as both Stalin and Hopkins were well aware. Molotov was also present, and two interpreters. At the first meeting, Hopkins told Stalin that a:

". . . body of American public opinion who had been the constant support of the Roosevelt policies were seriously disturbed about their relations with Russia. In fact, in the last six weeks deterioration of public opinion had been so serious as to affect adversely

9 Forrestal Diaries, p. 67
10 Sherwood, Roosevelt and Hopkins, p. 887

the relations between our two countries." [11]

Hopkins emphasized:

". . . in a country like ours public opinion is affected by specific incidents and in this case the deterioration in public opinion . . . had been centered in our inability to carry into effect the Yalta Agreement on Poland. . . . President Truman feels, and so does the American public, although they are not familiar with all the details, a sense of bewilderment at our inability to solve the Polish question." [12]

Whereupon, Sherwood quotes the following conversation:

"Marshal Stalin replied that the reason for the failure on the Polish question was that the Soviet Union desired to have a friendly Poland, but that Great Britain wanted to revive the system of **cordon sanitaire** [13] on the Soviet borders.
"Mr. Hopkins replied that neither the Government nor the people of the United States had any such intentions.
"Marshal Stalin replied he was speaking only of England and said that the British conservatives did not desire to see a Poland friendly to the Soviet Union.
"Mr. Hopkins stated that the United States would desire a Poland friendly to the Soviet Union and in fact desired to see friendly countries all along the Soviet borders.
"Marshal Stalin replied if that be so we can easily come to terms in regard to Poland." [14]

Soviet suspicions of England were fully shared by Hopkins. Before leaving for Moscow, Hopkins told Forrestal

". . . that he was skeptical about Churchill, at least in the particular of Anglo-American-Russian relationship; that he thought it was of vital importance that we [Americans] be not manoeuvered into a position where Great Britain has us lined up with them as a bloc against Russia to implement England's European policy." [15] (emphasis added)

Ambassador Harriman hypocritically seemed to agree, saying to Stalin:

11 Sherwood, Roosevelt and Hopkins, p. 889
12 Ibid., p. 890
13 Literally "health barrier." It refers to the chain of anti-Soviet nations in Eastern Europe after World War I set up by France and England to "quarantine" Communism. See Chapter 5
14 Sherwood, Roosevelt ad Hopkins, p. 890
15 Forrestal Diaries, p. 58

232

". . . we had, as Marshal Stalin knew, very intimate relations with Great Britain . . . nevertheless it was obviously desirable that the United States and the Soviet Union **should talk alone** on matters of special interest to them and that was also one of the reasons for Mr. Hopkins' visit." [16] (emphasis added)

Hopkins then invited Stalin to "mention any political questions concerning the United States which were worrying him." Stalin said he would do so, and at the second meeting he frankly and squarely placed the issues before Hopkins.

"Marshal Stalin said he would not attempt to use Soviet public opinion as a screen, but would speak of the feeling that had been created in Soviet governmental circles as a result of recent moves on the part of the United States government. He said these circles felt a certain alarm in regard to the attitude of the United States government. It was their impression that the American attitude towards the Soviet Union had perceptibly cooled once it became obvious that Germany was defeated, and that it was as though the **Americans were saying that the Russians were no longer** needed." [17] (emphasis added)

This is exactly what important American officials were saying; Stalin's analysis corresponded very closely with the facts. Admiral Leahy, General Deane, Forrestal and others are on record as saying the USSR was no longer needed. Harriman himself only a few days before (May 12) at a State Department meeting had suggested that the Yalta Agreement be re-examined" . . . in the light of the cessation of hostilities in Europe, which have changed the pattern of fact on which that agreement was drawn." [18]

In simpler English:—since the war is over, let's forget the Yalta agreement.

Stalin's statement makes a point of great importance in American-Soviet relations, and that is the question of public opinion. Hopkins talks of American "public opinion" being "disturbed," but the question may well be asked, who did the disturbing? The press, radio and films which shape public

16 Sherwood, **Roosevelt and Hopkins**, p. 892
17 Sherwood, **Roosevelt and Hopkins**, p. 893
18 **Forrestal Diaries**, p. 56

233

opinion are owned and controlled by big business interests. So Stalin said that "he would not attempt to use Soviet public opinion as a screen," thereby suggesting that Hopkins was doing so. [19]

Stalin went on to give several examples of U. S. hostility, including Argentina which "had raised the question of the value of agreements between the three major powers." Stalin made it clear that Argentina was a symbol and he was willing to forget about it. More important, however, was the manner in which Lend-Lease had been curtailed, as if "designed as pressure on the Russians in order to soften them up." [20] Whereupon, Hopkins in effect apologized both about Argentina and about Lend-Lease, saying that the Latin American countries had forced our hand on the first and that the second had been an accident.

Hopkins, having already apologized, went on to say that what disturbed him was the fact that Stalin should think the U. S. capable of such petty pressure tactics. The United States as a great power would not stoop to such measures. This interchange seems to have been in the nature of an education for Ambassador Harriman who had been recommending such tactics and was present throughout the meetings.

Stalin accepted Hopkins' apologies and went on to Poland. The discussions on Poland were the most important since here the Soviet Union had been accused by Truman of breaking agreements.

Stalin pointed out a basic historical fact, that "in the course of twenty-five years the Germans had twice invaded Russia via Poland," [21] and in the discussion Stalin sharply pointed out to Hopkins that:

". . . Soviet action in Poland had been more successful than Britsh

19 Sherwood, Roosevelt and Hopkins. The quotations for the following discussion may be found on pp. 889-895
20 Sherwood, Roosevelt and Hopkins, p. 896
21 Ibid., pp. 899-900

action in Greece and at no time had they been compelled to undertake the measures which they [British] had done in Greece." 22

This was by way of reminder to Hopkins that there had
been a definite agreement with the British on spheres of influences, an agreement accepted by FDR. With this in mind
he said that he did not "intend to have the British manage
the affairs of Poland" and that to him the Yalta agreement
meant "the present government was to form the basis of the
new. He said no other understanding of the Yalta agreement
was possible." 23

Hopkins cabled back to Washington and received instruc-
tions. On June 6, the U. S. accepted the Soviet position. The
Polish government was finally constituted by the addition of
several ministers to the Lublin government as the Soviet
Union had argued. By June 22 the government was formed.
This was a return by America to the Yalta agreements.

Once the Polish question was settled, the Soviet Union
showed its cooperation by agreeing to accept in good faith the
U. S. views on procedure in the UN. There was to be no veto
on procedural questions including the agenda. This last was a
big and specific concession to the United States. It saved the
San Francisco Conference which had been dragging along
inconclusively after Molotov had left.

THE MEANING OF THE HOPKINS MISSION

The success of the Hopkins Mission completely destroys
the theory that the Soviet Union started the Cold War at
the time of Roosevelt's death. It showed the Soviet Union
was willing to co-operate provided the United States lived up
to its agreements. Furthermore, it showed that the Soviet
Union was ready to trust President Truman.

In part this is due to Hopkins, who stressed throughout
the meetings Truman's "desire to continue President Roosevelt's policy of working with the Soviet Union and **his in-**

22 Ibid., p. 901
23 Sherwood, Roosevelt and Hopkins, pp. 909, 894

tention to carry out in fact as well as in spirit all the arrangements, both formal and informal, which President Roosevelt and Marshall Stalin had worked out together."[24] (emphasis added)

The fact that Truman had sent Hopkins lent weight to Hopkins' declarations of Truman's friendship. Ambassador Harriman cleverly stressed this point. He said:

". . . he wished to observe that President Truman in selecting Mr. Hopkins had chosen a man who, as the Marshal knew, had not only been very close to President Roosevelt but personally was one of the leading proponents of the policy of co-operation with the Soviet Union." [25]

Stalin couldn't know that it wasn't Truman who had selected Hopkins, but Harriman himself—who had then persuaded Truman.

The Soviets had reason to trust Hopkins, and Hopkins truly believed co-operation was possible. Said Hopkins:

". . . as the Marshal knew, he [Hopkins] had not been well and he would not be in Moscow unless he had felt the situation was serious." Hopkins added "he would not have come had he not believed that the present trend could be halted and a common basis found to go forward in the future." [26] (emphasis added)

At the same time Hopkins also knew that there were powerful anti-Soviet forces at work. He wrote a few weeks later:

"The thing the American people must look out for is that there is a minority in America who, for a variety of reasons, would just as soon have seen Russia defeated in the war. . . . There are plenty of people in America who would have been perfectly willing to see our armies go right on through Germany and fight with Russia after Germany was defeated." [27]

24 Sherwood, Roosevelt and Hopkins, p. 889. Hopkins couldn't really have believed all this since he had doubted Truman would send him. But he was acting as a mediator and putting forward his best arguments.
25 Ibid., p. 892
26 Ibid., p. 889
27 Ibid., p. 923

Nevertheless, he thought reaction could be defeated. In his eagerness to re-establish co-operation, Hopkins unwittingly gave Soviet leaders the wrong impressions, particularly about Truman. In this way, Hopkins played into the hands of American reactionaries by allaying Soviet suspicions.

This is not guesswork. There is startling confirmation of this not only in the fact that Ambassador Harriman chose Hopkins in the first place, but also by the Ambassador's own conclusions on the Hopkins Mission. At a Cabinet meeting, June 8, 1945, Harriman gave

". . . a report of the general effect of Hopkins' visit, which was about what was contained in Harry's own report. . . . He said that Harry's visit had already **dispelled the growing suspicion felt by Stalin and Molotov.**" [28] (emphasis added)

What could be more revealing? The men who were developing the Cold War had succeeded in lulling the Soviets into the belief that our policy was still Roosevelt's policy. That is why Soviet leaders had agreed on dropping the veto on questions of procedure within the UN.

Stalin was taking a calculated risk on the veto question. For the sake of co-operation, the Soviet Union put a weapon in the hands of the Anglo-American bloc. At the same time Stalin gave Hopkins a weighty warning, as important today as in 1945. Stalin told Hopkins that threats wouldn't work. If stopping Lend-Lease was a form of pressure,

". . . then it was a fundamental mistake. He said he must tell Mr. Hopkins frankly that if the Russians were approached frankly on a friendly basis much could be done, but that reprisals in any form would bring about the exact opposite effect." [29]

In view of what has happened in the last few years, of Soviet reactions to American threats, Stalin's warning seems prophetic. At this time also, Stalin made the remark already

28 Forrestal Diaries, p. 68
29 Sherwood, Roosevelt and Hopkins, p. 894

237

quoted in the last chapter:

"Despite the fact that they were simple people, the Russians should not be regarded as fools, which was a mistake the West frequently made, nor were they blind and could quite well see what was going on before their eyes."

And Stalin added that:

"It is true that the Russians are patient in the interests of a common cause but that their patience had limits."

These are clear, straightforward warnings and their specific formulations are worth re-reading. Stalin, who has been called "secretive," "devious," "inscrutable" and "enigmatic" by his enemies, actually speaks plainer language than Churchill ever did. These warnings provide the clue to Soviet attitudes throughout 1945-46.

The most important result which flowed from the Hopkins Mission is that its success made possible the Potsdam Conference. Newspapers headlined the fact that relations with Russia were on the "upgrade." Encouraged by Hopkins' results, progressive forces within the American government were able to carry out FDR's policies on Germany with Truman acquiescing. The Potsdam Conference is the last international conference where FDR's ideas prevailed. [30] It was also the last conference of the Big Three.

THE POTSDAM CONFERENCE

The Potsdam Conference was a success. The proof of this is the disappointment of the reactionaries. Writes Admiral Leahy:

"My general feeling about the Potsdam Conference was one of frustration. Both Stalin and Truman suffered defeats." [31]

30 In part this was also due to the fact that many of FDR's policies had been put into writing and directives issued even before his death. For example the Joint Chiefs of Staff directive 1067, which was the basic policy on Germany, was in the field in Europe months before Roosevelt died. It is interesting to observe the close correlation between JCS 1067 and the Potsdam Protocol
31 Leahy, I Was There, p. 426

Leahy suffered frustration because he was seeking an anti-Soviet victory and didn't get it. Obviously, if both Truman and Stalin suffered what Leahy considered "defeats," both sides must have made concessions. This means compromises—and compromises mean a successful conference.

Objectively, the areas of agreement among the Big Three were much larger than the areas of disagreement. The Soviet Union reaffirmed its intention of joining in the war against Japan, and the U. S. agreed on German reparations. The reparations question and related German questions were the heart of the Potsdam agreement and will be dealt with shortly.

The most important area of disagreement related to Eastern Europe. The U. S. did not succeed in increasing its power in the Military Control Commissions for Rumania, Bulgaria and Hungary; the USSR did not succeed in having these governments recognized by the West. Says Leahy:

"The result was complete impasse and may be said to have been the beginning of the cold war between th U. S. and Russia." [32]

This statement is one more proof, if any were needed, that the Cold War is an American idea. For at Potsdam the Soviet Union still was operating on the basis of friendly relations with the U. S. For example, both Admiral Leahy and General Arnold remarked on the great difference in the attitude of Soviet military men, a real feeling of comradeship. Says Leahy of the Staff talks, "the entire meeting was very friendly and none of the suspicions that so often frustrated our military mission in Moscow was apparent." [33]

To the Soviets the Potsdam Conference seemed a success. To the Americans, in Leahy's words, a frustration and the beginnings of the Cold War. How could such a thing be?

The reason is simple. The Potsdam agreement was de-

32 Ibid., p. 416
33 Ibid., p. 416

signed to de-militarize, de-nazify and de-cartelize Germany. This was pleasing to liberals all over the world, whether in Russia, France, England or the United States. For the same reasons it was displeasing to reactionaries all over the world.

THE POTSDAM AGREEMENT ON GERMANY
Looking back now, when Western Germany is being rearmed and neo-Nazism is showing increased vitality, the Potsdam agreement reads like a fantasy. But it is a fantasy signed by the heads of the most powerful nations in the world, America, England and Russia. It is worth looking at.

The Potsdam agreement, published August 2, 1945, is in several parts. Under Part III, Topic A, **Political Principles,** are ten sections, some with subsections. Here are sections 5 through 8:

"5—War criminals and those who have participated in planning or carrying out Nazi enterprises involving or resulting in atrocities or war crimes shall be arrested and brought to judgment. Nazi leaders, influential Nazi supporters and high officials of Nazi organizations and institutions and any other persons dangerous to the occupation or its objectives shall be arrested and interned.

"6—All members of the Nazi Party who have been more than nominal participants in its activities and all other persons hostile to Allied purposes shall be removed from public and semi-public office and **from position of responsibility in important private undertakings.** (emphasis added). Such persons shall be replaced by persons who, by their political and moral qualities, are deemed capable of assisting in developing genuine democratic institutions in Germany.

"7—German education shall be so controlled as completely to eliminate Nazi and militarist doctrines and to make possible the successful development of democratic ideas.

"8—The judicial system will be reorganized in accordance with the principles of democracy, of justice under law, and of equal rights for all citizens without distinction of race, nationality or religion.

Topic B, **Economic Principles** had nine additional sections. The key section reads:

"12—At the earliest practical date, the German economy shall be decentralized for the purpose of eliminating ... cartels, syndicates, trusts and other monopolistic arrangements."

Had these provisions been carried out, Western Germany today would not be again on the high road to military power, again rising to threaten peace. The Potsdam agreement on Germany is the last legacy from the Roosevelt days. The staff work for the conference had been going on for months under basic Roosevelt directives. In his brief spell of indecision, Truman carried on with FDR's existing policy. But already at Potsdam, the makers of the Cold War were once again getting the upper hand, this time permanently.

THE BRASSHATS TALK

The Potsdam agreement on Germany allayed Soviet suspicions precisely because it made sense from the standpoint of both American and Soviet national interests.

It seemed to prove that allied unity had survived FDR's death and to assure the Soviets that post-war co-operation was on a firm basis of mutual self-interest. But such was not the case.

At the very conference which seemed to guarantee peace, the Anglo-American brasshats were talking war. In the various memoirs, there are passages that make sad and bitter reading.

General Arnold had a long talk at Potsdam with the British Air Marshal, Portal. Arnold writes that "'we both believed our next enemy would be Russia, and a common line of thought emerged from our talk," namely, that the Russians understood manpower on the ground and were confident of having a good army but that they did fear long range bombers. Therefore:

"... to use our Air Force successfully we must have bases so located around the world that we can reach any target we may be called

241

upon to hit. On that Portal and I agreed."[34]

The entire military basis of the Truman Doctrine is in that one paragraph. The brasshats cannot conceive of a peaceful world. Arnold talked with Field Marshal Alexander (in 1952 still Minister of Defense under Churchill), who told him "the Russians were savages at heart." Field Marshal Montgomery added that he and Alexander "foresaw another war about twenty years hence."[35] Sir Alan Brooke and Admiral Cunningham agreed with him.

The political counterpart to the military picture of a world at war was the picture of a world dominated by the United States. At Potsdam, Byrnes, soon to be appointed Secretary of State, laid down the political line. Says Arnold:

"Jimmy Byrnes came out with something that struck me forcibly. He said what we must do now was not to make the world safe for democracy, but make the world safe for the United States."[36]

Byrnes is talking openly of U. S. world domination. The idea is not new with him. As far back as 1940, Virgil Jordan, President of the National Industrial Conference Board (an offshoot of the NAM), and a top spokesman for Wall Street, outlined the path of American imperialism. He said:

"Whatever the outcome of the war, America has embarked on a career of imperialism in world affairs and in every other aspect of her life. . . . At best, England will become a junior partner in a new Anglo-Saxon imperialism. . . . World events . . . have provided us not only with the occasion but with the economic tools, the social attitudes, and now the political manners and customs of modern imperialism. . . .

"Southward in our hemisphere and westward in the Pacific. the path of empire takes its way. . . ."[37]

Before Potsdam, one thing still restrained us from following the path of militaristic expansion, and that was the lack

34 Arnold, Global Mission, p. 586
35 Ibid., p. 588
36 Ibid., p. 589
37 Quoted in Perlo, American Imperialism, pp. 122-123

of overwhelming military power. The explosion at Alamagordo, New Mexico, made atomic power a reality. The Cold War makers saw an open road to world domination. As Admiral Leahy put it:

"One factor was to change a lot of ideas including my own. . . . The atom bomb." [38]

38 Leahy, I Was There, p. 429

ROOSEVELT THINKS IT GOOD IDEA TO LET NAZIS REPAIR SOVIET

March 3 1945

Says Ex-Troop~~~~~~ould Be Used,
Indicating ~~~~~~~
mise ~~~~

NOT D~~~~

Presid~~~~
Tr~~~~~
S~~~~

POTSDAM PROGRAM STILL UNREALIZED

feb. 18 1946

Centralized Rule of Germany, Other Goals Not Reached on Six-Month Schedule

By RAYMOND DANIELL
By Wireless t. The New York Times.

POTSDAM, Feb. 17—This was
~~ the month when the hig~~~~~

Soviet Plea for Billion Lost 6 Months; Parley Bid Sent

Mar. 2 1946

Shifting of Records Caused Misplacing of Request for Credit — Washington Warns Moscow Not to Loot Manchurian Factories

By HAROLD B. HINTON
Special to The New York Times.

WASHINGTON, March 1—The
Soviet Union has been invited to
enter into what was described as
"over all" negotiation for a credit
of $1,000,000,000, requested months
ago by Russian representatives in
this country, it was learned at the

lend-lease account, as well as possible future credits.

It was also learned today that
another communication, less cordial in nature, was sent to Moscow
about three weeks ago, warning
the Soviet authorities that the
~~~~tes Government would
~~~~~~position of Jap-

THE CRUCIAL
DOUBLE-CROSS

CHAPTER 11

"Mr. Byrnes speaks for a nation [the U.S.] which grew wealthy on the war to one which was fearfully devastated and impoverished. . . . Yet Mr. Byrnes can say that Soviet proposals for reparations . . . are 'inexcusable. . . .'"
Professor Frederick L. Schuman

"Soviet production of raw materials for export to the United States will adapt itself to what the United States requires."
Joseph Stalin to Eric Johnston, 1944

TRACING a reactionary foreign policy is an exercise in double-talk. Politicians who are deceiving the electorate don't talk about it, and when they do, they use euphemisms—flossy words to hide rotten meanings.

As every worker knows, when police beat up pickets they are "maintaining law and order," when bosses speed up the machines they are "increasing productivity," and layoffs are euphemistically known as "re-adjustment of inventories."

Likewise in foreign policy when Vandenberg wanted to repudiate the Yalta agreements he spoke of "overtaking Yalta," when Forrestal planned invasion of other countries he spoke of "applying force at a distance" and Truman says "police action" when he means war.

An interesting, and for this book, important euphemism is the difference between "loan" and "credit" in international relations. A "loan" is called a "credit" when the money is lent with such conditions as to constitute political domina-

245

tion. "Credit' sounds better than its true U. S. meaning: dollar imperialism. Ambassador Harriman, as a foremost banker, knew and stressed the difference in discussing post-war loans to the Soviet Union.

"Harriman suggested . . . an initial credit of five hundred million dollars and pointed out the need to distinguish between the Russian conception of 'loan,' which they could use as they saw fit, and 'credit,' use of which would be determined by the American government." [1]

This difference between a loan and dollar imperialism was an important item in the development of the Cold War. The Soviet Union wanted a loan, subject only to her paying it back. From a purely financial standpoint, the credit of the Soviet government was very high. It was Eric Johnston himself, then head of the U. S. Chamber of Commerce who recognized this in 1944, saying at a press conference:

"The credit of the Soviet Union is as good as any credits in the international field." [2]

Financial responsibility therefore was not the issue. Whether the Soviet Union would receive a post-war loan, as England did, was purely a political question closely connected with the question of German reparations. "Reparations" is a technical term for the payment of compensation for war damages. It is a stronger word than compensation for it has a moral implication of making amends, making good on a wrong. Given the damages done to the Soviet Union by the German armies, German reparations would have to be substantial to even begin "making amends." The U. S. attitude to reparations was a political question, just as the loans were, since both would affect the rate of Soviet reconstruction. Writes a student of the subject, Albert Z. Carr:

"It seems altogether probable that these two matters, an American credit and German reparations, were closely linked in Soviet politi-

1 Carr, Truman, Stalin and Peace, p. 25
2 Ibid., p. 23

cal thinking, for our attitude toward both questions **profoundly af-fected the rate of Russia's postwar recovery.**"[3] (emphasis added)

Carr is a man in a position to know the facts. He served as a special consultant to President Truman on these questions. Before that he had been assistant to Donald Nelson when Nelson was chairman of the War Production Board. Carr's book on Truman confirms this writer's opinion that the twin economic questions of loans and reparations are the keys to understanding how the Cold War was started. The reason is their importance to the USSR.

THE IMPORTANCE OF LOANS AND REPARATIONS

First and most obvious was the need of the Soviet Union to restore the incredible damage inflicted by the Nazis. Some twenty million people had been killed, a vast amount of land devastated, factories and machinery destroyed. Secretary of State Stettinius published figures estimating that 25 percent (one-quarter) of **all Soviet fixed capital**[4] had been destroyed —not counting livestock. Entire cities had been wiped out. The task of reconstruction was staggering.

Secondly, Soviet leaders were conscious that close economic relations with the United States would provide the basis for friendly political relations. During the war, military needs to defeat Hitler had provided the objective material basis for American-Soviet co-operation; after the war, trade could provide the objective material basis for friendship. Carr reports that:

"Stalin made no secret of his feeling that trade with the United States would provide a basis for political co-operation with the West."[5]

Stalin's view was shared by leading figures in the Roosevelt administration such as Nelson and Morgenthau. Secretary of the Treasury Morgenthau said it plainly in a letter

3 Ibid., p. 41
4 "Fixed capital" covers buildings, machines, installations of all kinds, railways, etc.
5 Carr, Truman, Stalin and Peace, p. 24

to Roosevelt on January 1, 1945. He wrote:

"I am convinced that if we were to come forward now and present to the Russians a concrete plan to aid them in the reconstruction period it would contribute a great deal towards ironing out many of the difficulties we have been having with respect to their problems and policies." [6]

Finally, economic aid would be a conclusive test of American intentions toward the Soviet Union. Both an American loan and German reparations would help to rehabilitate Russia rapidly, and of course, strengthen her. If we in America considered the USSR as an enemy we would not help her; conversely, if we helped her, it was proof positive that we did not expect military conflict.

There is a sharp difference between an American loan and German reparations. The Soviet Union had incontestable legal claims to payments by the Germans, and she had an army in Germany to enforce those claims. But the USSR had no legal claims to an American loan. She only had the same moral claims which England produced when she got her loan—the claims of a loyal ally, who had fought well and suffered greatly.

Therefore, an American loan would be a testimonial of American good-will and friendship. However, if we had refused the loan this would not necessarily indicate hostility provided we agreed to reparations. Soviet leaders were well aware that there was a constant tug of war in the U. S. between the friends and the enemies of American-Soviet cooperation. If a loan were refused, but reparations agreed to, it would indicate a cold but not necessarily hostile attitude. But if we blocked German reparations which were to make up in part for war damages in the USSR, this would indicate a calculated hostility.

This is particularly true because the smaller the reparations, the stronger Germany would be. For England and

6 Stettinius, Roosevelt and the Russians, p. 120

America to strengthen their bitter enemy, Germany, at the expense of the reconstruction of their loyal ally, Russia, within a couple of months of the end of the war, would be an unquestionable proof of hostile intentions. This was widely recognized by political observers and Carr poses the issue clearly:

"After World War I, fear of Soviet Russia had been a considerable factor in the decision of England and the United States to permit Germany to revive as a major power in Europe. Was this again to be the policy of the West? If so, **it would indicate an early resumption of political warfare against Russia.** The question of **German reparations** may well have been construed by Moscow **as a final test of fundamental attitudes** in Washington and London." 7 (emphasis added)

Let us take in turn the loan and reparations and see what happened.

THE BACKGROUND OF THE LOAN

As early as 1943, President Roosevelt sent Donald Nelson to Moscow on an exploratory mission concerning post-war problems. In pursuit of his policy of friendship, FDR had taken the initiative in seeing how America could help the Soviet Union with regard to loans. Donald Nelson, former head of Sears-Roebuck & Co., and at that time Chairman of the War Production Board, was himself in favor of closer economic co-operation with the USSR. When Nelson went to Moscow, Carr accompanied him.

On the way to Moscow they stopped in London and talked to the British Minister of Production, Oliver Lyttleton, as well as to Averell Harriman who had been head of the American Economic Mission in London and was just appointed Ambassador to Moscow. Lyttleton and Harriman were not enthusiastic about the idea of loans.

"As I listened," writes Carr, "I began to feel acute doubts about Nelson's chances of accomplishing anything useful in Moscow. Churchill, with his long political view—Lyttleton, a leader of Brit-

7 Carr, Truman, Stalin and Peace, p. 41

ish conservatism—Harriman, a friend of both Roosevelt and Churchill—all three were apparently expecting something less than harmony in the Allies' ranks after the war. Moreover, **these were all men of power, with the ability to translate ideas into policy.** I went away thoughtful from that meeting." [8] (emphasis added)

What Carr is saying is that these men who **in 1943** were expecting post-war friction were **also in a position to create it.** Nelson, however, went on to Moscow where he saw both Molotov and Stalin. Molotov and Nelson agreed on two basic points:

"1. It was in the mutual interest of Russia and America to work together in promoting sound industrial and commercial relations, so as to further their common objective of raising the living standards of their peoples and insuring a lasting peace.

"2. There seemed to be no economic reason why such an exchange should not take place, especially since no serious economic conflict existed between their two countries. The United States had a surplus of capital equipment, of manufacturing capacity, and of engineering and technical skills. Russia badly needed these same things, and had much to offer in the way of natural resources which the United States might advantageously use." [9]

Nelson then met with Stalin who indicated the large scale of purchases the USSR would make if American loans were forthcoming. [10] The meeting was extremely cordial. Stalin told Nelson:

"We like people from the United States. You come to us not as aristocrats but as businessmen. We like to do business with the United States better than with the British. We like American materials and American engineers. Everything you send us is of very good quality." [11]

Nelson asked to see the industrial development of Siberia and despite the rigorous wartime Soviet security, he was shown everything he wanted to see. According to Carr, he

8 Ibid., pp. 17-18
9 Ibid., p. 18
10 Stalin's list included: 250,000 to 300,000 kilowats of power (equipment), 10,000 locomotives, 50,000 freight cars, 30,000 kilometers of rails (about 20,000 miles)
11 Carr, Truman, Stalin and Peace, p. 20

saw more of Soviet industry than any American ever had. Nelson came back and informed Stalin the prospect for loans seemed good and Stalin told him, "We will guarantee our payments. Any obligations undertaken by this government will be repaid—and not by token payments." [12]

Shortly afterwards, Molotov spoke to Harriman about the long-term loan and Harriman cabled Washington that the USSR seemed "anxious to come to a prompt understanding" on the matter.

The groundwork established by Nelson was furthered in the summer of 1944 by a visit to Moscow by Eric Johnston, then president of the U. S. Chamber of Commerce. Johnston and Stalin went over the same ground as Nelson had. The Soviet Union offered raw materials in repayment. Said Stalin:

"Soviet production of raw materials for export to the United States will adapt itself to what the United States requires. We can furnish any quantity you wish, if we can get equipment to produce it." [13]

In January 1945 Molotov again mentioned the loan, this time to Stettinius and shortly after formally applied for a loan to the State Department. The request was for one billion dollars: the English, when they applied, asked for five billions of which they got nearly four in 1947.

THE LOAN AS AN INSTRUMENT OF POWER

The Soviet Union never got the loan.

As already mentioned, as early as 1944 Ambassador Harriman was stressing that America should give "credits," not loans. He again took this position on April 11, 1945. Using money as a lever to get political concessions worked on England and on other countries under the Marshall Plan. But it didn't work on the Soviet Union. Since the USSR has always insisted on non-interference in her internal affairs, Harriman's position was almost certain to insure rejection.

12 Ibid., p. 19
13 Ibid., p. 23

Influential Americans actually thought that Russia might be forced to knuckle under to American power because of Soviet economic weakness. Said Forrestal:

"The President mentioned the reports in the morning's newspapers of the deficiencies in the grain crop in Russia, the Ukraine, and that there were rumors of unrest within Russia because of short rations. He said . . . that it must have become clear to them (the Russians) by now that they, as well as others, would have to look to the United States as the sole source of relief on the question of food." [13a] (emphasis added)

Bread is a weapon, as Litvinov once told Herbert Hoover, and Truman here shows how it is used. But as so often in the past, American officials underestimated Soviet strength. Carr confirms this, writing:

". . . some high members of the Department of State and the armed services appeared to overestimate Russia's dependence on the United States for aid in postwar recovery. They seemed to believe that Russia could not survive economically without our aid. The actual position was that while the Soviets urgently wanted and needed American goods . . . this consideration . . . was not so important as to compel them to pay any political price we might ask." [14] (emphasis added)

Stalin had already hinted to Johnston that pressure wouldn't work when he said referring to the loans:

"We can get along without them, but it will be slower."

When it became obvious that the U. S. couldn't use dollars to apply pressure to the Soviet Union in the tradition of "dollar imperialism," the United States dropped the whole idea. The Soviet Union never got the loan; as a matter of fact, the State Department never even acknowledged the request. Many months after Potsdam, when the Cold War was in full swing, the State Department declared that the loan application had been "lost" in its file for six months. [15] The "explanation" was hardly credible, and in fact was more in-

13a Forrestal Diaries, p. 234
14 Carr, Truman, Stalin and Peace, pp. 25-26
15 N. Y. Times, March 2, 1946

sulting than the refusal to grant the loan.

THE QUESTION OF REPARATIONS

Reparations were vastly different from loans. The Germans were responsible for the war, and the Red Army was there to see that Germany paid.

The damage inflicted by Germany on the Soviet Union was so vast as to defy any simple description. Said Winston Churchill, "No government ever formed among men has been capable of surviving injury so grave and cruel as that inflicted by Hitler on Russia." Churchill is quoted by the American writer Edgar Snow, who adds, "Churchill was at least aware that the whole blitz over Britain was a siege of bad weather compared to Russia's ordeal. **All Britain's** civilian and military dead were fewer than the people killed in **one Russian city.**" [15a] Snow goes on to write eloquenty on Soviet losses:

"At costs which Americans have never more than dimly conceived, and have too conveniently obscured, the Russian people, not the atom bomb, cracked the heart of the Wehrmacht before we landed in Europe. More Russians were killed in the Stalingrad campaign alone . . . than all Americans buried by the war. . . . Two dozen Russian soldiers died for every American sacrificed. . . . "More than 800,000 square miles were occupied by the Germans . . . (the area) held one-third of Russia's population and its devastation meant the loss of half the Soviet coal mines, half the electric power, three-fifths of the iron mines and about half the steel and machinery industry. What the Russians liberated was for the most part a desert of worthless rubble, with its great cities from 30% to 90% destroyed. . . . "Shall we speak seriously of reparations as compensation for Russia's experience? Who can revive her dead? Material damages are estimated at 200 billion dollars, but it was more than money that went up in smoke. Suppose you had a house (four million **privately owned** dwellings were destroyed in Russia) and now you live in a hole in the earth. What damages do you claim when your child dies of pneumonia? Suppose you had a pair of boots stolen by Fritz and now you must wear straw wrapped around your feet. Is it only the price of the boots you lost?" [15b] (emphasis in the original)

Reparations were basic to Soviet plans for reconstruction.

15a Edgar Snow, Stalin Must Have Peace, New York, 1947, p. 63-64
15b Ibid., pp. 64-67

As American loans became more doubtful, German reparations assumed a greater importance to the restoration of Soviet devastated areas. By the time of the Yalta Conference in February 1945, the question of reparations was paramount in Soviet thinking. Says Byrnes flatly:

"During all the considerations of the German question at Yalta, reparations were the chief interest of the Soviet delegation." [16]

Carr makes the same point, more sharply:

"The records of Yalta show that Stalin at first yielded ground on political points. He accepted the American proposal on liberated areas. With reluctance, he agreed to let France control a 'zone of Germany. But when it came to reparations, he stood fast." [17]

The Soviet Union proposed that the allies should receive 20 billion dollars of reparations from Germany of which the USSR would receive half. In view of the destruction Germany had caused in the Soviet Union, 10 billion dollars was not an excessive amount. The Soviet proposal was that half of the reparations should be taken immediately from capital equipment and the rest, 10 billions, in yearly payments of one billion dollars. The amount could well be paid by the Germans, yet Byrnes called the proposals "inexcusable." Albert Z. Carr exposes Byrnes when he writes:

". . . the Russians guessed shrewdly the immense quantity of working industrial plants which would remain in Germany after the war, in spite of all the bombings, and the rapidity with which German recovery would take place." [18]

In spite of the clear justice of Soviet claims, Churchill fought against the proposal at Yalta. Roosevelt finally effected a compromise by saying that the 20 billions would be taken as a "basis for discussion." At Potsdam complete agreement was reached on the amounts and timing of the reparations. Specific quotas were set, and specific delivery dates. The relevant sections of the Potsdam agreement are as follows:

16 Byrnes, Speaking Frankly, p. 26
17 Carr, Truman, Stalin and Peace, p. 40
18 Ibid., p. 39

"Part IV, Reparations from Germany

"4—In addition to the reparations to be taken by the USSR from its own zone of occupation, the USSR shall receive additionally from the western zones:

"A—15% of such usable and complete industrial capital equipment . . . as is unnecessary for the German peace economy . . . in exchange for an equivalent value of food, coal . . . and such other commodities. . . .

"B—10% of such industrial capital equipment . . . to be transferred to the Soviet Government on reparation account without any payment or exchange of any kind in return.

"5—The amount of equipment to be removed from the Western Zones on account of reparations must be determined **within six months from now at the latest.**

"6—Removals of industrial equipment shall begin as soon as possible and be completed within two years. . . .

"7—Prior to fixing of the total amount of equipment subject to removal, **advance deliveries shall be made. . . ."** [19] (emphasis added)

This agreement is clear and unequivocal. The agreement was dated August 1, 1945. The whole program was to be settled by February 2, 1946 and advance deliveries were to begin before the February deadline. The decision was backed by the signatures of the Chiefs of State—Truman, Attlee, Stalin.

The agreement on reparations at Potsdam indicated to Soviet leaders that the United States was not anticipating an American-Soviet conflict and that the United States would not rebuild German might. Says Richard Sasuly, a student of the problem:

"The Potsdam approach to reparations was based on actual conditions as they existed at the end of the war. For this very reason it became the center of international political conflict. As the most war-damaged nation, the Soviet Union would receive the lion's share of German industrial equipment. The more you took from Germany, the more you gave to Russia; conversely, the less you bothered the Germans and the more war potential you left them,

---

19 Sasuly, I. G. Farben, p. 269. This excellent book is a case history of the formidable German chemical trust and its role in supporting Hitler and causing World War II. Sasuly was chief of financial intelligence in the Finance Division of the German Military Goverment

the less you helped to rebuild Russian industry." [20]

Besides Russia, all the other European nations would gain by Potsdam. As Sasuly points out:

"The reparations system drawn up at Potsdam made sense. By concentrating on the transfer of machinery instead of payments in cash or goods, the Potsdam system would simply shift the balance of industrial power from the world center of fascism to the countries which suffered the most from German aggression." [21]

Adds Sasuly pointedly:

"That is, the Potsdam system would do this—if applied."

ENTER THE ATOM BOMB

Into the complicated political and economic relationships existing at the war's end, was brought the sinister influence of the atom bomb. As we have already seen, the bomb was immediately conceived as an anti-Soviet instrument. Truman, Leahy, Byrnes, have already been quoted to this effect and Stimson vainly warned against this approach.

The political impact of the bomb was made clear within three weeks of the signing of the Potsdam agreement, within two weeks of the Hiroshima explosion and within a week of Japan's surrender. On August 18, 1945, Byrnes issued a statement attacking the Bulgarian elections and serving notice to the Soviet Union that all agreements were off. Writes Professor Schuman:

"The tragic impasse in American-Soviet relations had its chief original source in Byrnes' statement of August 18, 1945, seconded by Bevin's speech of August 20, wherein Washington and London, in the name of 'democracy' opened the diplomatic and propaganda campaign, which has continued ever since, to oust Soviet influence from Eastern Europe and the Balkans." [22]

Throughout the remaining months of 1945, and then on through 1946 Secretary of State Byrnes pushed his "atomic diplomacy." Our ambassadors in Poland, Rumania, Hungary strove openly to undermine the existing governments in the

20 Ibid., p. 219
21 Ibid., p. 223
22 Schuman, The Devil and Jimmy Byrnes, p. 7

most provocative manner possible, while Byrnes declared hypocritically that "America will never join any groups in those countries in hostile intrigues against the Soviet Union. . . ." [23]

Atomic diplomacy had its counterpart in dollar diplomacies. Britain and the United States cynically scrapped the reparations agreement signed at Potsdam by Attlee and Truman.

THE CRUCIAL DOUBLECROSS

The Potsdam agreement had a certain date written into it. Under Section 4, Part IV, a stated amount of equipment was to go from the Western Zone to the Soviet Union. Section 5 stipulated that this amount would be determined "within six months from now, at the latest," that is to say by February 2, 1946. Section 6 stated that all this equipment would be removed within two years. Section 7 said advance deliveries would be made before the lists were drawn up, that is before February 2, 1946.

These agreements were never challenged. There was no question of "misinterpretation." February 2, 1946, was a specific and agreed upon deadline. Plants were to be moved before that date; all reparations plants were to be listed by that date.

What happened is a matter of record:

"The Potsdam agreement," writes Sasuly, who was there, "was signed early in August. Later in August the Russians put in a request for forty-one plants in advance delivery."

This action was in accord with the agreement. Continues Sasuly:

"When the Foreign Ministers of the Big Three met in Moscow in September, nothing had been moved. The Soviet Union pointed to the advance delivery clause and asked for an immediate beginning of reparations. In October the Economics Directorate of the Allied Control Council agreed that thirty plants should be shipped at

23 N.Y. Herald Tribune Forum, October 31, 1945

once." [24] (emphasis added)

It looked as if the logjam had been broken. But now a most curious set of events took place. The French refused to be bound by the Potsdam decisions on the ground that they weren't represented.

Writes General Clay, the American Head of German Military Government:

"French unwillingness to abide by the Potsdam decisions was the major cause for dissent within the Control Council. . . ." [25]

As a result of the French veto, no four power control could be centralized and no over-all economic planning was set up. Byrnes later justified our breaking our word on shipping plants on the grounds that there was no over-all economic agreement. [26] In other words, plants weren't shipped because the French were blocking over-all control.

The Soviets remonstrated to Clay, saying that French obstructionism could easily be handled by the United States, since "France was receiving too much financial assistance from the United States to maintain such strong opposition without our acquiescence," but Clay answered that "our aid was not extended for such purposes." [27]

The protestation that the United States would not apply financial pressure is completely hypocritical. Byrnes applied pressure all the time. A classic and petty case took place at the Paris Conference. There, when Czech delegates applauded Vyshinsky's criticism of "dollar diplomacy," Byrnes boasts that he "immediately cabled instructions to the State Department to stop the extension of credits to Czechoslovakia." [28]

The French continued their obstruction unhindered by the United States, and by a strange coincidence, they did so

24 Sasuly, I. G. Farben, p. 217
25 Lucius D. Clay, Decision in Germany, New York, 1950, p. x, Introduction
26 Byrnes, Speaking Frankly, p. 167
27 Clay, Decision in Germany, pp. 39-40
28 Byrnes, Speaking Frankly, p. 143

for the six months up to the deadline of February 2, 1946. It's Clay who lets this tidbit slip out:

"Perhaps," he writes, "without the French veto we could have created central administrative agencies for Germany as a whole within the first six months. . . ."[29] (emphasis added)

Obviously, with French obstruction, no over-all figures could be obtained and no lists of plants could be prepared by February 2, 1946. French obstruction in those six months could not have taken place without the tacit approval, if not the active connivance of the United States authorities. But not only was the list not ready, no deliveries were made.

Sasuly gives the picture in two swift paragraphs:

"The Foreign Ministers met again in December, in London. Again nothing had been moved. Again the Russians asked for an immediate start. Again there was agreement. And again nothing happened.

"The February 2, 1946 deadline came and passed."[30]

A most solemn and vital agreement had been wantonly broken by the West. To the Soviets, it was a clear indication that the United States had joined England in an openly hostile operation.

Within a week, February 9, 1946, Stalin made a speech of major importance. It was a review of World War II as a grim test of the Soviet political and economic system. The war, Stalin said, showed that the Soviet state and socialism was here to stay. In view of the nature of the postwar world, however, it was not completely safe from attack. It was necessary to set certain goals over the next fifteen years, including trebling the output of coal, iron and steel and nearly doubling the output of oil. This was the only way, said Stalin, "to guarantee our country against any eventuality."

Forrestal called this speech "the Declaration of World War III."

29 Clay, Decision in Germany, ,p. 42
30 Sasuly, I. G. Farben, p. 217

Only in Forrestal's fevered mind could Stalin's warning **against** war be considered a declaration **for** war. What the speech meant was that the USSR would not quietly submit to a U. S. world domination. It was a warning to the West not to underestimate Soviet strength, just as in March, 1939, Stalin, in a similar speech, had warned Chamberlain and Hitler not to underestimate Soviet strength. [31]

COLD WAR: SHAMEFUL AND DANGEROUS

The breaking of the Potsdam agreement on reparations without provocation or excuse makes the Truman Administration seem as dishonest in world affairs as many of its corrupt officials have been dishonest in domestic affairs. The petty justification of Byrnes, hiding behind the French, is itself disingenuous. In regard to advance deliveries, the Potsdam agreement **specifically** exempted that equipment from the overall economic planning of Germany.

We broke our pledged word, and thereby strengthened our enemy, Germany. The road of German re-armament began by breaking the Potsdam agreement on reparations. In 1952 we can see how dangerous that road is.

But this breach of faith is particularly repugnant because in the words of Professor Schuman, it dismissed "the ghastly cost of the war to the Soviet Union." Adds Schuman:

"Mr. Byrnes speaks for a nation which grew wealthy on the war to one which was fearfully devastated and impoverished and gave thirty lives for every American life sacrificed to defeat the foe. Yet Mr. Byrnes can say that Soviet proposals for reparations from current German production are 'inexcusable' and that 'we should realize that, modern war being what it is, it is short sighted and futile for any country to seek approximate compensation for losses it has sustained." [32]

The United States increased its industrial capacity by over 50%. We can be proud of our great productive capacity, but not smug. The fact that we were fortunate enough not to

---

31 Stalin's March, 1939 speech is quoted in this book, Chapter 8. It is worth going back and re-reading it
32 Schuman, Devil and Jimmy Byrnes, p. 6

suffer devastation during the war should teach us a little restraint. Instead, Byrnes lectures countries like the Soviet Union on matters of war damages in the most arrogant manner.

Byrnes' entire book is permeated with an attitude of ruthlessness, of American supremacy toward the world which has since become a trademark of the Cold War and of American imperialism. Sumner Welles noted its appearance in American foreign policy, saying:

"It was only after Mr. Byrnes was appointed Secretary of State that 'telling' our American neighbors [what to do] became a feature of our policy." [33]

The result of this arrogance is that nation after nation has turned against the U. S. including the friends bought by American dollars. Writes Stewart Alsop, himself a staunch supporter of the Cold War:

"For the first time this country faces the prospect, in case of general war, of almost the whole world outside the Western Hemisphere, either actively united against us, or, like England, neutralized and rendered powerless to help." [33]

33 Ibid., p. 9
34 N. Y. Herald Tribune, August 18, 1950

TRUMAN CLEARLY STATES HIS 'MUSCULAR FORMULA'

He Will Continue to Seek Agreements With Russia, but on the Basis of Force to See They Are Kept

DEPARTURES FROM THE POLICY

By ARTHUR KROCK

WASHINGTON, Sept. 22—A routine question addressed to the President at this week's press conference drew from him 'he clearest and most concl...
ter foreign policy...
Thus again...
this country...
in the Legisla...

It is an...
tem, because...
his questione...
press confere...
are verbal...
ment which...
pers lack.

The master...
President desc...
formula" for b...
peace, with the...
ance, through a...
viet Russia which...
find't necessary...
ous to break...

ISRAEL AND THE U.S.

The Forrestal Error

By TED O. THACKREY
Editor and Publisher

Probably no single man exerted more influence on United States policy toward Israel, particularly in the days immediately before and immediate after her declaration of independence, than James Forrestal, as Secretary of the Navy and later Secretary of Defense. The influence was against Israel, and in favor of the Arab states.

To a marked degree United States policy toward Israel, though slightly softened in the intervening months, has continued to be based...
which guided Forre...

The matter mi...
as the tragic erro...
his life in a fre...
publication of a s...
Tribune on Wedn...

There is a curi...
notes accompan...
calculated to def...
to present it as...
have taken; an...
light of the fac...
are continuing...
name of our s...
Middle East's o...

"Futile Attem...
Retain Arab Fr...
the Herald Trib...
last Wednesday. An...
tal's activity "sprea...
Strategic...

U.S. Air Bases in Britain Growing; Improvements Indicate Long Use

Scarred Earth at Operational Fields Shows Building Is Going Ahead—'We Will Never Be Finished,' Is Comment of Officer

By CLIFTON DANIEL
Special to The New York Times

LONDON, July 13—The United States Air Force is here to stay—for a while anyway. That is the distinct impression one gets from a tour of the United States Air Force bases in the United Kingdom.

A force that first appeared here in 1948, ostensibly for training but actually to make a show of strength during the Berlin air lift, has become a permanent—or semi-permanent in the component in the western...

make preliminary preparations for a depot at Burtonwood to serve the Superfortress bombers that were being sent here for training.

That group of thirty men asked for 45,000 square feet of storage space at Burtonwood, which once had been a United States aircraft maintenance base with 16,000 employes, but since the war had fallen into disuse.

Today Burtonwood, whose vast repair shops resemble a great factory, is bustling again. The size of General Oliver's command, is a... Depot Wing, is a...

Keel Laid to Mighty Carrier Forrestal

NEWPORTS NEWS, Va., July 14 (P).—Giant cranes laid the keel plate today for the world's mightiest warship, a vessel to bring true the Navy's dream of in their innermost lairs can they escape the devastating power of this mighty weapon," he said.

Among 300 diknitaries present was John L. Sullivan Navy Secretary...

TRUMAN DOCTRINE — BY FORRESTAL

CHAPTER 12

"It was clear from this time on, he [For-restal] felt increasingly that policy could not be founded on the assumption that a peaceful solution of the Russian problem was possible."
The Forrestal Diaries, February, 1946

"The very persons who had been so con-genitally blind to the threat to us of Nazi Germany, were so quick to sense what they now were sure was a threat to our national interests from Soviet Russia."
William L. Shirer, April, 1946

WHEN Churchill at Fulton, Mo. for-mally launched the Cold War with his speech of March 5, 1946, American reactionaries were pleased. The speech was a good start in the development of a "war psychosis" in America. But behind the scenes, the British Foreign Office was planning something more concrete than speeches.

The British Foreign Office was headed at this time by Ernest Bevin, a right-wing trade unionist who faithfully fol-lowed the Conservative Party's policy. As CBS correspondent Howard K. Smith wrote, Bevin "dropped nothing of the pro-gram of his Tory predecessors but the aitches." In truth, Bevin was even more anti-Soviet than Churchill had dared to be. Churchill himself told Forrestal:

"He [Churchill] said there was considerable consolation in the victory of Bevin because Bevin was able to talk more firmly and clearly to Russia than he could have, by virtue of being a Labour government." [1]

That's pretty clear speaking. As a labor leader Bevin could more easily deceive the British workers into support of a Churchillian foreign policy.

One of the main problems facing the British Foreign Office was their intervention in Greece which cost them 250 million dollars a year. For three years the Greek resistance forces had been fighting British troops who had put a reactionary King back in the saddle.

The British had started shooting in 1944, to Roosevelt's complete disgust. Stettinius issued a statement deploring British action. Even conservative State Department officials on the spot in Athens were revolted. The writer was in London at the time as an intelligence official and the dispatches from the American representatives in Greece showed clearly that the British action represented imperialism at its worst. The day that the British troops opened fire on an unarmed demonstration, the American consular official **lowered the American flag to disassociate ourselves from British policy,** an action never made public.

The sordid story of Greek oppression by Britain has been fully told. An excellent summary is in a chapter of Howard K. Smith's book, **The State of Europe;** a longer, more detailed treatment is in Leland Stowe's **While Time Remains.** Both of these foreign correspondents strongly condemn British policy.

After Fulton, Mo., as the Cold War gathered momentum, the British sought for an opportunity to drop this situation in the lap of the U. S. In February 1947, the British told the State Department they couldn't afford to support their troops in Greece and what would the U. S. do about it? If the U. S.

1 Forrestal Diaries, p. 144

did nothing, said the British smugly, Communism would triumph in Greece.

Even General Marshall, then Secretary of State, was annoyed at this polite blackmail using the threat of Communism as a lever. He is quoted in **The Forrestal Diaries** as being angry at British "abdication" with the "obvious implications as to their successor." [2] Later, Marshall "wired Bevin in strong language, protesting against British action" in the way they told the U. S. "we would have to accept the responsibility for Greece." [3] Marshall, it should be noted, was protesting not the fact that the British were killing Greeks, but the manner in which they exploited American commitments to the Cold War, and assumed the U. S. would take over in Greece. The British assumed rightly: the U. S. went into the Near East and armed Greece and Turkey.

The announcement of the Greek-Turkish program was made by President Truman on March 12, 1947, in a speech that attacked the Soviet Union and served notice that we would fight them whenever possible. The declaration has become known as the Truman Doctrine which remains so far the clearest expression of the Cold War.

The Truman Doctrine was called the "Muscular Formula" by Arthur Krock, **N. Y. Times**. In England, a world-famous historian sees it as a doctrine of U. S. world domination "by the main force of a 'knock-out blow,' " saying:

". . . the President's move might turn out—however far this may have been from his intention—to have given the whole course of international affairs an impulsion away from the new co-operative method of trying to achieve political world amity, and towards the old-fashioned method of fighting out to the last round in the struggle of power politics and arriving at the political unification of the world by the main force of a 'knockout blow.' "[4]

This is a long, involved sentence, but the meaning is there:

2 Forrestal Diaries, p. 245
3 Ibid., p. 105
4 Arnold J. Toynbee, Civilization On Trial, New York, 1948, p. 137

the U. S. will unify the world by force. The verbose writer is Arnold J. Toynbee, the leading British historian, who can write briefly and to the point when he wants to. When Toynbee was in America and heard the talk of using England as an "unsinkable aircraft carrier" against the Soviet Union he coined a slogan that exposes the Cold War. Toynbee said that slogan for England should be:

NO ANNIHILATION WITHOUT REPRESENTATION.

The true meaning of the "muscular" Truman Doctrine is aggressive war. Its propagandist was Churchill, but the man who organized it, developed it and pushed it was James V. Forrestal, Secretary of Defense in the Truman Cabinet.

FORRESTAL AND THE TRUMAN DOCTRINE

The Truman Doctrine rested squarely on a series of actions which Forrestal had undertaken, starting the same week as Churchill's Fulton speech. Behind the "tough" words were the "tough" deeds. On February 28, 1946 (the Fulton speech was March 5), Forrestal approached Secretary of State Byrnes on the overt use of American military power in peacetime foreign affairs. Says a diary entry:

"I asked Byrnes if he was agreeable to the Navy preparing plans for a task force in the Mediterranean. He said to go ahead, with the suggestion it might accompany the battleship **Missouri,** which will take home the body of the Turkish Ambassador [who died at his post in Washington]. . . ."[5]

Byrnes here shrewdly points out how to hoodwink the American public so that it wouldn't know what was going on. A Navy Mediterranean Task Force was sent to Europe, and says Millis, "was to appear as a suddenly important prop" of the Truman Doctrine within a year.[6]

A few months later, September 12, 1946, when Henry Wallace as Secretary of Commerce urged a halt to the Cold War, Forrestal was instrumental (with Byrnes) in getting

5 Forrestal Diaries, p. 141
6 Ibid., p. 141

Truman to disavow Wallace and expel him from the Cabinet. [7] According to Millis, the result of this expulsion was "to firm and strengthen the Truman administration's foreign policy" and Forrestal immediately took two steps that led to the Truman Doctrine. Continues Millis, the editor of the Forrestal diaries:

"At a State-War-Navy meeting on September 25 ... Forrestal urged ... [to] make possible military aid to Turkey. **Here was the concept of** giving political precision to our use of our economic and military resources; a concept that first took important shape **in the 'Truman Doctrine'** of Greek-Turkish aid. ..." [8] (emphasis added)

After the concept, the action. Five days later (September 30, 1946) Forrestal took the second step by making public the U. S. Navy's policy. Says Millis:

"Forrestal was at last able to announce the consummation of an effort on which he had long been working—the re-establishment, as a permanent policy, of American naval power in the Mediterranean.
"[This] was widely received as a decisive new development of American policy." [9]

Small wonder that when the Truman Doctrine was announced, months later, Millis gives Forrestal full credit, saying that:

"... the new course ran closely parallel to the moral, strategic and tactical ideas which Forrestal had long been developing." [10]

Who was this man Forrestal whose influence on American foreign policy was so great? How did he get into a position of power?

FORRESTAL AS A SYMBOL

James V. Forrestal was a banker, president of the powerful Wall Street firm of Dillon, Reed and Co. This firm of investment bankers has a long history of reactionary inter-

7 Ibid., p. 210
8 Ibid., p 210
9 Ibid., pp. 210-211
10 Ibid., p. 253

national operations such as floating loans for German cartelists.

Forrestal was made Undersecretary of the Navy by Roosevelt, a symbol of the price Roosevelt paid for the wartime co-operation of Big Business. Forrestal was brought into the government as a watchdog of monopoly interests. The editor of the diaries, Walter Millis, makes this point very clearly saying that the 1940 re-armament program "could not succeed without the **whole-hearted co-operation of the large industrial and financial interests** with which the New Deal had so often been in conflict." [11] (emphasis added) and Roosevelt therefore needed someone who "could find the capable men who could be enlisted from the top ranks of industry, finance and the law," [12] that is, someone whom Big Business could trust.

James V. Forrestal was perfect for the job. He had wealth, power, position and the unquestioned confidence of the financial and industrial rulers of America. The same characteristics that made him useful to Roosevelt in wartime, made him the natural leader of postwar reaction. In Truman's Cabinet he rose from Secretary of the Navy to the first Secretary of Defense after the unification of the armed forces. He was here in a position of power next only to the President himself, and he used this position to the utmost.

Forrestal was the representative of Big Business in the government. He was the most powerful influence in postwar American foreign policy—class-conscious, hard-bitten, hard-driving organizer of reaction.

And reaction at the end of the war needed help all over the world.

REACTION IN TROUBLE
The unfolding of World War II brought shivers to reac-

11 Ibid., p. xxi
12 Ibid., p. xxiii

tionaries throughout the world. Stalin's pre-war warnings in 1934 were coming true: in case of war "many kings and heads of state would be missing" afterwards.

From Berlin to Manila, kings, quislings, dictators, armament makers and lesser fry were dead, dying or in exile. Mussolini hung by his heels in a Milan square, Hitler committed suicide in a Berlin bunker, Tojo was destined to hang. The King of Italy was on his way out, the King of Belgium never got back, nor did the King of Yugoslavia, and the King of Rumania was there only on sufferance. In France, Laval would be shot, Petain imprisoned.

The ruling classes in nearly every country were on the defensive. Even England, at its first opportunity threw out Churchill for a Labor government. In country after country Communist parties were in power or in coalition governments. France had a Communist Minister of Air, Italy a Communist Deputy Prime Minister.

The Soviet Union had come out of the war with tremendous prestige. All over the world the people had watched her epic fight, her endurance, her tenaciousness and courage with great admiration. MacArthur's phrases, usually so exaggerated, for once seemed appropriate. Said General Douglas MacArthur on February 23, 1942:

"The hopes of civilization rest on the worthy banners of the courageous Red Army. During my lifetime I have participated in a number of wars and have witnessed others, as well as studying in great detail the campaigns of outstanding leaders of the past. In none have I observed such effective resistance to the heaviest blows of a **hitherto undefeated enemy**, followed by a smashing counter-attack which is driving the enemy back to his own land. The scale and grandeur of the effort mark it as the greatest military achievement in all history." [13] (emphasis added)

The quality of the Red Army and its leadership was apparent even to reactionaries. U. S. Air Force General Chen-

13 Quoted in Schuman, Soviet Politics, p. 432

nault, friend of the vicious Chiang Kai-shek, has written in warnings to his fellow generals:

"Russian leadership was pared down to the hard, competent core that engineered Soviet survival. It is leadership of the very best. . . ."[14]

The leadership in the Soviet government impressed its most bitter enemies. Senator Vandenberg writes that Foreign Minister Molotov "is an earnest, able man for whom I have come to have profound respect"[15] and John Foster Dulles says that he has "seen in action all the great international statesmen of this country," but he has never seen "diplomatic skill at so high a degree of perfection as Mr. Molotov's."[16]

On Stalin there are dozens of tributes from friend and enemy alike. Roosevelt "liked him very much"[17] and Byrnes had to admit, "The truth is, he is a very likeable man."[18] Even Churchill paid grudging tribute, "Stalin has a very captivating personality."[19] Hopkins gave an incisive candid portrait of Stalin:

". . . he never wastes a syllable. If he wants to soften an abrupt answer or a sudden question he does it with that quick, managed smile—a smile that can be cold but friendly, austere but warm. He curries no favor with you. . . .
". . . there is no small talk in him. His humor is keen, penetrating. He speaks no English, but as he shot rapid Russian at me he ignored the interpreter, looking straight into my eyes. . . ."[20]

More important than Stalin's personality was Western judgment of his ability. General Deane who was strongly anti-Soviet nevertheless as a military man was professionally impressed. He says that Stalin "has a keen intellect" immediately understanding the "characteristics and use of

14 Chennault, Way of a Fighter, p. viii
15 Vandenberg, Private Papers, p. 184
16 Dulles, War or Peace, p. 29
17 Elliott Roosevelt, As He Saw It, p. 176
18 Byrnes, Speaking Frankly, p. 45
19 Churchill, Closing the Ring, p. 374
20 Sherwood, Roosevelt and Hopkins, p. 344

weapons" with a "quick grasp of the essential elements of any situation." Above all, Stalin was constantly applying "historical lessons to present events." [21] In similar terms Churchill speaks of Stalin's analysis of the North African invasion.

"I was deeply impressed with this (Stalin's) remarkable statement. It showed . . . (his) swift and complete mastery of a problem hitherto novel to him. Very few people alive could have comprehended **in so few minutes** the reasons which we had all so busily been wrestling with for months. He saw it all in a flash." [22] (emphasis added)

But the finest tribute came from the old-fashioned Tennessean, Cordell Hull. In a speech to Congress Hull said flatly:

"I found in Marshal Stalin a remarkable personality, one of the greatest statesmen and leaders of this age." [23]

The quality of Soviet leadership haunts uneasily the war dreams of reaction. But even more important, the victories of the Red Army revealed its strong industrial base. Lesser men might swallow the propaganda of the daily press about Soviet industrial incompetence, but top government and business people both in England and America knew full well what it took industrially and economically for the Soviet Union to beat the Nazi war machine. Says Stimson's biographer:

"The colossal achievements of the Soviet armies and the skill and energy of the Russian leaders were **perfectly apparent** to Stimson and Marshall. . . ." [24] (emphasis added)

Soviet development was indeed titanic. It has been well

21 Deane, Strange Alliance, p. 291
22 Churchill, Hinge of Fate, p. 482
23 Hull, Memoirs, p. 1315. Soviet leaders are modest, conscientious men of great ability and common sense as these statements show. Yet the American people have a directly contrary picture of Soviet leadership. The daily press compares these men to the insane, paranoiac Hitler, the dope-fiend Goering, the twisted Goebbels. Nowhere is the shameless distortion of the American press more sharply evidenced.
24 Stimson and Bundy, On Active Service, p. 605

summarized by Howard K. Smith: [25]

"To realize the dimensions of the achievement, it should be remembered that when seven years of war and revolution [1914-1921] were over, capital and machinery in Russia were on a par with the African Congo. **Steel production stood at three percent of the very low 1913 level.** When man declared armistice, God declared war: in 1921 there came a drought, the worst of the century. Two million people died and nineteen millions were in the last stages of starvation. There was cannibalism on the Volga.

"The Communists let things drift, and production found its 1913 level only in 1828. Then they began their plans for industrialization. In other words, they had not twenty-three but **only twelve years to prepare** for World War II. The measure of their success is in these comparative indices of industrial production for 1940, with the level of 1913 as index 100 in all cases:

France	93.2
United Kingdom	113.3
U. S. A.	120.0
Germany	131.6
U. S. S. R.	908.6

One item alone tells the story. Steel production is the heart of war production. In 1921 the newly born Soviet Union produced only one eighth (⅛) million tons of steel a year. By 1928 at the beginning of the First Five Year Plan, the figure was back to the pre-war level of four million tons a year. By 1940 in the middle of the Third Five Year Plan, the figure was 18 million tons, 1500 percent above 1921! When it is considered that for **ammunition alone** 2½ million tons of iron and steel were used in 1943, it is obvious that the power of the Red Army rested squarely on the success of the Soviet Five Year Plans.

The Soviet Union as a nation was certainly formidable enough, but what terrified reactionaries was the effect of its example. The success of socialism in the USSR stirred the imagination and inspired Socialists and Communists all over the world. In many countries today conditions are such that

25 Smith, State of Europe, p. 46

socialism is a real and pressing alternative to existing systems. Reactionaries try to say that socialism is imported from Moscow, but they don't really believe it.

When a strike takes place, the boss always says that his workers were worked up by an "out of town" influence; when the people of China win their revolution, reactionaries insist that it was imported from Moscow. It never seems possible to them that people can act for and by themselves whether in Malaya or Indo-China, the Philippines or South Africa, France or the United States.

Shrewd reactionaries know that domestic conditions make for socialism, and they know what the conditions are. That is why in the face of the postwar trend to socialism, they shuddered in fright. Wrote Senator Vandenberg in a letter to a friend:

"Weren't you stunned by Churchill's defeat? . . . I guess the whole world is on the leftward march. I want no part of it. Yet Americans can't surrender. So what? Ugh!" [26] (the emphasis is by the Senator)

To restore the pre-war system and put together reaction's Humpty Dumpty was a gigantic task. Vandenberg hated the idea of the job involved. But Forrestal was more self-confident. He thought the job could be done if big business was properly mobilized. Forrestal saw himself as the organizer of reaction, restoring the status quo ante. This was an impossible task and Forrestal broke himself trying to do it.

THE ORGANIZER OF REACTION

Forrestal had pretentions to historical erudition. He saw himself in a historical perspective and a curious episode in his diaries is extremely revealing. Forrestal was having dinner with Admiral Leahy and British Foreign Minister Eden. The conversation waxed historical. Forrestal spoke:

"I said I had come of late years to have a much clearer apprecia-

26 Vandenberg, Private Papers, p. 219

tion of what Metternich had been able to accomplish." [27]

Forrestal is referring to Count Metternich, an arch-reactionary Austrian diplomat who in 1815 tried to re-establish the corrupt monarchies that had been overthrown as a result of the French Revolution of 1789. He also tried to prevent the Spanish colonies in South America from freeing themselves.

Metternich tried to wipe out the effects of the French Revolution of 1789; Forrestal saw himself wiping out the results of the Soviet Revolution of 1917. Having given himself the same task as Metternich, to restore the shattered pre-war conservative governments, there is no wonder he appreciates Metternich.

Forrestal was a hard worker. His diaries show how indefatigable he was in furthering reaction in America and in the world. Nothing is too small for his attention. He accidentally hears of a couple of New Dealers in the U. S. Military Government for Japan. Instantly, he has them fired. At the other end of the scale nothing is too big for his fertile mind. Just as he sent a Navy to the Mediterranean, he sent a fleet of bombers to England, at the time of the Berlin crisis in the summer of 1948. He got the British to agree to "training" for two groups of B-29's.

Four years later this "training" was completely exposed. In July 1952 correspondent Clifton Daniel cabled a story on the U. S. Air Force in Britain, saying that although it had appeared in 1948 "ostensibly for training," the bombers were in England to stay. He continues:

"The first unit that came to Britain, a wing of bombs, was scheduled to stay only thirty days. Now, four years later, there are five wings of American aircraft. . . .
" 'We will never be finished,' an officer at Upper Heyford, one of the eight operational bases, remarked the other day." [28]

27 Forrestal Diaries, p. 48
28 N. Y. Times, July 14, 1952

Forrestal kept an eye on domestic affairs, but he considered the Soviet Union the mortal enemy and therefore spent most of his time on foreign affairs. Cold War was his specialty. There isn't an event described in this book, or a policy, or a propaganda line that Forrestal didn't influence. Very often, his influence was decisive for his power was enormous, both by virtue of his position in charge of all the armed forces of the U. S. and by virtue of his role as chief spokesman of Big Business within the government.

As the organizer of the Cold War, Forrestal tried to understand his opponent. He actually hired a professor to study Marxist philosophy for him.

Professor Edward F. Willett of Smith College prepared at Forrestal's request a paper on Dialectical Materialism, [29] the first time perhaps that a high American official thought to study Soviet philosophy. How good a job Willett did is not known, the study was never published.

However, Forrestal was so impressed with the study, that he had it mimeographed and sent copies to various people including columnist Walter Lippmann. Whether this philosophy struck a chord in Forrestal we don't know; what we do know is that he looked all over for a "theoretician" of the Cold War, someone who could "justify" and develop a line of attack against the USSR.

In February 1946 Forrestal found his man. He saw a State Department dispatch which pleased him greatly because, says Millis, "it was exactly the kind of job for which Forrestal had looked vainly elsewhere in the government." [30] The dispatch contained an analysis which according to Millis "ended

29 Forrestal Diaries, p. 127. Forrestal could have secured a better job, without cost, by reading Stalin's summary of Dialectical Materialism in Chapter 4, History of the Communist Party of the Soviet Union (Bolsheviks). For more extended study, Forrestal could have gone to the Jefferson School of Social Sciences in New York, or the Samuel Adams School in Boston, the Franklin School in Philadelphia or the California Labor School in San Francisco.
30 Ibid., p. 136

all hope of establishing conventional or 'normal' relations" with the USSR, or of reaching settlements "by a meeting of the 'heads of state' or by some similar form of reasonable give-and-take around a peaceful conference table." [31]

The name of this wonderful "theoretician" who saw no hope for the future was George F. Kennan, long a leading anti-Sovieteer in the State Department career corps. Forrestal's enthusiasm for Kennan is explained by the fact, says Millis, that Kennan's ideas "accorded very closely with those Forrestal had already been developing," [32] namely, that American policy towards the Soviet Union "could not be founded on the assumption that a peaceful solution of the Russian problem would be possible." [33]

In other words, both Forrestal and Kennan agreed that war with Russia was inevitable, "no peaceful solution was possible." Kennan emerges from the Forrestal Diaries as one of the chief American ideologists of the Cold War. [34]

GOVERNMENT AND BIG BUSINESS

Forrestal worked hard to make his ideas dominant inside the government as well as to get businessmen in key positions. He pounded away at his ideas systematically and with shrewd ingenuity. The way he worked on Truman is fascinating. Forrestal had a trick of asking "if" questions, provocative in the extreme, to get the President to think in terms of war. For example: on the 23rd of June, 1947, at a Cabinet luncheon Forrestal reports this:

". . . I asked permission of the President to pose a question which I had put to the Secretary of State last Thursday: What does this country do, politically or militarily, if it is confronted during this summer with a Russian **demarche** [diplomatic demand] accompanied by simultaneous coups in France and Italy "

31 Ibid., p. 138
32 Ibid., p. 139
33 Ibid., p. 135
34 In Europe, Kennan is not the oracle he is made out to be by Luce and others in this country. The conservative London paper **The Observer,** ran an article in March, 1952, entitled quite bluntly, "Mr. Kennan Is Wrong." (Richardson in the N.Y. Post, March 25, 1952)

This is certainly a provocative question, which Truman might justifiably rebuke. Instead we get a frightening glimpse into Truman's mind.

"The President replied that we would have to face that situation when it arose, and he then said that he and General Marshall had been talking about it just prior to lunch. He said that he was afraid the answer would have to be found in history—of the struggle between the Romans and Carthage, between Athens and Sparta, between Alexander the Great and the Persians, between France and England, between England and Germany." [35]

Everyone one of these struggles was for the domination of the known world of the time.

It is a characteristic of Forrestal that he was very conscious of what he wanted to achieve; the formalization of the kind of integration between Big Business, government and the armed forces which has been noted above, in chapter 4.

He told John Snyder, Secretary of the Treasury, that:

". . . in the competition between the Soviet system and our own, we shall have to harness all the talent and brains in this country just as we had to do during the war. I said I felt very strongly that the world could only be brought back to order . . . by businessmen." [36]

In a cabinet meeting a little later Forrestal pounds away at his favorite theme. He says that to check the Russians is a big job and to do it "we would have to turn to business." Whereupon Truman appointed a committee headed by John Snyder together with Harriman, Patterson, Acheson and Forrestal to make a "plan for laying out the facts before a selected group of business people." Adds Forrestal, "I said this selection should be made most carefully." [37]

While pushing reaction's policies inside the government, Forrestal maintained his close contact with Wall Street and acted as a sort of clearing center of high monopoly policies. In July 1945 he visited Dean Jay at Morgan's, who reported

35 Forrestal Diaries, p. 281
36 Ibid., p. 247
37 Ibid., p. 252

to him how the French capitalists were demoralized. [38]

During the Palestine controversy, Forrestal "instigated" Winthrop Aldrich of the Chase National Bank, to talk with Governor Dewey and report to Forrestal what Dewey thought on Palestine. [39]

Forrestal reported on the overall political situation to his former banking chief, Clarence Dillon; was constantly in touch with financier Baruch; was always available to advise Big Businessmen on foreign policy.

As a class conscious reactionary, Forrestal was acutely aware of the power of organized labor, particularly their power for maintaining peace in the world. He had to sit through a cabinet meeting under Roosevelt in March 1945 at which Secretary of Labor Frances Perkins reported on the World Federation of Trade Unions. Mrs. Perkins said that:

". . . The Russians, according to the American delegates, Mr. [James B.] Carey and Mr. R. J. Thomas, were extremely cordial in their relations with the Americans. She [Mrs. Perkins] said that one principal theme of discussion in the meeting was the enunciation of a principle that **labor in every country had in its hands the power to make war or peace, and that it proposed to use this power in the future.**" [40] (emphasis added)

This power of labor was and is a roadblock to reaction, although it has been weakened as a result of division in labor's ranks. What part Forrestal played in this split has not become known, but one unguarded entry in the diary indicates that he kept close touch with events in the labor field. This entry also shows how Forrestal kept the pressure on the CIO by playing on Philip Murray's vanity as a labor "statesman." At a luncheon with Murray, Forrestal turned the conversation on the split within the CIO asking about Joe Curran, president of the National Maritime Union who had fearfully switched from being union leader to a supine

38 Ibid., p. 77. The enormously powerful house of Morgan controls a major segment of our economy
39 Ibid., p. 364
40 Ibid., p. 34

supporter of the Cold War. Was Curran's "conversion" genuine, Forrestal wanted to know, and Murray said yes, he thought it was. Murray also had to confess that in contrast to Curran, many unions were not going along with the Truman-Forrestal "muscular" formulas and that CIO leaders "were encountering substantial difficulties from the United Electrical Workers (UE) and some other unions." [41]

Forrestal kept a close watch on the needs of reactionaries abroad. He was one of the prime movers behind the economic rebirth of the Axis nations, or as he put it, their "ability to get back to work," through American "financial help accompanied by American supervision." [42]

Forrestal's many activities and ideas, particularly the idea of integrating big business, big politicians and big brass-hats, were suspiciously reminiscent of Hitler and Mussolini. Forrestal was aware of this, telling Congressman Brown of Ohio that there was always danger of a Senate investigation "to prove that the Army and Navy and American business were combining on a neo-fascist program of American imperialism." [43] This is a pretty accurate description of what he was doing, and he should know. Forrestal always worried that he would be exposed, writing to Senator Ferguson:

"Needless to say, I shall appreciate your not giving this letter or these thoughts wide circulation or I shall be accused of being an appeaser, a Fascist. . . ." [44]

ORGANIZER OF THE "WAR PSYCHOSIS"

Probably the greatest domestic problem facing Forrestal was the friendly feeling of the American people for the Soviet Union. Byrnes says that "the Soviet Union had in the United States a deposit of good will as great, if not greater, than that of any other country." [45] This created a problem for the

41 Ibid., p. 406
42 Ibid., p. 248
43 Ibid., p. 244
44 Ibid., p. 57
45 Byrnes, Speaking Frankly, p. 71

organizers of the Cold War which Millis puts in a negative form, namely that the people of the United States were "not yet in the mood to face up to the basic issues of Soviet relation." [46] In plain English, the people of America were not in the mood to accept the Cold War, and to change this mood, "a campaign was worked up." [47]

Forrestal took the lead in this campaign. His work in the field of propaganda is steady, consistent and tireless. He dines with Henry Luce of Time and Life and complains that the U. S. press is too critical of its government. He lunches with Arthur Hayes Sulzberger, publisher of the New York Times and gets his support for the administration's China policy. He lunches with Wilbur Forrest of the New York Herald Tribune and suggests moderation in criticism. He lays down the line to Palmer Hoyt, of the Denver Post, that he should "continue to back up James F. Byrnes and not fall for the line of getting the Americans the hell out of China." [48]

He calls a large meeting with some two dozen foremost editors and publishers in the country. The list of guests is impressive:

Arthur H. Sulzberger, N. Y. Times; Geoffrey Parsons, N. Y. Herald Tribune; Walter Annenberg, Philadelphia Inquirer; Paul Bellamy, Cleveland Plain Dealer; Mark Ethridge, Louisville Courier-Journal; Paul Miller, Gannet Newspapers; Roy Roberts, Kansas City Star; John Cowles, Minneapolis Star-Tribune; Wright Bryan, Atlanta Journal; William Mathews, Arizona Star (Tucson); Clayton Fritchey, New Orleans Item; Roger Ferger, Cincinnati Enquirer; Paul Patterson, Baltimore Evening Sun; William Block, Pittsburgh Post-Gazette; Palmer Hoyt, Denver Post; Robert McLean, Philadelphia Bulletin; John Knight, Knight Newspapers, Inc.; Paul Smith, San Francisco Chronicle; John Cline, Washington Evening Star.

At the meeting Generals Marshall and Bradley brief the newsmen over the Berlin crisis; Forrestal leads a discussion on the use of the atom bomb and develops his anti-Soviet

46 Forrestal Diaries, p. 58
47 N. Y. Times, March 21, 1946
48 Forrestal Diaries, pp. 53, 117, 169, 193

propaganda with Bohlen of the State Department giving reports from Moscow. [49]

At this meeting as in all his propaganda work, Forrestal peddles his basic line, on record as early as February 1946, namely that "no peaceful solution of the Russian problem was possible."

The propaganda work of Forrestal and other Cold War makers soon brought results in the daily press and in the radio. As we have seen in detail in chapter 1, a gigantic "war psychosis" was developed based on deception and distortion.

One of the greatest hoaxes perpetrated on the American people at this time stemmed directly from Forrestal. He got an idea accepted so firmly that it is still held as an article of faith by many Americans. This is the idea that the United States demobilized so fast after V-J Day that we were practically disarmed and hence the Soviet Union became aggressive when she saw we were weak. [50]

This hoax was finally punctured by the Quakers in their excellent pamphlet **Steps to Peace:** [51]

"Another inaccuracy widely believed is that the United States disarmed unilaterally after World War II, thereby weakening itself and opening the way for Soviet expansion. The fallacy in this is in its frame of reference, for while it is true that we demobilized our army to a much larger extent than did the Russians, the military strength of the United States has never been measured by the size of its standing army. For geographic reasons we rely primarily on sea and air power, while the Soviet Union is primarily a land power. **If all categories of weapons are included,** as they must be in any fair analysis of military strength, the theory of America's unilateral disarmament collapses. In the years since the war, our production of atomic weapons has proceeded at an increasing tempo, accompanied by the maintenance of a far-flung network of air bases and the bombing planes necessary for their delivery. Our navy, by far the largest in the world, has been maintained on a standby basis. In no post-war years has our military budget fallen below eleven billion dollars. This is hardly unilateral

49 Ibid., pp. 487-488
50 Ibid., p. 129
51 Steps to Peace, American Friends Service Committee

disarmament." (emphasis added)

No account of the propaganda war against the American people would be adequate without a mention of the censorship pressures. Mr. William Shirer, who was himself to be silenced, has pointed up the attempts at censorship, the smears against those who opposed the Cold War and the consequences that might follow. His article is worth quoting at length to show how in 1946 the Cold War was in full swing, and how pressures were being applied to the mind of the American public:

"Bert Andrews[52] raised a vital issue . . . when he reported . . . that Mr. Truman, Mr. Byrnes, and Mr. Vandenberg, having agreed on a 'firm' policy toward Russia, wished to goodness that such dissenters as Senator Pepper and Secretary Wallace would either go along with that policy or keep their mouths shut.

"For if Mr. Andrews' report is correct . . . what the President, the Secretary of State and the Republican Senator from Michigan are proposing is a regimentation of public opinion on foreign policy such as has never been asked for by the heads of government in our history or in that of modern England, even in war time."

* * * *

"And it will not make for clarity and intelligence in our foreign relations if every person who airs doubts about the wisdom of some of our attitudes toward the Soviets is loudly branded as 'pro-Russian' or a 'Bolshevik.'. . . Every time I deviate from what may to called the Vandenberg-John Foster Dulles line on Russia . . . I get a bushel of abusive letters.

"Yet there are many able citizens—in Congress and out—who rather regret that Mr. Truman and Mr. Byrnes, green as they are in foreign politics, have taken over so many of the ideas of Mr. Dulles, especially in regard to Russia. . . . And one cannot but have reservations about an authority who right up to the outbreak of war saw no danger to America in the Nazi-Fascist conspiracy but who now presumes to see the imminent danger of a clash with Russia. . . ."

Mr. Shirer re-iterated an interesting fact:

"What surprised this reporter was that the very persons who had been so congenitally blind to the threat to us of Nazi Germany

52 Bert Andrews is a reporter for the Washington Post and the N. Y. Herald Tribune

were so quick to sense what they were now sure was a threat to our nation interests from Soviet Russia." 53

THE FINAL SYMBOLISM

James V. Forrestal died in May 1949 under far from ordinary circumstances. Usually, the subject of mental illness is considered too delicate to discuss. This would be true in Forrestal's case but for the fact that **his illness was a matter of public concern: Forrestal was still making decisions when already under severe strain.** 54 Millis, his friendly editor hints at it in the notes to the diaries.

"Early in January . . .one of the President's closest advisers noticed how **weary and nervous** Forrestal appeared; this man and a colleague remarked to each other that Forrestal's long-standing, unconscious habit of scratching the crown of his head had become so continuous **that a raw spot was beginning to appear.**" 55 (emphasis added)

Yet Forrestal remained in office three more months. His diary shows he was influencing policy on China, Israel and Russia. He was still in charge of the Armed Forces, deciding for example that the big bombers, B-36, should get auxiliary jet engines.

Forrestal became ill. Writes Millis:

". . . within a day or two psychiatric help seemed imperative. . . . On April 2, Forrestal was flown back to Washington and admitted to the Naval Hopital at Bethesda, Maryland.
". . . by the middle of May his physicians were looking forward to his discharge in another month or so, and as a necessary part of the treatment they risked a relaxation of the restraints that had been set around him. . . . It was a tragic miscalculation. On the night of May 21-22 he . . . fell to his death from its unguarded window." 56

53 **N. Y. Herald Tribune, June 9, 1946**
54 Reactionaries are conscious of the significance of the manner of Forrestal's death. They have deliberately sought to make a martyr of him, to idealize and enshrine him. A research laboratory at Princeton University was named after him. The Navy's new "super" aircraft carrier will be known as the Forrestal, as well as giving the name to that class of ships. Since these super-carriers are advertised as being capable to launch atomic bombers anywhere in the world, the name is appropriate enough, but no Secretary of Navy or Defense has ever been so honored
55 Forrestal Diaries, p. 547
56 Ibid., pp. 554-555

Mental illness has its roots deep in the past, yet the final breakdown is often related to current specific stresses and strains of the environment. Whatever tensions Forrestal's personality had suffered in the past, the world conditions around him must have intensified the pressures inside him.

For Forrestal's policy was not paying off. The policy of the Cold War, of atomic blackmail needed two things for success. One, support by the American people, and two, fear by the Soviet Government. Neither came through.

The whipping up of a "war psychosis" by the fraud of Soviet military threat did result in huge armaments, huge profits and the undermining of civil liberties in America. But even under the most powerful campaign of hate, the American people's resistance to militarism has been such that the military have not been able to seize control of the bomb, let alone use it. In this resistance the American people are allied to all the people of the world who, again and again, often through their governments, have expressed their horror of the bomb.

Nor was the Soviet Government frightened into submission.

Said Byrnes to Forrestal that the Russians were ". . . stubborn, obstinate and **they don't scare.**" [57] (emphasis added) Professor Blackett makes the same point ironically:

". . . the Russians have committed the unforgivable sin of not being as frightened of atomic bombs as the Americans." [58]

In the application of his policy of force, Forrestal again and again miscalculated. He was an intelligent man, but so hopelessly unable to understand deep social forces that his estimates of situations were sometimes downright childish. When Transjordan attacked Israel, for example, Forrestal expected the Arabs to win in three days. [59] Instead Israel beat

57 Ibid., p. 262
58 Blackett, Fear, War and the Bomb, p. 158
59 T. O. Thackery, N. Y. Compass, October 12, 1951

the Arabs.

Forrestal never did get his war. The "years of opportunity" he had talked about ran out very fast. Forrestal saw that capitalism and socialism were competing for the support of nations and people everywhere. He wrote in his diary, that today:

". . . the central problem is: Which of the two systems currently offered the world is to survive. . . ."[60]

Deep in his heart, Forrestal, like many reactionaries, had no faith in his own capitalist system. He was not willing to let the two systems compete peacefully, as Roosevelt was willing to do. He tried to solve the central question by force: Cold War as a preliminary to global atomic war.

Forrestal failed. Others in high places are still trying. They too must fail. Forrestal's death could well serve as a symbolic warning. The way of war disintegrates—the way of peace is the only human alternative.

60 Forrestal Diaries, p. 249

War of Prevention

Perils in Proposed Attack on Soviet Now Are Weighed Against Alleged Advantage

By HANSON W. BALDWIN

Fresh enemy divisions were re-ported massing on the Korean yesterday as the Chinese Co nists again complained tha aircraft had violated the churian frontier.

Two deductions can be

WEDNESDAY, JUNE 7, 1950.

Atom Bomb 'Over There' Urged by Official in '47

Special to The New York Times
WASHINGTON, June 6,—Paul H. Griffith, Assistant Secretary of Defense
that in 194
dent T
bomb
there'
United
"peop
to re

Army Convicts Gen. Grow For Misusing Secret Data

Reprimand and Bar From Command for 6 Months Given in Diary 'Theft'

B. HINTON
EW YORK TIMES.
July 29—Maj.
Grow was con-
court-martial
of secret of-
n a private
g failed to
rmation. He
su

MATTHEWS FAVORS U.S. WAR FOR PEACE

Navy Secretary Says at Boston We May
to Com

Special
BOSTON
A world af
ing to p
price of
rpel coop

Kimball Says He'll Cheer Any China Invasion

Won't Say if U. S. Will Aid Chiang Thrust, Feels Sure Navy Can Shield Formosa

By Mac R. Johnson
From the Her
Copyright, 1952. N
TOKYO, W
Secretary
Kimball
United S
the hell
munist
vade F
The
would
cheer

Gen. Robert W. Grow

War," and published in
The Army conducte

U.S. Has Right to Use Atom Bomb First

Dread that Russia will drop the first A-bomb is building up pressure for preventive war.

Ideas range from dropping bombs on the Kremlin now, to warning Russia that further satellite attacks will mean big war.

But odds are strongly against preventive action, despite talk. Reason in cold logic: Defense planners say U. S. isn't strong enough to assure a knockout victory.

U. S. NEWS & WORLD REPORT

AGGRESSORS FOR PEACE

CHAPTER 13

"To have peace we should be willing . . . to pay any price, even the price of instituting a war to compel co-operation for peace. We would become the first aggressors for peace."

Francis P. Matthews, U. S. Sec'y
of Navy, August 25, 1950

"I can break up Russia's five A-bomb nests in a week. And when I went up to Christ, I think I could explain to him that I had saved civilization."

Major General Orvil A. Anderson,
Commander of Air War College,
September 2, 1950

THE FRENCH have a saying: appetite comes with eating. The more you eat, the more you want to eat. American imperial strategists have developed a fine appetite. With the Truman Doctrine their "eating" became a devouring.

Across Europe, American reaction moved on the offensive. Direct American intervention smashed coalition governments in country after country. Part of the "war psychosis" propaganda in America is the idea that Communists in Europe turned against the existing governments to undermine them. This is not true. The record shows that in every instance, the initiative to break up existing governments came from the **right,** not from the **left.** The CBS correspondent in Europe, Howard K. Smith, has described the process.

In France, Premier Ramadier had asked for credit from

the United States. The reader will remember that a credit is a loan with strings attached. As Ramadier said, "each credit (from the U. S.) will be dictated by political realities. A little of our independence is departing from us with each loan we obtain." [1] Smith then goes on to show what these 'political realities' were:

"In May, 1947, two months after President Truman made his 'doctrine' speech, Ramadier suddenly dismissed the Communists from his Cabinet. In view of Ramadier's statement (given above), it looked to the Communists like a put-up deal ordered by America." [2] (emphasis added)

The pattern of credits as levers to control governments was repeated in Italy in the action of Italian Premier de Gasperi. Says Smith:

"When UNRRA deliveries ended in February, 1947, de Gasperi went to America to ask for a loan. After his return he summarily dissolved his coalition Cabinet and re-formed it, leaving out the left parties, as was done in France in the same month, May, 1947." [3] (emphasis added)

The pattern of U. S. interference broke down in the Eastern European countries. There the people's forces were strong enough to defeat reaction. But the try was made both in Poland and in Czechoslovakia. The events of Czechoslovakia particularly have been incredibly distorted in the American press, which glibly talks of a Communist "coup d'etat" or armed seizure of government. What are the facts?

Howard K. Smith, the American CBS correspondent who was there on the spot, has reported the events as he saw them. Although Smith himself is not immune to an anti-Communist bias, nevertheless he does give a glimpse of the truth. Smith starts by pointing out that "Czechoslovakia was ruled by a democratic coalition government led by the Communists," who together with the Social Democrats (Social-

1 Smith, State of Europe, p. 156
2 Ibid., p. 156
3 Ibid., p. 219

ists) had "a majority in the country of 51%." In spite of having a majority, Communists and Socialists allowed the other parties in the government for the sake of unity and the reconstruction of the country. However, after the Truman Doctrine was proclaimed, "the Communists foresaw a repetition in Czechoslovakia of what had happened in France," and the Minister of the Interior began to clean up the police force of right wing elements. [4]

This was in 1948, **almost a year after the Truman Doctrine was declared** and after U. S. had flagrantly intervened in France and Italy. As a matter of fact the Italian election of April 1948 was just getting underway and American money and threats of military intervention were openly being used. [5]

In such tense conditions the right wing parties in the Czech government precipitated a crisis by withdrawing from the government, which forced the Cabinet to dissolve. Their aim, says Smith, was to exclude the Communists. "If they could induce the Social Democrats to join them—they would have a majority and could form a government without the Communists." [6] Exactly as in France, exactly as in Italy.

This strategy failed. Says Smith who saw it happen, "a sea of 200,000 human beings" poured into Prague's main square. "This massive display had its effect," continues Smith, "fifteen parliamentary deputies from each of the two leading non-Communist parties and ten from the third hurried to Gottwald and offered co-operation." [7] The co-operation was accepted and the ministers who had resigned were kicked out of the government.

In the U. S. press all this was called "Russian Aggression

4 Ibid., pp. 341-343
5 It has since been revealed that Admiral Carney, at that time Vice-Chief of Naval Operations, had sent a Navy transport ship loaded with arms and ammunition to Italy, ready to intervene if the left-wing won the April election. Luigi Barzini, Jr., in the Italian conservative magazine, l'Europea
6 Smith, State of Europe, p. 343
7 Ibid., p. 346

against Czechoslovakia" and "Communist rule of terror." Smith who was there saw no terror. He saw support for the government and no sign of violence or resistance. He asks some questions which American reactionaries cannot answer.

"Why did President Benes . . . not resign if he was opposed? . . . He remained as the responsible head of the Communist-dominated state for months. Why did Czech moderate parties collapse so easily? Of their forty-odd deputies who rushed to support the Communists . . . many were men of high principle. One was a respected Catholic priest, Father Plohjar, who became Minister of Health in the new Gottwald Cabinet. How to explain the support given the new government by a universally respected Protestant theologian like Dr. Hromadka, Dean of Theology at the Charles University?" [8]

No right wing leaders in Czechoslovakia would have dared such gross provocation without the knowledge that the U. S. approved. In Poland the American ambassador openly supported the right wing parties. But in Poland, too, reaction had failed in the election of 1947, which also was completely misrepresented in the American press. The head of Polish reaction, Mikolajczyk, was made to appear as a fine democrat. This is the same man to whom Churchill had said, "get not only your foot but your leg in the door. . . . You can count now on the support and influence of both the British and the Americans." (see chapter 8)

This fine "democrat" interviewed by Howard K. Smith in the autumn of 1947 admitted that his Peasant Party "was inundated by the 15,000-odd landlords dispossessed in the land reforms, and by the anti-Semitic middle classes." Smith adds that "there is little doubt that his party in the provinces was linked to the rightist underground." The meaning of this "underground" becomes clear when Smith explains that

8 Smith, State of Europe, p. 347. A most absorbing novel by Stefan Heym, The Eyes of Reason, Boston, 1951, excellently portrays the Czecho-slovakian crisis

900 Communist and Socialist politicians had been murdered by "the rightist bands, some of whose local leaders were doubtless associated with the Peasant Party." [9]

Mikolajczyk lost. He ran away and he is now in America, stirring up hatred, dreaming dreams of going back to Poland in the baggage train of American and British armies. But little of the facts given above ever appeared in the American newspapers.

The effect of the Truman Doctrine was to sharpen struggles in every country. Since the U. S. allied itself with the rich and the powerful, the American ruthlessness alienated large sections of the population. The Czech Foreign Minister Masaryk, shortly before his death, told Dr. Jerome Davis that "the United States had promoted more Communism in Czechoslovakia than all the Russians combined, by cancelling a loan of fifty million dollars to the country while the anti-Communist bloc still controlled it."[10]

It would be impossible in this book to follow in detail, year by year and country by country the working out of the Truman Doctrine and of the Cold War. The purpose of this book is to show who started the Cold War, how and why. However, the most evil and dangerous consequence of the Truman Doctrine cannot be passed over, and that is the idea of preventive war. Preventive war has been defined by authoritative American officials including one Cabinet officer. Unequivocally and shamelessly, they have defined preventive war as a war of aggression by the United States.

PREVENTIVE WAR INHERENT IN THE COLD WAR

As this book has evidenced, atomic diplomacy marked the beginning of the Cold War and its subsequent manifestations. But the essence of atomic diplomacy is the monopoly of the atom bomb. From this fact there was for militarists but one conclusion: smash your potential enemy **before** he

9 Ibid., p. 331
10 Davis, **Peace, War and You**, p. 88

too, gets the bomb. Start a war of aggression, without reason, without justice, without need—just to maintain an atom bomb monopoly which would insure the domination of the world.

From the beginning of atomic diplomacy there was inherent in it the monstrous, evil idea of preventive war. **No other nation, not one, has talked about preventive war because no other nation, not one, has based its foreign policy on the atom bomb.** In the United States, however, the moment the Cold War began, the talk of preventive war started. Already in late 1945 the idea was widespread in Washington as Sumner Welles testifies.

"It must also be frankly stated that there existed another body of public opinion, in which **military and naval officials of the United States were included,** which insisted that, since the Soviet Union could soon develop the manufacturing processes of atomic energy, the only safe course for the United States was to **use the atomic bombs** as a means of forestalling the possibility of any later aggression against herself." [11] (emphasis added)

But in late 1945 and throughout 1946 while the idea of preventive war could be discussed, there was no possibility of carrying it into effect. A "war psychosis" first had to be created, and as we saw in the previous chapter, Forrestal led the way in organizing the propaganda campaign against the Soviet Union. Since the Soviet Union countered every aggressive move of the U. S. with a defensive move, as for example on the Baruch Plan, this was utilized by reaction to build up the war psychosis by presenting the Soviet moves as aggressive.

At the same time, the U. S. government began jailing those who were exposing the war drive. [12] After the Truman Doctrine had been imposed on the American people through

11 Welles, Where Are We Heading, pp. 347-348
12 The author of this book was indicted in January, 1947, after making a film exposing the drive to war and the reversal of Roosevelt's policies. The film, completed in late August, 1946, described U. S. foreign policy as "atomic diplomacy."

a combination of fear and hysteria, the idea of preventive war was no longer academic. It was later revealed that there was a "30-day war idea advanced in 1948 by individual Air Force officers." [12a] As we shall soon see, 1948 was a year of decision for American reaction, the year when the idea of preventive war seemed easiest of achievement. 1948 was a target year for action. The preparation for that year haunts the Forrestal Diaries, since Forrestal was the man for the work.

Forrestal was in charge of all the armed forces of the United States, the first time in American history that this has occurred, with the exception of the President as Commander-in-Chief. On July 27, 1947, the unification law having established a single Secretary of Defense, Forrestal was appointed to this key post. He received many letters of congratulations on his new position, but according to Millis, he only recorded one in his diary. That was from Myron Taylor, former head of U. S. Steel and the President's personal representative to the Vatican. Here is the letter which was so important to Forrestal:

"Dear Jim:
Congratulations on another great honor—stepping stones in a great career. May this one lead to world peace. **If that is impossible, then to effective war** and enduring peace in timely sequence.
Sincerely,
(signed) Myron Taylor." [13] (emphasis added)

Forrestal was thinking war, aggressive war. "In Forrestal's thought the atomic bomb had moved into the center of the international equation" says Millis commenting on the same page on a letter of Forrestal dated December 8, 1947. The letter said:

"As long as we can outproduce the world, can control the sea and can strike inland with the atomic bomb, we can assume certain risks otherwise unacceptable. . . .

12a U. S. News and World Report, September 8, 1950
13 Forrestal Diaries, p. 299

"The years before any possible power can achieve the capability effectively to attack us with weapons of mass destruction are **our years of opportunity.**" [14] (emphasis added)

What opportunity? What risks? Elsewhere Forrestal indirectly gives the answer. The risks inherent in a strategy of aggression. An entry in his diary for December 31, 1947 is illuminating:

"The most urgent strategic and tactical problem to be solved by the Air Force is the question of the usefulness and capabilities of the long-range bomber against jet fighter and radar defense." [15]

This is the problem of aggressive war. Given an opponent without atomic bombs you don't have to fear retaliation. You don't even think of defensive measures such as developing your own jet planes and radar defenses. You think aggressively, how to smash through the opponent's defenses of jet planes and radar. When Forrestal calls this the most urgent problem of the Air Force, he is saying in military jargon, that the most urgent task of the Air Forces was to be ready to wage aggressive war.

Another set of entries in the diaries confirm the fact that Forrestal is thinking of aggressive atomic war. They show the military concern with the **Eastern** Mediterranean, a key strategic area in any attack on the USSR, particularly its Baku oil fields. By October 1947 Kennan and Forrestal are agreeing "to reverse our policy" from hostility to friendship of Franco Spain because of our need of bases and access to the Mediterranean which "cannot be considered without considering Spain." [16] Some weeks later there is an entry on conferences between Secretary of Air Symington, General Spatz, commanding the Air Force, Admiral Souers of the Central Intelligence Agency, Forrestal and others concerning air bases in the Mediterranean. At one of those conferences:

14 Ibid., p. 351
15 Ibid., p. 355
16 Ibid., p. 328

"General Gruenther said he thought the question of air bases in North Africa implies a narrow limitation on our needs in the event of war. He said that what we were really talking about **was bases in the Eastern Mediterranean and in the Middle East.**" [17] (emphasis added)

While all this was going on, Forrestal was feverishly pushing for more atom bombs, "impressed with the importance of stepping up bomb production," [18] and to remove restrictions on the use of the atom bomb which were part of the secret wartime atomic agreements among the U. S. the U. K. and Canada. [19]

Why all these preparations, this sense of urgency? Why was it that Forrestal in late 1947 was "asking every casual visitor to his office whether in his opinion the public would support the employment of the bomb in the event of a major war?" [20] Why? Because 1948 was a target year, a target year for preventive war. **This shocking fact is revealed by James F. Byrnes, who as Secretary of State had made the diplomatic plans for a possible aggressive war in 1948.**

BYRNES WAR PLAN FOR 1948

Byrnes' plan gives both the timetable for the provocation of war and the way in which the war would be sold to the American people. This seems hardly believable, but the reader may judge for himself since the Byrnes' plan is here set down in full, in Byrnes' own words.

The essence of Byrnes' war plan is simple: make a separate treaty with the Western Zones of Germany, then push the Red Army out of the Eastern Zone **by force.** The timetable for this little operation was set to start in the spring of 1948. The United States was to call a peace conference in Germany for that time, **with or without the USSR,** and sign a peace treaty with **Western** Germany which would provide

17 Ibid., p. 357
18 Ibid., p. 339
19 Ibid., p. 339
20 Ibid., p. 339

for the evacuation of **all** German territory by foreign troops, **by force** if necessary.

The full immorality of this proposal for war is shown by the illegality of Byrnes' proposed "peace conference." Three nations had beaten the Nazis: England, the U. S. and the USSR. These three nations had zones of occupation in Germany [21] **achieved by right of victory** after untold suffering in a war started by the Nazis. A peace conference **without** the USSR was a fraud.

A "treaty" drawn up by such a conference couldn't possibly demand on any legal basis that the Soviet Union withdraw **its** troops from **its** zone. The USSR was in Germany with the identical rights as the U. S. **The entire premise of Byrnes' argument is therefore wholly false, false historically, legally, morally.** Now here is Byrnes' war plan based on this false premise. Byrnes writes:

"One may say: But suppose the Soviet Union declines to sign the treaty, what then?

"If Soviet troops are withdrawn from Germany, no action by other nations will be necessary. But if the Red Army is not withdrawn, we must, as a last resort, go to the Security Council of the United Nations. . . .

"Eastern Germany, like all other parts of Germany, is to be held by armies of occupation temporarily and only until a treaty of peace is agreed upon. For the Soviets to keep troops there after an overwhelming number of Allied Nations have reached a peace settlement would be evidence of their intentions to hold indefinitely territory allotted to them only for the period of occupation. Such action would constitute a threat to the peace of the world and the United Nations should therefore require the Soviet Union to withdraw from Germany.

"But, one may say, the Soviet Union will veto any action by the Security Council.

"Because I do not believe it wise to suggest a course of action unless one is willing to carry it through, it is proper to discuss the

21 France also had a zone, the result of diplomatic maneuvering by Churchill supported by FDR. Stalin had agreed to it at Yalta with reluctance, as a compromise concession. In Chapter 11 we saw how France sabotaged the four-power control of Germany, and how this was used as an excuse by the U. S. to break the Potsdam reparations agreement on plant deliveries

contingency that might arise. **We should not start something we are not prepared to finish.**

"First of all, let me say I do not believe the Soviet Union will force us **to take measures of last resort.** . . . If our action is to be effective, we must be clear in our minds and must make it clear to all that we are willing to adopt **these measures of last resort if, for** the peace of the world, we are forced to do so.

"I hope, believe, and I pray that the leaders of the Soviet Union will never force us to **this course of last resort.** But they must learn what Hitler learned—that the world is not going to permit one nation to veto peace on earth." [22] (emphasis added)

"Measures of last resort" is a long-established phrase in diplomacy meaning war. To keep the Soviet Union from "vetoing peace on earth" Byrnes is recommending that the U.S. start a war. In two other places in the book, Byrnes describes the military and political "tools" for this job. The military tool is of course the atom bomb; "we must use our best efforts to develop better bombs and more of them." [23] The political tool is the prestige of the United Nations which would "act" and then the United States would "use all of its power to support the action of the United Nations." [24]

This was precisely the political formula used by the U.S. in the Korean War.

When Byrnes' book was published with the above plan in it, the British were horrified that Byrnes should move so far, so fast and so openly. On the very next day, October 16, 1947, the authoritative London **Times** called this proposal, "little better than a simple recipe for war." The **London News Chronicle** said that Byrnes "has talked deplorable and dangerous nonsense." And the **London Daily** Mirror called a spade a spade: "Mr. Byrnes . . . is so frank as openly to advocate war with Russia. Is this wickedness, idiocy or a mixture of both?" [25]

22 Byrnes, Speaking Frankly, pp. 202-203
23 Ibid., p. 275
24 Ibid., p. 297.
25 Quoted in Schuman, The Devil and Jimmy Byrnes, p. 14

WHY BYRNES' WAR DIDN'T HAPPEN

A series of domestic and international developments frustrated the tentative plans of Byrnes, Forrestal and the rest of the preventive war clique. The most fundamental development was the rapid recovery of the Soviet Union from the devastation of the war and its existing military power. Furthermore in 1947 Molotov hinted that the Soviet Union had the atom bomb. The USSR certainly behaved with complete self-confidence. A prominent British journalist, Edward Crankshaw, looking back at 1948, wrote three years later that Molotov:

". . . bluffed the West into believing that the post-war Soviet Union, exhausted and demoralized, was ten times stronger than it was. It was apparent in his provocation of the Berlin crisis. . . ." [26]

Whether Soviet strength was real or a bluff, the fact is that the Western nations were restrained by their fear of Soviet strength and self-confidence of which the Berlin blockade was one example.

An important contributory reason was that at the very time of the Berlin blockade, the United States was in the midst of an election campaign, in which one party, the Progressive Party was appealing to the profound desire for peace among the American people.

Since the people of the United States are at this writing in the midst of an election campaign in which peace is the real issue, and since once again the Progressive Party is the only party whose candidates, Vincent Hallinan and Charlotta Bass, are standing squarely for peace, including an immediate truce in Korea, it is important to evaluate, however briefly, the role of the Progressive Party in the 1948 campaign.

Because of the impact of the Progressive Party for peace, Truman himself switched in the midst of his campaign and

26 N. Y. Times, Sunday Magazine Section, February 11, 1951

began to sound very "radical." He made a gesture of wanting to send Justice Vinson to Moscow, he said he got along fine with "Uncle Joe," and he attacked in the strongest terms the monopoly interests of America as parallel to the paymasters of the Nazis in Germany, the Fascists in Italy and the militarists in Japan. Said Truman:

"Now let's look at the group of men who are jeopardizing the future of the democracy of the United States through their concentrated economic power. . . .

"When a few men get control of the economy of a nation they find a 'front man' to run the country for them. Before Hitler came to power, control over the German economy had passed into the hands of a small group of rich manufacturers, bankers and landowners.

"These men decided that Germany had to have a tough, ruthless dictator who would play their game and crush the strong German labor unions. So they put money and influence behind Adolph Hitler. We know the rest of the story. . . .

"Today in the United States, there is a growing—and dangerous—concentration of immense economic power in the hands of just a few men." 27

Leaving aside Truman's blatant demagogy (since he has turned the government over to Big Business), the important fact is that the existence of the Progressive Party forced Truman to the "left," forced Truman to talk "peace" and may very well have been a major factor in preventing Truman from using Byrnes' war formula to fit the Berlin blockade.

THE KOREAN WAR

What Byrnes couldn't get in 1948, Dulles got in 1950 The Korean War has a trademark—MADE IN THE U. S. A. For a long time the "war psychosis" press succeeded in persuading large sections of the American people that the Soviet Union, through North Korean troops, had started the war as an act of aggression against the West. Today the truth is coming out: the United States, acting through the South

27 Truman election speech, Chicago, October 10, 1948

Koreans, started the war in part to save Formosa and the beaten Chiang Kai-shek.

This is the opinion of a leading British diplomat, Sir John Pratt. Pratt was former Adviser in Far Eastern Affairs for the British Government, and head of the Far Eastern Section of the British Ministry of Information. His background and knowledge are unimpeachable. This is what he says:

"Fighting began at dawn on Sunday, June 25, 1950, and that same afternoon the Security Council passed a resolution declaring North Korea guilty. Their decision was based on a telegram from the United Nations Commission in Seoul reporting that there was no evidence which side began the fighting. My suspicions were aroused by the haste with with this resolution was passed and by the fact that President Truman, without further reference to the United Nations, used it as a pretext for sending American troops to South Korea and the American navy to Formosa.

"The text of the United Nations telegram from Seoul was suppressed even in the Command Paper laid before the House of Commons. . . .

"The Russians had withdrawn from North Korea in 1948 but the Americans remained in South Korea and built up an army which they and Syngman Rhee confidently believed to be more than a match for the North Korean army. By November, 1949, according to the Economist, it was already a shooting war though the main armies were not engaged.

"In May, 1950, new elections were held in South Korea and the new National Assembly met in Seoul on June 19. Syngman Rhee's opponents had an overwhelming majority against him and started negotiations on the basis of a plan proposed by the North Koreans for unification of the country and for new elections to be held in August. It is difficult to believe that the North Koreans would sabotage this plan by launching an attack on the South Korean army.

"The solution of the puzzle must be looked for in Formosa.

"In January, 1950, President Truman and Dean Acheson announced that America was not interested in Formosa and would not intervene in any way in the civil war between the Nationalists on Formosa and the new government in Peking. The island had been returned to China in 1945; it had become once more a Chinese province and America 'would never quibble on any lawyer's words' about waiting for a peace treaty with Japan.

"The Republicans, however, were determined that Formosa should be 'included within the American perimeter of defense,' and their leaders supported Senator McCarthy in his campaign which a Committee of the Senate described as 'an effort to inflame the American people with a wave of hysteria and fear on an unbelievable scale.' In April, 1950, President Truman capitulated and appointed a Republican, Mr. John Foster Dulles, top consultant to the State Department.

"The 'liberation' of Hainan was effected by the forces of the Peking government with startling ease in April and the "liberation' of Formosa was timed for July. There was therefore little time to spare. In June Mr. John Foster Dulles, Mr. Louis Johnson (Secretary for Defense), and General Bradley (Chief of Staff), foregathered with General MacArthur in Tokyo and by June 23 it was known that they had agreed that Formosa must be 'included within the American perimeter of defense.' The fighting that broke out at dawn on June 25 saved Syngman Rhee from ruin and gave President Truman the pretext he required for seizing Formosa. No one who studies the evidence, of which the above is the barest outline, can doubt that **the Korean war began with an attack upon North Korea launched by Syngman Rhee with the support of his friends in the American Military Advisory Group.**" 28 (emphasis added)

Since Sir John Pratt wrote this indictment, one of the great newspapermen of America has proven this thesis to the hilt. I. F. Stone has written **The Hidden History of the Korean War,** a brilliant, thorough, analytical study of how and why the Korean War was started and carried on. Stone quotes Senator Connally, chairman of the Senate Foreign Relations Committee at the time, who granted an interview to the **U. S. News and World Report** of May 2, 1950. Said Connally:

"Well, a lot of them (certain people) believe like this: they believe that events will transpire which will maneuver around and present an incident which will make us fight. That's what a lot of them are saying: 'We've got to battle some time, why not now?' " 29

As if to prove Connally's point, preventive war talk was stepped up. Paul H. Griffith, former commander of the American Legion, told newspapers that he had already

28 Quoted in Davis, **Peace, War and You,** pp. 255-257
29 I. F. Stone, **Hidden History of the Korea War,** New York, 1952, p. 22

'Urged President Truman to order an atomic bomb dropped 'some place over there, as a demonstration of United States support of the 'people of the world who wanted to remain free.'
"Presumably Mr. Griffith meant that a bomb be dropped on the Soviet Union. . . ."[30]

There is no record of what Truman said. There is a record of what he did. Soon after, he appointed atomic bombardier Griffith to the post of Assistant Secretary of Defense.

This new outburst of preventive war talk occurred before the Korean War broke out. The war crowd, as Connally revealed, desperately hoped that events would "present an incident and make us fight."

Dulles turned up on the 38th parallel in Korea, on June 20, 1950. Newspaper photographers showed him peering through binoculars at North Korea. The next day he hurried to Tokyo to confer with General MacArthur, who was in conference with the very top U. S. military leaders who had just recently arrived in Japan: Louis Johnson (Secretary of Defense), and General Omar Bradley (Chairman of the Joint Chiefs of Staff).

Dulles, MacArthur, Bradley and Johnson: What did they talk about? The only clue we have is a statement that Dulles made to the Associated Press after leaving the conference. He "predicted 'positive action' by the United States to preserve peace in the Far East."[31]

How did war come to Korea? A fascinating clue is given by John Gunther, the author of all the "Inside . . ." books.

On the morning of June 25, 1950, Gunther was on the "inside" again, in General MacArthur's private railroad car in Japan. With him were "two important members of the occupation. Just before lunch," Gunther reports, one of them "was called unexpectedly to the telephone." He came back "and whispered, 'A big story had just broken. The South

30 N. Y. Times, June 7, 1950
31 N. Y. Times, June 22, 1950, quoted in Stone, Hidden History, p. 27

Koreans have attacked North Korea.' " [32] Gunther calls this report "wildly inaccurate" but he can't find any reason why an important occupation official should get a wildly inaccurate report in MacArthur's private railroad car. The best excuse he can think of is that:

"Nobody knew anything much at headquarters the first few hours, and probably people were taken in by the blatant, corrosive lies of the North Korean radio." [33]

I. F. Stone comments: "The conjecture that MacArthur might have been misled by the North Korean radio is fantastic." [34]

The Hidden History of the Korean War goes on step by step, from sensation to sensation, proving to the hilt that "the dominant trend in American political, economic and military thinking was fear of peace" [35] and that Korea was the way out for the warmakers. Stone quotes American General Van Fleet, commander in Korea, as saying in January 1952:

"Korea has been a blessing. There had to be a Korea either here or some place in the world." [36]

KOREA AND THE PREVENTIVE WAR

For two years the war in Korea has remained the most dangerous threat to global peace and the most powerful springboard for the advocates of preventive war. After the war started, the preventive war talk mounted in a new crescendo right up to the Cabinet itself.

In August 1950, a man who was then Secretary of the Navy, Francis P. Matthews, a Truman appointee, made a public speech and said:

"We should boldly proclaim our undeniable objective to

[32] John Gunther, The Riddle of MacArthur, p. 165, quoted in Stone, Hidden History, p. 45
[33] Ibid., p. 45
[34] Ibid., p. 45
[35] Ibid., p. 348
[36] United Press dispatch from 8th Army Hq., Korea, January 19, 1952, quoted in Stone, Hidden History, p. 348

be a world peace. To have peace we should be willing . . . to pay any price, even the price of **instituting a war to compel co-operation for peace. . . .**" This ". . . peace-seeking policy, though it cast us in a character new to a true democracy—an **initiator of a war of aggression**—it would earn for us a proud and popular title—we would become the **first aggressors for peace.**" [37] (emphasis added)

Matthews was not alone in this insane drive for global war. Two weeks later, Sept. 8, **U. S. News and World Report** had a whole article on the new upsurge of preventive war talk among top people. In addition to Matthews they quoted an influential Congressman, an Army general recently retired and an Air Force General on active duty, Orvil A. Anderson, at that time commander of the Air War College. General Anderson said that "Americans believe in taking the initiative"; he would be happy to bomb Russia, just "give me the order to do it," and ended up: "When I went up to Christ I think I could explain to Him that I had saved civilization."[38]

This was too much even for Truman. He suspended Anderson as commandant—that is, Anderson got another job—same rank, same pay. This type of "punishment" affords a real insight into the Administration's thinking: generals who demand preventive war are never seriously punished.

The most glaring recent example is the case of General Grow, who kept a diary early in 1951 while he was U. S. Military Attache in Moscow.

What Grow had written in his diary appalled the world when it came to light late in 1951: [39]

"War! As soon as possible!! Now!

37 N. Y. Times, August 26, 1950
38 N. Y. Times, Sept. 2, 1950. U. S. News did not print the whole statement.
39 Excerpts were first printed by British Major Richard Squires in Berlin. These have now been reprinted in the U. S. for the first time in a pamphlet called "The Diary of General Grow," Hour Publishers, 1952, with an introduction by Albert E. Kahn, author of High Treason. Major Squires had obtained photographs of the original diary and other private papers of Grow

"We need a voice to lead us without equivocation: Communism must be destroyed" (Entry dated February 5, 1951.)

Grow did not keep his recommendations to himself. He says he "threw a minor bombshell" by presenting to U. S. Ambassador Kirk in Moscow, a memorandum which predicted war before July, 1952. Grow then boasts that the Ambassador "accepted our paper as sound and worthy of serious consideration." He also boasts that his "letters are going to all important divisions, even to the President."

Grow also revealed his spying and target picking activities in Russia, writing of his travels: "Big power plant at Shatura . . . good target. . . . Only bridge is R. R. and is good target. . . . The bridge here is the best target in South Russia . . . located three A. A. A. positions."

Grow even discussed the methods of his proposed war.

"Our attack should be directed at enemy weakness . . . this war is total war and is fought with all weapons. We must learn that in war it is fair to hit below the belt."

Here it is in his own handwriting: [40]

[40] The army now denies that this passage, and the one that says "War Now" appear in the diary at all. However, they don't charge that the handwriting is a forgery, and they leave open the possibility that these passages came from Grow's private papers rather than the diary itself. The Army has refused to publish the diary, although it certainly is no longer a secret to the Russians

When the Grow diary became public, the first reaction in Washington was silence—no denials, no punishment. About six months later Grow was court-martialed, not for recommending war, but for failure to safeguard secret military information.

MONSTROUS CROP OF THE COLD WAR

The Cold War has given America the Korean War and the ever present possibilities of a preventive war—a war of aggression against the Soviet Union which would inevitably leave the U. S. fighting the whole world, as Hitler did—with the same disastrous results. The main reason why a preventive war has not been unleashed is because U. S. military "planners" are not sure they would win. Not morality but fear has thus far restrained U. S. militarists. This is coldly admitted by a big business magazine:

"Odds are strongly against preventive action, despite talk. Reason in cold logic: defense planners say U. S. **isn't strong enough to assure a knockout victory.** Military facts of life are being cited by U. S. defense planners as practical reasons why preventive armed attack on Russia is not to be attempted." [41] (emphasis added)

The Cold War has been underway since August 1945. Seven years later we can see the results. As of August 1952 what has a Republican-Democrat foreign policy yielded?

1—Over a quarter of a million American casualties in Korea (100,000 battle casualties, 120,000 non-battle.)
2—A nearly complete destruction of a country as big as Connecticut by high explosives and napalm bombs with a destruction of life far in excess of WORLD WAR II. Of a Korean population of 25 millions, it is estimated that 4 million, or one-sixth, have been killed.
3—An armaments race without precedent in history, a search for weapons of mass destruction such as the Hydrogen Bomb and bacteriological weapons that will dwarf the atom bomb.
4—The rise of militarism in America with the military dominant in foreign policy—government by generals with a General running for President.
5—The rearming of a Western Germany still ruled by the same

41 U. S. News and World Report, September 8, 1950

cartel and monopoly groups that boosted Hitler to power. A German army led by Hitler's generals; a German government staffed by Hitler's officials.

6—The rebuilding of Japanese armed strength under the identical monopolists and many of the same political leaders who attacked us at Pearl Harbor.

7—Friendship and alliance with the same General Franco of Spain who said in 1941, "What joy to see the German bombers one day punishing the insolence of the skycrapers of New York."

8—Alliance with the brutal colonial oppression of France, Britain and Belgium in Indo-China, Tunisia, Malaya, Egypt, the Near East, the Belgian Congo, and direct participation in colonial wars.

9—Economic crisis in Europe, fear of depression at home. Declining standards of living at home and abroad and super-profiteering for monopolies.

10—Attacks on civil liberties and free speech in the United States which have led to a "silence of fear" in the words of Supreme Court Justice Douglas. We have seen the Truman loyalty oaths, McCarthyism and a rapid drive to Fascism.

Yet we in America can be confident. The policy of the Cold War has failed so far in its inherent drive for an Atomic Global War. The reasons for this failure are basic and constantly operative. To know these reasons is to gain perspective and confidence. They will be briefly analyzed in the remaining chapters.

Bevan Charges U. S. Drives World to Ruin

LONDON, April 3 —Aneurin Bevan, Britain's left-wing Labor Party leader, accused the United States today of driving the world to ruin by overarming and hogging the world's resources.

He warned, in a new book, "In Place of Fear," which was published today, that the result of United States policy may be to drive the world into the clutches of Soviet communism.

Bevan said the West, through listening to the advice of military leaders, was playing into the hands of the Kremlin, and he said it was counting on economic ruin of the Soviet to achieve...

THE NEW YORK TIMES, WEDNESDAY, APRIL 16, 1952

Sixth Biggest British Union Backs Bevan; Places Social Welfare Over Armaments

LONDON, April 15—Britain's sixth biggest ... *Special to The New York Times.* ated a few months later when ...

5 More Unions Back Bevan on Arms Reduction

Their Resolutions Against Defense Plans Indicate Battle at Fall Meeting

By Gaston Coblentz
From the Herald Tribune Bureau
Copyright. 1952. New York Herald Tribune Inc.

LONDON, July 27—A group of British trade unions revealed today as having the imposingly large wing of British organized labor which would cut down on rearmament of the Soviet menace.

The disclosure came upon publication of an agenda which be fought out in September annual conference of British unions. They will be called to support or reject the policy of Left-Wing Laborite Aneurin Bevan that the rearmament program be ...

One of the main scheduled debates will deal with "international" issues, and the greater part of the resolutions under this head more or less agreed with Bevan's stand.

Four Uni...

Britain's Third Biggest Union Asks Arms Cut

Machinists, Lining Up With Bevan Policies, Demand Five-Power Peace Pact

By Gaston Coblentz
From the Herald Tribune Bureau
Copyright. 1952. New York Herald Tribune Inc.

LONDON, May 9—The third largest labor organization in Great Britain, the Amalgamated Engineering Union, aligned itself with Leftist Laborite Aneurin Bevan today by demanding a reduction in the British rearmament program.

The second of the country's "big-six" unions in a month to take such a stand, the engineers (machinists) went on record in a resolution adopted unanimously at an annual conference of the union's fifty-two national committee at Blackpool, in northern England.

The move coincided with reports of...

SATURDAY, MAY 10, 1952

BRITISH UNION ASKS FOR 5-POWER PEACE

Amalgamated Engineers Voice Concern at Rearming But —Views Lean to Bevan

Special to The New York Times.

LONDON, May 9—The National Committee of the Amalgamated Engineering Union, Britain's largest, unanimously voted a resolution expressing concern at Britain's present rearmament burden and calling for a peace among the five great powers—The United States, the Soviet Union, Britain, France and ...

The union, with 800,000 members in the metal using industry, is the largest participating in Britain's defense program. It representative turned down an amendment by forty-two to twelve calling for East-West negotiations to make possible armament reduction and the prohibition of atomic weapons.

Jack Tanner, president of the Union, who preferred the less emphatic break with British foreign policy, but went along with resolution, indicated that similarity in the views of unions ... to the views of the Laborites ... that ...

1952

Mi...
ers ...
ll res ...
serio ...
count ...

In ...
gamat ...
750,000 ...
closely ...
ganda ...
ing for ... Soviet propaganda ...
between the five great ...
Great Britain, ...
Russia, ...

PART III

THE DAILY COMPASS, WEDNESDAY, JANUARY 2, 1952

War Lessons—II

Toll Exacted by Foe's Jet Interceptors In Korea Indicates Danger to Bombers

By HANSON W. BALDWIN

I. F. STONE BEGINS A STARTLING SERIES

U. S. Has Lost Its Air Supremacy

By I. F. STONE

SOVIET JET OUTPUT 'FAR' AHEAD OF U. S.

Defense Chiefs Warn Congress Arms Fund Cuts Will Curb Air Power in Perilous Time

WASHINGTON, May 26 (UP)—
John D. Small, chairman of the
Munitions Board, told Congress
today that United States plane
production, particularly jets, still
was lagging "far behind" Russian
output although the program was
"pretty well off the ground."
Simultaneously

The End of the 'Buck Rogers' Strategy

Asian colored race fliers are operating successfully with the latest technological developments
in air warfare. Here is how the McGraw-Hill
correspondent described an MIG raid on our
B-29s. "The MIGs take off . . . climb into the sun
to high altitudes. There they are picked up by
other radar-tracking equipment and vectored into
attacking positions. They then press the attack
home against our B-29 medium bombers in a
high-speed downhill pass that is virtually impossible to stop . . . MIGs coming downhill can't be
headed off even if the Sabre pilots see them at
maximum visibility. By the time the Sabres turn
90 degrees to meet the attacks, the MIGs pass
and are on the bombers."

by Americans on the Red side. "Who flies the
MIG is still unprovable," a McGraw-Hill correspondent with the 5th Air Force reported in the
Dec. 17 issue of Aviation Week. "'For all we
know,' one F-86 Sabrejet pilot of the 4th Fighter
Interceptor Group says, 'there may be some ex-
American World War II fighter jockeys up there.'"
The men flying the Red jets could not have
asked for a more naive and sincere compliment.
The McGraw-Hill correspondent speculated that
the fliers probably include "Chinese, North Koreans, Poles, Germans, Mongols, Russians and
perhaps others." But no "Caucasians" have yet
been identified in downed planes.

1952

MILITARY
MADNESS

"We have no desire to delude ourselves as Hitler deluded the German people with his rash promises about German 'secret weapons.'"

Sec'y of the Army, Frank Pace Jr.

"We are still looking for a quick-and-easy war."

Hanson Baldwin of the *N. Y. Times*

AS SEEN in an earlier chapter, GM's president Charles Wilson said that if the armaments race continued the U. S. "would take the road to war—even as Hitler did." In May 1952 the U. S. Secretary of the Army made the statement quoted above, disclaiming any desire to behave like Hitler. The analogies to Hitler by American leaders are deeply disturbing. What kind of policies are being pursued which require reference to Hitler for clarification?

American political strategy is based on anti-Communism at home and abroad. This was also Hitler's main political theme. The parallel is obvious. What is not so obvious is that American military strategy has also followed Hitlerian lines of thought—the strategy of the blitz, the quick and easy victory. The up-to-date counterpart of Hitler's panzer blitz is the atomic bombing blitz. This has been America's strategy based on the long-range bomber.

That this has been U. S. strategy is admitted by the editor of Forrestal's diaries, Walter Millis, in the course of a review by him of a book of George F. Kennan, present Ambassador

311

to Moscow, and one of the chief architects of the Cold War. Millis says:

"A nation which, starting from the high moral idealism of the Kellogg pact [1], **ended with the atomic bomb strategy**— as stupid, barbarous and destructive as anything since the politics of Genghis Khan—must realize that something is wrong." [2] (emphasis added)

Why does Millis, who admired Forrestal so greatly, say that "something is wrong" with our atomic bomb strategy, when Forrestal himself played a key role in shaping that strategy, and when Millis himself called the atomic bomb "the real core of American military strength?" [3] Why does he now say it is "stupid, barbarous and destructive?" Is it because he is morally revolted at the thought of war? Not at all. In the very same review he says we "must frankly be willing to play power politics, or even fight limited wars. . . ."

The key to Millis' change of heart is the failure of atomic strategy. Long range strategic bombing with atomic weapons is not possible on a scale sufficient to give the U. S. victory in a global war. The military basis of total war against the Soviet Union has collapsed. There are four reasons for this collapse: (a) Soviet production of atomic weapons, (b) growing insecurity of American air bases in Europe and Near East, (c) Soviet radar defenses, (d) Soviet defensive jet supremacy. The last is of such importance that it will be treated separately.

BLOCKING THE AMERICAN STRATEGY

Soviet production of atomic weapons has an obvious importance as a retaliatory weapon. If we start atom bombing them, the Russians will atom bomb us. While atomic bombing is not decisive for either side, its possibilities impose a burden of defense which is formidable. More important, however,

1 A pact negotiated on the initiative of U. S. Sec'y of State Kellogg in 1923, which provided that the signatories would outlaw war and renounce it as an instrument of national policy
2 N. Y. Herald Tribune, Book Review Section, Sept. 30, 1951. Millis is one of the editors of the Herald Tribune
3 Forrestal Diaries, p. 462

Soviet possession of the bomb makes our air bases abroad insecure. Airbases designed for strategic offensives are large, difficult to hide, and eminently suitable targets for an atom bomb. Furthermore the Europeans in the front lines are growing more and more reluctant to play America's game when they would take the brunt of the atomic warfare.

As for the American bases in Europe and the Near East, they were considered insecure even before Soviet atomic power developed. These bases cannot be held against Soviet ground forces by any army now in existence on the continent of Europe, or even by any planned for 1954. [4]

Furthermore, even for this planned army, the United States is relying more and more on West Germany to provide the manpower, armaments and leadership for Western Europe's militarization. This means opposing a unified, democratic Germany and an alliance with former Nazi generals and cartelists whom we so recently fought.

This alliance may please American generals; it does not please the peoples of Europe who have been under Nazi domination. Not only do all European peoples oppose a new war, they all oppose German re-armament to such an extent that reactionary governments have to temporize. The morale of any European army which has strong German contingents will be very fragile.

Besides, what kind of a European army can be built up when millions and millions of people have pledged not to fight in any aggressive war against the Soviet Union. Inevitably huge sections of the French and Italian armies are Communist or Communist influenced. Who is going to make them fight the Soviet Union? Nazi generals? The entire idea is absurd.

4 1954 goal is 43 divisions, including 12 German divisions. All indications point to the fact that this goal will not be achieved. General Gruenther, American Chief of Staff, has "deplored the tendency of the European powers to lose sight of the 1954 goals." N. Y. Times, December 2, 1951. The U. S. News, August 15, 1952, says the target date for 1954 has been "abandoned"

One wonders why General Eisenhower who is such a busy man spent so much time in Europe, if the projected European Army cannot stop the Soviet Union. Walter Lippmann gives the answer:

"What then is the role of these ground divisions to which General Eisenhower has devoted so much energy. I do not know what he will say. But I venture to believe that their true role in the defense of Europe is to reinforce the authority of existing governments, making them strong enough to prevent the seizure of power by the Communist organizations." [5]

In other words, if the people vote Communist the Nazidominated European army will stifle the "seizure of power" in blood. This is exactly what Franco did—with the help of Hitler and Mussolini. The U. S. is following a deadly similar path.

It is obvious that the U. S. military no longer can count on European air bases. If these nearby bases are denied, the U. S. has lost an important element of the blitz strategy, namely the element of surprise. This element had already been seriously undermined by Soviet radar and jet defenses which are now first rate. This is not a guess: we know it because the A-bomb generals in Washington have been testing in peacetime the air defenses of the Soviet Union!

This frightening fact is revealed in **Look** magazine by Stephen White, its assistant managing editor. White reports that:

"American planes, by accident **and design** have probed the Russian radar screen and have discovered that fast Russian fighter planes rise into the skies long before the probers reach the borders of Russia." [6] (emphasis added)

White's article was the first open admission of such reckless provocation. It was confirmed a week later by columnist Joseph Alsop who has excellent contacts inside the Pentagon. Alsop stated flatly that both in Siberia and in Europe we have

5 N. Y. Herald Tribune, June 2, 1952
6 Look Magazine, June 3, 1952

been testing Soviet radar defenses. He writes:

"Our long range aircraft have been flying reconnaissance operations on the Siberian coast since **before** Korea; they have gone in far enough for interception to be attempted on more than one occasion. Equally, there can be little doubt that the Navy privateer shot down over the Baltic a couple of years ago was also on reconnaissance duty." 7 (emphasis added)

Warlike measures such as aerial reconnaissance have been carried out without the **knowledge or the consent** of the American people. They constitute reckless provocation by the U. S. against the Soviet Union. Yet when the Navy plane was shot down, screaming headlines accused the Soviet Union of provocation. The USSR was accused of brutality in shooting down "unarmed" planes. Recently a Swedish "unarmed" plane was also shot down. What people aren't told is that all reconnaissance planes are "unarmed," stripped down for speed.

In spite of the fact that the American government has been guilty of such unfriendly acts as air reconnaissance, Ambassador Kennan in Moscow protested to Russia in July 1952 against Soviet posters picturing Russian planes chasing American aircraft. Kennan said these posters feed the hatred against the U. S. The protest of Kennan is typical of the arrogance of the Cold War makers: Russia is unfriendly because she gets mad when American planes violate her frontiers! Inscrutable people these Russians.

The Kennan protest was headlined in all the newspapers which dwelt at length with the fact that three American planes have been shot down. The impression on the American public was that of Soviet unprovoked aggression. Not one newspaper however, saw fit to tell the American people what our planes had been doing, although obviously it was news. This incident is one of the clearest instances of how the daily press distorts the facts and feeds the "war psychosis" in

7 **Washington Post, June 13, 1952**

America.

Soviet radar defenses, Soviet atomic production and the growing insecurity of U. S. bases abroad all have contributed to making obsolete the American strategy of the atomic blitz. But the most important, overwhelming reason why U. S. atomic strategy has failed is the superiority of Soviet jet fighters as demonstrated in Korea.

On October 23, 1951, American B-29 superfortresses escorted by 100 American jet fighters set out to bomb an air strip at Namsi, deep in North Korea. They were met by 150 enemy jets and in the ensuing battle 3 B-29's were shot down and 5 so heavily damaged as to be counted a complete loss. [8]

Eight bombers were lost.

Eight seems a small number but it shook and rattled every A-bomb general in Washington, because only **eight** bombers had started out! The losses of October 23 were exactly 100%. As **Newsweek** put it, the losses had "approached the point of no return."

The significance of this event is grasped by one comparison: the **worst** losses in the air war over Germany, on the Schweinfurt raid, were only 40%, yet this figure was considered so prohibitive that no more daylight raids were made until long range fighter escort could be provided. The Schweinfurt losses of 40% **without fighter escort** was considered prohibitive; imagine then the Namsi losses of 100% **with fighter protection.**

U. S. LOSES AIR SUPREMACY IN KOREA

U. S. air supremacy over Korea was gone. No more daylight bombing with huge bombers. Bombing henceforth was done with small fighter bombers or at night as for example in the July raids on the Yalu River power stations. Moreover, we don't know what these raids cost American parents. Air Force generals have been cagy about our losses. Overall fig-

8 N. Y. Times, December 9, 1951

ures have come out only once in the entire Korean War—
March 1952, when Hanson Baldwin compiled a summary. His
figures are shocking. They showed that we lost **twice** as many
planes as the Chinese and North Korean Forces; "about 1800
to 1900 planes" for U. S. losses compared with 938 for the
enemy. [9]

Even these shocking figures do not tell the whole story.
Bombers have large crews, 14 men in a B-29. A jet fighter
has one man. The air battles take place over North Korean
territory. When a defensive fighter is shot down, the pilot may
parachute to safety. When an attacking plane is shot down,
its crew parachutes to imprisonment. Therefore, the ratio
of trained men lost is much greater than two to one, perhaps
as much as ten to one.

One final sobering thought. We have been fighting Chinese
and North Koreans whose air forces have been developed
over a period of some two years. Our airforce has been developing for almost forty years, with great installations,
tested training methods, developed schools, large teaching
staffs, and, above all, the tremendous battle experience
gained in nearly four years of global war over all kinds of
terrain in all kinds of weather.

Yet this modern airforce, meeting a hastily improvised
fledgling airforce, has not been able to maintain air supremacy. What would happen if we were to meet the Soviet air
force, as modern, as battle tested, as experienced as ours?
What would happen if we were to meet the Soviet air force
whose defensive **jet planes are better than ours, whose aviation industry is superior to ours?**

These startling facts are the basic reasons for the failure
of atomic strategy.

SOVIET TECHNOLOGICAL SUPERIORITY

Soviet technical achievements in jet planes outstrip the

9 N. Y. Times, March 27, 1952. These are total losses, combat and non-combat.

United States. The Soviet Union, for years described in our press as industrially backward, inefficient, incapable, suddenly blossoms out as superior to the United States which prides itself as the most highly developed, technically efficient industrial nation on earth. It seems incredible.

Yet the authority for this dramatic statement is none other than the Chief of the U. S. Air Force, General Hoyt S. Vandenberg. He said at a press conference:

"Soviet technicians have mastered **the design and production** problems of extremely high-speed aircraft to a degree which equals and in **some respects excels** all that we are able to demonstrate in warfare at the present time. Fortunately for us there is more to war than mere technical achievements."[10] (emphasis added)

The chief of our Air Force says that the Soviet Union "excels" the United States in jet design and production, that is, that in this field **the United States has been outstripped technologically**! The implications of this admission are so world-shaking and so important to the cause of peace that they deserve detailed attention.

Soviet jets are produced by Soviet designers and Soviet engineers. Soviet designers have out-designed British designers and got more power out of engines developed by the British themselves as told in **Aviation Week,** an American trade magazine of the aviation industry. [11] Another trade journal, **Aviation Age,** admits the ability of Soviet engineers:

"Russian airframe and engine designers . . . are very unusual people. Gifted, original, individualistic, and intensely practical, the lives they live are for the most part the exact antithesis to what most Americans would expect in a Communist state." [12]

Why should Americans expect "the exact antithesis," the opposite of the truth? Where do most Americans get their information? Where, but from the press and radio which systematically mislead our people on the Soviet Union with a stream of false ideas: that scientists in the Soviet Union

10 Press Conference, November 21, 1951, quoted by Stone
11 Quoted by Stone, N. Y. Daily Compass, January 3, 1952
12 Quoted by Stone, Hidden History, p. 342

are coerced, that they can only copy us, that socialism isn't working, that Soviet production is inferior, that Lend-Lease beat the Nazis in Russia and so on.

To the arrogant American generals it must have been a great shock to learn that Soviet designers and scientists are excellent. But, for the war-makers, there has followed even worse news. **The Soviet jet industry has surpassed the American in production methods and technical know-how!**

This seems truly fantastic. If there is one thing Americans are certain about it is that in production methods we lead the world. Yet the proof that we have been beaten in jet production methods comes from one of the most authoritative magazines in the business world, **Fortune** magazine.

Fortune is the aristocrat of the Henry Luce publications. It speaks to and for the brains in Big Business, the policy-making corporation executives. In December 1951 it published certain truths which could no longer be ignored:

"For the next year and a half, at the very least, nearly every airplane built in the U.S. will contain basic structural members produced by methods that should by now be obsolete.
"This means that thousands of planes for the ninety-five wing Air Force will cost more and take longer to build than is necessary. The reason: a **total lack** of closed-die forging presses of the size—25,000 to 50,000 tones—deemed essential for the efficient production of modern planes." [13]

Such presses are gigantic machine tools, taller than a six story house above ground, with an added three stories below ground.

The technical reasons for the need for big presses are simple. At modern jet speeds, wings and frames of planes must be very strong and very light. Welding is both too heavy and too weak. In America the problem has been met by machining wings out of solid slabs of aluminum, that is scooping the metal out bit by bit, like primitive man scooping out a canoe from a tree-trunk with a stone ax. In a press, the part

13 Fortune, December, 1951, p. 111

What's the meaning of this?

Russia has them...
We haven't!

Fortune...Reports Business News-in-Depth

Fortune ... Where Business Concentrates

Dec. 14, 1951
U.S. News &
World Report

...freeze designs... stimulate produ...

In the long run, probably the most vital problem of all arises from the fact that Russia is producing more engineers than we are. Production capacity basically is tied to the supply of trained technicians. Apparently the U.S. must make a major readjustment in its manpower policies, if it wants to catch up.

is forged at a saving of material (400% savings) and of time. Says **Fortune** that Soviet presses "turn out, **in minutes,** aircraft parts that required **scores of manhours** to produce by conventional methods. This was mass production on a scale to astonish **even** United States engineers." (emphasis added). Adds **Fortune** ruefully:

"It is never pleasant to discover that the U. S. has not been first with a major technological development, particularly one that has to do with mass production." [14]

To soften the bitter news, **Fortune** gives credit to the Germans for developing the big presses. It is the Soviet Union that worries them however. The article says:

"The U. S. lack of big forging presses might be less distressing if Russia were in the same fix. It isn't. Shortly after V-E Day the Russians hauled away Germany's enormous 33,000-ton forging press . . . the press is reliably reported in operation. It is also known that the Russians have been building the monster 55,000-ton press they found on Krupp drawing boards. In all, Russia may have **ten big presses,** and they could well explain how it has apparently raised production of jets to an impressive figure." [15] (emphasis added)

As against ten presses estimated for the Soviets, the United States has two, taken from Germany. These were minor (in this league) presses, a mere 16,000 tons. By 1952 the U. S. had built a press of 18,500 tons. The Soviets have been using a 33,000 tonner and building a 55,000 tonner!

The size of the presses is of key significance because 25,000 tons are the minimum for efficiency and for the larger parts, presses of 50,000 and 75,000 tons are essential. Beyond reasonable doubt, Soviet jet aviation industry is superior to the American, and this superiority is long-range. It takes from three to five years to build the huge presses that **Fortune** discusses.

Industrial achievements are always the result of trained

14 Fortune, December, 1951, p. 146
15 Ibid., p. 112

personnel. If Soviet jet planes are excellent, Soviet designers must be excellent, but for the designers to be effective, the engineers must be good and behind them are the scientists and the professors in the universities, the teachers in the secondary schools. The chain of intellectual development from child to plane designer must be strong in all its links.

SOVIET TRAINING BEHIND SOVIET TECHNOLOGY

If Soviet aviation industry surpasses the Americans, Soviet technicians must be well trained. Draftsmen and machinists, foremen and plant managers, apprentices and teachers, trade schools and management schools, secondary schools and primary schools, again, the entire chain of technical development must be strong in all its links.

Once these facts are clearly grasped, the following admission by a big business magazine stands out in its full astounding implications:

". . . Russia is producing **more** engineers than we are. Production capacity basically is tied to the supply of trained technicians. Apparently the U. S. must make a major re-adjustment in its manpower policies, **if it wants to catch up.**"[16] (emphasis added)

This statement is worth deep study. A magazine of big business, written for big business, warns the most highly industrialized nation in the world that it has **to catch up** with the Soviet Union in producing engineers!

For years Soviet science and Soviet education has been slandered and lied about in the popular press and radio of America. Today this still goes on, but here and there, reluctantly and unwillingly, part of the truth has to come out. Says columnist Marquis Childs that "Russian science had a long and distinguished record before 1917. Since 1917 the Bolsheviks have pushed it with every resource."[17] A British educator, Eric Ashby, President of Queens University at Belfast, visited the Soviet Union and wrote about it. Although he is

16 U. S. News and World Report, December 14, 1951
17 Washington Post, April 16, 1952

strongly anti-Soviet and anti-Marxist the university president makes these significant admissions:

".... the prestige of scientists has been deliberately boosted until the more distinguished among them are invested with the glamour reserved in the United States for film stars; working conditions for scientists are good . . . men of genius are given every encouragement and facility to work. . . .

".... in less than thirty years time, leadership in Soviet science will have passed to the post-war generation, to men who are well trained, hard-headed and realistic."[18]

The importance of science and engineering to plane design and production is obvious; not so well known is the importance of technical training for pilots. A modern military plane requires a high level of educational background and here too, it is the United States which is having difficulties, as revealed by the N. Y. Times' military expert, Hanson Baldwin:

"The newest planes are crammed with electronic gear. . . . Some youngsters who might qualify for this new art do not have the educational background, the incentive or the industry required to buckle down to the long and intensive training and study needed. . . ."[19]

To meet this problem, says Baldwin:

"Educational standards and aptitude grades have been reduced to a minimum. For instance college requirements have now been waived and high school graduates are accepted, yet the Air Force is having difficulty filling its quotas."[20]

In contrast, the Soviet Union seems to be having no difficulties in pilots, according to Air Secretary Finletter before a Congressional appropriations committee. [21] As to their quality since the war, no one knows since they haven't been in battle. There is no evidence of one single Soviet flier in combat anywhere since the war, except in defense of Soviet borders against reconnaissance planes.

There is however evidence of the quality of their pupils,

18 N. Y. Times, Magazine Section, January 6, 1952
19 N. Y. Times, May 2, 1952
20 N. Y. Times, May 1, 1952
21 Washington Post, April 17, 1952

the Korean fighter pilots trained by Soviet fliers. According to American fliers in Korea the enemy pilots are as good as the Americans. [22]

SOVIET JETS: FACTORS FOR PEACE

Soviet jet fighters have been developed for defense. An informed columnist, Alfred Friendly, states flatly that "the MIG-15 is an interceptor with a short range, 160 miles, and is not an offensive fighter." [23] In Eastern Germany, airfields are built with runways that "could handle fighters but were not strong enough to take bombers," forming "a network of defensive airstrips . . . to make a fighter screen against either atom bombers or conventional bombers." [24]

Walter Lippmann has drawn the obvious conclusion:

"What we think we know about their (Soviet) military preparations does not suggest that they have any intention of starting a world war for the military conquest of the world. . . . What the military preparations do suggest, is that the **Soviet Union is working to make it impossible for the United States to make war** successfully against it." [25] (emphasis added)

In the same article Lippmann also admits that our present war plans hinge "on strategic airpower with atomic bombs," and that present trends may make "strategic bombing of the Soviet vital centers too costly." Hanson Baldwin had already pointed out the lesson of Korea, that Soviet jets had, "forced some of our most ardent advocates of strategic bombing to take another good hard look at our prospects" since long range penetration of Russia without fighter support was out of the question, and "the supply difficulties of sending swarms of fighters deep into Russia would be terrific." Furthermore "it was very difficult for jets to prevent other jets from getting at . . . the bombers." [26]

22 Aviation Week, December 17, 1951, quoted by Stone in N.Y. Daily Compass, January 3, 1952
23 Washington Post, May 14, 1952
24 U.S. News and World Report, December 15, 1950
25 Washington Post, May 22, 1952
26 N.Y. Times, December 9, 1951, quoted by Stone, Hidden History, p. 344

When to the Soviet defensive jets one adds the radar warning screen which U. S. reconnaissance planes have found alert, and the radar controlled artillery whose accuracy we have ascertained in Korea and Indo-China, it is clear that the strategy of atomic bombing has failed.

SUPER-WEAPONS: THE HITLER DREAM

As the fallacies of American war planes become apparent a curious split has developed in the speeches, and perhaps the thinking, of top leaders in the United States. On one hand some have been hinting that we have and are developing super-weapons"; on the other hand others have been warning us that "super-weapons" do not win wars.

In January 1952, Charles E. Wilson, then Defense Mobilizer said:

"We are not preparing for the last war. We are preparing for a Buck Rogers' era." [27]

President Truman at West Point:

"'An atomic artillery piece has been developed and tested and will have to be reckoned with in the future. The Navy is working on its first atomic-powered submarine." [28]

The accent of these statements and actions was all on the word "super." It seems as if our leaders were trying to reassure us of our technological superiority. It is talk reminiscent of Hitler's boasts as he was losing, and indeed one high government official has made this parallel. Said Secretary of the Army Frank Pace:

"Most of our atomic weapons for Army use are weapons of the future. . . .
"We have no desire to delude ourselves as **Hitler deluded the German people** with his rash promises about German 'secret weapons.' " [29] (emphasis added)

That an American Secretary of the Army should use

27 N. Y. Times, January 22, 1952
28 N. Y. Times, May 21, 1952
29 N. Y. Times, October 14, 1951

Hitler as a warning to the American people is a fitting commentary to the kind of aggressive military thinking current in America today. At the same time, this statement is indirect proof of the failure of American strategy. If our military strategy were sound, we wouldn't be worrying about "delusions."

American atomic blitz strategy won't work. Our militarists have reached the end of the line. Hanson Baldwin, the N. Y. Times military writer, put it bluntly in an article entitled "There is No Military Miracle in Sight."

"We are still looking for a quick-and-easy war. And we are still looking for a cheap-and-easy means of security. But there is no such thing. There is no 'absolute weapon.' . . . Wars of today and the foreseeable tomorrow may start in the 'wild blue yonder' and end in the rubble of burning cities, but, in between, the ground army—the man in the mud—is very likely to be the arbiter of victory. There is no cheap-and-easy defense, or quick-and-simple victory; wars are still won by blood and sweat and tears." [30]

Ground armies, says Baldwin, are likely to be arbiters of victory. This thought chills American militarists because the U. S. achilles' heel in any aggressive war is lack of manpower! The U. S. population is some 150,000,000; the USSR and its allies have some 800,000,000. Experience shows that total mobilization yields roughly 1 in 10. During the war the U. S. had 15 million men under arms; the equivalent figure for the Socialist armies would be 80 million men!

But someone may say: What about the U. S. allies? The answer to that question is in Korea: 95% of all troops there are American troops. Allies fight well in a just, defensive war —they are totally unreliable in an unjust, aggressive war as Hitler learned with his Italians, and Rumanians, and Hungarians and Spaniards. Attacked by the U. S., Soviet allies will undoubtedly fight. At the same time, U. S. allies will melt away leaving perhaps Franco Spain, Royal Greece and feudal Turkey as the American prop. Their total population is less

30 N. Y. Times, Magazine Section

than one Chinese province.

The United States needs allies not only for manpower but for staging areas and military jumping off places. American troops have to go 6000 miles to get at the Soviet Union and its allies who will be on their home ground, defending their homes. U. S. military aggression has to have countries near the Soviet bloc which will court suicide in turning their land to America. To state the problem is to show how formidable it is. Walter Lippmann has revealed that the less blind of U. S. militarists are acutely conscious of the problem.

"The ill-informed and the irresponsible may talk wildly about 'dropping the bomb.' But those who understand the military position best know that without **the active assistance of a dozen nations** in Europe and Asia, not much of the military might of this country can be brought to bear upon the Soviet Union." [31] (emphasis added)

Where will the U. S. get these "dozen nations" if it starts a war of aggression? Already American aggressive plans and American aggressive talk have alienated those allies which American dollars had bought. Unmistakably, a political debacle is in the making.

31 Washington Post, January 1, 1952

ECONOMIC

BANKRUPTCY

CHAPTER 15

*". . . the present expenditure on arma-
ments is ruinous. It will ruin all the countries of the world unless we can find some
way out of it."*
Lord Blackford, House of Lords,
July 8, 1952

*"Actually the occupying powers . . . were
doing things for Hitler's New Order that
Hitler himself had never been able to do."*
J. S. Martin, Chief, Decartelization
Branch, Occupied Germany, 1945-47

THERE IS no longer any talk of eco-
nomic recovery in Europe. Instead, there is frantic talk of
staving off bankruptcy—at least until after the American
elections.

Walter Lippmann writes that:

". . . with some more palliatives the developing crisis can probably be postponed until after there is a new Administration to face
up to the new decisions. This is an optimistic estimate." [1]

Left, right and center, both here and abroad, are unanimous in their estimate of the economic realities in Europe:
imminent bankruptcy staved off by ever greater reliance on
U. S. dollars.

Churchill says that England's "head is above water but
it is not enough to float." [2]

Robert Boothby, a British Conservative, declares that

1 Washington Post, June 16, 1952
2 Ibid.

329

Europe is "in the midst of a 'deepening economic crisis.'" [3]

In France and Italy, the picture is the same. As is usual in the "free enterprise" countries, the burden is shrinking financial reserves and greater dependence on the U. S. dole.

ARMAMENTS vs. SOLVENCY

When Nazi Germany re-armed, Goering said "Guns or butter"; Germany couldn't have both. Today in Europe, however, "the problem is not guns or butter, **but guns or bread!**" [4] (emphasis in original). Europe's rickety economy cannot produce more guns without producing less bread. When the United States insisted on high-speed rearmament as the price of dollar aid, it inevitably caused an immediate cut in living standards.

No one today denies that armaments are responsible for Europe's crisis. Even Winston Churchill, late in July, asked Parliament for a "reshaping" of the arms program to prevent it from becoming "utterly beyond our economic capacity to bear."

Lord Blackford was more direct. He is a member of the British House of Lords, and one of the recognized spokesmen of the "City," London's financial powerhouse. He said,

"I have always thought that the present expenditure on armaments is completely ruinous. It will ruin all the countries of the world unless we can find some way out of it." [5]

Lord Blackford was followed by Lord Balfour, chairman of Lloyds Bank, who asserted that the British people must take further cuts in their standard of living. "The stark truth," he said, "has to be told to the people."

ECONOMIC WARFARE

Along with the preparations for hot war has come a

3 N. Y. Times, May 27, 1952
4 Andre Visson, Washington Post, December 28, 1951
5 Quoted by Gordon Schaffer in the National Guardian, August 7, 1952. This hard-hitting Progressive news weekly is indispensable reading. No American can be really well-informed on current affairs without it

policy of economic war. The chief feature of this is the boy-cott on East-West trade. The United States foreign aid legislation provides that dollars will be cut off to any nation which sells "strategic goods" to the Soviet Union or its allies.

What is included under the heading of "strategic goods?" As Edward Crankshaw, anti-Soviet British journalist wrote:

"Nor is it possible to distinguish with the least effect between war-like and unwarlike, strategic and non-strategic articles of trade. Because if a country, as Russia, can import unwarlike articles from abroad she can then afford to divert a corresponding sector of her economy from manufacturing those unwarlike articles to warlike ones. It is all or nothing. . . ." [6]

The U. S. is trying to force Europe to accept a policy of "nothing" traded with the east. Lippman describes the Ameri-can policy as one of "virtual embargo and blockade of the whole Communist orbit." [7]

The effect of this is literally to strangle the economy of western Europe. All the countries of western Europe must trade to live. Their normal source of raw materials is East-ern Europe and China. Their normal market for manufac-tures is Eastern Europe.

United States policy has cut them off from Russian grain and timber, and forced them to buy in the United States at higher prices. We have also cut them off from selling in a market that contains one-third the population of the earth, and not substituted any other market. Is it any wonder that Western Europe rumbles with discontent?

The **New York Times** reports from Geneva that . . . "there have been many rough sessions recently between United States and West European officials on the subject of East and West trade," and that "increased trade with the East is a growingly popular panacea in Left Wing and even

6 N. Y. Times, Magazine Section, April 6, 1952
7 N. Y. Herald Tribune, January 14, 1952

in business circles in Western Europe." [8]

This explains the relative success of the trade talks held in Moscow in April, 1952. Business men of all political complexions from all over Western Europe went to Moscow to try to revive East-West trade. The large number of deals that resulted showed that some businessmen are determined to break down the barriers to trade.

Still other businessmen trade with the east in defiance of U. S. threats, and sometimes win support of their governments. Both the Netherlands and Denmark have sold "prohibited" goods to the Soviet Union openly, and many other countries have done the same thing secretly.

Others who are not quite so bold merely plead. Crankshaw ". . . if Britain should become convinced that she **cannot survive** without Russian grain and timber and Russian and Chinese outlets for her exports, she **should be allowed** to work out her own salvation. . . ." [9]

The U. S.-imposed embargo on East-West trade has proved to be a bonanza for U. S. corporations. Banning purchases in the east means that Europeans have to buy from the U. S., and Europe has been flooded by U. S. goods. Since the end of the war, the U. S. has sold the rest of the world $47 billion dollars **more** than she bought. Europe is drowning in a sea of Coca-Cola.

The main instrument of U. S. conquest of the European market has been the Marshall Plan. When the Marshall Plan came to an end, this year, there were no triumphant statements from any capital of the world, including Washington. The reason is simple: the Marshall Plan has been a dismal failure.

MARSHALL PLAN: PROMISE vs. PERFORMANCE

Congress voted the first Marshall Plan appropriation in April, 1948. Congress and the American people were told

8 N. Y. Times, April 10, 1952
9 N. Y. Times, Magazine Section, April 6, 1952

that for about $20 billion spread out over four years, we could buy a political and an economic victory.

When the Marshall Plan was passed, the Communists had already been ejected from the governments of France and Italy, as a result of U. S. pressure. Marshall Plan dollars now were supposed to discourage Frenchmen and Italians from voting for their Communist parties, which had received more votes than any other parties in both countries. This was the political victory that the Marshall Plan predicted. It was supposed to be accomplished by raising the standard of living in Europe so that the workers would like "free enterprise" again.

A closely related promise of the Marshall Plan was that Europe would "recover" and become "self-sufficient," without continuous U. S. aid. Winthrop Aldrich, Chairman of the Chase National Bank, and one of our top financiers summarized the prevailing view in May, 1948:

". . . the European Recovery Program [Marshall Plan] would reach its goal if Europe achieved economic self-sufficiency by June 30, 1952." [10]

In August, 1952, nobody talks about these things any more. Europe was not made self-sufficient by the Marshall Plan, but is more dependent than ever, because of the Marshall Plan. One example illustrates the process.

In 1937 Western Europe imported 2,250,000 standards of timber from eastern Europe.

In 1951 Western Europe imported only 170,444 standards from Eastern Europe, but imported more than 600,000 standards from the United States and Canada. [11]

What about the promised political "victory?" That, too has failed. The European workers don't like monopolists any more than they did before, and they vote for the Communist parties in the same or even larger numbers. The reason is

10 Wall Street Journal, May 20, 1948
11 N. Y. Times, May 7, 1952

that under "free enterprise," foreign aid always aids the employer, never the worker. This has been admitted by conservative U. S. labor leaders who originally supported the Marshall Plan, and then went to see how it was working. Witness number one: John W. Livingston, Vice-President, United Automobile Workers Union, CIO:

"The Marshall Plan has been a 'miserable failure' insofar as skilled wage earners in Germany, Italy and France are concerned. . . . Huge profits of companies whose plants have been rebuilt and rehabilitated by Marshall Plan funds and extremely low wages have lowered worker morale to make effective and convincing Communist propaganda." [12]

Witness number two: Jacob Potofsky, President, Amalgamater Clothing Workers, CIO:

"Our money has been used primarily to strengthen the governments in power and the industrialists. The rich grow richer and the poor poorer. . . . European industry has retained the time-honored theory of unbelieveably high profits and low wages. Labor has not had the benefit of improved conditions since the end of the war." [13]

Witnesses number three, four and five: William Belandger, V-P, CIO Textile Workers' Union; Harold Gibbons, AFL Teamsters in St. Louis; Carmen Lucia, AFL Hatters Union:

"The American Unionists, fresh from a series . . . of French industrial centers, voiced frank alarm about the economic hardship endured by French workers' families. . . . All three were shocked to find that prices had been rising steadily in France during recent years while wages have been held down." [14]

The Marshall Plan was fine for capturing markets. It collapsed in its attempt to capture workers' support for "free enterprise" and the Cold War.

The U. S. has given up the attempt to win support from

12 N. Y. Times, August 15, 1950
13 Advance, organ of the ACW, October 1, 1951
14 CIO News, August 21, 1950. It should be noted that Philip Murray and other top CIO leaders forced a split in the CIO because unions like UE, ILWU, Furriers, Mine-Mill and others refused to accept the Marshall Plan and refused to accept Truman's policies

the peoples of Europe. Instead we have based our entire strategy on open support of the most hated people in Europe: the unreconstructed former Nazis who now run Western Germany.

All the rest of Europe is being organized to support Germany's mushrooming war industries. This policy was begun, in secret, even before the Marshall Plan. It was exposed by James S. Martin who was Chief of the Decartelization Branch of U. S. Military Government until July 1947, when he resigned in protest at Washington's sabotage of Roosevelt's plan to break up the German monopolies who financed Hitler's rise to power. Martin wrote of our 1947 policy:

"The effect in Germany was the same as if the original architects of the New Order [the Nazis] had been in charge. . . . [15]
"Actually, the occupying powers . . . were doing things for Hitler's New Order that Hitler himself had never been able to do. . . . What was emerging was a European economy dominated from a central hub of German heavy industry, with an outer ring of satellite areas supplying food, raw materials, and light industrial products." [16]

Today, with the North Atlantic Treaty Alliance and the Schuman Plan, this is open and official U. S. policy.

Why has the U. S. adopted such ruinous economic policies? Why did we start the Cold War and head straight for a military showdown with the Soviet Union—perhaps for global war itself? The only real answer is to look more deeply into the forces that shape our country's policies.

WHAT MAKES FOREIGN POLICY

Foreign policy cannot be explained, fundamentally, by saying that some Presidents are "good," and other Presidents are "bad." The foreign policies a nation follows are a result of the internal pressures of its economy, as we have seen in Chapter 3.

The U. S. economy has been coming more and more under

15 James S. Martin, All Honorable Men, Boston, 1950, p. 241
16 Ibid., p. 244

the sway of Big Business. A handful of monopolists, banks and insurance companies control most of our country's production. Monopolies have only one reason for existence: to make as much profit as possible.

To accomplish this they try their best to undermine workers' wages, speed-up the assembly lines and force workers into overtime work to make a living wage.

But there are limits to such measures: Many workers have strong unions. So monopolists turn to other methods to increase profits. They swallow up smaller businesses, they introduce labor-saving machinery. Basically however, this doesn't help. It is not machines but only workers who can produce more than it costs to support them, and therefore provide profits for the boss. So the mad rush to introduce machinery to displace labor really **reduces** the opportunities for profits in the long run.

Furthermore, the mechanization of production results in a flood of goods which impoverished workers can't buy. This is the so-called "air-pocket" in the economy discussed in Chapter 3. As we have seen, big business has turned to armaments to keep the economy going, and is trying to create the impression that armaments are the only way to prevent a depression. THIS IS NOT TRUE. A prosperous economy can be maintained, **without war,** by following the program laid down in Roosevelt's **Economic Bill of Rights**. On the same day that orders for military radar equipment are cancelled, orders can be placed for civilian radar equipment for safety in all our airports. Steel cancelled for battleships goes into cars; cloth cancelled for uniforms goes into clothes; lumber cancelled for barracks goes into homes.

Monopolists work hard to keep the American people from finding peaceful solutions. They want to control wages at home and scour the world for profits. Wall Street really regards the world as its oyster.

It captures foreign markets, and sells goods which workers at home can't afford to buy. It builds plants in foreign countries, especially colonial countries, and makes super-profits from those workers' pitiful wages. It buys raw mate-ilras from backward areas at ridiculously low prices, and sells them manufactures at ridiculously high prices.

This is the basis of the Cold War. The Soviet Union interferes with these Wall Street plans to rule the world. It stands as an example to the peoples of the world that they don't have to submit to the monopolists. And it stands as a great power which throws its political influence against imperialism, and offers countries, even capitalist countries, the alternative of profitable trade on an equal basis. The Soviet Union is a real obstacle to the monopolists. The key to postwar history is the drive of monopolists to smash that Socialist obstacle, if necessary by war.

This new surge of U. S. Imperialism [17] is coming on the world scene at a time when the older empires are bursting at the seams. Colonial peoples are in revolt, in Asia, the Middle East, and Africa. Wall Street hopes to pick up the pieces, but they are getting too hot to handle.

THE CRISIS IN COLONIALISM

Colonies have always meant super-profits for the British, French, Germans, etc. Today, however, an increasing number of colonies are becoming a drain on the imperialists. Indo-China, once France's richest prize, now drains away practically all the U. S. dollars France gets, and chews up her army piece by piece. Malaya, the pearl of Britain's oriental empire is in a similar state. Iran has seized foreign oil properties. In all of these countries, the people have refused to continue to make super-profits for foreigners. They are demanding freedom to improve their lot.

17 Victor Perlo's book, American Imperialism, contains a brilliant analysis of the methods of Imperialism, and its effects on the people, especially the Negro people. See Chapter 4, footnote 57

The economic success of the Soviet Union and the rapid development of the so-called "backward countries" under Socialism is a powerful incentive to the other colonial countries to follow their example. This danger is pointed out by Michael L. Hoffman in the **N. Y. Times** in May 1952.

"The Communist countries, while their known accomplishments do not appeal to the West, have done much better with their 'underdeveloped' regions than the non-Communist regimes of the Middle East and Asia have done with similar regions. However much the production results in the Soviet Union and its satellites are concealed or exaggerated, enough is known by the Western governments to establish beyond doubt that a process of growth has been initiated. **No such process is yet apparent** in most of the Arab world, India and Southeast Asia. . . . Western leaders who work in close contact with non-Communist and non-European peoples are increasingly aware of the **spreading belief that communism is bringing those aspects of modern civilization to underdeveloped regions faster than are the regimes modeled on the Western pattern.**" [18] (emphasis added)

If the colonial nations free themselves, imperialism will starve for profits. The U. S., as the strongest remaining imperialist nation, has the dirty job of trying to rescue the rotten structure of colonialism. Sometimes we try it by giving the British or French money and arms. As a last resort, we will fight ourselves. We're doing it in Korea, and may soon be doing it in Indo-China. The **New York Times** reported on July 31:

"The possibility that France may be compelled by public opinion at home to abandon Indo-China to the Communists has been raised in negotiations with the U. S. . . . Between the lines of the official French argument . . . is the suggestion that if France pulls out of Indo-China, U. S. troops must be moved in." [19]

The freedom of colonial countries would greatly increase world trade. Coupled with the trade of the Socialist bloc, this would solve Europe's economic problems.

Economists, businessmen, statesmen are all becoming

18 N. Y. Times, May 19, 1952
19. N. Y. Times, July 31, 1952

aware of the obvious. As a correspondent has put it, they are "much more worried about the red ink in the national balance sheets than the red tide beyond the Elbe." [20]

Increasing numbers of people see that U. S. economic policies are bringing them to ruin, and that the alternative of Soviet trade is their only salvation. That's why so many businessmen of all Western European countries went to the Moscow trade conference in April, 1952, and concluded up to 20 billion dollars in trade deals.

The leader of the British delegation was one of the most distinguished and respected of international statesmen, Lord Boyd-Orr, first Director-General of the United Nations Food and Agricultural Organization.

One day, late in July, a reporter from the **London Daily Express** went to visit Lord Boyd-Orr to find out what had happened to the 28 million dollars of trading deals the British had made with the Eastern nations at the Moscow conference.

Boyd-Orr's answer reveals that there is at least one man with some sense left in upper-class Britain. He said:

". . . the whole 10,000,000 pounds ($28,000,000) worth of contracts will go through, and if they are followed up vigorously by this country they should lead to 100,000,000 pounds worth of trade. I am the only sane Imperialist left." [21]

20 W. Richardson, N.Y. Post, August 20, 1952
21 London Daily Express, July 23, 1952

339

U.S. Officials Disturbed by 'Anti-Americanism' in Europe

By Ned Russell

American officials in Europe are becoming...

abhor and distrust everything American. In fact, Europeans...

distresses Europeans particularly... a withdrawal from the U. N. This probably is no more than a threat...

Anti-Americanism in India

Asian Attitude Based on U.S. Political Speeches, Hollywood Fi...

By Margaret Parton

NEW DELHI.—The easiest way to start a discussion among for... eigners or Indians these days...

American politicians as reported in the Indian press; (2) Hollywood films and (3) American weekly news...

British on Sovi... of Ma...

DISLIKE OF U.S. HELD INCREASING ABROAD

There are oth...

ARAB VIEW OF U.S. HELD AT LOW POINT

LAKE SUCCESS, Jan. 8 — Dr. Charles Malik, chief Lebanese delegate to the United Nations, expressed today the view that United States prestige in the Middle East had sunk to its lowest ebb in history.

He blamed the altered attitude...

The Washington Post

COMPLETE CAPITAL EDITION

Seventy-fifth Year in the Nation's Capital

WEDNESDAY, JULY 30, 1952   WTOP AM (1500; FM (96.3; TV (CH. 9)   FIVE CENTS

IRANIANS DEMAND U.S. ARMY ADVISERS QUIT THE COUNTRY

Deputies Call for Departure as Parliament Approves New Mossadegh Cabinet

POINT 4 ALSO ATTACKED

Henderson Talks With Premier —Only Opposition Deputy Is Ousted From Chamber

By ALBION ROSS
Special to The New York Times

TEHERAN, Iran, July 29—In... debate in which Premier Moha... med Mossadegh received a unan... mous vote of confidence from Pa... liament, deputies and galleries a... plauded today a demand by... Deputy, that United States m... named Damavandi, National Fr... tary advisers leave Iran.

Sixty-eight deputies were... ent and sixty-eight voted con... dence in the new Mossadegh Cab... inet and its program. The Oppo...

Iran Reported Ready To Ask Withdrawal Of U. S. Aid Missions

American Call On Mossadegh As Deputies Cry 'Kick Out Yanks'

TEHRAN, Iran, July 29 —Demands for the withdrawal of United States...

KOREA NEWS TURNS ARABS FROM WEST

U. S. Prestige Wanes Rapidly and Earlier Neutrality View Shifts to Isolationism

Special to The New York Times

LEBANON, July 19—The United States and the West are rapidly losing prestige in the Arab world as a result of the news from Korea. The strong attachment public opinion to neutrality, very evident here, the Korean war broke out, is turning into a passionate isolationism.

Though the government of certain Arab states have refused to go along with Egypt's complete isolation policy in regard to Korea, most every available report, completely convinced report, American difficulties in Korea... proof that the common enthusiasm for neutrality is justified.

The idea is steadily gaining ground that the United States is weaker than anyone thought that for the Arab states to throw in their lot with the West, or any contingency would be worse.

To the present feeling is added emphasis that had been placed previously on news and figures of American and the results... nander Western and the W...

SAIGON IRE VENTED ON U.S. NAVY CREWS

Sailors Were 'Shoved Around' by Rioting Ho Adherents— Schools in City Struck

SAIGON, Indo-China, March 30 (P).—The goodwill mission of two United States destroyers ended today, after a week-end of Communist-led anti-American rioting that saw United States sailors "shoved around" and left Saigon seething with unrest.

Students in all Saigon schools struck today... lice sent... three-... sixty night... under arrest...

The... the Rock... Stickell...
on schedule...

The agit... Chi Minh, a... of anti-Gov... so much dist... lation of r... state of c... around Vie...
over Unit...

1952

POLITICAL DEBACLE

CHAPTER 16

"The United States is involved in the affairs of its Allies to a degree that no other government was involved in the past. . . . The United States has done many things that would never have been tolerated. . . ."
James Reston, N. Y. *Times*,
March 22, 1952

"The American government's 'fiat' is virtually law for the other Western governments. . . ."
Prof. A. J. Toynbee, London *Observer*,
March 25, 1952

"An American today in Asia had better not go out at night. He is likely to get shot."
James A. Michener
The Voice of Asia, 1951

WENDELL WILLKIE, traveling around the world in the last war, found a vast reservoir of good will towards the United States among all the peoples of the world. In international relations such good will is clearly a great asset. In seven years of the Cold War and Korean War, this asset has been wantonly squandered. Today there is not a single government in the world, including Franco Spain, that trusts the U. S.; and as for the peoples of the world, the word "American" has become synonymous with corruption, reaction, arrogance, atomic madness, warmongering and napalm bombs.

England has been our closest ally. The Cold War was conceived by the Anglo-American bloc against the Soviet Union. With the existence of the atom bomb, England is now in the front line in case of war, and America's drive to war in a source of great fear not only to the British people, but to the British government as well. Coupled with American arrogance, America's warmongering has given rise to political movements marked by dislike and mistrust of the United States.

Professor Toynbee, a conservative British historian, has given voice to these attitudes, writing that political relations between the two countries are "unsatisfactory because of the disparity . . . in the extent of the respective risks" each country is taking. Britain is under the gun, in the way America isn't. Moreover, adds Toynbee, "the American government's 'fiat' (dictate) is virtually law for the other Western governments." [1]

Toynbee is saying that America gives the orders but doesn't have to suffer the consequences. To him, as to millions of British people, this doesn't seem right. As he said elsewhere, "No Annihilation Without Representation," an excellent slogan worth repeating.

NO ANNIHILATION WITHOUT REPRESENTATION

Again and again the deep distrust of American policy crops up. Again and again the resentment against American domination is expressed. In the European press it is found more frequently, but even in the American press the truth breaks through. Writing about the Ottawa Conference of the North Atlantic Treaty Organization (NATO) the N. Y. Times correspondent, Anne O'Hare McCormick, says that the smaller countries "complain that policies of vital concern to them . . . are decided without reference to their views," such as the policy of including Greece and Turkey into NATO. "a step

1 London Observer, March 25, 1951

that changes the character and scope of the Atlantic alliance was decided on in Washington." [2]

Two days later, the same correspondent reported that member countries of NATO were conscious that the Pentagon "makes policy for them too. Nothing is more apparent here than the general awareness that NATO decisions are essentially American decisions. When all the arguments are in, we cast the final vote." [3]

American power is applied with ruthlessness and arrogance. At the Ottawa meeting, U. S. General Bradley was called upon to explain a report. Whereupon he made a few remarks and "when called upon by some members to elaborate he declined to do so" with such language as to be "somewhat undiplomatic, if not curt." [4]

The result of American arrogance, American economic policy and the reckless American atomic policy has been to alienate British support. The British Labor leader Aneurin (Nye) Bevan who resigned from the British Cabinet in 1951 in protest against the scope of British re-armament under American pressures, has been obtaining mounting support.

The largest trade unions in England, in their conventions throughout 1952, have come out in support of reducing armament spending, even doing so over the opposition of their own leaders. For example, according to the N. Y. Times, the Amalgamated Engineering Union, with 800,000 members, "unanimously voted a resolution expressing concern" at Britain's re-armament and "calling for a peace pact among the five great powers—the United States, the Soviet Union, Britain, France and China." This resolution was taken against the wishes of the union's president, Jack Tanner, who nevertheless went along. Adds the news item, "The Amalgamated Engineering Union is the second of Britain's

2 N. Y. Times, September 17, 1951
3 N. Y. Times, September 19, 1951
4 N. Y. Times, September 18, 191

six biggest unions to take a position closer to Mr. Bevan.
. . . The Times of London said editorially that the implications of the vote were deeply disturbing." [5] Many unions followed suit and at this writing, Mr. Bevan has already become a major political figure within the Labour Party, on a straight anti-American, pro-peace platform.

Churchill has had to adopt many of Bevan's suggestions and much of Bevan's language. Correspondent Stewart Alsop in an article entitled "Churchill's New Bevanite Tinge" says " that on a whole series of measures the Churchill government has come out flat-footed against the American position." The most important of these, is the strategy of the atomic blitz. Continues Alsop:

"Churchill has pointed in apparent alarm to the 'great and ever growing' American air bases on British soil. The continued existence of these bases, as Churchill well knows, is at the very heart of the whole American strategic concept." [6] (emphasis added)

Since Churchill himself was one of the originators of the Cold War, it is clear that he only speaks in such a manner because he must. The British people, and perhaps Churchill as well, are increasingly aware that atomic war will mean destruction for themselves among the very first. In addition the British and other European peoples fear the re-armament of Germany. The re-armament of Germany has been one of the most important factors in the revulsion of the peoples of Europe against American foreign policy.

A NEO-NAZI GERMANY REARMS

Germany is now allowed to make tanks and artillery. [7] At the same time all restrictions on steel production in the Ruhr have been removed. [8] Finally Hitler's generals are back in power and pressing for release of the war criminals who are in jail. Says a N. Y. Times dispatch:

5 N. Y. Times, May 10, 1952
6 Washington Post, December 19, 1951
7 N. Y. Times, May 28, 1952
8 N. Y. Times, July 29, 1952

"In the opinion of Lt. General Adolf Von Heusinger and Lt. General Hans Speidel . . . it wil lbe **impossible to recruit desirable officers** for West German military contingents **unless a substantial number of war criminals are released** from Allied jails." [9] (emphasis added)

War criminals, it should be noted, were men found guilty of **specific atrocities** for which their **personal responsibility** was proven. The drive to get these "desirable officers" out of jail has been accompanied by a drive to rehabilitate Hitler's generals and make them palatable. Perhaps the most brazen attempt to date was the publication in August 1952 of the American edition of the memoirs of General Heinz Guderian, **Panzer Leader.** This book got a front page send off in the **N. Y. Times** Book Review of Sunday, August 10, 1952 with a friendly review by Drew Middleton. The book has a foreword by the British military historian, Liddell Hart who says:

"To understand him (Guderian) one must be capable of understanding the passion of pure craftsmanship. There one can find a **natural** explanation of his attitude to Hitler—**clearly more favorable** than that of most of the generals. . . .[10]
". . . he possessed most of the qualities that distinguished the 'Great Captains' of history. . . . Beyond these qualities Guderian had creative imagination, the basic characteristic of genius." [11] (emphasis added)

In rehabilitating this brass-hatted butcher, Liddell Hart finds he has "a sense of humor"; finds excuses for his waging aggressive war—"the greatest experts in the field of international law have found it difficult to frame an irrefutable definition of aggression" [12]; and finally as the most touching extenuation of a man who brought fire and blood to an entire continent, Liddell Hart tells us that Guderian is similar to "most soldiers of any country, at any time. Few qualms of conscience are to be found in the memoirs of those who exercised command in the wars for highly questionable causes

9 N. Y. Times, July 25, 1952
10 General Heinz Guderian, Panzer Leader, New York, 1952, p. 12
11 Ibid., p. 15
12 Ibid., p. 13

345

that Britain and the U. S. A. waged in the nineteenth century. There is a markedly 'Victorian' flavour about Guderian's turn of phrase and thought." [13]

Clearly Guderian is qualified to attend a 'Victorian' tea party and the peoples of Europe who suffered under his jackboot are crude, uncultured boors if they don't understand his endearing qualities.

The German generals have been very gentlemanly about their defeats and bear us no great ill will for having called them "war criminals." They did however, point out that the American generals behaved like the Nazis had when, at Koje Island, U. S. troops with flame-throwers, tanks and fixed bayonets moved against the Korean and Chinese prisoners of war.

General Guderian himself gives us the benefit of his mature thought: he thinks the Yalta agreements were unwise! Furthermore, he points out that Western leaders agree with him. Writes the Nazi general:

"Winston Churchill is no longer so certain that his actions at that time were wise. Both he-and Bevin have clearly modified the policy then adopted. Today many British statesmen no doubt wish that the decisions taken at the Yalta conference of February, 1945, had been other than they were." [14]

It is a revealing commentary on postwar Western policy that a Nazi general can afford to be so patronizingly agreeable and his book receive such deference in Britain and the U. S.

Under Hitler's generals, a German army is being recreated. The flimsy propaganda that the German divisions will not be "independent" but be part of a "European" army is believed by no one, least of all the government of the United States. Wrote correspondent William Stoneman from

13 Ibid., p. 12
14 Guderian, Panzer Leader, p. 285. Guderian, like Churchill, sees himself as a saviour of civilization, saying that he must defend Prussia, "which had remained attached to the ideals of Christian, Western culture through so many centuries of effort." p. 388

the NATO conference in Rome:

"As far as the United States is concerned it appears that she doesn't care whether the Germans form part of a real European army, a strictly phony European army or a good, old-fashioned German army. 'Give us those divisions and we'll ask no questions, is the attitude.'" [15] (emphasis added)

AMERICANS GO HOME

The responsibility for this German re-armament [16] rests squarely on the United States. The United States is also responsible for forcing the reluctant governments of Western Europe to accept German re-armament by threatening to withhold money. The interference of the United States has been so open and ruthless that even a great admirer of the Truman Doctrine was moved to remonstrate a little. In a long article in the **N. Y. Times,** James Reston a staunch supporter of the State Department gave eamxple after example of U. S. interference and said:

"Under the Nineteenth Century rules that governed relations between sovereign nations, the United States has done many things since the war that would never have been tolerated. . . .
"The French did not want to rearm the Germans. Neither did the British. . . . But Mr. Acheson, carrying the ball for the Pentagon, let it be known that unless the Germans were rearmed, the chances of getting Congressional support for the European aid program would not be good. Accordingly he kept pressing the point until he won. . . .
"The State Department does not explain why it is necessary to probe into the domestic questions in other capitals. It keeps denying that it intervenes; and this is a hard argument to make because it is apparent to everyone that the United States is involved in the affairs of its Allies to a degree that no other Government was ever involved in the past." [17]

Along with the rearmament of Germany, has come the rehabilitation of Fascist Franco of Spain, who has also been forced down the throat of our reluctant allies as a part of

15 Chicago Daily News, November 29, 1951
16 A thoroughly documented study, **Report on Germany,** showing the extent of neo-Nazism in Germany has been issed by the Faculty-Graduate Committee for Peace at the University of Chicago. It was reprinted, slightly abridged, in the **N. Y. Daily Compass,** March 9, 1952
17 N. Y. Times, March 22, 1952

the "free world." Ernest K. Lindley expressed the dominant U. S. view in **Newsweek** magazine:

"Let us put aside all ideological considerations except the fact that the Franco regime is anti-Communist." [18]

So was Adolph Hitler.

As a result of American imperialism and American arrogance the United States has lost friends wholesale. The most popular slogan in Europe today is:

AMERICANS GO HOME!

Europe has created this slogan but the entire world has embraced it. From Paris to Panmunjong Americans are not wanted. The daily press cannot keep this fact hidden, every day there are new incidents, demonstrations, even official protests by governments as when Iran on July 29, 1952 demanded that the U. S. military mission be withdrawn. [19]

Correspondent Ned Russell writes a long article entitled **Anti-Americanism in Europe,** Margaret Parton one entitled, **Anti-Americanism in India,** Arthur Krock one entitled **How to Win Friends Problems for U. S. 'Voice.'** [20] Traveling through the Far East, James Michener, author of **Tales of the South Pacific** was surprised at the depth of anti-American feeling.

He wrote in **Life** Magazine that in Asia:

"Along the entire eastern seaboard the American is utterly unwelcome. In countries like China, Malaya and Indo-China he runs the risk of being murdered. In great cities like Singapore, Saigon and Jakarta wise Americans stay indoors at night. Where he is not hunted, the American is reviled. Never in our national history have we been so feared and despised. . . . China, India, Burma and Indonesia . . . today condemn us as reactionary and imperialistic. We . . . are now ourselves branded as wilfull aggressors." [21]

Michener summed it up in a single sentence:

18 Newsweek Magazine, August 14, 1950
19 N. Y. Times, July 30, 1952
20 Washington Post, May 31, 1952; N. Y. Herald Tribune, September 11, 1950; N. Y. Times, August 5, 1951
21 Life Magazine, June 4, 1951

"An American today in Asia had better not go out at night. He is likely to get shot."[22]

AMERICAN POLICY IN COLONIAL COUNTRIES

U. S. political policy has been no more successful in colonial countries than it has been in Europe. Just as in Europe the U. S. has allied itself with Fascist Franco, a neo-Nazi Western Germany, a totalitarian Greece and a semi-feudal Turkey, so in Africa, the Near East and Asia the U. S. has allied itself with the colonial powers against the people of the various colonial countries.

We allied ourselves with French rule in Indo-China, and supported their war against the Viet Minh liberation movement. We supported them with arms and money. We taught them to use napalm (flaming jellied gasoline) to level villages. The New York Times reports from Indo-China:

"The type of mechanized warfare waged lately by the French Viet-namese forces is tough on the rural inhabitants and gives the Vietminh rebels talking points for their propaganda. To combat the Veitminh groups in the villages the French-Vietnamese use artillery and napalm and civilian casualties are inevitable."[23]

The result—a military stalemate, and the loss of all popular support. Life Magazine reports:

"The people of Indo-China, or Viet-Nam, are infected with revolt against the French and their weak emperor. Only by the force of arms, many supplied by the U. S., an expenditure of wealth equal to the total granted France under the Marshall Plan, and a fearful expenditure of lives have the French been able to retain islands of barbwire in what was once their most valuable foreign property."[24]

We allied ourselves with British rule in Malaya. We supported them with arms and money. There are 40,000 troops, 320,000 regular and auxiliary police and sizable air and naval forces being used by the British. [25] We have supported a British policy in Malaya that is so bankrupt, that they had to

22 James Michener, The Voice of Asia, New York, 1951
23 N. Y. Times, April 13, 1952
24 Life Magazine, December 31, 1951

349

introduce, late in 1950, a system of "Collective punishment" under which a community or village is held responsible for the conduct of all of its inhabitants and becomes liable to harsh penalties. Examples of "collective punishment" in Malaya follow:

"Army and police forces arrested today the 2,000 inhabitants of the village of Tras, in Pahang state, supply point for the guerilla gang that murdered Sir Henry Gurney, British High Commissioner, on October 6. The village, which has been condemned, will be fully evacuated in three days." [26]

More than 500,000 people have been uprooted and resettled in "protected villages." [27] Although the British in Malaya deny that they have planned to **poison** the crops in areas supporting the guerillas, they admit they are searching for a **non-poisonous chemical** which will **just destroy** the crops.

The result—military stalemate and the use of Nazi-like reprisals against whole populations.

The Philippines are sometimes held up as an example of America's "progressive" policy in Asia. The facts prove the opposite, as given by the **Atlantic Monthly** magazine, describing MacArthur's intervention in Philippine politics after the war:

"His whitewashing of charges of collaboration against Manuel Roxas was undoubtedly of great help in getting Roxas elected President.
"Once in that office, Roxas was able to stop the widespread movement to oust his collaborationist colleagues from the Senate and court positions which they had inherited from the pre-war period.
"The failure to expel these advocates of the pre-war political and economic status quo brought a number of Filipinos to believe that it was useless to work for social reforms through constitutional channels. That belief has become more general since last year's elections, when Quirino's party had recourse to dishonesty, intimidation and violence on a scale far greater than has ever before

25 Hugh C. Greene, former head of British Information Service in Malaya, "In Malaya the Front Is Everywhere," New York Times, Sunday Magazine Section, May 4, 1952
26 N. Y. Times, November 8, 1951
27 Hugh C. Greene, quoted above.

been recorded in Philippine elections." [28]

Thus, America's first acts in the Philippines aimed at restoring reactionaries and collaborators to power. And the terms under which the Philippines were given their independence made certain that economically they would remain a U. S. semi-colony. The Philippines were forbidden from establishing tariffs to protect any new industries, and had to agree to give U. S. corporations a free hand in the islands. This made certain that U. S. sugar and hemp interests would continue to dominate the Philippine economy, and that native industry would be choked off.

The reactionary role of America in colonial countries has been exposed by Supreme Court Justice William O. Douglas. After traveling through the Near East and Asia he came home and wrote a book. This is what he says:

"We tell about our high standard of living. . . . And it sounds like boasting or bragging.
"We finance agrarian projects for the **benefit of the landlords.** . . .
"We send technical experts abroad to help in seed selection, soil conservation, malaria control and the like. But we never raise our voice for reform of the vicious tenancy system of Asia under which increased production inures to the benefit of a few. . . .
"We talk about democracy and justice; and at the same time we support regimes merely because they are anti-Communist—regimes whose object is to keep democracy and justice out of reach of the peasants for all time, so as to protect their own vested interests.
"We put billions of dollars behind corrupt and reactionary governments which exempt the rich from income taxes and fasten the hold of an ogliarchy tighter and tighter on the nation." [29]
(emphasis added)

Douglas notes the failure of U. S. policy and sets it down to the fact that America is blocking people's revolutions. He writes:

"The revolutions which are brewing are not, however, Communist in origin nor will they end even if Soviet Russia is crushed

28 Atlantic Monthly Magazine, December, 1950
29 William O. Douglas, Strange Lands and Friendly People, pp. 317-318

through war. **The revolutionaries are hungry men who have been exploited from time out of mind. This is the century of their awakening and mobilization.** . . . The spirit that motivates these people is pretty much the same as the spirit that inspired the French and the American Revolutions. . . .
"For centuries Asia has been under the domination of the foreigner. . . . Those were mostly forms of imperialism that exploited the nations and left nothing for the peasants. That day is over and done with. Asia is united in one cause—to be rid of the foreigners' domination." [30] (emphasis in original)

CHINA AND JAPAN

The greatest setback to world imperialism since the Russian Revolution of 1917 has been the Chinese Revolution of 1949. It is an historic irony that American imperialism aided that Revolution to success by its wilful and blind support of the reactionary Chiang Kai-shek. It is a simple fact that **American arms and equipment** shipped to Chiang and captured by the Chinese People's Armies were instrumental in developing the great mobility and firepower of the Red armies which overwhelmed Chiang within a few months. The Chinese Communists used to call Chiang Kai-shek their "American supply sergeant." Says Professor Schuman, that the defeat of Chiang "was precisely due to the American method of fighting Communism."[32]

A myth has been created in America by the Republican Party that the U. S. aided the Communists and not Chiang. This is absolutely not true. At the end of the war, U. S. Marines helped Chiang, as Forrestal has admitted. [33] Some four billion dollars worth of aid were given to Chiang. The simple fact is that Chiang and his government, corrupt and vicious, could not stand up against the people's forces despite all the great help given by the U. S. [34]

---

30 Ibid., pp. 315-316
32 N. Y. Daily Compass, March 24, 1950
33 Forrestal Diaries, pp. 109, 174
34 The history of Chiang and the Chinese Revolution over the last twenty years has been thoroughly reported by Americans. For the postwar period culminating in 1949, Jack Belden's China Shakes the World and Israel Epstein's The Unfinished Revolution in China, are probably the best

In Japan, the U. S. forced on that nation a treaty which re-establishes the extra-territorial concession in Japan which China has just victoriously overthrown. America has military and naval bases in Japan, with American personnel not subject to Japanese courts and with the right to intervene in domestic affairs of Japan to put down "disorders." These were precisely the "rights" wrested by Western nations from a weak China in the nineteenth century.

These measures have not made Americans popular in Japan. Furthermore, the Japanese people have no desire to be involved in another war, and the Japanese leaders have no confidence in U. S. military might as against the Soviet Union. Colonel Tsuji Masanobo, formerly of the Imperial Japanese General Staff, and known to his countrymen as the "God of Strategy," gave a lecture in 1951 in which he said:

"Japan must refuse military bases to the U. S. or the U. S. will drag Japan into this war and leave her to the mercies of fate." [35]

KOREA

The military effects of Korea have already been discussed. Politically, Korea has provided the world with a bloody illustration of how the United States "liberates" a country and what kind of government it supports.

A **Washington Post** editorial plainly states the facts about Syngman Rhee's Korean government:

"Neither the United States nor the other United Nations members fighting in Korea can close their eyes to the virtual **police state** created by President Syngman Rhee. . . . Rhee, by defying the National Assembly and persecuting legislators into hiding, has set himself up as a dictator in all but name." [36]

Rhee's power is the result of his "merciless campaign . . . to liquidate his opponents either politically or physically." His "strong-arm tactics," adds the **Washington Post,** "are making the 20 million impoverished peasants ripe for the

35 N. Y. Sunday Compass, February 17, 1952
36 Washington Post, June 3, 1952

communism Rhee professes to fight. His regime is an embarrassment this country can no longer condone." [37]

Rhee's disregard for the sufferings of his own people shows his true character. The **Washington Post** reveals that "Rhee has intrigued ceaselessly to sabotage the truce talks in plumping for expanded war," and that this has been hidden because of "civil or military censorship." [38]

Walter Lippmann points out the ghastly futility of the war that Rhee wants to expand, writing:

"It is a ghastly business, this maiming and killing and getting maimed and getting killed in a war which as all the governments involved acknowledge, has now become useless and meaningless in that nothing further can be decided or gained by military action." [38]

The political repercussions of Korea can only be grasped by understanding what has been done to that unhappy country by American airpower. Said the American General O'Donnell, who was in charge of the Bomber Command in the Far East, at the beginning of the Korean War:

"I would say that the entire, almost the entire Korean peninsula is just a terrible mess. Everything is destroyed. There is nothing standing worthy of the name. . . . Just before the Chinese came in we were grounded. There were no more targets in Korea." [39]

One of the chief weapons employed in this destruction has been the napalm bomb.

On March 1, 1952, the **Manchester Guardian**, Britain's most distinguished liberal newspaper, quoted an eye-witness report by Rene Cutforth, Korean correspondent of the government owned British Broadcasting System, who described a napalm victim:

"In front of us a curious figure was standing a little crouched, legs straddled, arms held out from his sides. He had no eyes, and the whole of his body, nearly all of which was visible through

37 Ibid
38 Washington Post, April 8, 1952
39 I. F. Stone, Hidden History, p. 312

tatters of burnt rags, was covered with a hard black crust speckled with yellow pus. A Korean woman by his side began to speak, and the interpreter said: 'He has to stand, sir, cannot sit or lie.'
"He had to stand because he was no longer covered with a skin, but with a crust like crackling which broke easily. . . . I thought of the hundreds of villages reduced to ashes which I personally had seen and realized the sort of casualty list which must be mounting up along the Korean front."

The revulsion of the civilized world against such barbarian destruction has been expressed by a leading French magazine, Esprit, which is written for the well-to-do French upper class and has a strong Catholic tendency. A French author, Charles Faurel, writes:

"In Korea GIs have no pity. They think themselves a superior race and treat the 'natives' like filthy dogs . . . the GI refuses to see any human trace in the anguished faces (of refugees) turned toward them. . . . American intervention in Korea has ended in disaster. It has bled that country to death, killed many of its people, starved and terrorized it, and annihilated and ruined it. . . . Those who were waging that ferocious and barbarous war asked for more. Torch in hand, the American Army chased away the obstinate who had miraculously survived the massacre from the ruined villages. All along a 150-mile front Korea is but a huge fire, each house and each village aflame.

"It was an order motived by military considerations. It has been carried out under techniques borrowed from Attila's hordes. . . .

"This is what Europe can expect and hope from American intervention in its internal affairs. . . .

"If anyone ever dared to publish figures of the death toll and destruction suffered by North and South Korea civilians, as a result of the 'strategic' Allied bombings, you would understand why the people of the world are so reluctant to agree to a possible World War intended to liberate them at the price of total annihilation. . . .

"We are afraid of you (U. S.) because you are no longer satisfied with directing the foreign policy of Allied governments; now you want to step out of your borders and forcibly prevent the peoples of the world from enjoying freedom of speech. We are back to the days of the monarchy when the Prussians were called in to save the bastille."

After referring to the Japanese "peace treaty," Faurel concludes:

"We should think that in return for such generous help which American negotiators have asked for and obtained, Japanese police intervention might be asked in American elections.

"In the year of our Lord, 1951, such is Truman's version of the great Wilsonian concept of the right of peoples to self-determination!" [40]

The Truman Doctrine has arrayed the world against the United States. The political faliure of American policy outlined in this chapter has great repercussions on military strategy. Few U. S. bases abroad are secure against the people of that country. The attitude of the peoples of the world reflected in the slogan, **Americans Go Home,** is a powerful and positive force for peace.

40 N. Y. Daily Compass, January 13, 1952

PART IV

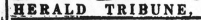

HERALD TRIBUNE,

Mass· Burials Under Study by Defense Chiefs

Expect 40,000 Deaths in 2 Days if Atom Bomb Hits Average U. S. City

WASHINGTON. (AP).—The Federal Defense Administration average Ameri-40,000 atomic

F. C. D. A. officials feel the first thing to do would be to get the bodies out of sight. If this were not done, the psychological effect on survivors would. be bad. On their morale and efficiency the continued existence

WE MUST
BE FRIENDS

CONCLUSION

"Man's dearest possession is life, and since it is given to him to live but once, he must so live as not to be seared with the shame of a cowardly and trivial past, so live as not to be tortured for years without purpose, so live that dying he can say 'All my life and my strength were given to the first cause in the world—the liberation of mankind.'"
V. I. Lenin, quoted by Sumner Welles

THIS BOOK is done. As I sit correcting the printer's proofs and finally get a picture of the whole I have a sense of amazement at the pattern it represents. Even to me it seems unbelievable that men, human beings, should gamble so recklessly with the peace of the world. Yet the record speaks for itself: these men stand condemned out of their own mouths.

A feeling of cold, lasting anger seizes my being. I have seen war at close range—its stupidities, its horrors, its inhumanities. Atomic war would be infinitely worse. I have seen the army's uncensored films on Hiroshima and Nagasaki —the mind shrinks from its satanic barbarism. All this is not academic stuff—for me or for you. On my worktable strewn with clippings, there is one I set aside from the **N. Y. Herald Tribune.** There it is on the opposite page.

In the next room my children are playing, Judith age 8, Tony age 5. Occasionally a piping shriek comes through, occasionally a spray of laughter. No, atomic war is not academic

—not to me, not to you, not to millions and millions of parents throughout the world.

Anger drives me, but confidence sustains me. The tap root of my confidence is the military and economic power of the socialist world. As each day, each hour, goes by without global war the power of the USSR, of China, of the Eastern European countries grows in gigantic strides. This is a power for peace. As Lippmann has said, the aim of the USSR is "to make it impossible for the United States to start a war" (see Chapter 14). 800,000,000 people consciously organized to prevent war is a formidable block to the warmakers.

Many in America have been so filled with slanders against the USSR that they have no conception of the depth of feeling in the Soviet Union regarding the prevention of war. Since Soviet intentions are so crucial, I want to show that practically and theoretically the Soviet Union wants peace and believes peace is possible.

THE SOVIET UNION NEEDS PEACE

The "war psychosis" created in America is a remarkable example of the power of press and radio to obscure obvious facts. A little thought should convince anyone that war is the last thing in the world wanted by either Soviet citizens or Soviet leaders. In the Second World War, the Soviet Union lost 17 million citizens. As shown in Chapter 11, huge areas of her territory were devastated, a large percentage of her industry was destroyed. Says American correspondent Edgar Snow:

"All those conditions have created in the mind and spirit of the Russian people an unprecedented receptivity, and an unprecedented need, for any proposals which offer mankind surcease from war and permanent peace. Far from ignoring that sentiment throughout the country, the Soviet government seeks . . . to harness it behind plans for reconstruction. . . ."[1] (emphasis added)

The title of Snow's book drives home the point, **Stalin**

1 Snow, Stalin Must Have Peace, p. 119

Must Have Peace. This book was published in 1947, but the attitude of the Soviet people and Soviet leaders hasn't changed. They are still emphasizing peaceful construction. In October 1950, the **N. Y. Times Moscow** correspondent, Harrison Salisbury, wrote a series of articles on Soviet conditions. He reported that even after the outbreak of the Korean War, the rebuilding of Moscow "far from being curtailed or reduced, has obviously been expanded." [2] In one article Salisbury reported that:

"The number one topic of conversation and interest in Moscow is the Government's vast new hydroelectric program. . . . These undertakings will not be completed until the middle fifties and will cost billions of rubles and millions of man-hours of labor. Moscow's man in the street regards this investment as evidence of his **Government's confidence in its ability to maintain and preserve world peace.**" [3] (emphasis added)

The observations of the two Americans, Snow and Salisbury, were confirmed in profuse detail by a French newspaperman Michel Gordey, foreign correspondent of the extremely conservative **France-Soir,** largest newspaper in France. Gordey himself has no love for the Soviets, he is the child of White Russians who fled from the Revolution in 1919. However he speaks Russian fluently and he visited Russia for two months. His experiences and observations were made into a book, **Visa to Moscow** which was published in the United States in 1952.

The book is remarkable in that Gordey, while disliking the Soviet system and taking every opportunity to discount what he sees, nevertheless cannot help himself and clearly admits that peace is the great need and desire of everyone in Russia, including the government. He says:

"The Soviet public feels a great fear and a deep horror of war. It has not forgotten the sufferings and the miseries of the last one. It is still mourning its 17,000,000 dead. . . . **This public is not ready**

2 N. Y. Times, October 11, 1950
3 N. Y. Times, October 12, 1950

—psychologically, physically, or morally—to venture upon an aggressive war.

"From the economic point of view, the present abundance of products available to Soviet consumers, the successive price cuts, the increase in the consumption of certain basic foodstuffs (such as butter, meat, bread, sugar)—these do not suggest preparation in the USSR for mobilization or military aggression." [4] (emphasis added)

Gordey is amazed by the extent and thoroughness of reconstruction in the Soviet Union. Leningrad which was practically destroyed, has been rebuilt so that there "was practically no trace of war. But the miracle does not stop there. The rebuilders have scrupulously respected the style of the former capital. . . . The sight of Leningrad is living evidence of the profound desire for peace of the Russian population." [5]

Gordey has a very cynical attitude to Soviet life, but even his cynicism is swept away by the Soviet attitude to children. The sophisticated Frenchman becomes almost lyrical:

"In all the Soviet cities I was able to visit, I saw the regime's great privileged class: the children. I could see for myself what extraordinary care surrounds their growth and the early years of their lives. I understood, far better than through speeches or theoretical articles, why the young citizens of the Soviet Union brought up under these conditions, cannot fail to be sincerely attached to the social and political regime under which they live." [6] (emphasis added)

It is no wonder that Gordey comes to this conclusion:

"The Soviet citizen does not feel himself to be enslaved or oppressed. . . . The fact must be added—and it is incontestable—that to tens of millions of citizens of the USSR, the Soviet regime has actually brought new liberties. Peoples formerly backward or oppressed have acquired or regained national cultures; they have progressed toward a material civilization unknown before 1917. The condition of the working class has also been improved, sometimes slowly, but always steadily (interrupted only during the last war). . . . As their material existence improves, they have the

4 Gordey, Visa to Moscow, New York, 1952, pp. 408-409
5 Ibid., p. 344
6 Gordey, Visa to Moscow, p. 259

sense of an increase in their liberty. . . .

". . . a very real and deep patriotism exists among the peoples of the Soviet Union. . . . It is supported by the material and cultural achievements which give these peoples the conviction that their national patrimony is worth defending." [7]

Such is the Soviet Union: a country that does not need war, a country of peace. It is time that we in America broke through the curtain of lies and slanders of the press, the radio, the magazines, the movies. It is time that we saw the Soviet leaders as they really are, [8] and the Soviet Union as it really is, a country whose government is owned by its people, and therefore is truly of, by and for the people.

Sumner Welles, FDR's Undersecretary of State, conservative as he is, has admitted the reality of Soviet life. He has written, after expressing his opposition to communism, that:

"Yet I also believe that Soviet Russia represents one of the greatest attempts to attain human betterment that the world has ever known, and that society in every part of the earth will eventually be profoundly affected by it. It was forged out of such suffering as the Western peoples have never dreamed of. In a quarter of a century it has given health, education, economic security and the hope of happiness to one hundred and eighty millions of human beings who had previously known only misery. It has not only created a new social structure out of the ruins of a barbaric feudalism, it has, within a short generation, changed the medieval agricultural economy of an entire continent into an economy of advanced industrialism." [9]

Welles then goes on to give this quotation from the founder of the Soviet Union, whom Welles calls the "greatest" communist of all—Lenin. Lenin said:

" 'Man's dearest possession is life, and since it is given to him to live but once, he must so live as not to be seared with the shame

7 Ibid., pp. 410-411. These quotations may lead the reader to think Gordey is pro-Soviet. I assure him that this is not so, and this is what makes the book valuable and worth the money—the grudging and reluctant admissions. For a less reluctant, and less expensive book, read George Marion, All Quiet in the Kremlin, which is published in a paper edition and gives a moving and thorough picture of contemporary Soviet conditions

8 See Chapter 12

9 Welles, Where Are We Heading, pp. 372-373

of a cowardly and trivial past, so live as not to be tortured for years without purpose, so live that dying he can say: "All my life and my strength were given to the first cause in the world—the liberation of mankind." ' "

IS CO-EXISTENCE THEORETICALLY POSSIBLE?

There is one final argument which must be answered because in my opinion it is the basic argument on the question of peace. The argument quotes the analysis in Marxist classics that war is the inevitable result of capitalism. Therefore, since the U. S. is capitalist, war is inevitable.

This argument is advanced by both the reactionaries and the ultra-"leftists." The reactionaries say that since Marxists believe war is the result of capitalism, therefore to be safe the Soviet Union must communize the world by force and Communist parties in capitalist countries must overthrow their governments. This is the basis of the prosecution of Communists under the Smith Act in the United States. The ultra-"leftists" say that it's all right to talk peace, but really war is inevitable because the capitalists are bound to start one. They imply that if a Marxist says peace is possible he is either kidding himself or kidding others. As so often in history, reaction gets strong support from ultra-"leftism."

First, it must be noted that the Soviet leaders have specifically repudiated the idea of spreading communism by war. This was precisely one of the key issues between the positions of Stalin and of Trotsky. Trotsky argued that the Revolution must be spread by the Red Army. Trotsky was defeated and exiled. The Communist Party of the Soviet Union for the last 25 years has stated unequivocally that communism cannot be spread by force.

The Communist Party of the Soviet Union rests on the theoretical basis of Marxism-Leninism. This theory holds that capitalism carries within it the seeds of its own collapse, that it is in a state of general crisis which breeds poverty and unrest, depressions and unemployment and therefore inevitably people under capitalism will be forced by their own

364

internal developments to turn towards socialism. Why, in the name of common sense, should the Communist Party of the USSR now reverse its policy of peace and avoiding war? Why should Soviet leaders start a war of aggression which would unite the world against them?

It simply doesn't make sense. Even John Foster Dulles has to admit this, in spite of the fact that he has been one of the propagandists who maintains that in Soviet theory war is inevitable. Says Dulles:

"The plainest of facts is that the Kremlin has not used its Red Armies for open military conquest even in these past years **when there were no military** obstacles in their path." [10] (emphasis added)

The plainest fact is that in Soviet political theory, war is not inevitable. Edgar Snow discusses this question thoroughly in his book and after analyzing Stalin's speeches points out that unquestionably peaceful collaboration is possible. He then quotes Molotov:

"The war vividly demonstrated that states with widely different political structures (i.e., imperialist and socialist) had extremely important interests in common. Mutual aid between them produced great results. The recognition (by the Soviet Union) of the principles of such international co-operation **has a profound meaning.** It reflects the firm will to achieve universal peace and readiness to enter into peaceful competition . . . between states and social systems." [11] (emphasis and parenthesis are Snow's)

In the Soviet Union today the theme that war is not inevitable is emphasized not only in their daily newspapers but in their most theoretical journals. For example the leading philosophical journal in the USSR, **Problems of Philosophy** is quoted in the **N. Y. Times** of September 24, 1951 as follows:

". . . in contemporary historical conditions it is impossible categorically to affirm that the coming of a new world war is inevitable. The Marxist-Leninist thesis of the inevitability of war in an epoch of imperialism, which was correct for some historical

10 Life Magazine, May 19, 1952
11 Snow, Stalin Must Have Peace, p. 45

conditions, cannot be carried over unconditionally into new historical conditions."

The article in the **New York Times** concluded that in the Marxist view, war is not inevitable and peace can be preserved.

The entire question has been squarely faced and dealt with by a leading Soviet philosopher in a recent book **The Marxist Dialectical Method**. [12] He writes:

"Marxism has firmly established that war is an inevitable accompaniment of capitalism. But Marxism never took the position that one cannot avoid this or another war by struggling against its outbreak and against those who instigate it.

"With exhaustive clarity this real possibility of preventing a new world war was shown by Comrade Stalin in his interview with a **Pravda** correspondent. There are, said J. V. Stalin, aggressive forces in the United States of America, in England, in France, who are preparing a new war, considering war 'as a paying proposition yielding enormous profits.' But the peoples of the world fight against the aspirations of the aggressive forces who are lighting the flames of a new war.

" 'How will this struggle between the aggressive and the peaceloving forces end?' asked Comrade Stalin and gave the answer: 'Peace will be preserved and consolidated if the peoples take the cause of preserving peace into their own hands and uphold it to the end.' "

There is little doubt that nothing in the Soviet Union precludes peaceful co-existence. Nothing in politics, nothing in economics, nothing in philosophy. On the contrary, Soviet leaders actively seek peace. Even General Eisenhower once testified to this, saying that "the Russians have nothing to gain from a war with the United States. Nothing guides Russian policy so much as a desire for friendship with the United States." [13]

12 This is the method that Forrestal tried to study. The Soviet book is reported in the **Daily Worker**, July 22, 1952, the only newspaper to my knowledge which saw fit to print such an important item
13 N.Y. Post, August 15, 1952, Murray Kempton's column. The Soviet Union hasn't changed but Eisenhower has. In his successful campaign to seize the Republican Presidential nomination he said on June 8, 1952, that "we have been too ready for too long to trust a godless dictatorship." Quoted in the same column, same day

The Soviet desire for peace is no pious, hypocritical mouthing of words. It is the guiding star of the foreign policy of a great and powerful nation, well able to steer a successful course amidst waters infested by Churchills and Harrimans and sundry "aggressors for peace." Here, as I have said, is the taproot of my confidence.

As I correct the printers' proofs of the last three chapters on the failure of the Truman Doctrine, I feel profoundly confident that war can be stopped. I feel confident because the failure of the Truman Doctrine is not a transient phenomenon.

The failure of Truman's "muscular policy" is due to deep causes which are on the upgrade in the world. The disgust of the peoples of the world with U. S. war plans will increase, not decrease. The heavy burden of armaments which is bankrupting Europe is having social and political consequences which favor irresistibly the cause of peace. Soviet technical supremacy will increase, not decrease. From the Transvaal in Africa to the Tonkin Delta in Indo-China, the oppressed peoples of the earth are on the march—not to be stopped. Everywhere the old order is changing. The Truman Doctrine tried the impossible—to freeze oppression in a world of change. It just won't work.

In our own United States resistance to war is growing, slowly but surely. There is a tendency to underestimate the resistance of the American people to war. Whenever the issue is concrete, such as the truce in Korea, the desire for peace is apparent. More important is the fact that for the United States to make aggressive war successfully, every organization capable of resistance must be controlled. This is what Hitler had to do. This is what American imperialists are trying to do. Chapter 3 spelled out the nature of the attack by reaction. While this attack has not failed as clearly as their foreign policy, nevertheless in my opinion it has failed. **Considering the power which reaction has thrown in**

367

its drive against civil liberties, the results must be considered a failure. Major independent unions are rejecting political control by Truman or anyone else; within the CIO there are rumblings of dissatisfaction; men have been imprisoned, but men have not been silenced. The very attack against civil liberties is developing a greater and greater resistance. On major issues, reaction has been beaten. Beaten on Universal Military Training, beaten on military control of the atom bomb, beaten on their attempts to stifle the growing peace movement in America. The Truman Administration using O. John Rogge as a tool tried to make peace treasonable by indicting Dr. DuBois and his co-workers for peace. The attempt failed; the tool miserably disintegrated; the judge didn't even send the case to the jury.

The organized work for peace has gone steadily forward, from the First World Congress for Peace in 1949 which Dr. DuBois called "the greatest meeting of men ever assembled in modern times to advance the progress of man," through to the Second World Peace Congress in Warsaw in 1950. A film, **Peace Will Win,** made at that Congress by Joris Ivens gives a tremendous sense of the power of the peace movement throughout the world. [14]

I say all this not to create a facile optimism. The situation is serious and dangerous in the extreme: yet the potentialities for peace are vast and waiting development. Beneath the outward manifestations of reaction, the situation in America is actually very fluid, with ever present possibilities of extremely sharp changes in the moods of the people.

Like an iceberg which is six-sevenths submerged the strength of the visible progressive forces is below the surface. The active fighters for peace are part of the people in shops and communities. At any moment, events at home or abroad may suddenly enable progressives to harness the deep desire

14 The film is available through the National Guardian, New York City

for peace and security which does exist in the American people. Reaction understands this very well: Forrestal was fearful of the day when a people's Congress would investigate his role and label him a fascist.

We must fight against lethargy and a feeling that nothing can be done. An example of this is the average person's feelings in the current 1952 election that a vote for Hallinan and Bass on the Progressive Party ticket is a wasted vote. It is my own personal belief that no more fallacious idea could be held. **Actually a Progressive Party vote counts for at least 10 combined Democratic or Republican votes as far as the issue of peace is concerned.** The statement is not exaggerated. The total Republican and Democratic vote in 1948 was 46 millions, and let's assume it will be the same in 1952. Does anyone doubt that a total of 5 million Progressive Party votes in 1952 (1 in ten) would have more weight for peace than all the rest of the votes; that reactionaries wouldn't be worrying about that vote and thinking several times over before starting a war; that a truce in Korea would come about more speedily? The plain fact is, every Progressive vote counts, and counts heavily, against war.

NEGOTIATIONS ARE POSSIBLE

The first step to peace is to sit down around a conference table and negotiate. Negotiations, it should be emphasized, do not require friendship. Negotiators can sit down unsmiling and bargain grimly, yet both sides are aware that a settlement must be reached. Every union man in America knows what that means from his own experience in collective bargaining.

In collective bargaining usually the employer distrusts the union and the union distrusts the employer. More often than not the large scale corporation hates the union; more often than not the feeling is reciprocated. Yet again and

369

again, year after year, the two sit down at the same table arguing about the most important interests for each side (profits for the corporation, wages for the workers), and year after year a settlement is reached.

Collective bargaining at home has reduced industrial strife, restrained the force and violence of the more ruthless employers. Collective bargaining internationally will reduce world strife, will restrain the more ruthless aggressors. I believe the USSR is ready to negotiate. Again and again Stalin has said this; twice the Soviet Union offered visas to prominent Americans to visit the Soviet Union—once to Baruch, once to Charles E. Wilson. Both times the State Department stepped in and stopped them.

I think it is up to the U. S. to accept the offers of negotiations. We must make our government officials negotiate for peace in the world. The first step is to expose the warmakers, what they have done, what they are doing. This is a necessary step, but it is only the first step. To make our political leaders sit down at a conference table we need the widest possible unity of all the people and all the organizations around this simple issue: truce in Korea, negotiations at the conference table.

Peace can be won even on a basis of distrust. Yet once peace is being built, that distrust will vanish. Trade will flourish, travel will increase, knowledge of each other will inevitably bring respect and friendship—as the Olympics have shown.

WE CAN BE FRIENDS

On July 23, at Helsinki an unbeaten U. S. crew won the eight-oar racing championship, with Russia "a surprisingly strong second." The words are from the Associated Press dispatch published in the N. Y. Times of July 25. The story continues, "After the race, the Russians asked the Americans to be their guests." The crew accepted the invitation. Thereby three Americans—Bill Fields of Forsythe, Georgia, Davey Manring of Cleveland and Bob Detweiler of Phoenix, Arizona —landed squarely in the history textbooks of tomorrow.

For these three Americans in one afternoon exposed the Eisenhowers and the Dulles, the Harrimans and the Trumans. The **AP** dispatch gives the details:

"Came the main dish—an inch thick filet mignon, potatoes and peas.

"Some steak" commented Fields.

"Yeah, Russian cows are just as good as ours," added Detweiler, who comes from Arizona cow country.

At the end of the repast, Vladimir Kuchmenko, the chief of Soviet rowing, rose to his feet.

"Welcome friends of America," he said in Russian as a girl interpreted. "We are happy for these friendships we have made on the water. We want the sportsmen of Russia and the sportsmen of America always to compete in this friendly spirit."

He offered a toast to "international understanding." Everybody rose and clinked vodka glasses. Manring rose to express thanks for the Russian hospitality.

"This has been a wonderful experience for all of us," he said. "We are glad to come here and meet your people and find they are just like us."

APPENDICES

APPENDIX I
FORESIGHT AND BACKTRACKING

In the preface to this book, it was explained why different types of quotations have been used in proving the argument. An additional comment is necessary on quotations from such men as Stimson and Wallace.

Henry L. Stimson in 1945 had considerably more foresight than most of America's governing class, when he predicted that atomic blackmail would lead to disaster. When Truman did just the opposite of what Stimson had recommended, and brought on the disaster he had predicted, did Stimson come out fighting? No, he remained silent, and later backtracked from his position.

In 1947 Stimson wrote that "since the early spring of 1945—even before the death of Mr. Roosevelt—the Soviet government has steadily pursued an obstructive and unfriendly course." [1] This argument has already been proven false elsewhere in this book. Besides, it is counter to Stimson's own attitude in the spring of 1945 when he warned against the adoption of a tough policy by the United States. Despite his turnabout, Stimson only backed down somewhat from his 1945 memorandum, but didn't repudiate it. His biographer, Bundy, writes:

"In 1947 Stimson was inclined to think the chances of a successful direct approach in 1945 [to Russia on the atomic bomb issue] had been smaller than he thought at the time; but the existence of any chance at all would have justified the attempt, so great was the objective at stake." [2]

Stimson says, in other words, maybe it wouldn't have worked but we should have tried it anyway. He knows that his 1945 memorandum was correct, and can't bring himself to throw it overboard completely.

Stimson's backtracking is a symptom of a fundamental political fact. Politicians rarely rise above their class. When events develop so that men like Stimson have to attack their class in order to defend their own views, they discard their views, however correct they may be.

1 Stimson, On Active Service, p. 649
2 Ibid., p. 648

372

Some of these politicians will stand behind the truth longer than others. Henry Wallace stood firm longer than most, but he, too, finally turned somersault, more spectacularly than Stimson because he had gone much further in criticizing U.S. policy. He resigned from the Progressive Party in 1950 and became an active supporter of the Cold War. By 1950, Wallace could no longer oppose the policies of our government without openly abandoning his class and exposing the nature of American imperialism. When faced with that choice, he crudely reversed his position, and the N. Y. Times editorialized with satisfaction that this "restores some of his stature." An example of his new stature was his attempt to prove that he always had wanted to help keep Chiang Kai-shek in power in China.

The fact that men like Stimson and Wallace backtrack under pressure doesn't destroy the validity of their former views. Even though they are no longer interested in fighting the Cold War, the people still are. The things that Stimson said in 1945 and Wallace said in 1948 are still true, and can still be used by the American people to oppose the ruinous policies of our leaders.

APPENDIX II
ATOMIC SECRETS

The Soviet Union did not have an atomic bomb immediately after World War II. What did they lack? Did they lack the scientific "know-how" or just the proper industrial plants?

General Smith, former U.S. Ambassador to Moscow, has already been quoted as telling Forrestal in 1948 that the Russians may well have the "notebook know-how," but not the "industrial complex to translate that knowledge into concrete weapons." This means that there were no scientific secrets connected with the atomic bomb, a judgment supported by almost all the top scientists in the field.

Dr. J. Robert Oppenheimer, foremost U.S. scientific authority on atomic weapons, said in January, 1951:

". . . there were no 'unpublished' secrets concerning atomic weapons, and no 'secret laws of nature' available to only a few." [1]

Supporting this was an editorial in the monthly periodical Atomics, in September, 1949, just after Truman announced that the Soviet Union had exploded an atomic bomb. It read:

". . . It should not be startling since it is only what every reputable scientist, knowing the principles of nuclear physics,

1 Speech to New York City Bar Association, January, 1951

has been predicting ever since we dropped the atomic bomb on Japan four years ago. **Since the discovery of Uranium fission in 1938 there has been no basic secret regarding an atomic bomb.** True, it was not until July 16, 1945, when the first experimental atomic bomb explosion took place at Alamogordo, that American scientists actually knew that an atomic bomb would work. **Only during the 21 days between that date and August 6, 1945, when the atomic bomb was dropped on Hiroshima, did we possess the secret of the atomic bomb. This secret was simply that we knew the bomb would work.** Scientists of other nations did not know it." [2] (emphasis added)

Even the U.S. Atomic Energy Commission itself has supported this view. A dispatch from Washington read:

"The Atomic Energy Commission Friday bared secret documentary proof that Russia has known the scientific secrets of atom bomb manufacture since 1940, the year the United States began attempts to develop the missile." [3]

The belief by most U.S. government leaders that we would have a monopoly of atomic energy for a long time was not based on any presumed secrets. It was based on the arrogant conviction that the Soviet economy was so much inferior to ours, that they couldn't possibly develop the "industrial complex" to achieve success in a short time.

John Foster Dulles, spokesman for the Republican Party on foreign affairs, admits both the mistake of top government officials and their arrogance. After mentioning that some industrialists told him in 1948 that the Russians would soon have the bomb, he writes:

"I was in a position to know, in the spring of 1949, that our top official experts were then convinced that it would probably be five years or more before the Russians would be able to make atomic bombs. . . .

"There seemed to be in official quarters a 'superiority complex.' . . ." [4]

American leaders would have done better to believe Molotov, when he hinted as early as 1947 that the U.S. monopoly on atomic energy was broken. The important point to observe, however, is that the deciding factor in everyone's mind was the industrial strength and technology of the Soviet Union, **not** the scientific knowledge which most experts assumed the Soviet Union had.

2 Atomics, September, 1949
3 International News Service, news story datelined Washington, D. C., December, 1950
4 John Foster Dulles, War or Peace, p. 111
5 Letter to New York Times, dated May 11, 1950

What then becomes of the argument that the Soviet Union "stole" the secret of the atomic bomb with the aid of spies? Harold C. Urey, one of the nation's top physicists, who worked on the development of the atomic bomb, wrote in May, 1950:

". . . let us not delude ourselves by thinking that our competitor succeeds only by stealing our secrets. It requires high intelligence to understand stolen secrets, and a high order of industrial competence to put them into practice."[5]

The question of atomic production is considered by all experts as primarily a question of industrial competence, rather than a question of scientific "secrets." This fact undermines and exposes all the spy scares which have been used in America to whip up a "war psychosis."

Particularly, it completely undermines the sentence of Judge Kaufman in the Rosenberg case when he sentenced to death Ethel and Julius Rosenberg. This was the first death sentence for espionage in this country's history by a civil court, in peace or in war.

In explaining his sentence, the Judge said the crime was ". . . .putting into the hands of the Russians the A-bomb years before our best scientists predicted Russia would perfect the bomb. . . ."

This conflicts with the facts. The speed of Russian atomic development depended primarily on the degree of their industrial development, as scientists, generals and diplomats all agreed. Furthermore, David Greenglass, who testified that he passed bomb sketches to a Russian agent at the instigation of the Rosenbergs was not a scientist but a virtual layman. And as the **Scientific American**, a leading science magazine, pointed out:

"What the newspapers failed to note was that without quantitative data and other necessary accompanying information the Greenglass bomb was not much of a secret."[6]

Time magazine commented that "some of his [Greenglass'] testimony made little scientific sense."[7]

All these authoritative opinions are evidence that the Rosenbergs could not have given anything to the Soviet Union that would have speeded up its atomic bomb program by years. To sentence them to death, in an action that has no precedent in our history, is even more shocking when it is remembered that no individual was sentenced to death for aiding an enemy in World War II. Spies for the Nazis got five to fifteen years sentences. "Axis Sally," convicted of treason to the United States, received a ten year sentence.

6 Scientific American, May, 1951
7 Time, March 19, 1951

The Rosenberg case dealt with the period from June, 1944, to January, 1945. At that time the Soviet Union was our fighting ally in a war for survival against Nazi Germany.

INDEX

Dewey, Thomas E., 278
Dillon, Clarence, 278
Dillon, Reed & Co., 267
Dolfuss, 138
Doolittle, Gen. James H., 105
Doolittle Raid, 163
Douglas, Justice Wm. O., 80, 351-352
Douglas, Paul H. (Senator), 93
Draper, William H., 104
Dulles, John Foster, 36, 84, 95, 96, 97, 100, 102, 103, 120, 153, 203, 230, 270, 301, 302
Duranty, Walter ("Stalin & Co.— Politburo"), 116

Eden, Anthony, 27, 188, 215, 273
Edwards, Frank, 68
Eisenhower, Dwight D., 23, 64, 104, 153-155, 157, 161, 175, 176, 179, 313
Epstein, Israel ("The Unfinished Revolution in China"), 353

Faurel, Charles, 356
Faymonville, Gen., 168
Finnish War, 136-138, 145
Flynn, Edward J. ("You're the Boss"), 223
Formosa, 300
Forrest, Wilbur, 280
Forrestal, James V., 22, 23, 25, 39, 40, 41, 42, 47, 48, 59, 60, 87, 90, 97, 101, 106, 161, 199, 200, 201, 202, 227, 229, 252, 260, 263, 264, 265, 266-268, 273-279, 280-285, 293-296, 298, 312, 353
Forrestal Diaries, 23, 41, 47, 48, 55, 87, 252, 264, 265, 266-268, 274-279, 280, 281, 283-284, 293-295, 353
France, 257, 258, 273, 287, 329
Franck, Prof. James (Report), 90
Franco, 122, 138, 183, 295, 341, 347
Friendly, Alfred, 101, 324

Gamelin, Comdr. Gen. (French), 139
General Electric, 31, 72, 74, 80
Germany, 118, 139, 140, 151, 238, 240, 241, 246, 259, 260, 268, 295, 296, 313, 330, 335, 344
Goebbels, Joseph, 83, 128, 143, 155
Goering, Hermann, 155, 330
Gordey, Michel ("Visa to Moscow"), 28
Gottwald, Clement (Czech), 289, 290
Graves, Gen. Wm. ("America's Siberian Adventure"), 115
Greece, 197, 221, 265
Griffith, Paul H., 301
Gromyko, Andrei, 103
Grow, Gen. Robert I. W., 59, 304-305
Grunether, Gen. Alfred M., 26

Guderian, Gen. Heinz ("Panzer Leader"), 346
Gunther, John, 303

Halsey, Admiral Wm. F., 105
Hall, Jack, 78
Hallinan, Vincent, 298
Harriman, Averell, 24, 36, 84, 100-101, 102, 106, 201, 202, 204, 223, 229, 233, 236, 246, 249, 250, 277
Hart, E. H. Liddell ("The German Generals Talk"), 155
Hazlitt, Henry, 74
Hill, Ernie, 27
Hillman, William, 54, 93
Hiroshima, 88, 89, 92, 95, 256
Hitler, 64, 77, 100, 101, 102, 107, 118, 118, 126, 138, 140, 260, 269, 279, 306, 311, 325, 335
Hoffman, Michael L., 338
Hoover, J. Edgar, 78
Hoover, Herbert, 21, 27, 33, 41, 60, 72, 138, 252
Hopkins, Harry, 87, 98, 99, 118, 161, 181, 185, 202, 230-235, 270
Hromadka, Dr. (Charles Univ., Czech), 290
Hull, Cordell, 132, 140, 161, 169, 170, 173, 210, 211, 271
Hungary, 256

Ickes, Harold, 204, 228
Imperialism, U.S., 110, 218, 337, 347-349
India, 86
Indo-China, 20, 130, 197, 273, 337-38
Iran, 337, 348
Israel, 283
Italy, 119, 123, 268, 289, 329

Japan, 115, 116, 117, 118, 119, 124, 353
Johnson, Louis, 106, 302
Johnston, Eric, 245, 251
Jordan, Virgil, 108, 242

Kahn, Albert E. ("High Treason"), 115
Kennan, George F., 24, 114, 276, 294, 311, 315
Kennedy, Joseph P., 136
King, Admiral Ernest J., 155
Kirk, Admiral Alan G., 24, 105, 304
Korea, 20, 69, 71, 78, 130, 300-307, 341, 354
Krock, Arthur (N.Y. Times), 80, 93, 265

Laski, Harold J., 27
Lattimore, Prof. Owen, 76

378

379